Psychotherapeutic Approaches to Schizophrenic Psychoses

ary

"*A wonderful book that should be read by all professionals that deal with schizophrenia! As a necessary counterweight to the current biology-dominated and drug-centred practice, it offers an almost complete anthology of the worldwide developments of truly integrative psycho-socio-biological approaches and their psychotherapeutic consequences on the individual, familial and socio-environmental level.*" **Luc Ciompi, Professor Emeritus of Social Psychiatry, University of Basel, Switzerland**

"*I am delighted to bring to the attention of psychiatrists and other mental health professionals across the world the work reflected in this book, as I am convinced that these approaches with their humanistic core have much to offer for upgrading person-centered clinical care for people experiencing psychoses.*" **Professor Juan E. Mezzich, M.D., Ph.D., President of the World Psychiatric Association**

Psychotherapeutic Approaches to Schizophrenic Psychoses brings together professionals from around the world to provide an extensive overview of the treatment of schizophrenia and psychosis.

Divided into three parts – past, present and future – the book begins by examining the history of the treatment of schizophrenia and psychosis, with reference to Freud, Jung, Harry Stack Sullivan and Adolf Meyer, amongst others.

Part II then takes a geographical look at treatment and its evolution in different parts of the world including the UK, USA, a large number of European countries, Eastern Asia and New Zealand.

Finally, Part III covers the range of interventions, from psychoanalytic psychotherapy to cognitive therapy to pharmacological treatments.

With contributions from leading figures in the field, this book will provide a varied examination of treatment, and spark much-needed debate about its future. As such it will be essential reading for all mental health professionals, in particular those involved in psychiatry, psychology and psychotherapy.

Yrjö O. Alanen is a psychoanalyst, family therapist and Emeritus Professor of Psychiatry at the University of Turku, Finland.

Manuel González de Chávez is Professor of Psychiatry, Complutense Madrid University and Chief of Psychiatric Services, University Hospital "Gregono Maranon", Spain.

Ann-Louise S. Silver is a psychoanalyst and Adjunct Professor of Psychiatry, Uniformed Services University of the Health Sciences, Bethesda, USA.

Brian Martindale is a psychoanalyst and Consultant Psychiatrist at the Early Intervention in Psychosis Services, Northumberland, Tyne and Wear NHS Trust, UK.

The International Society for the Psychological Treatments of Schizophrenias and other Psychoses book series

Series editor: Brian Martindale

The ISPS (the International Society for the Psychological Treatments of the Schizophrenias and other Psychoses) has a history stretching back more than fifty years during which it has witnessed the relentless pursuit of biological explanations for psychosis. The tide is now turning again. There is a welcome international resurgence of interest in a range of psychological factors in psychosis that have considerable explanatory power and also distinct therapeutic possibilities. Governments, professional groups, users and carers are increasingly expecting interventions that involve more talking and listening. Many now regard skilled practitioners in the main psychotherapeutic modalities as important components of the care of the seriously mentally ill.

The ISPS is a global society. It is composed of an increasing number of groups of professionals, family members, those with vulnerability to psychosis and others, who are organised at national, regional and more local levels around the world. Such persons recognise the potential humanitarian and therapeutic potential of skilled psychological understanding and therapy in the field of psychosis. Our members cover a wide spectrum of approaches from psychodynamic, systemic, cognitive, and arts therapies to the need-adaptive approaches, group therapies and therapeutic institutions. We are most interested in establishing meaningful dialogue with those practitioners and researchers who are more familiar with biological based approaches. Our activities include regular international and national conferences, newsletters and email discussion groups in many countries across the world.

One of our activities is in the field of publication. Routledge have recognised the importance of our field, publishing the ISPS journal *Psychosis: Psychological, Social and Integrative Approaches* www.isps.org/journal. shtml. The journal complements Routledge's publishing of the ISPS book series which started in 2004. The books aim to cover many topics within the spectrum of the psychological therapies of psychosis and their application in a variety of settings. The series is intended to inform and further educate a wide range of mental health professionals as well as those developing and implementing policy.

Some of the books will also promote the ideas of clinicians and researchers well known in some countries but not familiar to others. Our overall intention is to encourage the dissemination of existing knowledge and ideas, promote healthy debate, and encourage more research in a most important field whose secrets almost certainly do not all reside in the neurosciences.

For more information about the ISPS, email isps@isps.org or visit our website www.isps.org

Other titles in the series

Models of Madness: Psychological, Social and Biological Approaches to Schizophrenia
Edited by John Read, Loren R. Mosher & Richard P. Bentall

Psychoses: An Integrative Perspective
Johan Cullberg

Evolving Psychosis: Different Stages, Different Treatments
Edited by Jan Olav Johanessen, Brian V. Martindale & Johan Cullberg

Family and Multi-Family work with Psychosis
Gerd-Ragna Bloch Thorsen, Trond Gronnestad & Anne Lise Oxenvad

Experiences of Mental Health In-Patient Care: Narratives from Service Users, Carers and Professionals
Edited by Mark Hardcastle, David Kennard, Sheila Grandison & Leonard Fagin

Psychotherapies for Psychoses: Theoretical, Cultural, and Clinical Integration
Edited by John Gleeson, Eión Killackey & Helen Krstev

Therapeutic Communities for Psychosis: Philosophy, History and Clinical Practice
Edited by John Gale, Alba Realpe & Enrico Pedriali

Beyond Medication: Therapeutic Engagement and the Recovery from Psychosis
Edited by David Garfield and Daniel Mackler

Making Sense of Madness: Contesting the Meaning of Schizophrenia
Jim Geekie and John Read

Psychotherapeutic Approaches to Schizophrenic Psychoses

Past, Present and Future

Edited by Yrjö O. Alanen, Manuel González de Chávez, Ann-Louise S. Silver & Brian Martindale

Routledge
Taylor & Francis Group

LONDON AND NEW YORK

First published 2009 by Routledge
27 Church Road, Hove, East Sussex BN3 2FA

Simultaneously published in the USA and Canada
by Routledge
270 Madison Avenue, New York, NY 10016

Routledge is an imprint of the Taylor & Francis Group, an Informa business

Typeset in Times by Garfield Morgan, Swansea, West Glamorgan
Printed and bound in Great Britain by T J International Ltd, Padstow, Cornwall
Paperback cover design by Hybert Design

This publication has been produced with paper manufactured to strict environmental standards and with pulp derived from sustainable forests.

British Library Cataloguing in Publication Data
A catalogue record for this book is available from the British Library

Library of Congress Cataloging-in-Publication Data
Psychotherapeutic approaches to schizophrenic psychoses : past, present, and future / edited by Yrjö O. Alanen . . . [et al.].
    p. ; cm. – (ISPS–International Society for the Psychological Treatments of the Schizophrenias and Other Psychoses)
  Includes bibliographical references.
  ISBN 978-0-415-44012-7 (hardback) – ISBN 978-0-415-44013-4 (pbk.) 1.
Schizophrenia–Treatment. 2. Psychoses–Treatment. I. Alanen, Yrjö O. II.
International Society for the Psychological Treatments of the Schizophrenias and other Psychoses. III. Series: ISPS book series.
  [DNLM: 1. Psychotic Disorders–therapy. 2. Schizophrenia–therapy. 3.
Psychotherapy–history. 4. Psychotherapy. WM 203 P9739 2009]
  RC514.P71897 2009
  616.89'806–dc22
                                                              2008041589

ISBN: 978-0-415-44012-7 (hbk)
ISBN: 978-0-415-44013-4 (pbk)

Contents

PART I
The past: early history of the treatment of schizophrenic psychoses and the pioneers of the psychotherapeutic approach

Figures and tables

Figures

Tables

Contributors

Jukka Aaltonen, MD. Professor of Family Therapy (Emeritus), Department of Psychology, University of Jyväskylä, Finland; Psychiatrist, Psychoanalyst, Turku, Finland. Email: aaltonen@jyu.fi

Volkmar Aderhold, MD. Consultant and Trainer for treatment of patients with psychosis, Institute for Social Psychiatry, University of Greifswald, Germany. Email: volkmar.aderhold@uni-greifswald.de

Yrjö O. Alanen, MD. Professor of Psychiatry (Emeritus), University of Turku; Psychoanalyst, Turku, Finland. Email: yrjo.alanen@utu.fi

Marco Alessandrini, MD., Professor of Psychiatry, Head of Psychotherapy Service, Mental Health Center, University of Chieti, Italy. Email: lucesegreta@libero.it

Mike Ang, FRANZCP, Consultant Psychiatrist, Early Psychosis Intervention team, Waitemata District Health (WHDB), Auckland, New Zealand. Email: mike.ang@waitenadatadhb.govt.nz

Jacek Bomba, MD. Professor of Psychiatry, Jagellonian University, Krakow, Poland. Email: jazek.bomba@uj.edu.pl

Alison Brabban, DClinPsychol. Consultant Clinical Psychologist, Early Intervention in Psychosis Service, Tees, Esk and Wear Valleys NHS Trust; Hon. Clinical Senior Lecturer, University of Durham. Email: abrabban@btopenworld.com

Lyn Chua, PhD. Adjunct Assistant Professor, Department of Psychological Medicine, Yong Loo Lin School of Medicine, National University of Singapore. Singapore. Email: pcmcjl@nus.edu.sg

Johan Cullberg, MD. Professor of Psychiatry, Stockholm Center of Public Health; Psychoanalyst, Stockholm, Sweden. Email: j.cullberg@swipnet.se

Françoise Davoine, PhD. Psychoanalyst, Maitres de Conférences, Ecole des Hautes Etudes en Sciences Sociales, Paris, France. Email: gaudillierel@hotmail.com

Robert Dudley, PhD. Consultant Clinical Psychologist, South of Tyne Early Intervention in Psychosis service; Research Tutor on the Doctorate of Clinical Psychology, Newcastle University, UK. Email: r.e.j.dudley@ncl.ac.uk

Jean-Max Gaudillière, PhD. Psychoanalyst, Maitres de Conférences, Ecole des Hautes Etudes en Sciences Sociales, Paris, France. Email: gaudillierel@hotmail.com

Jim Geekie. Clinical Psychologist, St Lukes, Auckland, New Zealand. Email: jgeekie@adhb.govt.nz

Massimo di Giannantonio, MD. Professor of Psychiatry, Head of Mental Health Center, University of Chieti, Italy. Email: digiannantonio@unich.it

Manuel González de Chávez, MD. Professor of Psychiatry, Complutense Madrid University, Chief of Psychiatric Service, University Hospital 'Gregorio Maranon', Madrid, Spain. Email: mgchavez@teleline.es

Courtenay M. Harding, PhD. Professor of Psychiatry, Boston University School of Medicine; Senior Director, Center for Psychiatric Rehabilitation and Director, Institute for the Study of Human Resilience. Boston University, Boston, MA, USA. Email: charding@bu.edu

Svein Haugsgjerd, MD. Professor, Centre for Practical Knowledge, Bodo University College, Bodo, Norway; Psychiatrist, Psychoanalyst, Oslo, Norway. Email: sengell@online.no

Jarmo Hietala, MD. Professor of Psychiatry, University of Turku, Finland. Email: jahi@utu.fi

Klaus Hoffmann, MD, PhD. Medical Director, Forensic Psychiatry and Psychotherapy, Centre for Psychiatry, Reichenau, Germany; Head of the Institute of Psychoanalysis, Zurich-Kreuzlingen, Switzerland-Germany. Email: k.hoffmann@zfp-reichenau.de

Chan Hee Huh, MD. President, Korean Academy of Psychotherapists; President, ISPS Korea. Email: huhch@unitel.co.kr

Murray Jackson, FRCP, FRCPsych. Psychiatrist, Psychoanalyst, St. André de Roquepertuis, France. Email: murray.jackson@free.fr

David Kennard, DiplClinPsychol, PhD, M. Inst. GA. Consultant Clinical Psychologist and Group Analyst; Chair of ISPS, UK; Head of

Psychology and Psychotherapy at The Retreat, York, UK. Email: david@dkennard.net

Brian Koehler, PhD. Psychoanalyst, Professor of Postdoctoral Program in Psychotherapy and Psychoanalysis, School of Social Work, New York University, New York, USA. Email: brian_koehler@psychoanalysis.net

Tor K. Larsen, MD, PhD. Professor of Psychiatry UiB, Stavanger University Hospital, Regional Centre for Clinical Research in Psychosis, Stavanger, Norway. Email: tkmaclarsen@mac.com

Sonja Levander, PhD. Psychologist, Psychoanalyst, Stockholm, Sweden, Email: levander.lonnerberg@comhem.se

Dennis J. McCrory, MD. Chief Psychiatric Consultant, Massachusetts Rehabilitation Commission, Boston, MA; Council for Education, Training and Advocacy, Fountain House, New York City, NY, USA

Brian Martindale, FRCP, FRCPsych. psychoanalyst, Consultant Psychiatrist, at the Early Intervention in Psychosis Services, Northumberland, Tyne and Wear NHS Trust, UK; ISPS Book Series Editor. Email: Brian.Martindale@ntw.nhs.uk

Stavros Mentzos, MD. Professor and long-time Director (Emeritus), Department of Psychotherapy and Psychosomatics, University Clinic, Frankfurt am Main, Germany; Psychoanalyst. Email: s.mentzos@t-online.de

Viljo Räkköläinen, MD. Psychiatrist, Psychoanalyst, Professor h.c. Helsinki, Finland. Email: viljo.rakkolainen@columbus.fi

Patte Randal, LRCP, MCRS, DPhil. Medical Officer in Rehabilitation Psychiatry; Buchanan Rehabilitation Centre, Auckland, New Zealand

John Read, PhD. Associate Professor, Department of Psychology, University of Auckland, New Zealand. Email: j.read@auckland.ac.nz

Dale Rook. Occupational Therapy Professional Leader, Mental Health Services, Auckland DHS, New Zealand

Bent Rosenbaum, MD, MDSci. Psychiatrist and Psychoanalyst, Associate Clinical Research Professor, Faculty of Health Sciences, University of Copenhagen; Head of the Unit for Psychotherapy Education and Research, Psychiatric University Hospital Glostrup; Psychoanalyst, Glostrup, Denmark. Email: bent.rosenbaum@dadlnet.dk

Ann-Louise S. Silver, MD. Psychiatrist, Psychoanalyst, Professor of Psychiatry, Uniformed Services University of the Health Sciences, Bethesda, MD; Chairperson, ISPS-US, Columbia, MD, USA. Email: asilver@psychoanalysis.net

Laurie Stedman, LCSW-C, former social worker at the University of Maryland, USA (deceased)

Helm Stierlin, MD, PhD. Psychiatrist, Psychoanalyst, Professor of Basic Psychoanalytic Research and Family Therapy (Emeritus), University of Heidelberg, Germany. Kapellenweg 19, D-69121, Heidelberg, Germany

Melissa Taitimu (Te Rarawa, Te Aupouri), PhD. University of Auckland, New Zealand. Email: mtaitimu@gmail.com

Douglas Turkington, MD. Professor of Psychosocial Psychiatry and Consultant Psychiatrist, Department of Psychiatry, Newcastle University, UK. Email: douglas.turkington@ncl.ac.uk

Robert Whitaker. Author of *Mad in America: Bad Science, Bad Medicine and the Enduring Mistreatment of the Mentally Ill*, (2001). Cambridge, MA: Perseus. Email: robert.b.whitaker@verizon.net

Foreword

Towards personalizing and contextualizing psychiatric care

I feel honored and privileged to offer greeting words to the outstanding volume on integrative care for persons experiencing psychotic disorders that Yrjö Alanen, Manuel González de Chávez, Ann-Louise Silver and Brian Martindale are presenting to the world.

The first two parts of the book offer a remarkable account of the historical background and development of the subject. It begins with the work of early pioneers 100 years ago and proceeds to many parts of the world describing the contemporary situation of psychological approaches to the psychoses. I am not aware of any previous publication that has managed to bring together such important documentation and reviews of the development of the ideas and practice in this field. The editors are to be congratulated on bringing together authors with access to such knowledge to give a global view of both the common and the local factors in different regions of the world. They have been assisted by the existence of the increasingly influential International Society for the Psychological Treatments of Schizophrenias and other Psychoses (ISPS) and its national networks and I am delighted that ISPS is now an affiliated organization with the World Psychiatric Association (WPA). I look forward in the future to contributions from South America and Africa.

The third part of the book and the concluding chapter provide well-grounded optimism for the future developments in psychological therapies for the psychoses. This book is an outstanding testimony to a paradigm shift away from an era in which the mental health field was tending to look for a single explanation to an era in which it is increasingly recognized that complex interactions at many different system levels offer the best explanatory framework. The reductionistic approach contributed to exacerbating the alienation and isolation that is a core feature of psychosis. This book will assist in reversing that process. Its readers are able to study chapters by authors from many parts of the world bringing wisdom and rich experience of psychological work at individual, group, family and therapeutic community levels. There are also fascinating examples of increasingly sophisticated ways of thinking about medication and psychotherapeutic work – as well as detailed expositions of psychodynamic and cognitive frameworks.

In recent years I have become particularly familiar with the integrative approach originally developed in Finland three decades ago by the senior editor Professor Alanen and his team. This approach has some remarkable features: the focus on the needs of the individual patient in the context of their family for building assessment and care plans (which is connected to the term need adapted with which the approach is widely known) and on psychotherapy (particularly psychodynamic and family oriented approaches) and openness to incorporating biological and social therapies as needed for each person. Also potent is its careful and respectful attention to the experiences of the patient, who is therefore to be engaged as a whole person. Last but not least is the approach's strength in striving for continuity of care across time and clinical settings.

Other contributors, particularly from Scandinavia, make clear that this kind of approach is being widely adopted and carefully evaluated in an increasing number of countries, supporting its scientific validity and clinical effectiveness. Also encouraging are the positive statements repeatedly offered by patients and service users on their approach. Illustratively, Mrs Dorothea Buck cogently suggested at a WPA Thematic Conference in Dresden, Germany, in 2007 that focus on the subjective experience of patient be part of a new improved psychiatry.

I am pleased to note the consistency between need-adaptive assessment and care and the integrative principles underlying the initiative on Psychiatry for the Person of the World Psychiatric Association since both approaches articulate science and humanism. It is a fortunate coincidence that as the Alanen, González de Chávez, Silver and Martindale book is ready to be launched, Professor Alanen has been selected for his lifelong contributions as the first winner of the WPA Philippe Pinel Prize on Psychiatry for the Person: Articulating Medicine's Science and Humanism.

I am delighted to bring to the attention of psychiatrists and other mental health professionals across the world the work reflected in this book as I am convinced that these approaches with their humanistic core have much to offer for upgrading person-centered clinical care for people experiencing psychoses.

Professor Juan E. Mezzich, MD, PhD
President of the World Psychiatric Association
September 2008

Introduction

Schizophrenic psychoses pose one of the greatest challenges to psychiatric researchers and therapists. There is still much to be resolved in the pathogenesis and nature of these disorders. Even though the lifetime prevalence of the schizophrenia group of psychoses is little more than 1 per cent of the population, their social and economic significance is highly increased by the early onset in adolescence or early adulthood and the still frequently poor prognosis. For many young persons, their plans and hopes for the future become lost with the onset of the psychosis, causing great anxiety and suffering for them and also for their families.

During the most recent decades, psychological methods of treatment have developed and diversified considerably. However, their application and use in practice have not correspondingly increased compared with the dominant role of psychopharmacological treatment. From a global perspective, the great majority of professional staff working with persons suffering from schizophrenic psychoses – psychiatrists and psychologists, social workers and nurses – do not have adequate knowledge of the content and use of psychological approaches to schizophrenic psychosis.

In 2006, the three first editors of this book published the book *Fifty Years of Humanistic Treatment of Psychoses*, to celebrate the fiftieth anniversary of the International Society for the Psychological Treatments of the Schizophrenias and Other Psychoses (ISPS). During the XVth ISPS Congress in Madrid the book, published in both English and Spanish, was delivered to all congress participants and was received with great pleasure and satisfaction. The book was published in English by the Spanish foundation Fundación para la Investigación y Tratamiento de la Esquizofrenia y otras Psicosis and is now available from Karnac Books, London, as well as through www.paradox.es.

Encouraged by the good reception, we decided to edit another book with a wider perspective of the history of modern psychotherapy of schizophrenic psychoses. Dr Brian Martindale, Editor of the Routledge ISPS book series, soon joined our editorial group, also giving invaluable help on various matters relating to our common work. Because we discuss the past, present situation and future of psychotherapeutic work with psychotic patients, the book is titled *Psychotherapeutic Approaches to Schizophrenic Psychoses: Past, Present and Future.*

We consider our book very topical for many reasons. In the same way that the earlier book honoured the 50-year history of the ISPS, the present book will honour the 100-year history of the modern psychotherapy of schizophrenic psychoses. The pioneers we introduce in Part I of our book – Eugen Bleuler, C.G. Jung, Paul Federn, Adolf Meyer – began their work during the latter half of the first decade of the twentieth century. Freud's famous Schreber case was reported in 1911, and Harry Stack Sullivan began his work a decade later.

Another objective arises from the constant diversification of the psychological treatment modalities applied to patients with schizophrenic psychoses. Psychoanalytic (or, more widely, psychodynamic) individual therapy has been supplemented by group- and family-centred approaches and psychodynamic understanding by cognitive and behavioural techniques. The editors come from a psychodynamic orientation and are very aware of the need for more integrative development, to be better able to respond to the diverse needs of individual schizophrenic patients, their families and friends.

In Part II, developments in different parts of the world from the 1940s to the present are described. To avoid the boring repetition of similar themes from one country after another, we requested our contributors to approach their topics in the way they find most relevant. We have, for instance, two different chapters on the development in Great Britain, one to give a penetrating description of the Kleinian orientation, which has proved to be more and more important in the psychoanalytic understanding of psychotic patients, and another to give a more comprehensive picture of the current practice and development of psychological therapies with these patients in the UK. The French writers concentrate on the leading French psychoanalysts' ways of dealing with the problems of transference–countertransference that arise with psychotic patients, while the Italian chapter describes the ways in which psychotherapeutic activities have developed within the social psychiatric field. Considerable space has been dedicated to the German-speaking areas in Central Europe as well as to the Northern European countries. The impressive developments in these geographical areas are generally much less well known than the developments in the USA, a long time leading centre in our field. The global picture is complemented by very interesting contributions from areas culturally different from the western world. Regrettably, there are also areas that remained outside our review, such as the Netherlands, Australia and the rich South American tradition of psychodynamically oriented psychotherapy of psychoses.

Part III includes a detailed description of the present state and future views of the different modalities of treatment and their indications. Besides the role and development of individual, family and group psychotherapies, mostly from a psychodynamic point of view, there is a special chapter on cognitive behavioural therapy in psychosis. The challenges of pharmacotherapy are dealt with by a biologically oriented researcher-clinician on the one hand and by two psychoanalyst-family therapists on the other. They also try to find clues to differentiate between the kinds of cases where neuroleptics are not needed and cases where they are indicated. The other chapters in this section of the book deal with prevention and early intervention, psychotherapy and rehabilitation, the very topical Soteria model and its modifications, as well as a critical view of the myth and reality of the effects of neuroleptics. The book ends with an integrative review of the present treatment approaches and prospects of their further development, written by the editorial group.

Our book tries to capture the history and present state of psychological approaches across most of the world as seen from the standpoint of the ISPS network. We hope that the book will be read widely among the different groups of mental health professionals from all nationalities, and that it will prove a useful tool in the spread and generalization of integrated treatment programmes and in the teaching and training of mental health professionals in psychotherapeutic interventions and treatment modalities for psychotic patients.

We hope that the new generation of psychotherapists of different professional categories may witness a gradual rise of a more integrated and more humanistic age in the research and therapy of schizophrenic psychoses.

We express our great gratitude to all of our contributors, and to Professor Juan E. Mezzich, the Chairman of the World Psychiatric Association, for his great interest in our book and the Foreword he has written for us.

Yrjö O. Alanen, Manuel González de Chávez,
Ann-Louise S. Silver and Brian Martindale

The past

Early history of the treatment of schizophrenic psychoses and the pioneers of the psychotherapeutic approach

Chapter 1

Can we approach patients with schizophrenic psychoses from a psychological basis?

Yrjö O. Alanen

The schism between 'understanding' and 'explanatory' psychology

The diagnostic boundaries for schizophrenia have never remained fixed. Their criteria have been different at different times, in different countries and in different psychiatric cultures. The clinical heterogeneity of schizophrenic patients makes us ask whether it is even justifiable to speak about an illness called 'schizophrenia'. Such diagnostic practice certainly has disadvantages for both research, where notably dissimilar patients are placed into the same diagnostic clusters, and for individuals, who continue too often to carry the diagnostic label even after their recovery. Eugen Bleuler (1911), the originator of the name 'schizophrenia', himself concluded that schizophrenia is not a uniform disorder but rather a group of disorders including 'a nuclear group' with well-known clinical subgroups and 'a borderline group' difficult to distinguish from neuroses and manic-depressive psychoses. In line with him, we should at least prefer the term 'the group of schizophrenic psychoses'.

In the study of etiological factors as well as in treatment, the heterogeneity of schizophrenic psychoses should be taken into account much more than is usually done today, including the patients' individual psychological characteristics and life situations.

Can schizophrenia be approached via psychological understanding, or is it a disorder exclusively due to biological factors? The controversy that leads to questions of this kind has a long history with many cultural implications (see Chapter 2).

An influential statement on this topic was made by the German psychiatrist and philosopher Karl Jaspers (1913/1949), who introduced the concepts of 'explanatory' and 'understanding' psychology in the early twentieth century. The former concept referred to disorders explained by organic brain pathology, while the latter pertained to mental conditions regarded as psychologically understandable. Jaspers was inclined to place schizophrenia in the category of explanatory psychology. This was the tradition cherished almost exclusively by academic psychiatrists in Europe during the twentieth century. It was already adopted by Emil Kraepelin, 'the great classifier', who in the 1890s regarded the disease he called 'dementia praecox' as a brain process of unknown causation, leading to demented end states.

Eugen Bleuler (1911) was influenced by the work of Freud and Jung (see Chapter 4). He noticed that the outcome of the disorder was not necessarily as inevitable as Kraepelin had taught. Still, Bleuler also described the basic or 'primary' symptoms of schizophrenic psychoses – autism and disintegration of cognitive and affective functions – as being most probably due to organic causes, but attributed the content of the 'secondary symptoms' – including delusions and hallucinations – to the patient's individual complexes. The primary symptoms of schizophrenia were later discussed and redefined in attempts to distinguish 'real' schizophrenias from more benign schizophreniform psychoses (e.g. Langfeldt, 1939; Schneider, 1929/1962). In European psychiatry, even the term 'Praecox-Gefühl' ('praecox feeling') was presented as a criterion of the diagnosis of schizophrenia. It referred to the examiner's intuitive experience of being unable to establish any empathic understanding with the patient.

In the USA, such pioneers as Adolf Meyer (1906, 1910), Harry Stack Sullivan (1931, 1962) and Frieda Fromm-Reichmann (1959) made the tradition more favourable for an approach to schizophrenic psychoses based on understanding psychology (see Chapters 6 and 7). Following this tradition, the understanding of schizophrenic patients developed. However, the belief that schizophrenia is an organic disease and should be treated as such became dominant even in the USA, especially during the 1990s, called 'the decade of the brain'. However, we should still not forget the words written by Meyer almost one hundred years ago:

> The comfort of working under the cover of fatalistic and analyzed conceptions of heredity, degeneracy, and mysterious brain diseases . . . is a powerful and unconsciously cherished protection . . . We are, I believe, justified in directing our attention to factors *we see* at *work* in the life history of the cases of so-called dementia praecox.
>
> (Meyer, 1910, his italics)

The contradiction between the American and European concepts of schizophrenia some decades ago was most clearly illustrated by the results of the well-known British-American collaborative research project (Cooper *et al.*, 1972), which showed 'schizophrenia in London to be quite different from schizophrenia in New York'. This result could probably be interpreted from the standpoint of the different developments in the 'understanding psychology'. In the USA, psychiatrists were more inclined to view schizophrenic psychoses as understandable. They also found similar (though less pronounced) psychodynamic characteristics in patients now most often diagnosed as 'schizotypal' or 'borderline' personality disorders. Parallel to this, the American concept of schizophrenia gradually expanded. In the UK, the dominant opinion was that schizophrenia is psychologically non-understandable and the enlargement of the category of 'understandable disorders' narrowed down the concept of schizophrenia.

This, and other corresponding studies, led to a resumption of the Kraepelinian symptom-based classification, as manifest in the diagnostic and statistical manuals (DSM) compiled by the American Psychiatric Association (fourth edition, 1994). From the point of view of epidemiological research, this was necessary, but we should bear in mind that the planning of treatment also requires different approaches.

Some therapists have been inclined to completely deny schizophrenia being an illness and have rather spoken of a person's desperate attempt to protect himself or herself in an anxiety-provoking environment that threatens to destroy individuality (e.g. Laing and Esterson, 1964). However true this may be, one must acknowledge the huge regression of psychological functions and loss of social abilities experienced in such autistic decline.

How can we understand the schizophrenic person?

Sigmund Freud's essay on the autobiography of Dr Daniel Paul Schreber, the eminent lawyer who experienced schizophrenic psychosis, was the first in-depth account of the inner psychology of a schizophrenic person (Freud, 1911c; see Chapter 3). Freud distinguished two phases in the psychodynamic development of Schreber's psychosis: first a loss of differentiation of personality functions, including regression to early narcissism with abandonment of object relations; then attempts to find restitutional solutions, which were peculiar but still psychologically relevant. These basic interpretations have been confirmed by numerous psychoanalysts working with schizophrenic patients.

Why is such understanding still so difficult to adopt, even for psychiatrists and other mental health workers? A number of factors nurturing such antagonism can be listed:

- The commitment of medical research and education to the natural sciences tradition makes it difficult to appreciate work representing different theoretical outlooks.
- The expansion of brain research seemed to give support to the belief that schizophrenia is an organic disorder unrelated to psychological factors.
- The major influence of the pharmaceutical industry.
- The belief that psychotherapeutic work with psychotic patients could not possibly be widely applied in public health care because of the extensive staff resources that would be needed.

- The results of rigidly planned controlled psychotherapy trials have not been promising.
- Freud's belief in the irreversible nature of the narcissistic regression has engendered a pessimistic attitude towards psychotherapeutic treatment of schizophrenic patients.
- Studies of the psychological etiological factors of schizophrenia arouse anxiety and resistance, especially when they are (erroneously) perceived as accusing parents for their child's illness.
- Our defence mechanisms emphasize the difference between us and our patients, favouring superficial drug treatment, which helps us to avoid encountering the patients' deep-rooted problems.

One point should be added connected with the 'praecox feeling' mentioned above. Many people, even professionals, really find their schizophrenic patients more difficult to understand than those suffering from neuroses or narcissistic disorders, and this is not only due to their own unconscious defence mechanisms. In order to understand the psychic functions of schizophrenic patients, therapists need, besides adequate training, a genuine interest in these patients, a good capacity for empathy and a good ability to access their own unconscious 'psychotic domain', as manifest in our dreams. These qualities will provide us with insight into the patient's anxiety and regressive, concrete thinking that is still amenable to symbolic interpretation. Many psychiatrists and other professionals – even therapists – find this line hard to cross.

Based on schizophrenic patients' regressive state and the nature of transference–countertransference experiences, psychoanalytic investigators have concluded that severe frustrations of gratifying experiences within the early mother–child relationship are the deep-lying source of schizophrenic psychoses. An empathic, 'holding' (Winnicott, 1960) way to relate with the patient may gradually open the possibility for new restoring growth of the personality within a reliable, 'mirroring', symbiotically oriented interrelationship. The development of psychoanalytically oriented psychotherapy with its different schools and modifications will be described in several chapters of this book.

However, some remarks should be added here. It is important to note that the 'blame' for early frustrations in the future patient's life should not be placed on his or her mother's shoulders. The innate inclinations of children, e.g. their pronounced autistic tendencies and low-level tolerance of anxiety, should also be taken into account here, and it should further be emphasized that the early mother–child relationship never develops in a vacuum. The nature of the mutual relationship between the mother and the father has an impact on it, as do the overall environmental circumstances. The parents' own childhood experiences and development may also be crucially important. The author of this chapter has described the origin of schizophrenia as a multifactorial and multilayered process including both biological and psychosocial factors, which are weighted differently in different cases (Alanen, 1997). With regard to psychological predisposing factors, not only the crucial early human relationships but also the subsequent developmental phases and experiences have importance. Especially the two individuation–separation phases, the first in early childhood and the second in adolescence, may significantly increase the risk of psychosis or its avoidance.

The interaction between the individual's genotype and the longer term family environment has been most clearly shown by the extensive and methodologically comprehensive adoption study by Pekka Tienari and his group (Tienari *et al.*, 2003, 2004; Wahlberg *et al.*, 2004; Wynne *et al.*, 2006). They found that schizophrenia spectrum disorders (schizophrenic and paranoid psychoses and closely related personality disorders)[1] in adults were more common in those who had been adopted away from a mother with a schizophrenia group illness than among the control adoptees. But a crucial finding was that this only occurred at a statistically significant level when the atmosphere of the growing environment had included disordered features. Both a low genetic liability and a healthy rearing environment protected adoptees against severe psychiatric morbidity. The integrative approach tends to level off the sharp distinction earlier made between biological and psychological etiological factors (see Chapter 25).

To illustrate what has been said above, a couple of examples of the idiosyncratic concrete expressions of schizophrenic patients will be given.

I still remember very well a young man's first admission because of schizophrenia. I met him during my psychiatric training in Lapinlahti Hospital in Helsinki in the 1950s. According to the referral letter, he had been calling his superior at his workplace Christ. In our conversation he appeared evasive, avoided eye contact and mostly did not answer my questions. Since some kind of positive atmosphere seemed to be developing, I asked why he had called his superior by that name. The man glanced at me under his eyebrows and said, after a pause, 'You can find those Christs here and there.' It gradually became clear that he meant innocent victims; his superior was one of them, and so was he himself.

The other example comes from my book (Alanen, 1997).

One of the patients in our hospital in Turku claimed that wars and unemployment would have been eliminated from the world if his relationship with his first ever female friend had continued. If this had been so, we may think, it might have prevented his illness – at least temporarily – and his later violent tendencies and unemployment. We can thus see that even this ostensibly senseless association has a kind of sense, when we recognize the regression of the patient's experiential world to an omnipotent level.

We may thus find ways to approach the patient's world through symbolic understanding. However, successful therapeutic work with such patients requires intimate examination and knowledge of their personality development, family environment and current problems, which may lead to empathic mutual interaction of long duration.

Note

1 The term schizophrenia spectrum was initiated by Kety *et al.* (1968). Tienari *et al.* (2003) designated as the putative broad spectrum they would evaluate: *DSM-III-R* schizophrenia; schizotypal, schizoid, paranoid, and avoidant personality disorders; schizoaffective, schizophreniform and delusional disorders; bipolar disorder with psychosis; depressive disorder with psychosis; and psychotic disorder not otherwise specified.

References

Alanen, Y.O. (1997). *Schizophrenia – Its Origins and Need-Adapted Treatment.* London: Karnac.

American Psychiatric Association (APA, 1994). *Diagnostic and Statistical Manual of Mental Disorders, DSM-IV*. Washington, DC: APA.

Bleuler, E. (1911). *Dementia Praecox oder die Gruppe der Schizophrenien*. Leipzig, Vienna: Deuticke. [English edn *Dementia Praecox or the Group of Schizophrenias*. New York: International Universities Press, 1950.]

Bullard, D. (ed.) (1959). *Psychoanalysis and Psychotherapy. Collected Papers by Frieda Fromm-Reichmann*. Chicago: Chicago University Press.

Cooper, J.E., Kendell, R.E., Gurland, B.J. *et al.* (1972). *Psychiatric Diagnosis in New York and London*. Maudsley Monograph no. 20. London: Oxford University Press.

Freud, S. (1911c). Psycho-analytic notes upon an autobiographical account of a case of paranoia (dementia paranoides). *Standard Edition* XII: 1–79. London: Hogarth Press.

Jaspers, K. (1913). *Allgemeine Psychopathologie*. 5th edn 1949. Berlin-Heidelberg: Springer.

Kety, S.S., Rosenthal, D., Wender, P.H. and Schulsinger, F. (1968). The types and prevalence of mental illness in the biological and adoptive families of adopted schizophrenics. *Journal of Psychiatric Research* 6 (Suppl. 1): 345–362.

Laing, R.D. and Esterson, A. (1964). *Sanity, Madness and the Family, Vol. I: Families of Schizophrenics*. London: Tavistock Publications.

Langfeldt, G. (1939). *The Schizophreniform States*. Copenhagen: Munksgaard.

Meyer, A. (1906). Fundamental conceptions of dementia praecox. *British Medical*

Journal 2: 755–759. Also in: E.E. Winters (ed.) *The Collected Papers of Adolf Meyer*. Baltimore, MD: Johns Hopkins University Press.

Meyer, A. (1910). The dynamic interpretation of dementia praecox. *American Journal of Psychology* 21: 385. Also in: E.E. Winters (ed.) *The Collected Papers of Adolf Meyer*. Baltimore, MD: Johns Hopkins University Press.

Schneider, K. (1929). *Klinische Psychopathologie*. 6th edn 1962. Stuttgart: Thieme.

Sullivan, H.S. (1931). The modified psychoanalytic treatment of schizophrenia. *American Journal of Psychiatry* 88: 519–540. Also in H.S. Sullivan *Schizophrenia as a Human Process* (ed. O.A. Will Jr). New York: Norton.

Sullivan, H.S. (1962). *Schizophrenia as a Human Process* (ed. O.A. Will Jr). New York: Norton.

Tienari, P., Wynne, L.C., Läksy, K. *et al.* (2003). Genetic boundaries of the schizophrenia spectrum: evidence of the Finnish adoptive family study of schizophrenia. *American Journal of Psychiatry* 160: 1–8.

Tienari, P., Wynne, L.C., Sorri, A. *et al.* (2004). Genotype-environment interaction in schizophrenia-spectrum disorder: long-term follow-up study of Finnish adoptees. *British Journal of Psychiatry* 184: 216–222.

Wahlberg, K.-E., Wynne, L.C., Hakko, H. *et al.* (2004). Interaction of genetic risk and adoptive parent communication deviance: longitudinal prediction of adoptee psychiatric disorders. *Psychological Medicine* 34: 1531–1541.

Winnicott, D.W. (1960). The theory of the parent–infant relationship. *International Journal of Psycho-Analysis* 41: 585–595.

Wynne, L.C., Tienari, P., Sorri, A. *et al.* (2006). I. Genotype-environment interaction in schizophrenia spectrum: genetic liability and global family ratings in the Finnish adoption study; II. Genotype-environment interaction in the schizophrenia spectrum: qualitative observations. *Family Process* 45: 419–447.

Chapter 2

Treatment of psychoses before the twentieth century

Manuel González de Chávez

Primitive societies

Primitive societies, with a dominant magical or magical-religious ideology, already distinguished involuntary behaviours that violated their rules in ways that we now know to call psychotic disorders (Opler, 1959; Kiev, 1964; Kleinman, 1980; Jenkins and Barret, 2004). They attributed a wide range of unnatural causes, such as loss of soul, sin from breaking taboos, introduction of objects, harmful spirits or demons in the body, harmful effects of witchcraft and magic from other human beings and also resentment and dissatisfaction from the deceased.

The sorcerer or wizard was the therapeutic agent. He wore masks, clothes, talismanic objects and other attributes of his occupation, such as bags of plants and medicinal drugs. His activity was performed through community acts that took various ceremonial forms such as dances, songs, orations or spells aimed at identifying the agent or pathogenic cause by exhorting a public confession of the breaking of taboos, sins, impieties and other acts of negligence or by means of trances in which the sorcerer communicated with the spirits or offended gods. The appropriate remedy, together with sacrifices and purifications, was then applied, invoking the soul to return to the suffering subject or expelling the spirits or demons by exorcisms, drugs or trepanations. The tribal attitude towards the disturbed subjects depended on the attributions given to their illnesses. When it was considered that they were caused by the possession of a malignant spirit that they could not eliminate, the possessed person could be sacrificed or expelled from the community.

Early civilizations

In a subsequent phase of human history, the ideology became increasingly less magical and more characteristically religious, as occurred with the Incas, the Maya and Aztecs and in Mesopotamia, old Egypt, Iran and Palestine and also during earlier settled cultures as in what is now India,

China and Japan. These were complex agrarian and slavery-based societies, governed by a military and sacerdotal minority sector that enforced all the power, symbolized through the presence of an emperor, pharaoh, Inca or king, who was either identified with divinity or embodied it. In all these societies, insanity, differentiated from other diseases and behaviors, was understood in religious codes, with supernatural causalities and remedies similar to those of tribal societies. There was already a description of different types of disorders. For example, the Maya distinguished insanity, melancholy, hallucinations and several other syndromes. The Egyptian papyruses and the long treatises of Hindu medicine included several mental problems. Almost two thousand years before Christ, one part of one of these treatises, Yajur Veda (Buthavidja) was totally dedicated to psychic diseases, in the traditional concept of demoniacal possessions (Sigerist, 1951; Laín Entralgo, 1972).

These civilizations frequently equated disease with sin, and punishment was considered as a therapeutic remedy. In some civilizations the patients were shut away in prisons. In ancient Iran, many diseases were treated by whippings: the whip being one of the main therapeutic instruments. However, other more pleasant remedies, such as music, changes of setting, bright light, and the recommendation of better living habits were also applied to mental patients. In all of them, the sacerdotal clan of physicians generally acted as the helpers of the gods and a great part of medical knowledge consisted of a health theology that was associated with the gods and their revelations.

Israel had specific characteristics as a population that had been enslaved several times by their powerful neighbors, but above all they had a written history of great value that reveals the attitudes, conceptions and management of insanity, of both Palestine itself and the civilizations close to Mesopotamia, Persia and Egypt. In Israel, there were no real doctors but rather healers or helpers of Yave. They were the ones responsible for curing and they were forbidden to use any type of magic or witchcraft. In general, mental patients were considered as possessed by the devil. An attempt was made to expel the devil with psalms, exorcisms and spells, although purifying ablutions and music were employed. An example of the latter was by David to cure Saul's melancholy. The Hebrews also tried unsuccessfully to clearly mark the borders of insanity, as shown by the favorable or miserable fate of those who acted as prophets (Rosen, 1968).

The Babylonians, Sumerians, Hittites and Egyptians initiated the practice of 'incubation', using dreams to obtain knowledge of diseases and their treatment. At that time, dreams were considered to be independent of the person who dreamt them. They were believed to be a special form of communication with human beings used by the spirits, the dead or the gods. 'Incubation' acquired great prevalence in the therapeutic practice of many populations, including Ancient Greece. The patients spent the night in caves or in the temples of the oracles or of gods such as Asclepius, and during the dream, the divinity, or one of its manifestations, its serpents or dog informed them of the pathway to follow to recover their health. The dream interpreters, the oneirocritics, were real professionals (Meier, 1967; Laín Entralgo 1972; Rocatagliata, 1973).

Greek and Roman civilization

However, not only dreams were considered to be independent of those dreaming them. In ancient civilizations, even in the Homeric world of archaic Greece, there was no unified conception of the persons or of human consciousness (Jaynes, 1976). The mind still did not have a definite position (varying from the brain to the heart or the diaphragm). The activity initiating agents were external, such as gods, demons, other persons or parts of the body itself. Insanity was caused by the gods, generally as a consequence of violation of the rules. There were divine causes of insanity that could be prophetic (inspired by Apollo), religious (by Dionysus), poetic (by the Muses) and erotic (by Aphrodite and Eros). The therapy was the return to the social order and it was represented in the epic and in tragedy and was approached by means of oracles, dreams, music, catharsis or dances such as those of the corybantic (Dodds, 1951; Simon, 1978).

When Greek society changed from being rural to urban, many philosophers defended the primacy of reason in human behavior and self-control. The genesis of insanity was in impossible desires, in frustrations of reality, violent emotions and lack of control of the passions. Insanity was the victory of exaggerated passions over reason and an error of judgement that led to disorganized behaviour. In Plato's Dialogues there was already a model of an individual, conflicted and hierarchical mind that initiates and considers one's own activity. In addition to insanity that was divine in origin, diseases and physical causes were considered as were ignorance, irrationality, cowardice, injustice and intemperance. In these last causes, the philosopher was the therapist who, using dialogue and rhetoric, could achieve harmony, using rationality against irrationality, knowledge against ignorance, and virtues against vices. Plato finally conceived the idea of a specific philosophical-therapeutic institution in 'The Laws': the sophronisterion (Laín Entralgo, 1958; Simon, 1978).

Beginning in the sixth century BC, mercantile plutocracy displaced the landed aristocracy and with their economic and social power being based on manufacturing trade, facilitated interest in the development of techniques to understand the rational knowledge of nature. This would later give Greece a character that was distinctive from that of the other ancient civilizations. Greek Hippocratic medicine would exceed the theurgist and pure empirical model and be based on technical knowledge stemming from methodical observation giving a concept of health and disease relating to the good order and harmony of human nature and the balance of the humors and elements that were its constituents.

Without resorting to the gods, Hippocrates had already distinguished 'phrenitis' (acute mental disorder with fever), 'mania' (sudden onset insanity but without fever) and 'melancholy' (that included most of the chronic psychic disorders). He described what we now call schizophrenia as 'desipience', 'hebetude' or 'desipientia stupida', and attributed their origin to an excess of phlegm or pituita, in the same way that phrenitis and mania were caused by excess yellow bile and melancholy by an increase of black bile (Howells, 1991).

As insanity was understood as a natural disease produced by an imbalance of the humors that was influenced by passions or moral causes, therapy was aimed at recovering the balance of nature by eliminating excess black bile in melancholy, excess yellow bile in anxiety, mania and aggressiveness and the abundance of phlegm in the 'hebetude'. Purgatives, enemas, emetics, bleedings and sedative drugs such as adormidera and mandragora were used. Remedies and rules of life adapted to each patient were also recommended: music, philosophical conversations, rhetorical exercises, attending theater – tragedies or comedies as appropriate – physical exercises, baths, changes in lighting, bed or house. There were other procedures that psychiatry subsequently would call 'shock therapy', such as cold water, hunger, darkness, sudden frights, blows, whipping and other 'punishments', with the aim of producing 'deep shock' that would lead to rebalance of the sick nature.

Enclosure and mechanical restraints were a common practice for all those who were not calm or docile. In the upper classes, servants and guardians were in charge of restraint. Whenever possible, this was done within the home itself, using ropes, chains, shackles and other instruments. The 'furious' were locked up in prison, if the family could not do it in their own home. The poor insane and calm persons roamed about and were subject to practical jokes and maltreatment. Popular attitudes toward the insane were greatly influenced by previous magical-religious notions and archaic fears that the evil could be contagious or transferred. Thus, these persons were often spat on and avoided.

For more than twelve centuries of the Greco-Roman and Byzantine period, schizophrenia, which was called by different names ('fatuitas', 'hebetude', 'morositas', 'desipience', 'stupiditas', 'stultitia'), was well known and distinguished from paranoia ('fanaticism', 'paraphrosyniae') or catatony ('cathoco', 'congelatio'; Rocatagliata, 1973). There are six centuries full of historical events and intelligent clinical deductions and observations between the physiological and corporal works of Hippocrates that broke off from magical medicine, and that of Galen, which incorporated the work of Aristotle and all the philosophy and subsequent knowledge of human psychology. Cicerone, as the Stoics and Epicureans, advocated a psychological or psychogenetic psychopathology, in which the disorders were caused by dynamic conflict. The experience of disturbing events gave rise to exacerbated passions because man reacts in a particular way and may feel frustrated, guilty or humiliated by what has occurred. They considered the gradual process between inclination ('inclinatio'), propensity or temperament, 'aegritudo' and reactions which would presently be called adaptation reactions or neurosis, and 'morbus' that includes the current concept of psychosis. When the violent agitation of emotions became chronic, body function was thought to be affected. 'This entered into the medulla, veins and humors', altering the balance and becoming a disease. Mental disorder is linked to the person who experiences it in its origins and content and has a 'moral' significance. Delusion is the dreaming of a subject who is awake, in the same way that dreaming is the delusion of the subject who is sleeping. The true therapy must go to the roots of the disease, to the exaggerated passions. Those who control their passions are saved from insanity (Cicerone, 45 BC; Rocatagliata, 1973). Galen already had an integrating concept of normal and pathological behavior, a consistent system with reciprocal connections between passions and humors, which is why his work endured from the second to the eighteenth century (Galen, 1963; Siegel, 1973).

The medieval period

Medieval Christian medicine is a combination of Galenism and that of the Christian world from which the first initiatives of charity health care institutions, derived from a solidary attitude towards the poor and the sick, essential for eternal salvation, arose in the Byzantine Empire. In Byzantium, the first hospitals were established in the episcopal cities, hospices were close to the churches, and there was a close relationship between monasteries and hospitals and between monks and the ill. In the coexistence of secular physicians and monks who practiced medicine, there was a greater trend towards the monk who assisted, directed and administered health care institutions, which were mainly religious institutions.

Monastic medicine would be dominant for several centuries and would add to Galenic medicine the biblical tradition of disease as sin, punishment, desire, sample or proof of divine will and the omnipotence of a god that must be invoked to recover health (Laín Entralgo, 1961). Monastic medicine was well connected with the popular medicines that also coexisted in the Roman Empire and with the Hebrew and 'pagan' practices that were widely Christianized. Primitive invocations were brought up to date in prayers and supplications. Even 'incubation' was Christianized. There were churches where the ill spent the night or where places were reserved for the possessed. Exorcisms became part of the liturgy as well as medicine. The pagan gods of health were converted into 'curing saints' and their new images and relics replaced the old fetishes and amulets. There were many pilgrimages of the insane to famous sanctuaries, in some of which their miraculous fountains and holy water evoked the purifying rites of archaic medicines (Rosen, 1968; Kroll, 1973; Clarke, 1975).

There were theoretical difficulties in distinguishing between the physical, the moral and the mental and between insanity, sin and demoniacal possession in the merger of Christianity with the synopses of Galenic medicine when divine or diabolical interventions and original sin were added to the already intricate relationships between mortal body and incorporeal soul (Kroll and Bachrach, 1984; Kemp and Williams, 1987). The classifications followed the classical tradition and Galenic remedies continued to be used together with religious ones, with the great extension of some violent practices such as 'capipurgia', application of hot irons on the skull, or the trepanations so greatly popularized in pictorial works.

Islam, in its territorial expansion, also incorporated Hellenic medical science and Byzantine experience. Arab doctors, in the Hippocratic tradition, considered insanity as a bodily disease. They were not mere transmitters of Galenic knowledge but rather they discussed, extended and modified it according to their experience. Many of the Arab doctors criticized violent therapeutic procedures and tended to recommend patience and persuasion, exercises, baths, dancing, relaxation, theater in the hospital gardens or prolonged sleep with drugs. The Islamic Society had an attitude of tolerance and help towards these persons and they even respected them, because it was common to suspect that there was an underlying message or divine charisma.

Islam maintained the rule of assisting patients or the helpless through the civil administration, so that they constructed large hospitals in the main cities. They were secular and medical institutions, in the modern sense, with an internal division into departments (surgery, ophthalmology, orthopedics, etc.), daily medical visits, auxiliary staff and regulated teaching of medicine. The hospitals of Baghdad, Damascus, Cairo and Fez had departments for the demented. Using the same criteria, smaller hospitals were created for specific diseases and others for mental patients, among which Maristan of Granada (Spain), founded in 1367, may have been the first mental hospital to be constructed in Europe (Hammarneh, 1962; Ammar, 1968; Ullman, 1978).

In Spain, familiar with Islamic institutions during the eight centuries in which it had formed a part of the Islamic area, hospitals were subsequently constructed for the insane in other cities such as Valencia, Zaragoza, Seville, Toledo, Valladolid and Barcelona. Knowledge of the Arab world began to become widespread in the rest of Europe during the Crusades. In the fifteenth century, with the boom of commerce and the rise of the mercantile bourgeoisie, civil hospitals and institutions were created for the insane in many European cities. These new civil hospitals and institutions for the insane replaced the confinement sites, churches, monasteries and general hospital cells where the patients were restrained with chains, ropes and beds enclosed with windows where the patient could be observed (Ullesperger, 1954; Clarke, 1975).

Renaissance

In the Renaissance, monastic medicine declined and secular medical schools flourished. Greco-Roman naturalistic concepts were taught once again in these schools, often collected from Arabic translations. Renaissance medicine, with its autopsies and anatomical studies, would combat the supernatural character of diseases with the 'Vesalius knife'. However, until the final hegemony of the bourgeoisie several centuries later, natural and supernatural views and approaches to insanity and other deviant behaviors overlapped and conflicted, so lay and religious fields coexisted. The borders of demonology and witchcraft with insanity were unclear, but it would be very simplistic to reduce them to mental disorders (Zilboorg, 1941) because they were a product of a convulsive history of theological cosmogonies and ecclesiastic institutions for religious control and social power. Insanity, as well as irrationality, was greatly used in literature and philosophy to fight for a new ethics of reason (AAVV, 1976).

Sixteenth and seventeenth centuries

Medicine of the sixteenth and seventeenth centuries still accepted the natural and supernatural among the causes and remedies of insanity (Hunter and Macalpine, 1963). The Hippocratic classification (phrenitis, mania and melancholy) was the most common one, although 'black bile', the supposed cause of melancholy and other chronic insanities, was not found by the anatomists in any part of the body. The clinicians of the period tried to maintain the authority of the classical authors, transforming 'humors' into 'vapours'. Paracelsus spoke of 'lunatics' (whose loss of the senses originated by their own fault, that made them fall under the influence of the moon, its phases and movements), of 'insania' (inherited and a product of inadequate sexual intercourse of the parents), of 'vesania' (due to poisonings or to abuses), 'witchcraft' and finally 'melancholy' (due to the nature or complexion of the subject; Midelfort, 1999).

The famous *Anatomy of Melancholy* of the erudite Robert Burton (1621) is a valuable synopsis of historic knowledge that collects all types of divine and human, dietary, pharmaceutical and surgical causes and remedies. However, it is also a treatise of moral and philosophical therapy with a large repertoire of strategies against adversity, persuasive speeches and comforting advice; patterns of 'psychological healing', personal and humanitarian help through words that are real predecessors of many common therapeutic factors in our current psychotherapies (Jackson, 1999).

However, up to the time of the Enlightenment and even after it, there were many brutal treatments based on body punishments, physical tortures, surprise, terror and horror, such as immersing the patients in frozen water, until they were close to asphyxiation, in order to 'suffocate the mad ideas', exhausting them until they were tired and nauseous with rotating machines or wheels, provoking new diseases that were supposedly inconsistent with insanity, silencing them with 'facial masks', using electric shocks, blood transfusions from animals to renew their humors and rubbing them with abrasive ointments ('oleum cephalicum') or making incisions in their heads in order to expel the harmful vapours. These were historical predecessors of other subsequent treatments, such as cardiazol shocks, malaria therapy, insulin comas, electroshocks and psychosurgery.

At the beginning of industrialization, upper class mental patients were visited by a doctor in their homes or in small private institutions such as the 'petit maisons' or 'madhouses' (Hunter and Macalpine, 1963; Parry-Jones, 1972). The poorer ones in Europe had very few specific institutions and also lived in prisons, general hospitals, hospices or 'workhouses', a new proto-type of bourgeois institution which rejected the ancient religious charity and was based on the new values of re-education by work. It was indus-trialization, with the inflow of the popular classes to the large cities, that generated new health care demands. These demands were collected by the more reformist sectors of the bourgeoisie and the medical professionals. From the middle of the eighteenth century, construction of both general and specialized new hospitals began in many cities. Psychiatric asylums should be situated within this history of hospital construction (Rothman, 1971; Jones, 1972; Castel, 1976; González de Chávez, 1980).

Eighteenth century

The Reformation and Counter-Reformation had a decisive influence on the unequal development of health care institutions (Midelfort, 1999). During the eighteenth century, under the initiative of the reformist bourgeoisie, several psychiatric asylums were constructed both in London and the rest of England, including The Retreat in York where Tuke later prac-ticed. (Bethlem Asylum had long been in existence.) This period of con-struction also occurred in other countries, adding to the asylums that already existed in Catholic Mediterranean Europe and in Latin America. It was very late in this century (1793) when the renowned Philippe Pinel went to Bicêtre to work.

Eliminating the use of chains in prisons and asylums for the insane formed a part of the same historic process. Chiarugi in the Ospédale Bonifacio of Florence (1788) and Joly in Geneva (1787) had done so before Bicêtre and Salpetriere. From 1792, William Tuke had demonstrated in The Retreat at York that patients did not need restrictions, limitations or punishments. Pinel visited European asylums, praised Tuke and recognized the importance of moral treatment and English institutions (his main source: British Library, 1798; see Swain 1977, p. 36), describing the organization, functions and success of The York Retreat in his own writings. Being unaware of his subsequent myth, Pinel himself wrote about elimination of the chains in barely one page, describing how patients, some of whom had been chained up for many years, were released by the order and happy initiative of Pussin, his talented assistant, whom he always praised and referred to as his true teacher in this aspect. Subsequent French alienists decontextualized the whole historic process, reducing it to a single action of one man, and took this 'moment' as the founding point of psychiatry, creating a myth of its origins (Swain, 1977; Micale and Porter, 1994).

Chains would also disappear from prisons in the group of institutional reforms undertaken by the bourgeoisie. These reforms were a sign of humanization and a sample of the values of the new moral and institutional force based on reason and persuasion, will and control of emotions and passions that played an etiological role in mental alienation. Passions were classified by Pinel as spasmodic, debilitating and oppressive or serene and expansive, collecting classical traditions together with the philosophical etiology of that time. Those exaggerated and uncontrolled passions that disrupt reason and cause alienation are always the same manifestations in human life: love, lust, desires, wishes, pains, suffering, shame, sadness, horror, fear, uneasiness, despair, rage, anger, hate, revenge, envy, jealousy, ambitions, pride, conceit, arrogance, greed, etc. However, 'moral treatment' did not have an ethical meaning. This was a 'psychic' treatment which was differentiated from 'physical' treatments and aimed at understanding and control of oneself. Walter Riese proposes that 'psychotherapy' would be the least ambiguous and most accurate translation of 'moral treatment' (Riese, 1969).

Treatments of insanity – both physical and psychic – or as was said 'of the body and for the spirit' – had coexisted throughout the history of humanity (Ellenberger, 1970; Ehrenwald, 1976; Jackson, 1999). The so-called 'psychotherapy' of the present and 'moral treatment' of the past would not be understandable without this historical continuity, even in England where 'moral treatment' acquired its institutional character for the first time. Certainly, many of these 'psychic', 'moral' or 'spiritual' remedies already had a great tradition outside of medicine. It is not surprising that they demonstrated their superiority over the medical treatments used at that time in a Quaker institution, The York Retreat. This is the example usually referred to but both within and outside of England other similar public and private institutions existed. They renounced the restraints and restrictions of the patients, demonstrating how the relationships inside the asylum improved with knowledge and affection, with more humanitarian communication with the patients and more interest in understanding their difficulties. The crises that led to mechanical restraint of the insane were consequences of the relationships and attitudes which were held towards them. In general, the concept of insanity at that time was predominantly psychogenic and social (although attempts were made to establish their connection between physiology and behavior). Re-education was no more than the correction of biology by other means.

'Moral treatment' had several versions, 'non-restraint' being one of them – not the most extensively adopted although greatly accepted. However, there were also different kind of tendencies towards 'pure order' and institutional discipline, a mixture of 'theopathology', and practical disinterest in brutal remedies which were used with the patients, such as swinging them from the neck and making them circulate with rotary machines to make them 'correct erroneous ideas', 'destroy the links of morbid associations and break the force and effects of vicious mental habits'. These procedures were published in scientific journals to demonstrate empirically that they were 'safe and effective' remedies (Hunter and Macalpine, 1963). John Conolly, one of the most clear-thinking men of psychiatry of that time, commented that these treatments were an unspoken recognition of the lack of efficacy of medicine and a proof of the obstinacy of vain and ignorant men who wanted to use force to obtain all that they could not get with their science (Conolly, 1856).

'Moral treatment' was the 'scientific' therapy that demanded and justified building specific institutions for 'lunatics' or the 'alienated' where 'discipline of their will, control of their passions and reasonable order of their ideas' were to be achieved. The development of asylums also meant new legal regulations, the first associations of alienists and their first scientific journals, with the knowledge facilitated by clinical observation in the asylum and by rationalist and empirical methodology. These were decades of institutional reform and therapeutic optimism.

Another kind of treatment centre had come into being in Belgium in the famous village of Gheel, a site for medieval pilgrimage in which a tradition of custom and care for patients by the inhabitants had developed. Families had, by delegation and payment, converted into 'nourriciers', true foster carers and guardians with whom the patients lived and worked. It was said that in Gheel it was not possible to distinguish between the insane and sane (Roosens, 1979).

During the nineteenth century, asylum psychiatry went from having greater optimism to the most desperate pessimism. Reality showed that treatment of mental patients was very secondary to other dominant interests and that the responsible authorities haggled about financing and gave priority to custodial functions. The bourgeoisie abandoned the principles and 'abstract ideas' of the Enlightenment, with which they had fought against the 'Ancien Regime', and adopted defensive positions with respect to the contradictions and inequalities of capitalism and the revolutionary attacks of the proletariat. They embraced positivism and certain aspects of evolutionism that 'justified' the predominance of the most competent in the inevitable fight for life. They used governmental powers widely to channel all types of the deviated and helpless to asylums, which lacked personnel and material resources, were precarious, overcrowded and inoperative. Here, a moral re-education of the confined was an illusory effort.

Industrial capitalism, motivated by profitability, favored scientific discoveries and technical innovations. Positivist medicine was no longer 'merely conjectural knowledge' and achieved important advances with the microscope and laboratory, especially in hygiene and bacteriology. Psychiatry tried to follow the same example. The brain lesions found in patients with general progressive paralysis who abounded in the insane asylum encouraged those who took the 'somaticist' position; these had been in the minority at the beginning of the century but now began to prevail. The recognition of general progressive paralysis stressed the diagnostic importance of the evolution of the disorders and the polymorphism of some clinical pictures that were thoroughly analyzed in their symptoms with descriptive psychopathology (Berrios, 1996).

However, the question of unity or heterogeneity was not clear. 'Alienation' or 'insanity' were common terms until 'psychosis' replaced them. Ernst von Feuchtersleben used it in 1845 in his book *The Principles of Medical Psychology*, in which he described the therapeutic uses of that time: the more or less persuasive armamentarium of rewards and punishments and 'psychic remedies' that were added to the varied pharmacopeias of narcotics, sleeping pills, stimulants, emetics and other 'body remedies', including wine and opium (Goshen, 1967).

The therapeutic-pedagogic-re-educating homologation of the insane with the child was quite common. It was practiced by both so-called 'psychic' psychiatrists of the Enlightenment or of Romanticism, who believed in the independence of reason or the spirit, as well as by the psychosomatic psychiatrists with their dual remedies for the body and the mind. The others, 'somaticists' and materialists, were more occupied with their microscopes than with their patients, defending the unity of mental and somatic phenomena. For them soul was only the sum of brain states; there were no more diseases than those of the brain (Ellenberger, 1970; Engstrom, 2003).

Hypnotism was the provocative shadow of 'somaticist' materialism and opened the way to many questions on the functioning of the normal and pathological mind, the causes of mental disorders and underlying mechanisms in psychological treatments. In the later decades of the nineteenth century, human sciences were released from the experimental laboratories of psychophysiology and there was an increase of interest in unconscious mental activity, introspection, suggestion, persuasion and dreams (Whyte, 1960; Ellenberger, 1970; Pigman, 2002). This is the background history to the contemporary development of dynamic psychiatry, the psychotherapies and psychoanalysis.

References

AAVV (1976). *Folie et Dèraison à la Renaissance*. Bruxelles: Université de Bruxelles.

Ammar, S. (1968). La medicine de l'âme chez les Arabes. *L'Information Psychiatrique* 44: 855–862.

Berrios, G. (1996). *The History of Mental Symptoms*. Cambridge: Cambridge University Press.

British Library (1798). Tome VIII. Lettre du Dr. Larive aux rédact de la Bibl. Brit. sur un nouvel établissement pour la guérison des aliénés.

Burton, R. (1621). *The Anatomy of Melancholy*. Oxford. [Spanish edn: Madrid: AEN. 3 volumes, 1997, 1998, 2002.]

Castel, R. (1976). *L'Ordre psychiatrique*. Paris: Editions Minuit.

Cicerone (45 BC). *Tusculanae disputationes*. [Spanish edn: Madrid: AEN, 2005.]

Clarke, B. (1975). *Mental Disorders in Earlier Britain*. Cardiff: University of Wales Press.

Conolly, J. (1856). *The Treatment of the Insane without Mechanical Restraints*. London. [Italian edn: Torino: Einaudi, 1976.]

Dodds, E.R. (1951). *The Greeks and the Irrational*. Berkeley: University of California Press.

Ehrenwald, J. (1976). *The History of Psychotherapy*. New York: Jason Aronson.

Ellenberger, H.F. (1970). *The Discovery of the Unconscious*. London: Allen Lane.

Engstrom, E. (2003). *Clinical Psychiatry in Imperial Germany*. Ithaca, NY: Cornell University Press.

Galen (1963). *On the Passion and Errors of the Soul*. Columbus, OH: Ohio State University.

González de Chávez, M. (ed.) (1980). *La transformación de la asistencia psiquiátrica*. Madrid: AEN.

Goshen, C.H. (1967). *Documentary History of Psychiatry*. New York: Philosophical Library.

Hammarneh, S. (1962). Development of hospital in Islam. *Journal of the History of Medicine and Allied Science* 17: 366–384.

Howells, J.G. (ed.) (1991). *The Concept of Schizophrenia: Historical Perspectives*. Arlington, VA: American Psychiatric Publishing.

Hunter, R. and Macalpine, I. (1963). *Three Hundred Years of Psychiatry*. Oxford: Oxford University Press.

Jackson, S.W. (1999). *Care of the Psyche*. New Haven, CT: Yale University Press.

Jaynes, J. (1976). *The Origin of Consciousness in the Breakdown of the Bicameral Mind*. Boston: Houghton Mifflin.

Jenkins, J.H. and Barret, R.J. (2004). *Schizophrenia, Culture and Subjectivity*, Cambridge: Cambridge University Press.

Jones, K. (1972). *A History of Mental Services*. London and New York: Routledge.

Kemp, S. and Williams, K. (1987). Demonic possession and mental disorder in medieval and early modern Europe. *Psychological Medicine* 17: 21–29.

Kiev, A. (ed.) (1964). *Magic, Faith and Healing*. New York: Free Press.

Kleinman, A. (1980). *Patients and Healers in the Context of Culture*. Berkeley: University of California Press.

Kroll, J. (1973). A reappraisal of psychiatry in the Middle Ages. *Archives of General Psychiatry* 29: 276–283.

Kroll, J. and Bachrach, B. (1984). Sin and mental illness in Middle Ages. *Psychological Medicine* 14: 507–514.

Laín Entralgo, P. (1958). *La curación por la palabra en la antigüedad clásica.* Madrid: Revista de Occidente.

Laín Entralgo, P. (1961). *Enfermedad y pecado.* Barcelona: Toray.

Laín Entralgo, P. (1972). *Historia Universal de la Medicina.* Barcelona: Salvat.

Meier, C.A. (1967). *Ancient Incubation and Modern Psychotherapy.* Evanston, IL: Northwestern University Press.

Micale, M. and Porter, R. (1994). *Discovering the History of Psychiatry.* Oxford: Oxford University Press.

Midelfort, H. (1999). *A History of Madness in Sixteenth-Century Germany.* Palo Alto, CA: Stanford University Press.

Opler, M.K. (ed.) (1959). *Culture and Mental Health.* New York: Macmillan.

Parry-Jones, W. (1972). *The Trade of Lunacy.* London and New York: Routledge.

Pigman, G.W. (2002). The dark forest of authors: Freud and nineteenth century dream theory. *Psychoanalysis and History* 4: 141–166.

Riese, W. (1969). *The Legacy of Philippe Pinel.* New York: Springer.

Rocatagliata, G. (1973). *Storia della Psichiatria Antica.* Milan: Ubrico Hoepli Editore.

Roosens, E. (1979). *Des fous dans la ville? Gheel et sa therapie seculaire.* Paris: PUF.

Rosen, G. (1968). *Madness in Society.* London and New York: Routledge.

Rothman, D. (1971). *The Discovery of Asylum.* Boston: Little Brown.

Siegel, R. (1973). *Galen on Psychology, Psychopathology and Function and Diseases of the Nervous System.* Basel: Karger.

Sigerist, H.E. (1951). *A History of Medicine. I Primitive and Archaic Medicine.* Oxford: Oxford University Press.

Simon, B. (1978). *Mind and Madness in Ancient Greece.* Ithaca, NY: Cornell University Press.

Swain, G. (1977). *Le sujet de la folie.* Paris: Privat.

Ullesperger, J. (1954). *La historia de la psicología y la psiquiatría en España.* Madrid: Ed. Alhambra.

Ullman, M. (1978). *Islamic Medicine.* Edinburgh: Edinburgh University Press.

Whyte, L. (1960). *The Unconscious before Freud.* New York: Basic Books.

Zilboorg, G. (1941). *A History of Medical Psychology.* New York: Norton.

Chapter 3

The Schreber case and Freud's double-edged influence on the psychoanalytic approach to psychosis

Yrjö O. Alanen

Sigmund Freud (1856–1939), the founder of psychoanalysis, also contributed highly significantly to our psychodynamic understanding of schizophrenia. This came about even if Freud's experience of psychotic patients was not extensive. He did not work in psychiatric hospitals and the classical psychoanalytic method that he developed and to which he was committed was not applicable to the treatment of psychoses in the way it was to neuroses. Freud's actual experience of psychosis psychotherapy remained scanty, and, together with his theoretical inferences, this is an important reason why his influence on the psychoanalytic approach to schizophrenic psychoses became two-edged.

The early papers of Freud, published in the 1890s, include two brief case reports of the psychology of psychoses. The first of them deals with hallucinatory confusion state where disappointment is replaced with wish fulfilment (Freud, 1894a), the second with 'dementia paranoides' (paranoid schizophrenia) where Freud demonstrates the connection between the psychotic symptoms and repressed experiences in infancy (Freud, 1896b). Freud has stated that in later years he saw numerous psychotically ill patients sent to him by colleagues for consultation. However, the main purpose of these consultations was to make sure that he was not dealing with an underlying or incipient psychotic patient, thus unfit for the analysis. One can still notice that his criteria were not very strict: some of his well-known patients, e.g. the Wolf Man (Freud 1918b), had, in the eyes of later psychoanalysts, psychotic features. It was also later found that – despite his opinion that the inability to form transference was peculiar to schizophrenic patients – Freud conducted an analysis with at least two patients that he himself regarded as schizophrenic though with unsuccessful results (see Boyer, 1980; Roazen, 2001).[1]

Freud's treatise on Schreber's memoirs

Freud's major contribution to the understanding of psychoses was not, however, based on a patient Freud had treated personally, but on his famous analysis of the autobiographic memoirs *Denkwürdigkeiten eines Nervenk-ranken* [Memoirs of a Mental Patient], published in 1903 by Dr Daniel Paul Schreber (1842–1911), a notable German lawyer who suffered from para-noid schizophrenia. The Schreber case, 'Psycho-analytic Notes upon an Autobiographical Account of a Case of Paranoia (dementia paranoides)', was published by Freud (1911c), eight years after the patient's autobio-graphy, and it has later been studied also by several other psychoanalysts.

Schreber was 51 years old at the onset of his serious psychosis in 1893 after he had been nominated to a new, demanding official post (presiding judge, 'Senatspräsident', Court of Appeals, in Dresden, the capital of Saxony). This was not, however, his first 'nervous disease'. Nine years earlier he had been successfully cared for over six months in the same hospital headed by Professor Flechsig in Leipzig because of 'hypochondria' – most probably a depressive psychosis. In the beginning phase of that hospital treatment he made serious suicidal attempts, something which was repeated in the beginning phase of the recurrence of his illness.

Professor Flechsig also came to play an important role in Schreber's new psychosis, which gradually developed from a deep depressive state with paranoid features to typical paranoid schizophrenia with auditory hallu-cinations and delusions of persecution, odd somatic and megalomanic delusions and peculiarities of language including frequent neologisms ('Grundsprache' as called by Schreber himself). He first felt himself to be persecuted by Flechsig, 'the murderer of his soul'. Later on, Flechsig was replaced by God and the hostile persecution by the idea that God intended to make him female and he would be able to give birth to new human beings conceived out of a cosmic union with God. Schreber was treated in different mental hospitals in Saxony until 1902 when he was discharged following his own pleadings, partially recovered but without any relin-quishment of his delusional beliefs. In 1907 he was again hospitalized, two weeks after his wife's stroke; his mother had died earlier in the same year. Schreber died in a mental hospital in 1911.

According to Freud, Schreber's psychosis was psychodynamically domi-nated by repressed homosexuality. He invites attention to the point that Schreber tells of having had dreams of a recurrence of his old nervous disease well before the onset of his new psychosis – but after having been nominated to his new post and whilst waiting to be transferred to take it up. Schreber had also awoken from another dream thinking that it would actually be wonderful to be a woman, who would be the submissive party in sexual intercourse – an idea quite incompatible with his conscious male identity.

Schreber had a favourable (even if, most probably, deep down ambi-valent) relation with Flechsig after his previous episode of treatment. In his memoirs he particularly underlines his wife's gratitude towards this doctor, 'who had given her husband back to her'.

Freud postulated that the dreams of recurring illness reflect Schreber's desire to return to Flechsig's treatment. The desire, however, aroused a panic in him, because the repressed homosexual feeling associated with his affection for Flechsig threatened to break through. The paranoid delusions that Schreber had of Flechsig are understandable on the basis of two important defence mechanisms, *denial* and *projection*, as if Schreber was saying to himself: I do not love him – I hate him – because he hates me. According to Freud, these defence mechanisms are the key for understanding all kinds of paranoid psychoses.

Noteworthy is that the most serious deterioration of Schreber's psychotic state set in only after three months' hospitalization when his wife, who had until then stayed with him every day for several hours and having her lunch with him, left for a four-day visit to her father, in order to have a well-deserved rest. His wife's presence apparently had had a protective influence on her husband's fragile self-integrity. Schreber describes his experiences after her return from the holiday:

> I could no longer see in her a live person but only a miracled-up human figure in the manner of 'fleetingly made men'. Decisive for my mental breakdown was a particular night in the course of which I had a quite unusual number (perhaps half a dozen) of nocturnal emissions. At about that time also the first indications of contact with supernatural forces appeared . . . especially with Professor Flechsig who spoke with my nerves without being present in person.
>
> (quoted from Niederland, 1984: 16)

During the later course of the psychosis, Schreber experiences God as stimulating 'nerve fibres' all over his body receiving stimulation also himself. God is gradually changing Schreber's nerve fibres to female ones, and he expects new children to be born out of himself conceived by God. Schreber feels himself to be the most important person in the world because of the task given to him by God.

According to Freud's ingenious conclusion, the new symptom development actually had a restitutional function. The homosexuality was now permissible, although at the cost of a deepening regression and chronicity of the psychotic condition.

> The attraction, however, lost its terror for the nerves involved if and when they encountered a feeling of soul voluptuousness in my body, in which they in turn participated. In my body they thus found a complete or almost complete substitute for the lost heavenly bliss which is equivalent to voluptuous desire.
>
> (quoted from Niederland, 1984: 18)

Schreber repeats that his transformation into a woman is essential for the regeneration of mankind. God's attitude toward this earth and to all human beings is derived from his relationship with Schreber.

Freud interpreted that both Professor Flechsig and God were, for Schreber, figures on to whom he projected emotions originally felt for his father in childhood. It was a question of transference. This was also well fitted to the fact that – as reported to Freud by a Dresden physician – Schreber's father had been a significant personality, a physician like Flechsig and a well-known pioneer of health education and gymnastics, inspirer of 'Schreber Associations' devoted to the systematic cultivation of these activities.

Psychologically significant is also the knowledge that Schreber and his wife did not – despite their devoted wishes – have any children, but experienced several miscarriages which troubled and frustrated both of them. We may think that Schreber's delusion of himself giving birth to children conceived by God also had, in a way, the meaning of correcting this situation. In 1903, after Schreber's discharge from hospital, the couple adopted a ten-year-old girl who, as an old lady, told to Niederland of her adoptive father's warmth and kindness – he was 'more of a mother to me than my mother'.

At the end of his essay Freud (1911c), based on his libido theory (Freud, 1905d), postulated that schizophrenic psychosis involves a conversion of libido (i.e. pleasure-seeking drives) away from external objects and directing it toward one's self. In paranoid psychosis this regression is still partial, while in dementia praecox (actual schizophrenia) it is complete. This leads to the conclusion that the disposing fixation of the libido in schizophrenia must be earlier than in paranoid psychosis. The unconscious homosexual urges, which we so often – according to Freud, regularly – find in paranoid psychoses, obviously do not have a parallel role in schizophrenia. While presenting these ideas, Freud also referred to his pupils, especially to the work of Karl Abraham (1908).

According to Freud, the psychodynamics of psychoses thus consists of two stages: the first stage of the abandonment of object love and its redirection toward one's self is of basic significance; this is often followed by symptom formation that could be interpreted as an effort to revive the lost objects, yet in a manner that is egocentric and megalomanic and simultaneously isolated from the real objects. Schreber's delusive fantasies and visions of God were symptoms of precisely this kind.

Later studies on the Schreber Case

Niederland's findings

Among the later psychoanalysts dealing with Schreber's psychosis, the careful studies by William G. Niederland are especially important. Through historical studies of Schreber's life, including his hospital treatments, he could throw new light especially on his family background and father relationship. Even if much knowledge of Schreber's father could be found from public sources, details of the family life were insufficient in Daniel Paul Schreber's *Memoirs* – the chapter dealing with them had been censored as 'unfit for publication'.

Niederland's studies, beginning during the 1950s (Niederland, 1951, 1959, 1960, 1963, 1984) confirmed the basis of Freud's transference hypotheses of Schreber's delusions – probably even stronger than what Freud could have wished. Daniel Paul Schreber's father, Dr Moritz Schreber (1808–1861), was in his time a very well-known figure in Saxony and also in surrounding Germany, the writer of a popular manual on bringing up children, *Kallipädie*, and also the founder of so-called 'Schrebergarten': small rented pieces of land, filled with various useful plants and flowers.[2] As a physician, Dr Moritz Schreber became the principal of the Dresden institution for orthopaedics. What is most relevant for us is that he seems to have been a very dominating personality, with obvious (though probably unconscious) sadistic features. The educational methods he described in his pedagogic books and writings were extremely authoritarian and hard, with the purpose of achieving the child's absolute obedience and to cure the child of evil inclinations. He had constructed several pieces of equipment (pictured in Niederland's book, 1984) to serve these purposes; for example, a posture chair ('Geradehalter') with a head holder, which forced the child to sit upright and immobile while doing his homework, as well as an apparatus for the purpose of maintaining a perfect posture in the sleeping child. Probably one of the aims of these mechanical devices was to prevent masturbation, which at that time was generally held as an important cause of mental dullness and nervous disorders.

As emphasized by two later biographers of the Schreber family (Israëls, 1989; Lothane, 1992), an authoritarian character was typical of the cultural environment and ideas on child education in Germany during the eighteenth century. However, Niederland's findings still clearly confirm Moritz Schreber's domineering personality and unusual interest in heavy-handed training of his children. The father demanded, for example, that from the age of two the children should be washed daily with cold water. The moral principles he applied for the children's upbringing were extremely strict. In his manual, Dr Schreber (senior) writes that the methods and equipment pictured 'were also regularly and actively personally applied by him in rearing his own children – with telling effect, as he reports with paternal pride' (Niederland, 1984). It is noteworthy that many of these childhood experiences had rather direct points of contact with the son's delusional ideas of 'divine miracles' brought about by God in his body: 'hardly a single limb or organ in my body escaped being temporally damaged by miracles, nor a single muscle being pulled by miracles'. Undoubtedly, like his son in his delusions, Moritz Schreber also had his own idea 'to create a better and healthier race of men'.

It is interesting and easy to understand that – besides ideas of submitting to the will of God and submitting to him sexually – the *Memoirs* also include aspects that are covertly disparaging and derogatory to both father and God, as referred to already in Freud's treatise. So Schreber junior, for example once writes that the God in his heaven does not really understand the people living on earth.

Niederland also gives us some interesting information of Moritz Schreber's own developmental background. He was a man of small stature, in his youth physically underdeveloped and of delicate health. One of Schreber senior's books contains a brief case history entitled 'Confessions of One who had been Insane', which, according to Niederland, was probably largely autobiographical. In the book he depicts a youth inclined to attacks of melancholia, morbid brooding and tormenting criminal impulses. (This case history can be found in totality in Israëls' 1989 book.) Anyway, Moritz Schreber succeeded in overcoming his problems through persistent training, great personal effort, and methodical muscular exercises. Apparently he transmitted the solution for his own problems on to the next generation, coercing his sons to have the same treatment in their childhood.

Niederland (1984: 74) defines Schreber senior as 'a symbiotic father', 'whose all pervasive presence, usurpation of the maternal role, and other domineering features (overtly sadistic as well as paternalistically benevolent, punitive as well as seductive) lent themselves to their fusion with the bizarre God hierarchy characteristic of the son's delusional system'. The family tragedy did not save even the elder brother of the writer of the *Memoirs*: he committed suicide at the age of 38. The three daughters of the family had a better history.[3]

But what about Daniel Paul Schreber's mother? The information about her seems very scanty, compared with that about her husband. Freud does not even mention her in his treatise. Niederland has, however, found a letter written by Schreber's elder sister Anna in 1909, two years after the mother's death. According to her: 'Father discussed with our mother everything and anything; she took part in all his ideas, plans, and projects; she read the galley proofs of his writings together with him, and was his faithful, close companion in everything.'

It is understandable – states Niederland – that a loyal daughter would tend to depict the parental relationship in a harmonious fashion. The picture of a paternalistic atmosphere, ruled by the father with mother as his loyal follower, and also it is to be noted a person giving him important support, still seems very clear. Undoubtedly, this became most important after Moritz Schreber had an accident in 1851 in which an iron ladder fell on his head. After this, he had continuous attacks of headache and often isolated himself in his room to write his booklets and other presentations.

Anna tells how her mother, after her father's death, 'in her grief, destroyed everything that reminded her of him' (Israëls, 1989) – was this a reflection of inner ambivalence?

Niederland (1963) assumes that most probably there was a regressive fusion of primitive mother and father images with each other, reflected in Schreber's psychotic delusions. Some peculiar complexities of Schreber's deity, especially the division into anterior and posterior 'forecourts', etc., may represent such condensed, archaically distorted (and, at the same time, concretized) parental fusions in the son's delusional system. A couple of years before Niederland, Robert B. White (1961) had presented the hypothesis that primitive, oral, destructive-dependent impulses towards Schreber's mother-figure were a crucial component of his psychotic conflict. According to White, Schreber's delusion of being a woman was at one level an expression of the wish to regain a primitive and least differentiated relation with the mother: 'Schreber was simultaneously the foetus and the mother who carries the foetus.'[4]

These ideas seem believable. In our Finnish family studies (Alanen et al., 1966) we also met rather often – besides possessive mothers – such 'symbiotic fathers' acting as the pathological centre of the family dynamics, with excessively intrusive relations to their children (or one of them), based on narcissistic projective identifications. Through their behaviour, they also push aside the mother, trying to take her place in the family dynamics.

The significance of the father transference is also striking in an interesting passage of *Memoirs*, in which Schreber describes his pre-psychotic problems connected with his promotion to the new position: 'The burden was the heavier, and put great demands on tact in personal intercourse, as the members of the five-man court, of which I had to assume the presidency, were nearly all my seniors, far superior to me in age (up to twenty years) and, moreover, more familiar with the practice of the court to which I was a newcomer.' Along with Niederland (1951) we may conclude that he found himself surrounded by threatening father figures in whose midst he saw himself as a filial intruder, helpless and in danger. I suppose that he also had a heightened unconscious need for internal identification with strong and friendly male objects, which possibly contributed to the sexualization of his relationship to Professor Flechsig.

Compared with Freud's treatise, Niederland's findings and views emphasize the importance of interactional family processes in the development of Schreber's personality and his psychosis, thus preceding the family studies on schizophrenic psychoses which originated at the same time. Freud's emphasis was to study and interpret the internal psychodynamic development of the patient and his disorder, even if he was the first to notice the importance of Schreber's father relationship as the basis of his psychotic-level transferences to Flechsig and God. In Freud's later writings on psychoses, his goal in understanding was even more wholly directed (and restricted) to the internal psychodynamics. We may also note that the significance of countertransference, especially heightened in the psychotherapy of psychotic patients as emphasized by later psychoanalysts, was hardly dealt with by Freud during that time.

Lothane's (1992) book gives a thorough review of the later psychoanalytic literature around Daniel Paul Schreber. Among them, I would especially draw attention to Theodore Lidz's (1975) review of Niederland's findings, including his point that Niederland should have emphasized that Schreber's delusions were more the result of repressed feelings of hatred than of suppressed and projected homosexual tendencies, as was one-sidedly pointed out by Freud. Lidz also states that 'the passive homosexual stance of the patient (Schreber) might have been a result of his father's subjugation; or, of the patient's wish to have been a girl who would not have been so menaced by castration threats'. He emphasizes the fact (also pointed out by Niederland), that in reality Flechsig had utilized castration as a treatment of mental disorders in his hospital, 'which may have had much to do with Schreber's delusion of having been "unmanned" and turned into a woman'. Such knowledge certainly had its reflections in Schreber's transference from his father to Flechsig and in the repressed hostile part of these inner object representations.

Most recently, John Steiner (2002) published an interesting treatise on the Schreber case, examining the gradually deepening regression of Schreber's illness from a melancholic depression towards paranoia and subsequently towards a psychotic organization experienced as a psychic retreat. Steiner especially emphasizes Schreber's hospital experiences of rejection, first on the part of Flechsig (who had promised a cure and then lost interest in Schreber), later on the part of his wife, as major causes of his regressive development. The wife's change from a living human person to a 'miracled-up' scarcely living figure, stimulated by her visit to her father (see earlier), as perceived by Schreber, may certainly reflect hateful feelings reactivated by this 'desertion' (and jealousy).

Freud's later writings on schizophrenia

In his widely read essay 'On Narcissism: An Introduction' (1914c) Freud further specified his views on early libido and its relation to schizophrenia. He distinguished between ego libido and object libido, love of oneself and love of others. The first postnatal stage of libido is objectless, characterized by 'pure autoeroticism'. This is followed by primary narcissism, where the object of libido is oneself. It is only after this that libido begins to be directed increasingly toward other people, while the ego libido is retained at the same time and constant partial and reciprocal shifts take place between it and object libido. Schizophrenic psychosis (for which Freud had proposed the term paraphrenia) is characterized by megalomania (reflecting an excessive investment of the ego with libido) and turning away from the external world. 'In consequence of the latter change, they become inaccessible to the influence of psychoanalysis and cannot be cured by our efforts.'

Freud even more strongly emphasized his therapeutic pessimism with regard to schizophrenia in the following year in his essay 'The Unconscious' (Freud, 1915e). In the last part of it he makes a clear difference between the preconditions for treatability in 'transference neuroses' (anxiety hysteria, conversion hysteria and obsessional neurosis) and schizophrenic psychoses. Here, no attention is given to the fact that the psychotherapeutic relationship is an interactional two-person process that is also influenced by the way in which the other person, the therapist, approaches the patient.

I may here refer to an illustrative case report of the analysis of a schizophrenic woman published by Herbert Rosenfeld (1987). The patient's narcissistic withdrawal appeared to be a particular (and interactional) form of defensive object relationship that helped the patient to reject and split off any awareness of her inner reality containing emotions of love or hate to objects close to her, even so far as to lead to fear of losing her awareness of her identity as a separate person.[5]

One implication of Freud's standpoint was that the early mother–child relationship gradually became of central importance in psychoanalytic notions of schizophrenia. The essence of the disorder – the decisive libido fixation – had come about at a very early stage. The development of the object libido had been stunted or seriously handicapped from the very beginning, and it had been ready, when faced with frustration, to withdraw into the state of primary narcissism, unlike in neuroses, where the critical origins of disordered development occurred later. Abraham (1916) described a case of 'dementia praecox' he had analysed, pointing convincingly to the importance of the oral zone, through the patients' fixation to oral forms of gratification. Some years later, he presented a comprehensive classification of stages of libidinal organization, comparing it to the findings of embryologists (Abraham, 1924). We should keep in mind that Freud never ignored the biological research into mental phenomena but tried, for example, in the frames of his instinct theories, to find integrating points of contact between the two approaches.

In the 1920s, having published his theory of the structure of psychological functions (id, ego, superego), Freud (1924b) in his short paper 'Neurosis and Psychosis' proposed a different definition of 'perhaps the most important genetic difference' between a neurosis and a psychosis: neurosis is the result of a conflict between the ego and the id, whereas psychosis is the analogous outcome of a similar disturbance in the relations between the ego and the external world. In neurosis the ego (the psychological functions oriented towards the internal control and external adjustment of the personality) represses the anxiety-provoking drives, whereas in psychosis the ego is overrun by the id, becomes distorted by some aspects of reality and thereby loses its commitment to external realities. Freud also emphasized the role of the superego in all forms of mental illnesses, especially in depressive disorders (melancholia) that corresponded to a conflict between the ego and the superego.

When presenting this formula Freud emphasized that there may be 'good grounds for being suspicious of such simple solutions of a problem', expecting, however, that it will turn out to be correct in the roughest outline. In another short paper, 'The Loss of Reality in Neurosis and Psychosis', published in the same year (Freud, 1924e), Freud discussed the fact that not only in psychoses but also in neuroses the patient's relation to reality is in some way disturbed. A couple of years later he returned to these problems at the end of his paper 'Fetishism' (1927e), even stating that he now had reason to regret that, in proposing the essential difference between neurosis and psychosis in the papers referred to above, he had ventured so far. A careful reading of the paper on fetishism still shows that it was a question only of a relative change of his views. He referred to two young men who had failed to take cognizance of the death of their father and yet neither of them had developed a psychosis. Further study led, however, to a solution of this apparent contradiction by showing that it was only one current in their mental life that had not recognized their father's death; there was another current which took full account of the fact. 'I may thus keep to the expectation that in a psychosis the one current – that which fitted in with reality – would have in fact been absent', writes Freud. In this essay, he introduces the term *split* to describe the psychological defence mechanism used by these young men – a term which later received a crucial position in the psychological understanding of psychoses.

In his posthumous treatise 'An Outline of Psycho-Analysis' Freud (1940a) states that the precipitating cause of the outbreak of a psychosis is either that reality has become intolerably painful or that instincts have become extraordinarily intensified. The ego's detachment from reality could, however, only rarely or perhaps never be carried through completely. One learns from patients after their recovery that at the time in some corner of their mind there was a normal person hidden 'who, like a detached spectator, watched the hubbub of illness go past him'. Freud then continues:

> We may probably take it as being generally true that what occurs in all these cases is a psychical *split*. Two psychical attitudes have been formed instead a single one – one, the normal one, which takes account of reality, and another which, under the influence of instincts, detaches the ego from reality. The two exist alongside of each other. The issue depends of their relative strength. If the second is or becomes the stronger, the necessary precondition for a psychosis is present. If the relation is reversed, then there is an apparent cure of the delusional disorder. Actually it has only retreated in the unconscious – just as

numerous observations lead us to believe that the delusion existed
ready-made for a long time before its manifest irruption.

(Freud, 1940a: 202)

We may still agree with Boyer (1980) who ends his treatise on Freud's
contributions to schizophrenia by stating that even if in his last writings
Freud 'indicated awareness that in the schizophrenias total withdrawal of
instinctual cathexis does not take place, he never totally abandoned his
(early) theory of the psychoses'.

Freud's two-edged influence

Through his study of Schreber's memoirs, Freud was the first to publish a
solid and comprehensive study of the psychodynamics of a disorder within
the group of schizophrenic psychoses. In other chapters of this book we will
read about how this work was continued by later psychoanalysts and other
psychodynamically oriented researchers.

However, Freud's influence on the psychoanalytic study and treatment of
schizophrenic psychoses became two-edged because of his views on the
therapeutic inaccessibility of schizophrenic patients, so strongly emphasized
especially in the papers he wrote following the Schreber treatise. In his later
writings the contrast between 'transference neuroses' and 'narcissistic neuroses' became somewhat smoother, but the views expressed earlier over-
shadowed them in the greater part of the psychoanalytic community.

Freud's pessimistic views about the psychoanalytic therapy of psychoses
were weighty enough to keep the interest of most psychoanalysts to these
patients largely theoretical. The possibility that an empathic therapeutic
encounter could be able to create new hope and a therapeutic relationship
even in the mind of a patient withdrawn from contact with other people was
largely ignored. During the very early years of psychoanalysis a growing
interest to treat psychotic patients was not uncommon but, following the
'Master's' standpoint, this usually soon faded, only to begin to be slowly
awakened again two or three decades later.

Practical matters such as the unsuitability of the classical psychoanalytic
technique for the treatment of these patients had its role: this technique was
the only one taught to the candidates in most psychoanalytic training
institutes – that which was considered 'pure gold' compared with other
approaches which were regarded as mixed with 'the copper' of supportive
elements. And, as with Freud, not many analysts were working in the wards
of mental hospitals. The role of society's large-scale resistance to views on
the psychological origins of patients with schizophrenia is a topic whose
study is still in its beginnings.

Nevertheless there were exceptions: psychoanalysts who tried to treat
psychotic patients soon noted that these patients – or a great deal of them –

were capable of developing a transference relationship to their therapist. For many seriously disturbed psychotic patients with lack of a sufficient organization of ego functions the treatment was possible only when they were persuaded not to lie on the couch, at least in the beginning phase of the therapy. A concrete face-to-face contact could best help them to develop an enduring transference and an internalization process with the therapist, so important in the treatment of schizoprenic patients.[6]

The most important precondition for the psychoanalytically oriented psychotherapy with schizophrenic patients is the therapist's capacity to develop an empathic countertransference, and to create an interactive relationship. The patient's transference is often ambivalent and vulnerable to frustrations, but when met with empathic understanding a strong and durable dependency on the therapist can be awakened. Pioneers of psycho-analytic psychosis psychotherapy – G. Benedetti (1979), e.g. with a special strength – have emphasized that the development of a therapeutic relation-ship and its advance is always a two-way process, not only based on the patient's transference but as much on the therapist's countertransference to the patient. When reading Freud's early papers, one notices that he only rarely referred to countertransference processes and then mostly warning of injurious effects of transference phenomena based on the analyst's early experiences now directed at the patient.

It also became clear that the libido theory as such, even in modified forms, has its limitations, especially in the understanding of psychotic disorders. Freud's hypothesis of a purely autoerotic first phase has not proved to be correct in the light of empirical studies of small babies (e.g. Stern, 1985). Freud's structural theory has been supplemented by object relation theories (especially the internalized and externalized object rep-resentations), which are crucial for our understanding of psychotic patients and their psychoanalytically oriented treatment (see e.g., Klein, 1946; Volkan, 1990, 1995; Jackson, 2001).

Other psychotherapeutic approaches more or less connected with Freud's work have been developed. I have sometimes wondered whether a family-centred therapy with Daniel Paul Schreber and his wife would have been able to save this famous patient from the fateful regression into which he fell in the hospital due to the temporary 'rejection' on the part of his wife – without believing that such intervention would have made unnecessary a lengthy transference–countertransference relationship with a psychoanaly-tically oriented individual therapist.

Notes

1 According to Freud's letter to a colleague (see Boyer 1980: 64–68) the unsatis-factory result of one of these treatments, conducted around 1930, may have confirmed Freud's pessimistic opinions of psychosis psychotherapy. Boyer thinks

that the discontinuation of the treatment of this patient was due to Freud's sudden abandonment of the classical psychoanalytic technique (because of the fear of a new psychotic breakdown which he thought he would be unable to manage). The patient may have sensed this as a sign of his pessimism and left the treatment at his own initiative.

2 According to H. Israëls (1989), the fame of Moritz Schreber as the founder of these gardens was undeserved, even if they were linked with his name.

3 Gustav Schreber, a lawyer like his brother, committed suicide by shooting himself in 1877. According to Lothane (1992) he was depressed but was also 'alleged' to suffer from syphilis.

4 Murray Jackson noted to me that he certainly agrees with this interpretation. He strongly emphasizes the significance of 'double identifications' among Schreber's inner object relationships. Schreber's delusion of the 'regeneration of mankind' is, according to Jackson, also a wish to give mother babies in reparation of his attacks on real or imagined displacing siblings.

5 I am indebted to Dr Gustav Schulman for this point and the reference to Rosenfeld.

6 Some experienced therapists (e.g. Boyer, 1983; Volkan, 1990) have also published positive reports on psychotherapy of these patients in the conventional psychoanalytic setting.

References

Abraham, K. (1908). The psychosexual differences between hysteria and dementia praecox. In *Selected Papers of Karl Abraham, M.D.* London: Hogarth Press, 1949, pp. 64–79.

Abraham, K. (1916). The first pregenital stage of the libido. In *Selected Papers of Karl Abraham, M.D.* London: Hogarth Press, 1949, pp. 64–79, 248–279.

Abraham, K. (1924). A short study of the development of the libido, viewed in the light of mental disorder. In *Selected Papers of Karl Abraham, M.D.* London: Hogarth Press, 1949, pp. 418–501.

Alanen, Y.O., Rekola, K., Stewen, A. *et al.* (1966). The family in the pathogenesis of schizophrenic and neurotic disorders. *Acta Psychiatrica Scandinavica* 42 (Suppl. 189).

Benedetti, G. (1979). The structure of psychotherapeutic relationship in the individual treatment of schizophrenia. In C. Müller (ed.) *Psychotherapy of Schizophrenia*. Amsterdam: Excerpta Medica, pp. 31–37.

Boyer, L.B. (1980). Historical development of psychoanalytic psychotherapy of the schizophrenias: the followers of Freud. In L.B. Boyer and P.L. Giovacchini *Psychoanalytic Treatment of Schizophrenic, Borderline and Characterological Disorders*. 2nd edn. New York: Jason Aronson, pp. 35–70.

Boyer, L.B. (1983). *The Regressed Patient*. New York: Jason Aronson.

Freud, S. (1894a). The defence-neuropsychoses. *Standard Edition*, III: 41–61. London: Hogarth Press.

Freud, S. (1896b). Further remarks on the defence-neuropsychoses. *Standard Edition*, III: 157–183. London: Hogarth Press.

Freud, S. (1905d). Three essays on sexuality. *Standard Edition*, VII: 123–243. London: Hogarth Press.

Freud, S. (1911c). Psycho-analytic notes upon an autobiographical account of a case of paranoia (dementia paranoides). *Standard Edition*, XII: 1–79. London: Hogarth Press.

Freud, S. (1914c). On narcissism: An introduction. *Standard Edition*, XIV: 67–102. London: Hogarth Press.

Freud, S. (1915e). The unconscious. *Standard Edition*, XIV: 159–204. London: Hogarth Press.

Freud, S. (1918b). From the history of an infantile neurosis. *Standard Edition*, XVII: 3–122. London: Hogarth Press.

Freud, S. (1924b). Neurosis and psychosis. *Standard Edition*, XIX: 149–154. London: Hogarth Press.

Freud, S. (1924e). The loss of reality in neurosis and psychosis. *Standard Edition*, XIX: 183–190. London: Hogarth Press.

Freud, S. (1927e). Fetishism. *Standard Edition*, XXI: 147–158. London: Hogarth Press.

Freud, S. (1940a). An outline of psycho-analysis. *Standard Edition*, XIII: 139–207. London: Hogarth Press.

Israëls, H. (1989). *Schreber: Father and Son*. Madison, CT: International Universities Press.

Jackson, M. (2001). *Weathering the Storms. Psychotherapy for Psychosis*. London: Karnac.

Klein, M. (1946). Notes on some schizoid mechanisms. *International Journal of Psycho-Analysis* 27: 99–110.

Lidz, T. (1975). Review of the Schreber Case by William T. Niederland. *Psychoanalytic Quarterly* 44: 653–666.

Lothane, Z. (1992). *In Defense of Schreber. Soul Murder and Psychiatry*. Hillsdale, NJ: Analytic Press.

Niederland, W.G. (1951). Three notes on the Schreber case. *Psychoanalytic Quarterly* 20: 579–591.

Niederland, W.G. (1959). Schreber: father and son. *Psychoanalytic Quarterly* 28: 151–169.

Niederland, W.G. (1960). Schreber's father. *Journal of the American Psychoanalytic Association* 8: 492–499.

Niederland, W.G. (1963). Further data and memorabilia pertaining to the Schreber case. *International Journal of Psycho-Analysis* 44: 201–207.

Niederland, W.G. (1984). *The Schreber Case. Psychoanalytic Profile of a Paranoid Personality Expanded Edition*. Hillsdale, NJ: Analytic Press.

Roazen, P. (2001). *The Historiography of Psychoanalysis*. Edison, NJ: Transaction Publishers.

Rosenfeld, H.A. (1987). *Impasse and Interpretation*. London: Tavistock.

Steiner, J. (2002). Gaze, dominance and humiliation in the Schreber case. *International Journal of Psychoanalysis* 85: 269–284.

Stern, D.N. (1985). *A View from Psychoanalysis and Developmental Psychology*. New York: Basic Books.

Volkan, V.D. (1990). The psychoanalytic psychotherapy of schizophrenia. In L.B. Boyer and P. Giovacchini (eds) *Master Clinicians on Treating the Regressed Patient*. Northvale, NJ: Jason Aronson.

Volkan, V.D. (1995). *The Infantile Psychotic Self and Its Fates: Understanding and*

Treating Schizophrenics and other Difficult Patients. Northvale, NJ: Jason Aronson.

White, R.B. (1961). The mother-conflict in Schreber's psychosis. *International Journal of Psycho-Analysis* 42: 55–73.

Chapter 4

The Burghölzli School

Bleuler, Jung, Spielrein, Binswanger and others

Klaus Hoffmann

It is Burghölzli's achievement – recognised throughout the world – to be the first university clinic to take up psychoanalysis and apply it to gain knowledge of the true mental illnesses. Although psychoanalysis was not introduced at that time to treat the true mental illnesses, its study led to the psychological understanding of the language, asocial behaviour, motoric manifestations of illness, and other symptoms of many mentally sick persons. On the basis of psychoanalytic study, a much closer relationship between doctor and patient, so essential for treatment, could be established than ever before.

(M. Bleuler, 1951: 378)

Psychoanalytic therapy of psychoses in the German-speaking world, indeed in the world in general, began at the University Psychiatric Hospital in Zurich, Burghölzli. Actively supported by its then director Eugen Bleuler, Karl Abraham, Carl Gustav Jung, Abraham Arden Brill, Max Eitingon, Alphonse Maeder and Ludwig Binswanger worked with psychotic patients using Freud's method of free association and attention to the expressions of the unconscious as early as from 1903. Freud favoured this as, inter alia, the following postcard message to Bleuler dated 30 January 1906 shows: 'Honoured colleague, after Jung's splendid study of dementia praecox, now your so comprehensive essay – I'm confident that we'll soon conquer psychiatry' (M. Bleuler, 1979: 21).

Eugen Bleuler (1857–1939)

In keeping with his character, Bleuler's external life followed a straight line. Born at Zollikon on 30 April 1857, he spent a happy, busy youth in his then still rural hometown, and he retained its simple earthiness all his life. 'At school he hesitated between the study of medicine or history. If he – for the good fortune of our field – chose the former, his interest in the genetic aspects remained a constant guide in his activities' (Maier, 1941: 10). From March 1885 as assistant to Auguste Forel (1848–1931) at Burghölzli, he was already recommended by the latter in 1886 to head up the Rheinau Clinic, which function he exercised until 1898. At Rheinau, Bleuler devoted himself very intensively to the chronically ill patients and practically lived with them. Then, from 1898 to 1927, he worked as director of the University Psychiatric Hospital Burghölzli in Zurich. In addition he was the full-time president of the board of the model Zurich detoxification clinic at Ellikon an der Thur.

Bleuler was the first psychiatry professor in the world openly to support Freud's psychoanalysis and to try, together with his colleagues, to put it into practice in his clinic. Already in 1896 he had reviewed Breuer and Freud's studies of hysteria positively, and he praised Freud's *The Interpretation of Dreams* (Falzeder, 2004). His first psychoanalytic work 'Freudian Mechanisms in the Symptomatology of the Psychoses' appeared in 1906. Bleuler reached the greatest nearness to Freud in his 1910 paper: 'The Psychoanalysis of Freud: A Defence and Critical Remarks' (Bleuler, 1910; see Walser, 1976: 1195). Bleuler was one of the first authors and co-editors of the *Yearbook of Psychoanalytic and Psycho-Pathological Research.*

In 1911 Eugen Bleuler's famous monograph *Dementia Praecox or the Group of the Schizophrenias* came out, in which he labelled the illness described by Emil Kraepelin as dementia praecox with the new concept of the group of schizophrenias and thereby also emphasised the individual variety of the symptoms. In his foreword, Bleuler also wrote: 'An important part of the attempt to extend the pathology is nothing other than the application of Freud's ideas to dementia praecox' (Bleuler, 1911/1988: XV). From his rather biological-monistic viewpoint, Bleuler defined the psychotherapy which deals with the patient's affects as the true therapy in psychiatry.

Shortly after the Nuremberg Psychoanalytic Congress in 1910, Bleuler distanced himself from the psychoanalytic movement, although Freud wanted to name him president of the Swiss association. For Bleuler, it was developing into a new *Weltanschauung* and overemphasised sexuality. Freud deeply regretted this step of Bleuler's and defended himself against the latter's reproaches.

One can hope that the complete correspondence between Freud and Bleuler will soon be available (see Falzeder, 2004). Alexander and Selesnick (1965) show in a few excerpts from letters how Freud presents his arguments to Bleuler for the founding of a psychoanalytic association. According to Freud, only Bleuler could be the mediator, the promoter of tolerance in the world of psychiatry; later Freud thought that Binswanger could take over this task. After Jung's separation from the psychoanalytic movement Bleuler wrote to Freud:

Scientifically I still do not understand why it is so important to you that the whole edifice of psychoanalysis should be accepted. But I remember

I told you once that no matter how great your scientific accomplishments are, psychologically you impress me as an artist. From this point of view it is understandable that you do not want your art product to be destroyed. In art we have a unit which cannot be torn apart. In science you made a great discovery which has to stay intact. How much of what is loosely connected with it will survive is not important.

(Alexander and Selesnick, 1965: 6)

No psychoanalytic case histories of Bleuler have been preserved. We can assume that on his rounds and also on walks he talked with his patients and brought his knowledge to bear in doing so. One can hardly speak of a methodically structured psychoanalysis in today's sense. But Bleuler remained just as committed to a psychodynamic understanding of the more serious psychic disturbances as to a practical clinical access to the patients. In 1916 he wrote his psychiatric textbook, which went through many new editions thanks to the work of his son, Manfred Bleuler.

Carl Gustav Jung (1875–1961)

On 10 December 1900, Jung, son of a minister of the Reformed Church, started to work at the University Psychiatric Hospital in Zurich. In 1902, he finished his medical dissertation about the psychology and pathology of occult phenomena and experimental findings with word associations. He studied Freud, mainly his book *The Interpretation of Dreams* (Freud, 1900).

Jung's works *The Psychology of Dementia Praecox* and *The Content of Psychosis*, which appeared in 1907 and 1908 respectively, 'did not yet aim explicitly at a therapeutic method, but were the fruit of very intensive and enthusiastic analytic work with schizophrenics at Burghölzli' (Müller, 1958: 456). Affectivity, for him, was the central feature of mental life; complexes resulting from (and later in) affective interpersonal conflicts were the core reasons for neurotic and psychotic developments. This was shown in several case reports. One finds quite similar ideas with Bleuler.

Without the concepts of ego strength and weakness which were developed later, Jung soon realised: 'A verbal suggestion can seldom be placed in dementia praecox, and when it does succeed, the results are uncontrollable and seemingly haphazard. Thus foreign elements are mixed in with normal suggestibility with early patients' (Jung 1907/1990: 87). Despite this clearly recognised limitation, Jung tried to formulate a sense of life for the patient mainly from the content of his spoken words, less from his everyday life and his communication structure. He saw psycho-pathological features like hallucinations more in terms of the traditional Freudian drive concept as wish fulfilment, less as signs of loneliness, despair and suffering (Jung, 1907/1990: 166).

Through his association experiments, Jung developed the essential bases of the psycho-pathological structure of the schizophrenias. These experiments, directed and documented by Jung, led him to the discovery of emotionally charged complexes. 'These are autonomous contents of the unconscious which operate in the experiment as disturbances' (Wehr, 1985: 80–81).

> Even if we are far from explaining the inter-relations of that dark world exhaustively, we may already now maintain with certainty that in dementia praecox no symptom exists that could be described as psychologically groundless and senseless. Even the most absurd things are nothing but symbols of thoughts which are not only generally and humanly understandable, but which inhabit every human breast without exception. Thus we discover in the mentally ill not something new and unknown, but the underside of our own nature, the mother of the life problems on which we all work.
>
> (Jung, 1908/1990: 198)

Later, Jung stated both honestly and sceptically:

> It is probably still too early to speak of a psychotherapy of the psychoses. . . . At the moment I would put the main emphasis on the investigation of function and significance of the psychological factor in the aetiology and course of the psychoses.
>
> (Jung, 1919/1990: 246)

> The psychogenesis of schizophrenia also explains why certain lighter cases . . . can be psychotherapeutically cured. But one should not be too optimistic with respect to this possibility of cure. They are rare cases, for the nature of the illness and the decay of the personality hinder precisely the active agency of the therapy, namely the exertion of psychic influence.
>
> (Jung, 1928/1990: 259)

Sabina Spielrein (1885–1941)

More is known today about Sabina Spielrein having been a patient and mistress of Jung (e.g. Carotenuto, 1986; Minder, 1994; Spielrein, 2006; film by E. Marton, 2002). Less is known about her two important contributions to psychoanalytic work with psychotic patients, which were republished in the collection of her writings in 2002.

Born in 1885 into a wealthy Jewish merchant family at Rostov on the river Don, in today's Russia, she was brought to Burghölzli by her mother in 1904 because of mental problems that had lasted for several years. Jung treated her from the beginning, diagnosed a 'psychotic hysteria', and spoke about her case at the First International Congress of Neurology and Psychiatry in 1907 (Carotenuto, 1986). The quite ambivalent relationship with her father, who tyrannised her, played an important role in the treatment. Spielrein was an inpatient at Burghölzli from 17 August 1904 to 1 June 1905; Jung continued to treat her as a private patient. In 1908, Jung began an affair with Spielrein, about which Jung's wife informed Spielrein's mother, who in turn wanted to consult Bleuler about it. Jung feared for his career and turned to Freud for help:

> It is a terrible story. And particularly so in that it demonstrates the complicity of men against a woman who has succumbed to seduction by a man – demonstrates this in the style of the Victorian double standard. . . . Jung and Freud alike condemn Sabina Spielrein and appeal to her reason and insight to see that she must withdraw in favour of Jung's career and marriage.
>
> (Carotenuto, 1986: 9)

Sabina Spielrein had started to study medicine at the University of Zurich in 1905. Despite the problems, she continued to work scientifically and finished her medical studies in Zurich. In 1911, she completed her dissertation about the psychological content of a case of dementia praecox. She then became a fairly well-known psychoanalyst, among other things the training analyst of the prominent Swiss developmental psychologist Jean Piaget. From October 1911 to April 1912 she attended the Wednesday Society in Vienna. In 1912 Spielrein married the Russian physician Paul Scheftel, produced two daughters, practised in several cities in Switzerland and Germany, and returned to her hometown, Rostov, in the Soviet Union in 1923. With Freud's support, she became a member of the Russian Psychoanalytic Society. She practised there as a child psychoanalyst, founding a special nursing home for children, until psychoanalysis was forbidden by Stalin in 1936. Spielrein continued to teach at the University of Rostov until 1941, when she and her daughters were killed by the Nazis in the local synagogue.

Spielrein's 1911 case history of a psychotic woman, which contains detailed ideas on her religious and sexual delusions, is one of the very few dissertations in early psychiatric and psychological history dealing with a psychoanalytic approach to psychoses. According to Lütkehaus (2002), the publisher of Spielrein's collected works, 'her own illness was the basis of understanding, nearness as the basis of empathy'.

Spielrein (1911/2002) tells the story of her patient, the content of her delusions, and the therapist's attempts to influence her. The patient is unhappily married and had had an abortion, she being Protestant, the husband Catholic. She often fears that the hospital will 'catholicise' her and produces pictures touching this theme. The 'hot love' she desires from her husband cannot be realised because she no longer has any feelings of love for him and because she is no longer 'pure'. Spielrein takes up her patient's pictures and translates them into the language of their relationships. The death of the foetus also signifies its ascendance: The patient also uses it as a sexual object. Spielrein shows how she herself is used in the transference of her patient, who wanted to kiss her and asked her to cure her sexuality so that she could join her husband again.

> I don't believe that I have brought out a systematic and exhaustive analysis of this case. With a patient who is so disassociated and without a real interest in giving true explanations of her inner life, but who rather stops short at the raw materials and leaves it to the listener to make sense of them, an analysis that gets to the bottom of things is simply impossible with our current means. . . . Freud and Jung have shown us that the delusional system of our patients is by no means senseless but that it follows the same laws as a dream, for example, which always reveals itself in the end as a meaningful arrangement of complexes.
>
> (Spielrein, 1911/2002: 87)

In 'Die Destruktion als Ursache des Werdens' ['Destruction as the cause of becoming'], Spielrein (1912/2002) again brings the case history of a schizophrenic woman, showing that destruction is part of vital energy and necessary to create a new life.

> I was forced to see that the main characteristic of an individual lies in dividedness. The closer we get to conscious thinking, the more differentiated our ideas become; the deeper we penetrate into the unconscious, the more general and typical our ideas become. The depths of our psyche know no 'I', but simply its summation, the 'we'.
>
> (Spielrein, 1912/2002: 106)

This is also precisely the case with patients suffering from dementia praecox. Spielrein describes the philosopher Friedrich Nietzsche in detail as a case in point (Spielrein, 1912/2002: 117f). She defines an instinct to preserve the species which stands in contradiction to the self-preservation instinct, basing it on the observation that one must give up part of one's own world in order to enter into relation with others. Literary models are for her among others the death and resurrection of Jesus as well as the Nibelung saga in Richard Wagner's presentation.

Using Jung's concept, Spielrein spoke about her ideas concerning the death drive at the Wednesday Society in Vienna on 29 November 1911:

Destruction is thus the cause of becoming; the old form must be destroyed so that the new can take shape. There is therefore no absolute concept of death, and what is dead with respect to the old form is living for the new. Death per se is no doubt horrible, but in the service of the sexual instinct it is beneficial.

(Nunberg and Federn, 1979: 315–316)

Freud was sceptical towards the mythological tendencies of this paper, in his view overly influenced by Jung. In 'Beyond the Pleasure Principle' (1920), where he introduced the death instinct, Freud mentioned Spielrein:

In a paper rich in content and thought, but for me unfortunately not entirely clear, Sabina Spielrein has anticipated a good portion of this speculation. She describes the sadistic component of the sexual drive as 'destructive'.

(Freud, 1920: 59, note 2)

Freud noted the difference here from his dual theory (sexuality = life), but he did not discuss Spielrein's approach further. For her, destruction was inherent in sexual energy (Nitzschke, 2000).

Ludwig Binswanger (1881–1966)

Ludwig Binswanger was born into a rich psychiatric family tradition. His grandfather, bearing the same name Ludwig Binswanger (1820–1880), was a member of a Jewish South German country family of small factory owners who studied medicine in Munich, became a general practitioner and psychiatrist, but could not enter government medical service in Bavaria because he was Jewish. He took an active part in the 1848 revolution in Munich, fighting especially for equal rights for Jews, and got himself into even more difficulties than before.

Switzerland was then more liberal than the German states. After moving there, Ludwig Binswanger senior worked as director of the new cantonal mental hospital at Münsterlingen, near the German border town of Constance. In 1857 he bought the sumptuous Bellevue Villa in Kreuzlingen, very close to Constance, and founded a private asylum for mentally affected patients. In his practice, he followed the no-restraint policy of the English psychiatrist John Conolly.

Under his son Robert Binswanger, director from 1880 to 1910, Bellevue Sanatorium grew; more villas were built, the clientèle became more and more upper class and the site increasingly well known. In 1881, Josef Breuer, Freud's early mentor and co-worker, sent his patient Bertha Pappenheim, known as Freud's case Anna O, to Bellevue for a morphine aversion treatment. In the following years, Freud sent several patients who needed long-term treatment to Bellevue.

The young Ludwig Binswanger grew up in the sanatorium environment alongside its patients. After his medical studies in Lausanne, Heidelberg and Zurich, he entered the Burghölzli Clinic. Jung supervised his dissertation and joined him in carrying out association experiments. It was together with Jung that Binswanger visited Freud for the first time in 1907. During 1907 and 1908 he worked under his uncle Otto Binswanger, professor of neurology and psychiatry at Jena University in Germany.

In 1908, Ludwig Binswanger returned to Kreuzlingen and went to work for his father. On the latter's death in 1910, Ludwig took over the sanatorium, which he led until his retirement in 1956 (see Hoffmann, 1996, 1997). During over forty years the Bellevue Sanatorium became one of the very few psychiatric sanatoriums where psychoanalysis became the main method for treating psychoses. Well-known personalities such as the Russian dancer Vaslav Nijinsky, the painter Ernst Ludwig Kirchner, who created 22 of his most important wood engravings at Kreuzlingen, and many others were treated there. Bellevue also became one of the centres of Central European cultural life, from 1919 to 1932, as Binswanger organised regular scientific gatherings for philosophers, psychiatrists and jurists. For Binswanger, psychoanalysis and philosophy were important means of understanding his patients and Binswanger always saw himself as a clinician.

Although he worked closely with Jung in 1907, Binswanger stayed in contact with Freud after the 1914 split with the Zurich group. Despite their differences, mainly on philosophical issues, Freud and Binswanger remained good friends. This is evident in the Freud–Binswanger letters (Fichtner, 1992).

Binswanger treated psychotic and substance-addicted patients psychoanalytically. However, for Binswanger, the treatment of psychoses also included the active use of all the sanatorium's resources. Nurses cared for and observed the patients at times very intensively, and even entered into physical confrontations with them in order to bring the patients' psychotic aggression into the arena of real encounters with other human beings. As a documented and published example, the report written by the male nurse Fritz Wieland about Vaslav Nijinsky is quoted:

> In desperation and great anxiety he pulls his hair out and must finally be restrained. Later I was able to quieten him by talking to and stroking him. . . . At 10 o'clock he suddenly jumps up, again tears his hair out, whispers almost inaudibly: 'I'm being killed.' The patient makes a fist, stands up and threatens to strike. That can only be prevented by holding him fast, and after I talked with him for some time, he calms down. Later he comes to me, sits on my lap like a little monkey and lets me feed him.

> (Ostwald, 1991: 311)

The way that Binswanger dealt with everyday life in his sanatorium and took into account the approaches of individual psychotherapy in so doing is shown in his writing about work therapy at Bellevue:

> Thus for the first time a systematic work therapy, under the direction of my wife, was introduced. . . . Here too we try to avoid forced uniformity and schematising and let the greatest possible individualisation prevail in every respect. Whether a patient should work at all or not, whether in the carpentry shop, the weaving room, the book bindery, or farming, alone or with others, whether with or without care personnel, with this or that teacher, or preferably has private instruction in languages, literature, history, or music, whether he should continue with his scientific or artistic work, go on with his business correspondence or not, whether he is better off working in the clinic or outside it, in the same location or a distant one, etc.: All this is just a small section of the decisions that the medical and care staff together with the work therapists have to take with regard to the treatment of patients.
>
> (Binswanger, 1957: 32)

Binswanger indicated that after inpatient treatment lasting for months or even years patients continued to be treated on an outpatient basis, with the patients coming to him. Binswanger's process notes are in the University Archives at Tübingen and can be opened only several years hence.

In 1942, at the height of World War II, Binswanger published *Grundformen und Erkenntnis menschlichen Daseins* [Being-in-the-World], where he formulated the philosophical principles that also ruled his clinical practice. Psychosis is an illness manifesting itself in the interpersonal encounter and can be treated in this interpersonal encounter as well:

> What we in psychiatry label with such clear moral expressions as irresponsibility or non-committal speech, as 'unrestrained' chattering and, depending on the other characteristics, diagnose as a symptom of feeble-mindedness or dementia, a schizophrenic process or a manic flight of ideas, concerns the moral no less than the intellectual sphere and is based in each case on a particular form of existential bringing forth of history.
>
> (Binswanger, 1942/1993: 295–296)

Through love and through good new object relations, psychotics can become healthier again.

Karl Abraham (1877–1925) and other colleagues

Karl Abraham worked at Burghölzli from 1904 to 1907, after which he opened the first psychoanalytic practice in Berlin and later founded the important Berlin Psychoanalytic Institute. Abraham described libidinal traumatisations as causes of psychotic illnesses, both in the schizophrenic and manic-depressive forms; for this reason he considered psychoanalytic treatment to be highly effective. He limited himself here – always with clear methodical restrictions – to individual cases observed and treated by himself, and consistently made it clear that, in his opinion, serious psychic illnesses arose from a combination of constitutional and experiential factors, but that psychoanalytic treatment frequently led to ego-strengthening and hence to significant improvement. This approach has once again become very topical at the present time, since post-traumatic stress disorders, including those with psychotic symptoms, have moved into the centre of interest, and works on neurobiological modifications in these disorders have been published. Abraham described what is today universally recognised: the repetition compulsion, that psychic traumas are unconsciously re-enacted in the illness and treatment and thus endanger the success of the latter (Abraham 1907a, 1907b, 1912).

Following the initial enthusiasm it seems that a 'sobering up' occurred, above all in the Zurich School:

> For it became apparent that although a surfeit of 'material' was available that with schizophrenics positively teemed with sexual symbols, even the keenest interpretative work was unable to change much in the real process of the illness. In 1910 Alphonse Maeder had published a case of melancholy depression with a surprisingly good result, but this patient, a farmer from the vicinity of Zurich, had been treated as an out-patient and was therefore not comparable to the cases that had to be hospitalised because of their strong danger to themselves. Nonetheless, Maeder's case is likely the first detailed report of the successful psychoanalytic treatment of a psychotic.
>
> (Müller, 1958: 456)

However, several reports of psychoanalytic observations of psychotic patients were published in the *Yearbook of Psychoanalytic and Psycho-Pathological Research*. In 1912 Jan Nelken described an eight-month treatment of a catatonic patient whose sexual complexes were of central importance. The therapist used the patient's pictures and linked them to biblical topics. Incest fantasies and grandiose feelings were analysed. Nelken related to the delusional and catatonic conditions of his patient and brought them into the therapeutic process. Also in 1912, Grebrelskaja reported on a paranoid patient where homosexuality and a persecution delusion were the trenchant topics. Psychotic contents were interpreted in the light of psychoanalytic findings, but there was no account of the treatment.

Summary

The first attempts to understand schizophrenic symptoms psychoanalytically and to present them as case histories took place in the years just before World War I. Eugen Bleuler's clinic in Zurich was the first and for long time the only official psychiatric clinic which took an active interest in Freud's theories. After World War I, Binswanger in Kreuzlingen, Georg Groddeck (1866–1934) in Baden-Baden, István Hollós (1872–1957) in Budapest, and Frieda Fromm-Reichmann in Heidelberg were the European pioneers in inpatient psychoanalysis of psychoses.

References

Abraham, K. (1907a). Über die Bedeutung sexueller Jugendtraumen für die Symptomatologie der Dementia praecox. In K. Abraham *Gesammelte Schriften*. Frankfurt am Main: Fischer, 1982, pp. 125–131.

Abraham, K. (1907b). Das Erleiden sexueller Traumen als infantile Sexualbetätigung. In K. Abraham *Gesammelte Schriften*. Frankfurt am Main: Fischer, 1982, pp. 165–179.

Abraham, K. (1912). Ansätze zu einer psychoanalytischen Erforschung des manisch-depressiven Irreseins. In K. Abraham *Gesammelte Schriften*. Frankfurt am Main: Fischer, 1982, pp. 146–162.

Alexander, F. and Selesnick, S.T. (1965). Freud–Bleuler correspondence. *Archives of General Psychiatry* 12: 1–9.

Binswanger, L. (1942). *Grundformen und Erkenntnis menschlichen Daseins*. Zürich: Max Niehans. Also in L. Binswanger *Ausgewählte Werke, Band 2*. Heidelberg: Asanger, 1993.

Binswanger, L. (1957). *Zur Geschichte der Heilanstalt Bellevue in Kreuzlingen 1857–1957*. Zürich: Selbstdruck.

Bleuler, E. (1910). Die Psychoanalyse Freuds. Verteidigung und kritische Bemerkungen. *Jahrbuch für psychoanalytische und psychopathologische Forschungen* II: 623–730.

Bleuler, E. (1911). *Dementia praecox oder die Gruppe der Schizophrenien*. Leipzig: Deuticke. Unaltered reprint Tübingen: Edition Diskord, 1988. [English edn *Dementia Praecox or the Group of Schizophrenias*. New York: International Universities Press, 1950.]

Bleuler, M. (1951). Geschichte des Burghölzli und der psychiatrischen Universitätsklinik. In Regierungsrat des Kantons Zürich (ed.) *Zürcher Spitalgeschichte* II: 377–425.

Bleuler, M. (ed.) (1979). *Beiträge zur Schizophrenielehre der Zürcher Psychiatrischen Universitätsklinik Burghölzli*. Darmstadt: Wissenschaftliche Buchgesellschaft.

Carotenuto, A. (1986). *Tagebuch einer heimlichen Symmetrie–Sabina Spielrein zwischen Jung und Freud*. Freiburg im Breisgau: Kore.

Falzeder, E. (2004). Sigmund Freud und Eugen Bleuler. Die Geschichte einer ambivalenten Beziehung. *Luzifer-Amor* 17: 85–104.

Fichtner, G. (ed.) (1992). *Sigmund Freud–Ludwig Binswanger. Briefwechsel 1908–1938*. Frankfurt am Main: Fischer.

Freud, S. (1900). Die Traumdeutung. *Gesammelta Werke* II/III. London: Imago, 1940.

Freud, S. (1920). Jenseits des Lustprinzips. *Gesammalte Werke* XIII. London: Imago, 1940.

Grebelskaja, S. (1912). Psychologische Analyse eines Paranoiden. *Jahrbuch für psychoanalytische und psychopathologische Forschungen* IV: 116–140.

Hoffmann, K. (1996). The Scientific association of the Lake of Constance psychiatrists. *International Forum of Psychoanalysis* 5: 271–276.

Hoffmann, K. (1997). Ludwig Binswanger's Collected Papers – Introduction and Critical Remarks. *International Forum of Psychoanalysis* 6: 191–201.

Jung, C.G. (1907). Über die Psychologie der Dementia Praecox. In C.G. Jung *Psychogenese der Geisteskrankheiten*. Freiburg im Breisgau: Walter, 1990, pp. 1–175.

Jung, C.G. (1908). Der Inhalt der Psychose. In C.G. Jung *Psychogenese der Geisteskrankheiten*. Freiburg im Breisgau: Walter, 1990, pp. 171–215.

Jung, C.G. (1919). Über das Problem der Psychogenese bei Geisteskrankheiten. In C.G. Jung *Psychogenese der Geisteskrankheiteni*. Freiburg im Breisgau: Walter, 1990, pp. 235–252.

Jung, C.G. (1928). Geisteskrankheit und Seele. In C.G. Jung *Psychogenese der Geisteskrankheiten*. Freiburg im Breisgau: Walter, 1990, pp. 253–259.

Lütkehaus, L. (2002). Vorwort. Produktive Krankheit–lebendige Theorie. In S. Spielrein *Sämtliche Schriften*. Gießen: Psychosozial, pp. i–vii.

Maeder, A. (1910). Psychoanalyse bei einer melancholischen Depression. *Zentralblatt für Nervenheilkunde* 21: 50–58.

Maier, H.W. (1941). Bleulers Leben und praktisches Wirken. Ansprache an der Trauersitzung des Psychiatrisch-Neurologischen Vereins in Zürich am 9. Februar 1940. *Schweizer Archiv für Neurologie und Psychiatrie* 46: 10–15.

Marton, E. (2002). *Ich hieß Sabina Spielrein* [*My Name was Sabina Spielrein*]. Film.

Minder, B. (1994). Sabina Spielrein. Jungs Patientin am Burghölzli. *Luzifer-Amor* 7: 55–127.

Müller, C. (1958). Die Pioniere der psychoanalytischen Behandlung Schizophrener. *Nervenarzt* 29: 456–462.

Nelken, J. (1912). Analytische Beobachtungen über Phantasien eines Schizophrenen. *Jahrbuch für psychoanalytische und psychopathologische Forschungen* IV: 504–562.

Nitzschke, B. (2000). Sabina Spielrein–Die Liebe einer Psychoanalytikerin. In B. Nitschke *Das Ich als Experiment: Essays über Sigmund Freud und die Psychoanalyse im 20. Jahrhundert*. Göttingen: Vandenhoeck & Ruprecht, pp. 95–111.

Nunberg, H. and Federn, E. (eds) (1979). *Protokolle der Wiener Psychoanalytischen Vereinigung III, 1910–1911*. Frankfurt am Main: Fischer.

Ostwald, P. (1991). *Vaslav Nijinsky – A Leap into Madness*. New York: Carol Publishing.

Spielrein, S. (1911). Über den psychologischen Inhalt eines Falles von Schizophrenie (Dementia praecox). *Jahrbuch für psychoanalytische und psychopathologische Forschungen* III: 329–400. Also in S. Spielrein *Sämtliche Schriften*. Gießen: Psychosozial, 2002, pp. 11–97.

Spielrein, S. (1912). Die Destruktion als Ursache des Werdens. *Jahrbuch für psychoanalytische und psychopathologische Forschungen* IV: 465–503. Also in in S. Spielrein *Sämtliche Schriften*. Gießen: Psychosozial, 2002, pp. 98–143.

Spielrein, S. (2002). *Sämtliche Schriften*. Gießen: Psychosozial.
Spielrein, S. (2006). *Nimm meine Seele–Tagebücher und Schriften*. (Ed. T. Hensch).
    Berlin: Edition Freitag.
Walser, H.H. (1976). Psychoanalyse in der Schweiz. In D. Eicke (ed.) *Die
    Psychologie des 20. Jahrhunderts II*. Zürich: Kindler, pp. 1192–1218.
Wehr, G. (1985). *Carl Gustav Jung. Leben, Werk, Wirkung*. Munich: Kösel.

Chapter 5

The pioneering work of Paul Federn

Yrjö O. Alanen

At the beginning of the twentieth century, early case reports dealing with the psychotherapy of psychotic patients were presented by several psycho-analysts from different orientations, e.g. Jung, Maeder, Spielrein and the Swede Poul Bjerre (see Chapters 4 and 12). The most significant pioneer in this area was, however, Freud's faithful student and fellow worker Paul Federn (1871–1950) from Vienna. For rather a long time he was also the only European psychoanalyst whose interest in the development of psycho-analytic treatment of psychoses appeared to be sustained.

In 1906 Federn began to treat his first schizophrenic patient, a female artist who had deteriorated over many months into an agitated and hallucinating catatonic state. During his visits to the hospital, Federn gained the patient's confidence by his kindness. The treatment was continued while the patient lived in Federn's house and his wife acted as the therapeutic assistant. The patient recovered and later married twice without suffering from relapses of psychosis. Even in many of his later cases, Federn considered it important to rely on the help of a maternal female assistant – sometimes the patient's mother or sister – who was in charge of the patient during the therapy. The best known of these assistants was the nurse Gertrud Schwing, whose work *Ein Weg zur Seele des Geisteskranken* [An Approach to the Mind of the Psychotic], published in 1939, has been translated into several languages. With Federn's help, Schwing was the first nurse to become a member of the International Psycho-Analytical Association.

Federn was an outstanding clinician who, besides his office work, also took care of his contacts with the Viennese psychiatric university clinic, led first by Wagner von Jauregg and then Pötzl. There is an anecdote according to which Professor Wagner von Jauregg – who received the Nobel Price for his introduction of malaria treatment for brain syphilis – once told the parents of a young girl he had diagnosed as schizophrenic, 'Your daughter is incurably ill, but you may look to see if Dr Federn can help her.'

Federn, originally an internist, had become acquainted with Freud right at the beginning of the century, and was one of his first students in Vienna. Freud was Federn's analyst in the way then practised; according to Weiss

(1952) Freud was to him a father figure to whom he always felt great loyalty. Federn only hesitantly admitted the existence of some discrepancies between his own and Freud's concepts of ego psychology and the psychoanalytic therapy of psychoses and always emphasized that he was continuing Freud's way of thought. Maybe one can rephrase this by stressing that Federn's work, in fact, extended the psychoanalytic approach, originated by Freud, to the treatment of psychoses.

After Federn's death, his scientific papers and lectures on the psychotherapy of psychoses were published in *Ego Psychology and the Psychoses*, edited by his friend and pupil Edoardo Weiss (Federn, 1952). It is noteworthy that Federn – besides two short papers in 1933 in German on the indications and technique of psychosis analysis – despite his otherwise relatively extensive literary production, only published the major reports of his abundant Viennese experience on the psychotherapy of psychoses during the last decade of his life, having moved to the USA. The most important of these papers is 'Psychoanalysis of Psychoses' (Federn, 1943). It deals with both schizophrenia and manic-depressive psychoses. This paper was supplemented by 'Principles of Psychotherapy in Latent Schizophrenia' (Federn, 1947). These papers reflect the views of a clinician with astute observations and sensitive understanding of his patients, combined with a pragmatic technique always aiming to find the best way to help them.

Federn pays crucial importance to the positive relationship between the analyst and his psychotic patient: 'Whenever a psychotic feels that you understand him – he is yours.' He demonstrates that the schizophrenic patient's withdrawal from real objects is not complete. They are able (contrary to Freud's notions) to establish a transference relationship to their therapist with both healthy and disturbed parts of their personality. Although these transference relationships may easily break down as a consequence of frustrations, they may also persist life-long. For the success of therapy, positive transference is necessary and should generally not be analysed, whereas negative transference should always be interpreted; if this is not done or if it fails, the therapy may easily be interrupted. Federn is pessimistic about the possibilities of the working through of a transference psychosis in which the analyst becomes a persecutor. This may easily make further work impossible and lead to the need for a change of therapist.

Federn developed his therapeutic technique so as always to meet the demands of the patient's present psychological condition. He emphasizes that the patients also have valuable defences which must not be interfered with, and the repression often needs to be reinforced instead of being exposed. Sincerity of the analyst is inevitable: 'There are no white lies allowed with psychotics.' The classical psychoanalytic technique used with neurotics, with free association and lying on a couch, must of necessity be abandoned. Federn had many experiences of the treatment of patients who became psychotic in the middle of a classical psychoanalysis with some of his colleagues. In his writings he pays much attention to signs of latent or approaching psychosis warning about such unhappy developments.

When positive transference prevails and dangers are avoided, there are plenty of starting points for analytic work aiming to help the psychotic patient 'to decipher the meaning of his astonishing products by the use of his logical understanding and self-observation and translate with him the eruptive products of his unconscious, one after other'. This includes the patient's understanding of his injuries from, and conflicts with, the external world; how his past ego states and situations have returned and need to be repressed, or recognized as remembrances; and how the strangeness and absurdities of his mental state are due to specific inner processes.

During the analytic work, the psychoanalyst first shares and accepts the patient's psychotic falsifications, his griefs and fears. When convinced that the patient feels himself to be understood, the analyst will present the true reality, as opposed to falsifications. He then gradually shows: (a) which actual frustration, grief, or apprehension is represented by falsifications; (b) which deep fear, conflict, or frustration is a primary cause of the falsification; and (c) which ego boundary changes have made the process of falsification possible. These points form the essence of the psychoanalytic process with a schizophrenic patient.

Federn (1952: 120) states that when we treat the schizophrenic 'we treat in him several children of different ages'. He is fully aware of the import-ance of the family environment in the pathogenesis of schizophrenia: 'Every psychosis is consciously or unconsciously focused on conflicts or frus-trations in family life.' However, he does not see the influence of the family exclusively in a negative way:

> In no single case have I succeeded without the steady cooperation of the family or of someone in their place . . . Unless unsatisfactory conditions in family life are changed, the cure of psychotics turns out to have been a Sisyphean labor which ends in hospitalization or foster family life.
>
> (Federn, 1952: 121)

This does not mean that he should not recognize the impact of constitu-tional factors, best inferred from his ego psychological conclusions.

Federn's theoretical notions about the ego of a psychotic patient were creative and have, in many respects, had influence on the later development of psychoanalytic research into ego psychology and narcissism. This holds true even more so with regard to Kohut's self psychology (even if Kohut himself does not refer to Federn's work). According to Federn, the libidinal charge (cathexis) of the ego does not increase upon abandonment of external objects but should rather be described as being too weak in the

psychotic state. The concept of 'ego' characteristically received a phenomenological emphasis in Federn's writings. It approaches the 'ego-feeling'
('Ich-Erlebnis') whose intensity varies continuously in all individuals, being
weak in, for example, dream states. The common notion of ego weakness
being typical of psychotic individuals was first introduced by Federn. Every
psychosis is, he states, a mental disorder of the ego itself. The ego of
psychotics is unable to draw a boundary line that would differentiate
between the internal fantasies and external experiences. Delusions and
hallucinations are not exclusively an attempt to regain the lost objects in a
fantasy world. They may also be a consequence of the ego's more common
qualitative inability to draw boundaries between the 'real' external world
and the 'imaginary' internal images. Federn also points out that the ego
states can be repressed and more primitive ego functions used as defences
against the contemporary difficulties.

Federn's work became the foundation for the development of the
psychoanalytically oriented psychotherapy of schizophrenia. Some psychoanalysts have considered his way of including supportive elements in the
therapy perhaps too cautious, but – most often – they still retain their value
in practice. I have myself experienced Federn's wise teaching as very
important, both in my own work with people with schizophrenia and in my
endeavours to extend the scope of psychosis psychotherapists to include
professionals without a specific psychoanalytic training, especially psychiatric nurses with a warm personality and a talent to understand the quality
of problems of psychotic patients. With these kind of aspirations I was also
encouraged by these words of Federn: 'I would like to see nurses trained in
and through psychoanalytic societies, or at least with their help. We cannot
wait for exceptions like Gertrud Schwing among nurses, or Anna Freud
among pedagogues, for thousands of such helpers are needed to fight
widespread psychosis' (Federn, 1952: 135).

In this matter, as in many others, Federn was ahead his time. Like Freud,
he also (according to Weiss) could refer to a period of 'splendid isolation'
he had during the first decade of his work with psychotic patients. Later,
some followers of this work appeared, among them the Hungarian psychoanalyst Istvan Hollós, the author of the book *Hinter der gelben Mauer*
[Behind the Yellow Wall], published in 1928. During the last century of his
life, Federn's work was widely appreciated in the USA.

References

Federn, P. (1943). Psychoanalysis of psychoses. I. Errors and how to avoid them; II.
    Transference, III. The psychoanalytic process. *Psychiatric Quarterly* 17: 3–19,
    246–257, 470–487.
Federn, P. (1947). Principles of psychotherapy in latent schizophrenia. *American
    Journal of Psychotherapy* I: 129–144.

Federn, P. (1952). *Ego Psychology and the Psychoses* (ed. and introduction by E. Weiss). New York: Basic Books.

Hollós, I. (1928). *Hinter der gelben Mauer*. Stuttgart: Hippokrates Verlag.

Schwing, G. (1939). *Ein Weg zur Seele des Geisteskranken*. Zurich: Raschers Verlag.

Weiss, E. (1952). Introduction. In P. Federn *Ego Psychology and the Psychoses*. New York: Basic Books, pp. 1–21.

Chapter 6

Pioneers of psychoanalytically oriented treatment of psychosis in the USA

Ann-Louise S. Silver

Even before Freud, Jung and Ferenczi arrived in the United States in 1909, participating in the Clark University's twentieth anniversary conference, psychoanalytic thinking had influenced many Americans working with the severely mentally ill. Many were infused with hopefulness that having a method of understanding the symbolism in patients' delusions and non-verbal gestures would give them access to increasingly solid communication with their patients, which would encourage restored cohesiveness and calmness. If we can understand dreams, we can understand psychosis; if neuroses can resolve, so can psychoses. Various forms of psychotherapy had gained popularity in the preceding decades, including hypnosis and sugges-tion: 'Into this therapeutic ferment dropped just the right catalyst, the Swiss psychotherapist Paul Dubois' book *The Psychic Treatment of Nervous Disorders* (1905) . . . [which] quickly [became] the "Bible" of the nascent psychotherapy movement in America' (Gach, 1980: 143). But Dubois' book provided encouragement without the conceptual framework Freud would supply. 'American physicians were ready for a theoretical model which explained psychological facts psychologically and which prescribed a clinical technique for their patients' (Gach, 1980: 145). Clifford Beers' moving autobiography, *A Mind That Found Itself* (1907), stirred the con-science of the mental health profession while providing the spark of hope for more recoveries.

Care of the mentally ill took place in very many small sanatoria around the country owned and operated by physician 'alienists' – those caring for people alienated from their communities. Many very sick people remained at home, often sequestered from the world. Some were in almshouses or jails, while others lived in public hospitals run by the various states. Their superintendents had joined The Association of Medical Superintendents of American Institutions for the Insane, founded in October 1844 at the home of Thomas Kirkbride, superintendent of the Pennsylvania Hospital for the Insane. This organization evolved into the American Psychiatric Associa-tion in 1921. During the first half of the twentieth century, the state institutions became warehouses both for long-time US citizens and for the many immigrants who broke down in the upheaval of failed transitions. Doctors sank into their own demoralization, overwhelmed by the numbers and by the frequent language barriers. I strongly recommend Constance McGovern's (1985) *Masters of Madness: Social Origins of the American Psychiatric Profession*. It provides fascinating background on the origins of the state hospital system and the life of the alienist.

James Jackson Putnam

James Jackson Putnam (1846–1918) is credited as the first American to get interested in psychoanalysis, treating a neurotic patient in 1906, the same year that he wrote the first psychoanalytic paper to be published in English – 'Recent Experiences in the Study and Treatment of Hysteria at the Massachusetts General Hospital; with Remarks on Freud's Method of Treatment by "Psycho-analysis"' – in *The Journal of Abnormal Psychology* (1906). In May 1911, Putnam became the first president of the American Psychoanalytic Association. Ernest Jones (1920: 8) credits him with launching the mental hygiene movement in the US, along with Clifford Beers. There are 88 surviving letters between Putnam and Freud (Hale, 1971). George Prochnik's (2006) *Putnam Camp: Sigmund Freud, James Jackson Putnam, and the Purpose of American Psychology* gives the reader a sense of this great man and his times, along with a fuller picture of Freud's time in the US.

Adolf Meyer

But the primary intellectual bridge-builder between European and American psychiatry was Adolf Meyer (1866–1950). Swiss-born and Burghölzli-trained (August Forel was his principal teacher of psychiatry), he arrived in the US in 1892 at age 26, and worked closely with John Dewey and George Herbert Mead at the Chicago School of the Social Sciences (which would later inspire Harry Stack Sullivan). By the time of the Clark University lectures Meyer was Director of the Pathological Institute of the State Hospitals in New York City. He moved the institute to Ward's Island, to be closer to the hospitalized patients. He was editor-in-chief of the *Bulletin of the New York State Hospital*, where we find the first US psychodynamic reports of treatments of people diagnosed with 'dementia praecox', beginning in 1908. Meyer wrote the lead article, beginning:

> There prevails a widely spread idea that it is no easy matter to interest physicians and medical students in mental disease. In the first place medical training is usually directly opposed in its whole tendency to consideration of mental conditions. In the little instruction the student gets, he is apt to be made to understand that it is unscientific to think of mental disorders in any other terms than disorders of the brain itself, or

cerebral disorders induced by disease of various internal organs . . . the attitude of fatalistic indifference of a large majority of physicians is euphemistically and systematically justified with . . . dogmatic excuses for inactivity if not ignorance.

(Meyer, 1908: 5–6)

He urged teamwork of clinician and patient in developing a detailed understanding of the contributing factors to the patient's difficulties, along with exploration of the patient's strengths and successes: 'To be helpful to the practitioner we must have a good *history with special attention to the early developments, and to the possibilities of early management*' (Meyer, 1908: 8, original italics). These reports are stunning in the detail of their histories as well as the inclusion of process notes from particular sessions. They bubble with the enthusiasm that therapist and hospitalized patient shared as they gained insight into the patient's dynamics, and real reintegration followed (Silver, 2002). The staff's ferment spread from these New York hospitals to the rest of the country.

Meyer was one of the speakers at the famous 1909 Clark University twentieth anniversary conference, receiving an honorary doctorate along with Freud, Jung, William James and about 25 others.[1] His presentation was 'The Dynamic Interpretation of Dementia Praecox'. He advocated against Kraepelin's dogma of inevitable deterioration and emphasized that clinical observations do not warrant this gloom:

We find in evidence factors which are apt to shape or undo a life – specific defects or disorders of balance, with special tendencies and *habitual* ways of bungling and substitutions and a special make-up which is liable to breakdown in specific manners.

(Meyer, 1948: 251–252)

The comfort of working under the cover of fatalistic and analyzed conceptions of heredity, degeneracy, and mysterious brain diseases – and the relief from responsibility concerning a real understanding of the conditions at hand, and concerning the avoidance of preventable developments – is a powerful and unconsciously cherished protection.

(Meyer, 1948: 257)

I should like to make all feel the sanctity and paramount interest of the concrete cases.

(Meyer, 1948: 258)

While Meyer was among the eight founders of the American Psychoanalytic Association, which held its first meeting in Baltimore, Maryland on

9 May 1911, he became increasingly ambivalent about the specialty, given his impression that Freud was inadequately supportive of his analysand and emissary of psychoanalysis in the US, Horace Frink. He was later disenchanted with Ernest Jones, both these men falling victim to sexual indiscretions and their consequences (Edmunds, 1988; Maddox, 2006).

> Meyer integrated functions of teaching, research, and patient care. At the Phipps Clinic in Johns Hopkins, Baltimore [which opened in April of 1913] Meyer trained two generations of psychiatrists, elevated modes of diagnosis and treatment, and conducted extensive research in neuroanatomy, neuropathology, and psychiatry. His major contributions include propounding the doctrine of psychobiology, standardizing case histories, reforming state insane asylums, and co-founding the mental hygiene movement.
>
> (Johns Hopkins Medical Institutions' archives)

Johns Hopkins University was a revolutionary place, designed to exceed the rigid recommendations of the (Abraham) Flexner Report of 1910, also called the Carnegie Foundation Bulletin #4. The report urged strictly scientific standards in medical education. It demonstrated that the majority of US medical schools were far below these standards. Half of these schools closed in the years immediately following the report. It gave a glowing report to Johns Hopkins, which Flexner visited in December 1909, when plans were under way for the Phipps Clinic, its psychiatric hospital. Meyer went on to train the majority of future heads of psychiatry departments around the United States. He set US psychiatry on a firm professional base. His classical European education, strong ties with leading educators in Europe, his comfort in leadership positions and in didactics, and his unstinting energy gave him more authority than any of his contemporaries in psychiatry. He insisted that those he trained learn psychodynamics; however he never treated a patient with psychoanalysis.

Even in the early 1900s, psychiatry struggled with the tension between biological and psychological orientations and emphases. Meyer tried to maintain a middle ground, eclectic and inclusive – 'mind, and behavior and organs as a biological whole' (Lief, 1948: vii). Alfred Lief, who edited Meyer's papers, quotes Meyer telling him, as they planned this book of his selected papers: 'The main thing is that your point of reference should always be life itself and not the imagined cesspool of the unconscious' (Lief, 1948: vii). He maintained a humble attitude regarding all we do not know: 'My struggle in this country has been with a false conception of science. . . . Psychiatry has to be found in the function and the life of the people' (Lief, 1948: viii). Meyer had ridden his own pendulum, swinging from a strong enthusiasm for psychoanalysis in the early years of the twentieth century to a position of disillusionment.

Isador Coriat (1875–1943), a student of Adolf Meyer at the Worcester State Hospital, in 1917 reported on the successful treatment of five patients suffering from schizophrenia. His 1910 book, *Abnormal Psychology*, is dedicated not to Freud or Meyer, but to Morton Prince (1854–1929). Prince had inaugurated *The Journal of Abnormal Psychology* in 1906, where psychoanalytic articles were included, and had launched and presided over the American Psychopathological Association, founded on 2 May 1910. Rosenzweig states that 'it appears to have arisen as a counterforce to the Freudian approach' (1992: 209). Prince was especially interested in dissociation, hysteria and multiple personality disorder, but felt Freud overemphasized sexual tensions in these and other conditions.

Another Meyer student was C. Macfie Campbell (1876–1943), Meyer's assistant at the Psychiatric Institute on Ward's Island, New York. In 1909 he wrote up two cases in which the patients' delusions are clearly wish fulfillments. He said that when one learns the patient's history, the steps in the development of the psychosis become understandable. He said he should have titled his paper 'A plea for a more thorough analysis of cases of dementia praecox and allied conditions'. I echo this plea a full century later. Campbell wrote five books, one titled *Destiny and Disease in Mental Disorders: With Special Reference to the Schizophrenic Psychoses* (1935). Intriguingly, the third section is titled 'Our Kinship with the Schizophrenic'. In this book, Campbell says:

> As to the nature of the conflict, as one goes over a series of cases one meets the same topics again and again; they are the fundamental issues of human life. We meet the insistent urge of the appetites, especially the sexual appetite and all its components. We meet the strong desire to be of value and to have prestige and to escape from a feeling of guilt or of inferiority. We meet the craving for a sound bond of affection between oneself and the family and one's fellows.
>
> (Campbell, 1935: 87–88)

> In the schizophrenic psychoses external danger and the resultant fear seem to have small part. The patient is not concerned about the preservation of his life, but is preoccupied with the question of personal value and with the relationship between himself and the social group.
>
> (Campbell, 1935: 197)

Jelliffe and White

Enormously influential in launching the psychoanalytic interest in the psychoses in the US were William Alanson White (1870–1937) and Smith Ely Jelliffe (1866–1945). The two met in 1897 while working at the Binghamton State Hospital; both were writers who grew up in Brooklyn,

NY. Karl Menninger, founder of the Menninger Clinic, credits Jelliffe with igniting his analytic interest (Burnham, 1983: 157), and Jelliffe introduced White to psychoanalysis as well. Jelliffe is the originator of the term 'psychosomatics'. He treated Eugene O'Neill and encouraged his writing of his autobiographic play *Long Day's Journey into Night* (Silver, 2001). He and his wife had translated Paul Dubois' bestseller years earlier (Gach, 1980: 145). In 1907, he and White published Jung's *Psychology of Dementia Praecox* (Jung, 1907) as number three in their monograph series of the Nervous and Mental Disease Publishing Company – 'the first Freudian book published in America' (Gach, 1980: 142). In 1913, just one year after the appearance of the German *Imago* and a few months after the *Zeitschrift* began, the two launched the first US analytic journal, *The Psychoanalytic Review* (using their own funds).

Unfortunately for them, their place in history was limited by their including C.G. Jung's very long Fordham lectures in the first volume, to Freud's marked displeasure. Jelliffe had invited Jung to speak at Fordham University in New York City, not realizing that he would be announcing his break from Freud. I recommend John Burnham's (1983) fascinating biography of Jelliffe, which includes Jelliffe's correspondence with Freud and Jung. *The Psychoanalytic Review* was truly international, including new papers by the European pioneers of psychoanalysis along with abstracts of papers published at psychoanalytic conferences there and from the European analytic journals. There is a heavy emphasis on psychoanalysis and psychosis, since William Alanson White was the superintendent of the federal mental hospital St Elizabeths. Many on the St Elizabeths staff contributed articles to *The Psychoanalytic Review*, and many were among the early members of the Washington-Baltimore Psychoanalytic Institute, which split in 1946. Lucille Dooley was a leader in this early group, and was very helpful to Frieda Fromm-Reichmann when she arrived in 1935 (Noble and Burnham, 1989). The strong psychoanalytic connection with both St Elizabeths and with the Sheppard and Enoch Pratt Hospital in Towson, Maryland, now in the northern Baltimore suburbs, created the necessary atmosphere for the flowering of ideas with the arrival there of Harry Stack Sullivan in December of 1922 and Frieda Fromm-Reichmann to Chestnut Lodge in 1935 (discussed in Chapter 7).

Jelliffe wrote and spoke eloquently and prolifically; his students nick-named him 'Windy Jelliffe'. A founder of the New York Psychoanalytic Society, Jelliffe found himself extruded as he supported lay analysis, maintained an interest in applying psychoanalytic understandings to the treatment of psychosis, and tried to remain on friendly terms with both Freud and Jung, especially as the New York group became increasingly orthodox. Jelliffe's first wife, Helena Leeming Jelliffe, also a trained scientist, helped with translations and book reviews for the journal, but did not receive printed credit for her contributions. She died in 1916 of a brain haemorrhage.

Edward Kempf (1885–1971) was the first psychoanalyst on the St Elizabeths staff, arriving there in 1911 from Johns Hopkins. He even believed he was the first analyst in the world to apply analysis to the treatment of psychosis (Kempf, 1919). His 1920 text, *Psychopathology*, was the first US analytic text with application to psychosis. He emphasized that an active method of analyzing was necessary to help the psychotic patient overcome suppressive attitudes of his or her family members (Silver, 2002: 55). Harry Stack Sullivan's biographer, Helen Swick Perry, credited Kempf with contributing to ideas that formed the basis of Sullivan's theoretical and clinical work (Engel, 1990).

By the 1920s, the eugenics movement was taking hold, its enthusiasts advocating the removal of the mentally unfit into mental hospitals where they could not reproduce, or were even 'prophylactically' sterilized (Whitaker, 2002). Those hospitalized included many from the flood of immigrants, some of whom had broken down under the enormous stress of this transition, in which their hopes for financial and social security had been dashed, and as they struggled to learn English well enough to venture outside their immediate neighborhoods. The enormous numbers being warehoused, usually in deplorable conditions, made the standards set by Meyer and his students impossible to maintain in these state or public institutions. The small private sanatoria, many of which had closed in the aftermath of the Flexner Report, varied according to the treatment philosophies of their medical owners; many maintained a psychodynamic orientation. As the popularity of psychoanalysis grew, clinicians could maintain lucrative private practices working with those suffering from neuroses. Many clinicians left their state hospital jobs to establish such practices, and treatment of the more challenging psychotic patients fell away, as classical psychoanalytic teaching maintained these sufferers were unanalyzable. However, exceptions could also be found (see Chapter 7).

Note

1 An interesting footnote to the Clark Lectures is that simultaneously Bertha Pappenheim, Breuer's and Freud's famous Anna O, was on a lecture tour in Canada, Chicago and New York, advocating for material help for impoverished and poorly educated women in Eastern Europe (Guttmann, 2001).

References

Beers, C. (1907). *A Mind That Found Itself: An Autobiography*. Norwood, MA: Plimpton Press.

Burnham, J. (1983). *Jelliffe: American Psychoanalyst and Physician and his Correspondence with Sigmund Freud and C.G. Jung* (ed. W. McGuire), Chicago: University of Chicago Press.

Campbell, C.M. (1935). *Destiny and Disease in Mental Disorders: With Special*

Reference to the Schizophrenic Psychoses. Thomas W. Salmon Memorial Lectures. New York: Norton.

Edmunds, L. (1988). His master's choice. *The Johns Hopkins Magazine*. Baltimore: Johns Hopkins Press, pp. 40–49.

Engel, M. (1990). Psychoanalysis and psychosis: the contribution of Edward Kempf. *Journal of The American Academy of Psychoanalysis* 18, 1: 167–184.

Flexner, A. (1910). *The Flexner Report on Medical Education in the United States and Canada 1910*. New York: Carnegie Foundation for the Advancement of Teaching.

Gach, J. (1980). Culture and complex: on the early history of psychoanalysis in America. In E. Wallace, E. Pressley and L. Pressley (eds) *Essays in the History of Psychiatry: A Tenth Anniversary Supplementary Volume to the Psychiatric Forum*. Columbia, SC: Wm. S. Hall Psychiatric Institute of the South Carolina Department of Mental Health, pp. 135–160.

Guttmann, M. (2001). *The Enigma of Anna O.: A Biography of Bertha Pappenheim*. Wickford, RI: Moyer Bell.

Hale, N. (1971). *James Jackson Putnam and Psychoanalysis: Letters between Putnam and Sigmund Freud, Ernest Jones, William James, Sandor Ferenczi and Morton Prince, 1877–1917*. Cambridge, MA: Harvard University Press.

Jones, E. (1920). James Jackson Putnam. *International Journal of Psychoanalysis* 1: 6–16.

Jung, C. (1907). *The Psychology of Dementia Praecox*. Tr. A.A. Brill and Frederick Peterson. New York: Journal of Nervous and Mental Disease Publishing Company.

Kempf, E.J. (1919). The psychoanalytic treatment of dementia praecox. Report of a case. *Psychoanalytic Review* 6: 15–58.

Lief, A. (ed.) (1948). *The Commonsense Psychiatry of Dr. Adolf Meyer: Fifty-two Selected Papers*. New York: McGraw-Hill.

McGovern, C. (1985). *Masters of Madness: Social Origins of the American Psychiatric Profession*. Hanover, CT: University Press of New England.

Maddox, B. (2006). *Freud's Wizard: Ernest Jones and the Transformation of Psychoanalysis*. Cambridge, MA: Da Capo Press.

Meyer, A. (1908). How can our state hospitals promote a practical interest in psychiatry among the practitioners? *State of New York, State Hospitals Bulletin* 1, 1: 5–20.

Meyer, A. (1948). The dynamic interpretation of dementia praecox. In A. Lief (ed.) *The Commonsense Psychiatry of Dr. Adolf Meyer: Fifty-two Selected Papers*. New York: McGraw-Hill, pp. 247–259. Also in *The American Journal of Psychology* 21: 385, July, 1910.

Noble, D. and Burnham, D. (1989). A history of the Washington Psychoanalytic Institute and Society. In A.-L. Silver (ed.) *Psychoanalysis and Psychosis*. Madison, CT: International Universities Press, pp. 537–573.

Prochnik, G. (2006). *Putnam Camp: Sigmund Freud, James Jackson Putnam, and the Purpose of American Psychology*. New York: Other Press.

Putnam, J. (1906). Recent experiences in the study and treatment of hysteria at the Massachusetts General Hospital; with remarks on Freud's method of treatment by 'psycho-analysis'. *Journal of Abnormal Psychology* 1: 26.

Rosenzweig, S. (1992). *Freud, Jung and Hall the King-Maker: The Expedition to America (1909)*. Seattle: Hogrefe & Huber.

Silver, A.-L. (2001). American psychoanalysts who influenced Eugene O'Neill's *Long Day's Journey into Night*. *Journal of The American Academy of Psychoanalysis* 29, 2: 305–318.

Silver, A.-L. (2002). Psychoanalysis and psychosis: players and history in the United States. *Psychoanalysis and History* 4, 1: 45–66.

Whitaker, R. (2002). *Mad in America: Bad Science, Bad Medicine, and the Enduring Mistreatment of the Mentally Ill*. Cambridge, MA: Perseus Books, pp. 42–72.

Website

Adolf Meyer. http://www.medical archives.jhmi.edn/sgml/AMG-B10.htm. Accessed 29 October 2008.

Part II

From past to present

World developments from the 1940s to the present

Chapter 7

United States of America

Psychodynamic developments, 1940s to the present

Ann-Louise S. Silver and Laurie Stedman

From the mid-1930s through the 1970s, psychoanalytic perspectives dominated the theoretical literature on the treatment approaches for psychotic
disorders, even though the majority of psychoanalysts agreed with Freud
that psychoses were beyond the disorders reachable through psychoanalytic
techniques. They believed the problem lies with the patient's disorder,
which involves 'withdrawal of cathexis from the outside world'. Sadly
and regrettably, the patient was beyond our reach. C.G. Jung and Karl
Abraham, however, wrote more optimistically on psychoanalytic treatment
of psychosis, Abraham focusing on manic-depressive psychosis. Arlow and
Brenner, in their widely studied classic *Psychoanalytic Concepts and the
Structural Theory* (1964), explicitly disagreed with Freud regarding the
schizophrenic's withdrawal of cathexis.

The cultural psychosis of war, quintessentially expressed in the Holocaust, left people with a great need for explanations of the human psyche
and its disruptions. However, the atmosphere of war also fed a sense of
urgency. 'Between 1937 and 1940 the use of insulin and shock therapy
swept across the United States with startling rapidity' (Grob, 1985: 105),
replacing the preceding use of metrazol, but preceding the prefrontal
lobotomy craze. Still, psychoanalytic theory was the most inclusive and
thoroughgoing system of explanation around.

Concurrently, continuing debates centered on whether there is a unified
disorder of schizophrenia, and if so is it a reaction to chronic severe stress,
is it an organic illness, or is it an accumulation of self-defeating behavior
patterns? Are we all vulnerable? Is 'schizophrenia' a conflict or a deficit
disorder? Why is it very frequently diagnosed in one culture (or one clinic)
and relatively rarely in another? However, for the vast majority of those
suffering from psychosis, these theories hardly influenced their institu-
tionalized daily lives. Effectiveness was greatly impaired by competition
between mental health specialties, medical doctors 'guarding their turf',
often impeding the work of psychologists, social workers, nurses and case
managers, many of whom would have blossomed as therapists to those
struggling with psychosis had they received adequate support. Now, we are

beginning to see collaboration between psychodynamic and cognitive behavioural approaches, this another self-defeating competition. Aaron Beck, the founder of cognitive behavioral therapy, was the keynote speaker at the ISPS-US annual meeting in March 2008.

The existential approach to schizophrenia was developed mainly in Europe. It asked how does the patient feel, not how does he or she behave? Binswanger emphasized that the patient feels he is externally controlled, and has lost his freedom. Minkowski stressed the distortions of time and space. Leslie Farber (1966), from Chestnut Lodge, contributed through articles of an existential orientation, which appeared in magazines read by the general public such as *Atlantic Monthly*, *Harper's*, and *Commentary*, thus informing readers in general of the relevance of psychoanalysis to the treatment of psychotic conditions.

The key influence of Sullivan and Fromm-Reichmann

But the most influential psychiatrists during the 1940s through 1980s were the unlikely duo of Harry Stack Sullivan (1892–1949) and Frieda Fromm-Reichmann (1889–1957). Their personalities and backgrounds were quite disparate. Their influence extended far beyond their lifespans and geographic locations. Sullivan's biographer, Helen Swick Perry, titled her (1982) book *Psychiatrist of America: The Life of Harry Stack Sullivan*. It was runner-up for the Pulitzer Prize in Biography. It is outstanding in that it provides mini-biographies of those who influenced Sullivan, and summarizes the various schools of thought. For an excellent integration of Sullivan's writings and an analysis of their impact, I recommend Barton Evans III's (1996) *Harry Stack Sullivan: Interpersonal Theory and Psychotherapy*. Sullivan's revolutionary interpersonal theory of personality underscored the impact of society and culture on the individual's personality development, in health or illness. It dwelt on anxiety in infancy and childhood rather than on Freudian infantile sexual drives. Sullivan introduced the concepts of self-dynamism and selective inattention. Sullivan's impact continues to grow, as evidenced by the popularity first of object relations and self psychology theories and now of relational psychoanalysis, although quite often recent authors have not traced the lineage of their ideas in their publications.

A negative aura surrounds Sullivan, due to his irascible personality, his problematic alcohol consumption, his reporting that he had once suffered from schizophrenia, and his probable bisexuality. And he enjoyed disagreeing with tenets of Freudian theory. He was scathingly critical of his own writings, markedly inhibiting his productivity. And he could turn that sarcasm on his students, many of whom dreaded and hated him. But he could be deeply empathic. He bypassed Freud in his writings, ignored drive theory and was then ignored by psychoanalytic theorists. People worried that being 'Sullivanian' would be bad for their analytic professional health.

But Sullivan had a very loyal following, students who recorded, transcribed and then organized and edited his lectures posthumously for publication (Sullivan, 1953, 1954, 1956, 1962, 1964). These students each made formidable contributions of their own. They included Mabel Blake Cohen, Janet Rioch, David Rioch, Clara Thompson, Dexter Bullard, Sr, Otto A. Will, Jr, and Donald Burnham; Helen Swick Perry was their editorial consultant. Sullivan's theories were instrumental in the development of theories of personality disorders and of brief psychotherapy and of systems-oriented family therapy and group psychotherapy.

His theories formed the working bridge joining psychiatry and the social sciences as early as the 1920s, as evidenced in the colloquium he organized in 1939 at the American Psychiatric Association, igniting a new scholarly interest in really listening to psychotic speech. Published in 1944, *Language and Thought in Schizophrenia*, Kasanin, the book's editor, introduced the term schizoaffective psychosis to describe patients who seemed at first to 'be schizophrenic' but then recovered.

Sullivan worked closely with Edward Sapir, a prominent University of Chicago professor of cultural anthropology, and Harold Lasswell, a pioneer of political psychology. Sullivan introduced the concept of 'security operations'. He is best remembered for his aphorism, or 'one-genus hypothesis', that 'we are all more simply human than otherwise, be we happy and successful, contented and detached, miserable and mentally disordered, or whatever' (Sullivan, 1947: 16). Winnicott and Searles (1965) developed and amplified his notions that countertransference is inescapable as well as the most important means of understanding the patient. And our countertransference grows from our own experiences of anxiety and from our cultural backgrounds and inculcated prejudices and biases. Sullivan had been impressed by the congruence of his own ideas and those of Sándor Ferenczi whom he heard speak when Ferenczi came to the United States in 1926 (Silver, 1993).

'Sullivan was on a lifelong search for the mothering one, and when he felt sustained, he was able to care deeply and empathically for colleagues and patients alike' (L. Stedman, unpublished). His theories emphasize the severe effects of maternal anxiety on the infant's development. He himself was his parents' third baby, all three born in February, the older two boys having died before reaching their first birthdays, two and four years before his own birth. There is some evidence that when he was two and a half years old, his mother was hospitalized after trying to harm herself and Harry. His childhood was extremely lonely. He had one friend once he began in school, a neighbor, both of them very bright. This chumship saved him.

Sullivan went off to college on a coveted Regents Scholarship, awarded to the best student in each county in New York State. But at college, he became involved with a group of students stealing money from other students' mail and was suspended for a semester. He never returned, resurfacing in Chicago to go to the Chicago College of Medicine' and Surgery. The Flexner Report (1910) describes it as an independent school, with no records of the credentials of any of its 33 students. The school closed a few years after the report was published, Sullivan receiving the last diploma issued. He went on to a variety of jobs, arriving at St Elizabeths Hospital, the US mental hospital in Washington, DC under the leadership of William Alanson White in 1921, at the age of 30. White had pioneered the use of dynamic psychotherapy in the treatment of psychosis (see Chapter 6). Sullivan published his first two papers on schizophrenia in White and Jelliffe's journal *The Psychoanalytic Review* (they can be found in Sullivan, 1947). He then worked for eight years at the Sheppard and Enoch Pratt Hospital, running a ward for schizophrenic men, which had an all-male staff, where status roles were downplayed and the staff was trained to be empathic and non-judgmental. Personal validation was emphasized, and the need for personal security. Transference reactions were intense, and treatment results were impressive. Clara Thompson was his psychoanalyst and later a close ally.

He ultimately found his calm mother, whom he had written was crucial in the infant's stability and future mental health, in Frieda Fromm-Reichmann. She had a pattern of adopting and supporting men of great talent. 'I used to call them my victims,' she said (Silver, 1989: 475). They included Kurt Goldstein, Georg Groddeck, Erich Fromm (to whom she was married for over four years), and finally Sullivan. She was childless, yearning for a child of her own. Her posthumous paper. 'Loneliness' (Fromm-Reichmann, 1959) would have been thoroughly endorsed by Sullivan.

Fromm-Reichmann arrived at Chestnut Lodge in Rockville, Maryland in 1935, having fled Frankfurt, Germany, to Alsace-Lorraine and then to Palestine. Her former husband, Erich Fromm, had contacted Ernest Hadley, Sullivan's close collaborator, who was analyzing the Lodge's owner and medical director, Dexter Bullard, Sr, at that time. Hadley asked Bullard if he could use a German-Jewish immigrant as summer help and at first he said no, but when he and the only other doctor there, Marjorie Jarvis, both wanted to take vacations in August, he reconsidered. When he and Fromm-Reichmann met, and he saw how articulate, enthusiastic and well-informed she was, he was ecstatic. She was just what he needed to make the hospital analytic in orientation. Within five years, doctors were clamoring to come to the Lodge for advanced training, and there was an impressive waiting list of patients whose families saw the Lodge as their last hope. Fromm-Reichmann's biography, *To Redeem One Person Is to Redeem the World*, by Gail Hornstein (2000) provides an excellent view of Fromm-Reichmann's life and contributions.

Fromm-Reichmann was both petite (4'10" tall) and fearless. People naturally treated her with great deference and respect. She, like Sullivan, was outspoken, as is clear in her comments to presenters at the Lodge's weekly staff conferences (Silver and Feuer, 1989: 23–45). She stressed the importance of personal analysis for anyone wanting to be a therapist to patients suffering from schizophrenia. The therapist must be as calm and secure as possible, aware of her vulnerabilities and of the defeating aspects of becoming defensive. Psychotic people have extraordinary sensitivity, and can see through the other person's lies and maneuvers in an instant. One must earn the patient's trust simply by being fundamentally trustworthy, and this comes through unstinting self-scrutiny. Her text, *Principles of Intensive Psychotherapy* (1950), was required reading for everyone training in any branch of mental health from when it appeared through to the early 1980s. It has remained in continual print for over 50 years, filled with pearls such as:

> The purpose of interpretation and interpretive questions is to bring dissociated and repressed experiences and motivations to awareness and to show patients how, unknown to themselves, repressed and dissociated material finds its expression in and colors verbalized communications and behavior patterns such as their actions, attitudes, and gestures.
>
> (Fromm-Reichmann, 1950: 70)

Fromm-Reichmann enjoyed giving talks at professional meetings, talks which inspired the listener to aim for a higher level of humane interaction. The Lodge became the world's beacon for psychodynamic treatment of the severely mentally ill. Bullard was able to be very choosey in whom he hired. Sullivan was never on the Lodge staff, but gave a series of weekly seminars at the Bullards' residence on the Lodge grounds. Beginning in 1956, the Lodge began holding yearly symposia which became something of religious retreats for the mental health community, attracting up to 600 people each year. However, beyond that the place was too insular. We did not reach out to the local mental health community on a more regular basis, nor foster an exchange of staff, nor hold seminars open to the local mental health community. The medical staff generally believed they were treating patients far sicker than those the others treated, but I do not believe this was so.

Frieda Fromm-Reichmann's selected papers were published after her death, edited by Dexter Bullard (1959).

Other Chestnut Lodge therapists

The staff at the Lodge was extraordinarily prolific, producing substantial research, technical and philosophic papers. Donald Burnham, Arthur

Gladstone and Robert Gibson published *Schizophrenia and the Need-Fear Dilemma* (1969). Ping-Nie Pao published *Schizophrenic Disorders: Theory and Treatment from a Psychodynamic Point of View* (1979). Clarence Schulz and Rose Kilgalen published *Case Studies in Schizophrenia* (1969). Schulz had moved on to Sheppard Pratt by the time the book came out, but he reports on treatments at Chestnut Lodge. A work that came directly from Sheppard Pratt (as did Harry Stack Sullivan's early seminal papers) was Lewis Hill's very popular *Psychotherapeutic Intervention in Schizophrenia* (1955). The classic text by Alfred Stanton and Morris Schwartz, *The Mental Hospital* (1954), brings together and validates Sullivan's social theories and Fromm-Reichmann's clinical skills and their impact, as it depicts the group dynamics on a unit at Chestnut Lodge. This book could be seen as a sequel to Sullivan's research papers from his years running an innovative unit at the Sheppard and Enoch Pratt Hospital in Towson, Maryland in the early 1920s (Sullivan, 1962). The Washington School of Psychiatry, which Sullivan founded in 1943, retains its interpersonal academic orientation.

Harold Searles (his *Collected Papers on Schizophrenia and Related Subjects* was published in 1965) worked unstintingly, producing an extraordinary body of works, most notably seeringly honest about his moment-to-moment responses to his patients. His talks at professional meetings always drew standing-room-only crowds, as did his 'one shot interviews', where he and the patient he was meeting for the first time as the interview began, would get into topics that the long-term therapist had heard nothing about. I attended such an event in an auditorium seating close to 1000 people. 'Will you be all right?' Searles asked as the interview concluded. 'Don't worry about me. I'll be fine. I'm going shopping,' the patient responded.

Other centres and therapists

While the Baltimore-Washington area formed the center for psychodynamic work for psychosis, it was certainly not the only center. In Boston, the Massachusetts Mental Health Clinic, under the leadership of Elvin Semrad in the role Fromm-Reichmann held at the Lodge, and Jack Ewalt in Dexter Bullard's spot, became a superbly inspiring program for those training in the Harvard psychiatric system. Elvin Semrad (1909–1976) died suddenly at age 67, as did Frieda Fromm-Reichmann. He had served as president of the Boston Psychoanalytic Society, was a Professor of Psychiatry at Harvard and was the Clinical Director at the Massachusetts Mental Health Center for two decades. Semrad had become the most influential teacher of psychiatry in the Boston area and one of the most important teachers of his generation. He wrote or co-authored over 200 papers. Born in Abie, Nebraska, he called himself 'just a hayseed from Nebraska' (Rako and Mazer, 1980: 12). Semrad also said that 'the patient is the only textbook we require' (p. 13). He had been trained by John Whitehorn (1894–1973), Adolf Meyer's successor as Chair of the Department of Psychiatry at the Johns Hopkins Hospital. Whitehorn saw anxiety as central to all mental difficulties, and the therapist's interest in the patient as the key to recovery. He was ambivalent about psychoanalysis, as was Meyer, but saw it as central to strengthening dynamic psychiatry.

After Semrad's death, his students collected his pithy aphorisms into a now classic book, *Semrad: The Heart of a Therapist* (Rako and Mazer, 1980). For example, at a case conference he commented:

> There's no doubt that the genesis of her present situation is in her development, but therapeutically that's not the issue. The issue is the overwhelming pain she can't face right now.
>
> (Rako and Mazer, 1980: 139)

> Regarding schizophrenic inpatients; I haven't met a patient here who hasn't had some idea of what pain in their life they're avoiding. And the thing is that they cannot bear that pain and they go through all sorts of antics to get somebody to make it better, which looks very infantile. But if they can bear it themselves, they don't have to be so infantile. I wouldn't analyze anybody for avoidance problems; for not being able to bear the pain of their life and the issues around which it centers. I would help them develop some structure so that they could acknowledge and bear it and put it into perspective.
>
> (Rako and Mazer, 1980: 169)

In Topeka, Kansas, Karl Menninger oversaw the now relocated Menninger Clinic (Friedman, 1990). In Stockbridge, MA, the Austen Riggs Center became a pre-eminent clinic and training center, especially with the arrival of Otto Will and Martin Cooperman, from Chestnut Lodge. Riggs is now the only large treatment center that has been able to continue a strong psychodynamic program in the current climate in the United States. The Boyer House, in San Francisco, also provides psychotherapeutic treatment for psychotic patients. Hyman Spotnitz, MD, based in New York City and still working in his mid-nineties, is the founder of the school of Modern Psychoanalysis. He has emphasized the vital role of psychoanalysis in the treatment of psychosis, and has trained many professionals in this work, done usually on an outpatient basis in these therapists' and analysts' offices. He has given clear and sensible instruction in his text *Modern Psychoanalysis of the Schizophrenic Patient* (1985). John Rosen, founder of the school of Direct Analysis has documented his approach in *Direct Analysis: Selected Papers* (Rosen, 1953). ISPS-US pillars Bertram Karon and Ravela Levin both had the opportunity early in their careers to work at his treatment center which was located in Bucks County, north of Philadelphia.

Large studies have reviewed the effects of psychodynamic treatments. Bertram Karon and Gary Vandenbos's classic book *Psychotherapy of Schizophrenia: The Treatment of Choice* (1981) not only documents the effectiveness of this approach, but also teaches how it should be done. Robert Wallerstein's *Forty-Two Lives in Treatment* (1986) is 'the most comprehensive as well as most ambitious psychotherapy research program ever conceived and carried out' (Wallerstein, 1986: vii). They found that those receiving supportive psychotherapeutic approaches did about as well as those in more insight-oriented treatments (60 per cent had moderately to very good treatment results, about the same as the analytic group (Wallerstein, 1986: 725). Tom McGlashan's Chestnut Lodge follow-up study presented results famously claiming inadequate results for patients treated between 1950 and 1975 (McGlashan, 1984, 1986a, 1986b). Many of us felt he 'set the bar' for moderate improvement inappropriately high. Birgitte Bechgaard (2003) has presented an elegant rebuttal to his article's gloomy pronouncements.

Silvano Arieti (1955), in his enormously successful book *Interpretation of Schizophrenia*, provided encouragement for therapeutic efforts for psychotic patients, but he emphasized the work as important in the training of the clinician, while being pessimistic about the success rate (Silver, 2005). He had established himself as a world authority in psychiatry through his multi-volume *American Handbook of Psychiatry* (1959). L. Bryce Boyer (1983) in San Francisco and Peter Giovacchini (1978) in Chicago (see also *Master Clinicians on Treating the Regressed Patient*, 1990, which they edited together), and Michael Robbins (1993), formerly at the Massachusetts Mental Health Clinic and now based in Amherst, MA, each contributed enormously to the field through their teaching, supervising, and writing. Vamik Volkan's (1995; Volkan and Akhtar, 1997) clinically based examination of 'the infantile psvchotic self' and its relation with adult psychosis is one of the most interesting recent developments in the understanding of psychotic breakdown. Both Volkan and Boyer clearly show not only the influence of the US tradition in treating psychosis, but also that of British object relations theories.

Of course, there are very many authors not mentioned here. I recommend that the reader consult the *Psychoanalytic Electronic Publishing Company's PEP Disk, Version 6*, to search through the many fascinating papers found there.

In the late 1950s chlorpromazine was seen by many as the long-awaited treatment if not cure for psychosis. Simultaneously, a groundswell of interest in deinstitutionalization, moving patients into the community to supervised living arrangements, with care given in community health centers, caught the interest of the public, and in 1963 President John F. Kennedy signed the Community Mental Health Centers (CMHC) Act (Public Law #88–164). It was not long before people noticed a rapid increase in the numbers of homeless and mentally ill showing up in the nation's jails and prisons, an enormous tragedy that is not yet resolving (Whitaker, 2002).

The pharmaceutical industry became increasingly aggressive in its advertising, and increasingly allied with and financially supportive of the National Alliance for the Mentally Ill, an organization whose members are mainly parents who have a child struggling with psychosis. They were up in arms over the parent-blaming which ran through the analytic literature. 'Schizophrenia, a brain disease' became their shared motto. From the 1980s onward, we have seen a marginalization of psychodynamic approaches to the psychotic conditions, which has led to closures of many hospitals such as Chestnut Lodge, and the reconfiguration of general hospital psychiatric units into extensions of the emergency rooms, where patients are 'stabilized' rather than treated with an aim of even getting acquainted. To 'treat' has come to mean to medicate. For a while, the recommendations coming from the American Psychiatric Association were that psychodynamic individual and family treatments should not be done, even in combination with medications.

Lately, a report from the Medical Directors Council of the National Association of State Mental Health Directors (July, 2006) has reported on the very high mortality rates among patients suffering from psychoses in various states in the United States, such that their lifespans are shortened by 25 years. While some are dying of suicide, accidents, homicide, or the attrition caused by living homelessly, the overwhelming majority are dying of cardiovascular and metabolic disorders. It seems to me that the newer antipsychotic medications or their combination with other psychiatric medications are strongly implicated. As this crisis becomes documented, and as we are learning of various pharmaceutical companies that withheld studies which might have warned the profession of these outcomes, the psychiatric community has needed to rethink its push for efficiency. We are seeing an increasing openness among those in the psychiatric research community to reconsider the role of the psychotherapist, of whatever professional or para-professional stripe, and the recent convention of the American Psychiatric Association showed clear evidence of a resuming interest in psychodynamics and psychotherapy in general. Perhaps we will see increased interest of psychotherapy for the psychoses as well.

References

Arieti, S. (1955). *Interpretation of Schizophrenia*. New York: Robert Brunner.

Arieti, S. (ed.) (1959). *American Handbook of Psychiatry*. New York: Basic Books.

Arlow, J. and Brenner, C. (1964). The psychopathology of the psychoses. In J. Arlow and C. Brenner *Psychoanalytic Concepts and the Structural Theory*. New York: International Universities Press, pp. 144–178.

Bechgaard, B. (2003). Lessons in how to ruin a study in psychotherapy effectiveness: a critical review of the follow-up study from Chestnut Lodge. *Journal of the American Academy of Psychoanalysis and Dynamic Psychiatry* 31: 119–140.

Boyer, L.B. (1983). *The Regressed Patient*. New York: Jason Aronson.

Boyer, L.B. and Giovacchini, P.L. (1990). *Master Clinicians on Treating the Regressed Patient*. Northvale, NJ: Jason Aronson.

Bullard, D. (ed.) (1959). *Psychoanalysis and Psychotherapy. Selected Papers of Frieda Fromm-Reichmann*. Chicago: University of Chicago Press.

Burnham, D., Gladstone, A. and Gibson, R. (1969). *Schizophrenia and the Need–Fear Dilemma*. New York: International Universities Press.

Evans, Barton, III (1996). *Harry Stack Sullivan: Interpersonal Theory and Psychotherapy*. London and New York: Routledge.

Farber, L. (1966). *The Ways of the Will: Essays toward a Psychology and Psychopathology of Will*. New York: Basic Books.

Flexner, A. (1910). *The Flexner Report on Medical Education in the United States and Canada 1910*. New York: Carnegie Foundation for the Advancement of Teaching.

Friedman, L. (1990). *Menninger: The Family and the Clinic*. New York: Alfred A. Knopf.

Fromm-Reichmann, F. (1950). *Principles of Intensive Psychotherapy*. Chicago: University of Chicago Press.

Fromm-Reichmann, F. (1959). Loneliness. *Psychiatry* 22: 1–15.

Fromm-Reichmann, F. (1989). Reminiscences of Europe. In A.-L. Silver (ed.) *Psychoanalysis and Psychosis*. Madison, CT: International Universities Press, pp. 469–481.

Giovacchini, P. (1978). *Treatment of Primitive Mental States*. New York: Jason Aronson.

Grob, G. (1985). *The Inner World of American Psychiatry, 1890–1940: Selected Correspondence*. New Brunswick, NJ: Rutgers University Press.

Hill, L. (1955). *Psychotherapeutic Intervention in Schizophrenia*. Chicago: University of Chicago Press.

Hornstein, G. (2000). *To Redeem One Person Is To Redeem the World: The Life of Frieda Fromm-Reichmann*. New York: The Free Press.

Karon, B. and Vandenbos, G. (1981). *Psychotherapy of Schizophrenia: The Treatment of Choice*. New York: Jason Aronson.

Kasanin, J. (1944). *Language and Thought in Schizophrenia: Collected Papers*. Berkeley: University of California Press.

McGlashan, T. (1984). The Chestnut Lodge follow-up study: I and II. *Archives of General Psychiatry* 41: 573–601.

McGlashan, T. (1986a). The Chestnut Lodge follow-up study, III and IV. *Archives of General Psychiatry* 43: 20–30, 167–176.

McGlashan, T. (1986b). Predictors of shorter-, medium-, and longer-term outcome in schizophrenia. *American Journal of Psychiatry* 143: 50–55.

National Association of State Mental Health Directors (July, 2006) *Morbidity and Mortality in People with Serious Mental Illness*. http://www.nasmhpd.org/nasmhpd_collections/collection4/meeting_presentations/Summer%202006%20commish/NASMHPD%20Morbidity%20and%20Mortality%20Slides%20071006.pdf. Accessed 29 October 2008.

Pao, Ping-Nie (1979). *Schizophrenic Disorders. Theory and Treatment from a Psychodynamic Point of View*. New York: International Universities Press.

Perry, H.S. (1982). *Psychiatrist of America: The Life of Harry Stack Sullivan*. Cambridge, MA: Belknap Press of Harvard University Press.

Rako, S. and Mazer, H. (eds) (1980). *Semrad: The Heart of a Therapist*. Northvale, NJ: Jason Aronson.

Robbins, M. (1993). *Experiences of Schizophrenia: An Integration of the Personal, Scientific, and Therapeutic*. New York: Guilford Press.

Rosen, J. (1953). *Direct Analysis: Selected Papers*. New York: Grune & Stratton.

Schulz, C.G. and Kilgalen, R.K. (1969). *Case Studies in Schizophrenia*. New York: Basic Books.

Searles, H. (1965). *Collected Papers on Schizophrenia and Related Subjects*. New York: International Universities Press.

Silver, A.-L. (ed.) (1989). *Psychoanalysis and Psychosis*. Madison, CT: International Universities Press.

Silver, A.-L. (1993). Countertransference, Ferenczi, and Washington, DC. *Journal of the American Academy of Psychoanalysis* 21, 4: 637–654.

Silver, A.-L. (2005). In the footsteps of Arieti and Fromm-Reichmann: psychodynamic treatments of psychosis in the current era. *Journal of the American Academy of Psychoanalysis and Dynamic Psychiatry* 33, 4: 689–704.

Silver, A.-L. and Feuer, P. (1989). Fromm-Reichmann's contributions at staff conferences. In A.-L. Silver (ed.) *Psychoanalysis and Psychosis*. Madison, CT: International Universities Press, pp. 23–45.

Spotnitz, H. (1985). *Modern Psychoanalysis of the Schizophrenic Patient: Theory of the Technique*, 2nd edn. New York: Human Sciences Press.

Stanton, A. and Schwartz, M. (1954). *The Mental Hospital*. New York: Basic Books.

Sullivan, H.S. (1947). *Conceptions of Modern Psychiatry*. New York: Norton.

Sullivan, H.S. (1953). *The Interpersonal Theory of Psychiatry* (eds H.S. Perry and M.L. Gawel). New York: Norton.

Sullivan, H.S. (1954). *The Psychiatric Interview* (eds H.S. Perry and M.L. Gawel). New York: Norton.

Sullivan, H.S. (1956). *Clinical Studies in Psychiatry* (eds H.S. Perry, M.L. Gawel and M. Gibbon). New York: Norton.

Sullivan, H.S. (1962). *Schizophrenia as a Human Process* (ed. H.S. Perry). New York: Norton.

Sullivan, H.S. (1964). *The Fusion of Psychiatry and Social Sciences*. New York: Norton.

Volkan, V.D. (1995). *The Infantile Psychotic Self and Its Fates. Understanding and Treating Schizophrenics and Other Difficult Patients*. Northvale, NJ: Jason Aronson.

Volkan, V.D. and Akhtar, S. (eds) (1997). *The Seed of Madness: Constitution, Environment, and Fantasy in the Organization of the Psychotic Core*. Madison, CT: International Universities Press.

Wallerstein, R. (1986). *Forty-Two Lives in Treatment: A Study of Psychoanalysis and Psychotherapy*. New York: Guilford Press.

Whitaker, R. (2002). *Mad in America: Bad Science, Bad Medicine, and the Enduring Mistreatment of the Mentally Ill*. Cambridge, MA: Perseus Publishing.

Chapter 8

Great Britain

Part 1: The contribution of Kleinian innovations to the treatment of psychotic patients

Murray Jackson

The evolution of key concepts

Modern psychoanalytic thought about psychosis is founded on the work of Sigmund Freud, C.G. Jung and Karl Abraham. Freud (1925) believed that psychotic patients were too withdrawn from reality to be accessible to psychoanalysis, at least as practised at that time, but that study of their minds would pay dividends of knowledge. He observed:

> So many things that in neurosis have to be laboriously fetched up from the depths are found in psychosis on the surface, visible to every eye. For that reason the best subjects for the demonstration of many of the assertions of psychoanalysis are provided by the psychiatric clinic . . . in the long run even the psychiatrists cannot resist the convincing force of their own clinical material.
>
> (Freud 1925: 60)

Jung, in contrast to Freud, had a great deal of contact with the severely disturbed hospitalised patients. His personal experience of a psychotic episode helped to inspire his work and informed his development of the concept of the archetype. This concept, which has generally held little interest for psychoanalysts, has recently attracted the attention of some psychoanalysts who see it as having much in common with the concepts of primal (unrepressed) phantasy and of internal part-object relations.

Abraham undertook individual psychotherapy with manic-depressive and schizophrenic patients. His belief that the roots of psychosis lie in disturbances in the early emotional development of the infant inspired Melanie Klein's explorations of the mind of the infant.

Between the two world wars, psychoanalysis began to flourish in the US. The foundation of the Washington School of Psychiatry in 1936 by William Alanson White and Harry Stack Sullivan, as well as the work at the Chestnut Lodge hospital, inspired generations of psychiatrists. From this Washington base and a few other centres, important work with psychotic patients emerged associated with many pioneers, past and present, and such differing theoretical developments as ego and self psychology.

Before World War II the arrival in the UK of Melanie Klein in 1926 and Anna Freud in 1938 launched an era of revolutionary, often strongly conflicting, contributions to child development and the treatment of psychotics. Klein's analytic treatment of two- and three-year-old children led her to greater understanding of the harsh 'archaic' superego involved in many adult mental disturbances. She believed that all infants must pass through a period of innate destructive feelings of hatred towards the imagined 'bad' mother and when these remain unresolved they form a contributory factor to the development of psychotic illness in adolescence and adulthood. She regarded these impulses as an innate and biologically driven expression of Freud's 'death instinct', a view that has remained a central focus in the Kleinian approach to psychosis.

Kleinian innovations

By the beginning of World War II, Klein (1881–1960) had already put the first two years of life firmly on the map of mental development as a source of psychical conflict. She had explored the processes of symbol formation and the early stages of the Oedipus complex and had contested Freud's concept of an orderly chronological sequence of stages of psychosexual development (oral, anal, genital), regarding them as overlapping. She now turned her attention to psychotic states, which she considered to be rooted in the pathology of early infancy, where the basic matrix of mental function is formed, and the capacity to think, speak and to form symbols are acquired, all of which functions tend to be disturbed in psychosis. In order to understand the mental mechanisms involved in psychosis, she believed it is necessary to understand the development of the early ego and its object relationships. On this conceptual basis she published the first of the three papers that were to define her unique approach to psychotic states and provide the foundation of the Kleinian school.

In the first paper, *A Contribution to the Psychogenesis of Manic-Depressive States* (Klein, 1935), she formulated the concept of the depressive position, which subsequently became the hallmark of Kleinian theory. From the beginning, the infant forms an image of a good (gratifying, nurturing) 'breast-mother' and in opposition a bad (frustrating one), and under normal circumstances the infant, late in the first year of life, becomes able to recognise that these 'part-objects' are the same. At that point ('position') the infant becomes capable of feelings of responsibility for the damage done in his imagination (which she called 'phantasy')[1] to the bad mother, and a psychologically justified concern for her survival begins to replace concern for himself and his own survival (in what she later described as a paranoid world), and reparative motivations are mobilised, leading to wishes to put right the damage done in phantasy.[2] Klein observed what she considered to be feelings of depression at this point, and called this psychodynamic constellation *the depressive position*, a maturational achievement not to be confused with clinical depression, contending that it is the degree of success or failure to negotiate this position that determines relative normality or psychosis. This structural model came for Kleinians to incorporate and replace Freud's concept of primary processes of thought, and relocated the origins of the Oedipus complex (which he regarded as the key organising system of the personality) to the period of infancy. As an ever-present 'position' this dynamic constellation provides a conceptual link between infant development and adult psychosis. Klein described several crucial primitive defences against infantile anxiety (also to be found later in life) such as denial of psychic reality, splitting, projection and introjection, which she regarded as the basis of paranoia. This was a consolidation of her early formulation of infantile psychotic anxieties, and she observed that obsessional mechanisms can be seen to play an important part in modifying these anxieties.[3] Believing that every infant employs these mechanisms and that they can be seen in the adult psychotic, she called them *psychotic anxieties*.[4]

It was in this paper that she elaborated on Freud's observations on mania and formulated her concept of the manic defences, employed when the depressive position cannot be mastered, and seen in its purest form in manic-depressive psychosis. In order to avoid the fear that the object has, in phantasy, been destroyed, the subject denies the importance of the object, disparaging it in a contemptuous manner, and in an excited and triumphant fashion dissociates himself from concern about its fate.[5] At the same time an unconscious awareness of his destructive hostility gives rise to a hunger for objects, to be clearly seen in the restlessness, hypersexuality and omnipotent thinking of the manic-depressive patient. She also spoke of the mild hypomania of relatively normal people and of the frequent association of manic pathology in exceptionally creative individuals.

The second paper, *Mourning and its Relation to Manic-Depressive States* (Klein, 1940), was a sequel to the previous one. Having sustained a series of grievous personal losses and struggled with her own mourning, she developed her idea that mourning at any age is linked to the normal infantile development of the depressive position. She concluded that the mourner is compelled to relive the threat, first active in infancy, of the loss of the mother, brought about by destructive impulses. A manic denial of the hostility towards the lost object may lead to a pathological bereavement reaction. Working through mourning involves repeated recognition of both the loving and hateful feelings toward the lost object, leading to the mobilisation of reparative feelings.[6] Paranoid fears diminish, loving feelings such as sorrow and regret overcome aggressive hatred and vengeful grievance, and the (integrated) object is eventually installed permanently in the subject's inner world as a predominately loving and supportive figure. This view contrasted with Freud's, according to whom the mourner must, step by step, give up the attachment to the lost loved object.

The third paper, *Notes on some Schizoid Mechanisms* (Klein, 1946), developed the idea that normal developmental processes of infancy underlie psychosis and in conjunction with the previous two formed the basis of subsequent Kleinian work on psychosis. In this paper she introduced the concept of *projective identification*, an elaboration of the familiar mechanism of projection. This new concept emphasises the importance of the individual's inner world, a figurative space which contains images of the self and its internal objects, imaginative representations of other people and things, past and present, which are a permanently active and influential part of his inner scenery. Projective identification, associated with splitting of the self and object, can serve different motivations. It has been regarded as the normal basis of communication between mother and baby, and as the basis of empathy. In its pathological form it consists of an omnipotent imaginative belief that it is possible to transfer aspects of the self, usually but not exclusively unwanted, into the mental representation of another person or thing. This can be seen as an evacuative or attributive process of denial, in which unwanted elements are expelled, aimed at avoiding the necessity of recognising a 'bad' part of the self. This process changes the perception of the object, which may then be considered to be threatening, and also of the self, which has thereby been deprived of a necessary element which has been condemned by the superego, according to the principle of idealisation, as 'all good' or 'all bad'. Splitting, unlike the more mature defence of repression, effectively eliminates unwanted thoughts and feelings (and parts of the self) which become wholly unavailable to the subject's awareness, but wholly available to a process of further disposal by projection.

When Klein became aware of the work of Fairbairn (1952) she adopted his term 'schizoid' and renamed the paranoid position *the paranoid-schizoid position*.[7] This involved extending the connotation of 'schizoid' beyond its customary use in psychiatry and focused on the mechanisms of pathological splitting of self and object. This work suggested a close connection between manic-depressive and schizophrenic psychoses, based on regression and progression between the paranoid-schizoid and depressive positions. In this model it is the depth of fixation of conflict and the individual's potential for regression which determines the clinical patterns, in contrast to Kraepelin's now outmoded dichotomous view of dementia praecox and manic-depressive psychosis as separate disease entities.

After the war several psychiatrists who had acquired much relevant experience in the British Army came under the influence of Klein and went on to train as psychoanalysts and to make major contributions to psychosis theory. Tom Main (1957) developed a psychoanalytically based milieu at the Cassel hospital. W.R. Bion (1967), after making unique contributions to group analytic theory at the Tavistock Clinic, went on to apply Klein's work to psychotic disorders. John Bowlby (1988), at first much influenced by Klein, came to criticise what he saw as her neglect of factors of attachment and separation and laid the basis for modern attachment theory.[8]

Since this chapter is focused on Kleinian and 'post-Kleinian' developments it will not deal in detail with the other theoretical streams that emerged from this powerful base. However, mention must be made of the outstanding work of Thomas Freeman (1988) who, in close association with Anna Freud and her followers, made a unique contribution to the study and treatment of severe psychotic states in a hospital setting. Freeman had the rare opportunity for a British psychoanalyst of having have full clinical control over inpatients, and he inspired many (including the author), whose theoretical interests may sometimes have differed in some respects.

In the late 1950s the British object relations school, having discovered the potential of the mechanism of 'projective identification' as a tool for understanding early object relations in childhood development, primitive mechanisms of defence and psychotic states of mind, produced a wealth of literature from the Kleinian group which has continued to the present day. The work of Hanna Segal (1981; see Bell, 1997), Herbert Rosenfeld (1987), Donald Meltzer (1994), Winnicott (1975), and Bion (1967; see Bléandonu, 1994) has been the most influential. Amongst the many new fertile ideas have been Segal's concept of *symbolic equations*, and Rosenfeld's descriptions of *omnipotent destructive narcissistic object relations*. Winnicott, originally a follower of Klein, considered psychosis to be the consequence of a failure in the maternal caring environment, in which the mother failed to protect the infant from premature exposure to reality, an 'impingement' which can fracture the fragile infantile sense of self.

Bion considered this failure in terms of *maternal containment*, whereby a mentally healthy mother helps the infant to acquire the basis of a stable sense of identity and mastery of overwhelming storms of affect. He studied the consequences of such failure and concluded that many psychotic manifestations result from destructive attacks of the psychotic self on the capacity for painful self-reflective thought.

Bion formulated the concept of *psychotic* and *non-psychotic selves*, which allowed a greater understanding of the widely accepted view that there is always an island of sanity somewhere to be found in the madness of the psychotic mind. He applied this insight to the minds of normal people, where he saw a universal, albeit usually non-pathogenic, psychotic part. His prolific and highly influential work included study of the origins of conceptual thinking, the formation and functions of delusions and hallucinations, the formation of the *psychotic organisation* (also pursued by Rosenfeld, and later by John Steiner) and other themes relevant to the understanding of psychotic processes.

Kleinian contributors to the field of schizophrenic and other psychoses have sometimes been criticised by psychiatrists on the grounds that their observations and therapy are based on borderline disorders, rather than those 'true' psychoses that form a large part of clinical psychiatry in hospital practice. Whatever justice there may be in such criticism, it cannot apply to some of the work of Segal and Rosenfeld, both of whom have reported experience with severely psychotic hospitalised patients. Kleinians, however, maintain that borderline patients use the same psychotic mechanisms as the disturbed psychotic, and trace the origins of both to the pathology of infancy.

The application of Kleinian concepts in clinical practice

For complex reasons Kleinian workers relatively rarely report work with hospitalised psychotic patients. When the British National Health Service (NHS) was founded in 1947 the British Psychoanalytic Society, jealous of its independence from state funding and of the spectre of managed care, elected to remain outside its aegis. Such a fate has subsequently befallen some other psychoanalytic societies which, whilst benefiting from public health provision, have become subject to its constraints.

Although this has meant that in the British health system the most disturbed patients have in general been deprived of the most knowledgeable psychotherapists, psychoanalytic influence, by way of teaching and supervision of psychiatrists and psychotherapists, although limited, has been profound.

Relatively few Kleinian practitioners have had the opportunity, or the responsibility, of full clinical control in the management of hospitalised psychotic patients. Inspired by the work of Tom Hayward in the Shenley Hospital, a great deal of work was done with ambulant psychotic patients in 'Villa 21' under the direction of Michael Conran (1991), a psychoanalyst of the Independent group of the psychoanalytic society. In the forensic field, Kleinian psychoanalysts have been influential in promoting the understanding and psychotherapy of criminal offenders, a significant proportion of whom are psychotic. Hyatt Williams (1998) contributed extensively to the understanding of the minds of murderers, and Leslie Sohn and Patrick Gallwey have long conducted teaching seminars on severely disturbed criminal offenders and supervision of psychoanalytic psychotherapy.

In the Maudsley Hospital an outpatient psychotherapy unit had for many years been active in the assessment and treatment of borderline and psychotic patients, and the contributions of Kleinian analysts such as Henri Rey and Michael Feldman had a significant impact in the essentially biomedical and psychosocial culture of the Institute of Psychiatry.

In 1972 an experimental inpatient unit was set up in the Maudsley Hospital, in association with the outpatient psychotherapy unit and the Institute of Psychiatry. This unit, run in collaboration with a conventional psychiatric unit directed by Professor Robert Cawley, was inaugurated by

Kleinian analyst John Steiner, and continued by Murray Jackson for 13 years. It was dedicated to the application of psychoanalytic principles and assessed and treated as wide a range of psychiatric conditions as possible. Secondary and tertiary referrals of psychotic and borderline patients formed the greatest part of the intake. This unit was unique in the NHS and has been reported in detail (Jackson and Cawley, 1992; Jackson and Williams, 1994). Nurses were trained in basic psychodynamic concepts and principles of milieu therapy, and attempted, with varying degrees of success, to create a psychoanalytically informed atmosphere within which the ward could maximise its therapeutic function. However, despite its being widely regarded as successful, the unit did not survive Jackson's retirement from the NHS, and the ward was fragmented and restructured along psycho-biosocial lines, losing its psychoanalytic perspective.

Outside of such a specialised experimental context, Klein-oriented work with disturbed psychotic patients has flourished in many parts of England,[9] Scotland and Northern Ireland. At the present time Richard Lucas (2003), who has written widely on manic-depressive, puerperal and schizophrenic psychoses, is the only Kleinian analyst working in the British NHS as a psychiatrist with full clinical control of a hospital ward and the same full load of clinical work and responsibilities as other hospital-based general psychiatrists. Another contemporary source of Klein-oriented influence is found in the work of Brian Martindale (2007) who, having access to supportive psychiatric resources, has long been dedicated to the integration of psychoanalysis with other theoretical perspectives and treatment methods. Kleinian workers have made important contributions to the treatment of psychotic children, and the work of the Tavistock Clinic has become an important source of learning and treatment.

The spread of Kleinian thought

Although the influence of Kleinian thinking on contemporary British hospital psychiatry has been limited, Kleinian views about the nature and treatment of the primitive states of mind characteristic of borderline and psychotic patients have been widely influential far beyond the shores of the UK where they were developed. In the USA, Kleinian and 'neo-Kleinian' theory has been increasingly adopted in their work with psychotic patients by such pioneers as Searles (1965, 1986), Ogden (1989), Boyer (1983), Grotstein (1985, 2001) and Volkan (1995; Volkan and Akhtar, 1997), and in the Argentine by David Rosenfeld, Jorge Badaracco and many others.

Contributions to non-clinical spheres

Kleinian developments have also extended far beyond the clinical sphere, influential contributions having been made to social theory (Alport, 1989;

Rustin, 1991; Lubin, 1996; Bell, 1999), and to cultural issues such as art, aesthetics and literature. Kleinian workers have also contributed extensively to exploration of the unconscious dynamics of political violence (Covington *et al.*, 2002).

Discussion

British psychiatry is today predominately a psychosis service, with relatively little direct psychoanalytic input, and the aim of the International Society for the Psychological Treatments of the Schizophrenias and other Psychoses (ISPS) to bridge the increasing gap is therefore of particular importance. In recent years there has been a drift away from the psychoanalytical basis of the ISPS, and although much progress has been made by cognitive behavioural therapy (CBT) workers in helping to alleviate the distress of many psychotic patients, and of psychiatrists in detecting and treating first episode psychosis, the relevance of psychoanalysis is in danger of being marginalised.

In the foregoing outline I have emphasised that however much other vulnerability factors may be involved and later experience promote or obstruct normal development, it is in the mother–baby relationship in the first year of life that Kleinian and object-relation theorists believe that the seeds of later psychosis are to be found. However, focusing on the deepest developmental roots does not detract from the contribution of the branches of later and less deeply rooted processes. When confronted with psychotic material many Kleinians today try to link the patient's current situation to early infantile experience, and it can be helpful to speculate at the outset of a psychosis about what the experience of the patient as a baby, and the mother–baby relationship, might have been.[10] Evidence of emotional deprivation, maternal depression, trauma, physical and sexual abuse and other potentially psychotogenic factors are not always easy to discover. Often evidence may only emerge in the course of treatment when it can be seen how early pathogenic processes have influenced later developmental phases in an epigenetic manner and how they are continuing to exert their influence in the patient's present disturbance.

The Kleinian tradition of presenting detailed case material to illustrate writings can help to bring life to some of their more difficult and abstract formulations. The experience of some personal psychotherapy can enable those workers, of whom there are many, to resolve sufficiently the conflicts that may have influenced their choice of this demanding but rewarding specialty. Undertaking the individual psychotherapy of a selected psychotic patient under expert supervision can be an important learning experience for both patient and therapist. Learning to listen to, learn from, and talk to and with psychotic patients is not a skill to be quickly achieved, but the quality of the therapist's relation with the patient depends on it. Countertransference processes may exert powerful pressures on him to respond in non-therapeutic ways, and the more he is aware of the irrational 'psychotic' aspects of his own personality, the better will be his understanding of the patient and the safer will be the patient in his hands. The therapist's reward for this self-knowledge will be a greater freedom and confidence in his work and a capacity to work more with psychotic patients in the future if he so chooses. Psychotherapy, with or without medication, can very often resolve an acute psychotic episode relatively quickly, but when this has been achieved the therapist is left with the task of evaluating the character of the patient's underlying personality. This may be found to range from normal to severely disturbed, requiring the therapist to recognise that some personalities are so damaged that they are inaccessible to psychotherapeutic influence, which if ignorantly pursued can do more harm than good.

Grotstein (2001) has formulated the idea of 'rehabilitative psychoanalysis', in recognition of the fact that recovery from a psychotic episode may leave the patient with nightmarish memories that he will struggle to forget. Although some patients will show a wish to understand the meaning of what happened to them, many fear that talking about their experience will bring a recurrence. Some live with a sense of doom that they regard as a meaningless biological anomaly which will overwhelm them. Such states can be considered as post-traumatic stress disorders, of a severity greatly influenced by the level of sensitive understanding that they have received in the psychotic episode. Manic-depressives who have recovered from an episode of mania or hypomania may have to face the depressing realisation that what they thought was abundant good health was, in fact, severe illness. This may induce suicidal despair and contribute to a swing into psychotic depression.

Learning to use psychoanalytic concepts confidently with psychotic patients is a hard-won skill which requires many years of experience. Although based on research it is a very different activity from the 'evidence-based' approach of medical research. Among the many pathways to the learning of relevant and useful psychodynamic knowledge it is the psychosis workshop (or seminar) that many consider the most valuable teaching-learning device. Such an event needs to be conducted by a clinician of experience, who has sufficient understanding of the psychoanalytic model. The members can be drawn from all the professionals working with psychotic patients, any of whom can present material for discussion within the group.

In this context participants can sharpen their capacity to listen to psychotic patients and to consider the meaning and significance for the patient of what they are hearing. Making an initial emotional contact with the patient, forming the basis of future trust, discovering the crucial significance of transference and countertransference, the interplay of psychotic and non-psychotic parts of the personality, and the decoding of bizarre or baffling symbolic communications are key topics that can be explored in a rational and controlled manner in such a setting. Although acquiring such skills can be richly rewarding, it can often be extremely emotionally disturbing for the therapist, particularly if he is working in isolation, and the group situation can offer powerful support (Garelick and Lucas, 1996; Lucas, 2003).

When a patient is being seen for the first time by a psychoanalytic psychiatrist for purposes of evaluation or therapy in the presence of the nurses and other members of the multiprofessional team who are caring for him, some powerful and significant processes may be discovered, as the following examples illustrate.

Case examples

A patient came into hospital having changed his name by deed poll to Jesus Christ, complaining that he was angry with God. It soon became clear that he couldn't cope with his present extreme stress which included his inability to manage his financial affairs, and in his psychotic way he hoped that, by changing his name, God would help him. However, he was disappointed and angry to find that this change of identity hadn't resolved his financial troubles. The psychiatrist could now begin to understand that it was his psychotic difficulties in the struggle to cope with his limited mental resources that were his essential problem, and not just simply the obvious stress of financial disorder.

A patient on admission angrily said, 'I am God's older brother.' The psychiatrist replied that he must really be 'fed up with his younger brother getting all the publicity!' The patient stopped, smiled and a mutual warmth developed between them from that time onwards. Previously, he had taken his brother's car and driven it into a wall, fortunately without any resulting serious injury. He thought he was omnipotent, that at the time he could do anything.[11]

A young chronic schizophrenic patient was told by the senior psychiatrist of a Scandinavian hospital that he was to be interviewed the following day by a visiting specialist. Very little contact had been made with him for many months, and he sat in his chair strumming his guitar and smiling remotely. He didn't respond to my invitation to talk, so I asked him what he dreamed last night. Somewhat to my surprise he smiled broadly and said that he had dreamed of two elephants talking on the telephone. I said that I wondered if he had been thinking that these two heavyweight psychiatrists had been speaking on the telephone yesterday in order to arrange this unexpected meeting. He burst into laughter, put down his guitar and began to talk freely.

Comparable examples could be multiplied indefinitely. I quote them in order to illustrate the interplay of the psychotic and non-psychotic parts of the personality and to show how it is possible to make an immediate contact of emotional warmth with such patients. Occasional moments of humour offer some light relief from the staff's constant exposure to tragedy and confusion, and it is the immediate warmth of contact that is so important in establishing the beginnings of a human and humane relationship between the two participants and the attendant staff. Many pitfalls await the inexperienced interviewer who may be tempted to enjoy his moments of cleverness. When emotional contact is made with a patient it will usually be followed sooner or later by a retrogressive movement that can be considered as the psychotic part of the personality struggling to regain control over the patient's mind.

> The gratifying contact with the guitar-playing young man led to the beginnings of a possible exploration of his denial of his appalling plight. However, it was not long before he picked up his guitar and began to show his sense of superiority and contempt of the interviewer and the staff. This did not need to be considered simply as a setback so much as an illustration that he might respond to a trial of individual psychotherapy.

> An interview with a chronic schizophrenic woman had been moving and illuminating for both patient and staff. However, the nurse who escorted her back to the ward reported that the patient told her that she [the patient] had never heard such nonsense, and that the psychiatrist must be mad. This projective expulsion of her painful awareness of her madness at the point of parting illustrated the fact that defences are old friends not to be relinquished lightly. I have taught that this reversal is to be expected and have often warned both the patients and the staff that it would happen sooner or later.

Lucas has reported many such dramatic examples of denial and submission, showing the power of the psychotic part and the need to intervene where possible. Rosenfeld's concept of omnipotent destructive narcissism allows further understanding of the controlling qualities of the psychotic part.[12]

Conclusions

The foregoing examples are but a few of the more obvious ways in which skilful interview technique can be learned and applied in various contexts with psychotic patients. Modern developments in psychoanalysis, based on Freud's original work, object relation theory in general and Kleinian and 'neo-Kleinian' developments in particular have transformed our understanding of psychotic psychopathology in a revolutionary fashion. Psychoanalytic concepts, and particularly those presented in this chapter, can help those working with psychotic patients in several ways:

1 They help to give meaning to confusing or bizarre communications, and this can be a relief to all concerned. By furthering understanding of the patient's preoccupations and problems they help to reduce the risk of inappropriate behaviour by professional staff towards the patient, and of unexpected aggressive outbursts of patients towards the staff. Intimate contact with psychotic patients can be extremely disturbing in all life situations, even to the most mature of personalities, and mental health workers who actually have to care for them can be exposed to huge emotional demands. The nursing staff in particular have to contend not only with exposure to the repeated impact of human tragedy, but also very often with the patients' projective processes. Work that is oriented to these principles based on the concepts of projection and countertransference can help increase confidence in their work.

2 They can act as a foundation for the creation and implementation of comprehensive treatment plans. A psychoanalytically informed perspective enables a variety of treatment modalities to be employed in a truly complementary and rational manner. Individual psychotherapy, behavioural, cognitive, cognitive analytic, family or group analytic therapy, and psychopharmacological procedures may be used with confidence when appropriate to the patient's needs and capacities at a given point in treatment.

3 They permit the differentiation of psychotic patients who are likely to benefit from sufficiently long individual psychotherapy or formal psychoanalysis from those who may not, and can help in understanding why one form of treatment proves beneficial and another does not.

4 They help in the early detection of incipient psychosis, where impaired ego function may go unnoticed or be mistaken for precocious imaginative talent (De Masi, 2003).

The symbolic transformation of the primitive levels of mental processes of early life into progressively higher and abstract forms creates a layering of mental structure and a diversification of mental functioning, leading under normal circumstances to a stable and flexible mental structure. When these developmental pathways take pathological forms they remain embedded in the internal world, to be reactivated at a later date if the subject meets particular stresses in the external or internal world. Such a reactivation requires the mobilisation and intensification of defence mechanisms in the attempt to manage the crisis. In the most extreme cases these emergency defences lead to that state of confusion of internal and external reality and of the sense of self which we call psychosis.

Contemporary psychoanalytic understanding of psychotic disorders has undergone great development since the founding work of the great pioneers, Freud, Jung and Abraham. Kleinian developments since the last war have had a dramatic impact on psychotherapists working in the UK, other parts of Europe and Scandinavia, and in the USA, and have offered a new perspective and a relatively optimistic therapeutic orientation which provides new interest for clinicians and new hope for psychotic patients.

Notes

1 Klein adhered to Freud's use of the term 'phantasy' in order to preserve the differentiation of 'primal' infantile thought processes which have never been conscious from those of 'fantasy', which are conscious or repressed into the unconscious.
2 Winnicott called the depressive position 'the stage of concern'.
3 For an example of infantile anxieties underlying obsessive-compulsive neurosis in adult life, see Jackson (2001).
4 Misunderstandings arose as the consequence of her using a psychiatric term for a normal developmental process, despite the fact that she made it clear that infantile psychotic anxieties simply resembled those of the adult, and did not imply that the infant was psychotic, but that it was the excessive use of these mechanisms that was pathological (see Hinshelwood, 1989).
5 Manic disparagement of the object can also defend the subject from envy of the object, reasoning that if the object is totally devoid of any desirable quality there is nothing for the subject to envy. For a clinical illustration see Jackson (1993).
6 Klein's concept of reparation in the depressive position is an innovation of the greatest importance, one which led Rey to teach that attention to reparative processes is the hallmark of good psychotherapy.
7 Although Klein disagreed in some important respects with Fairbairn's work, she gave him full credit for the profound implications of his concept of schizoid object relations. Rey has offered a detailed and original description of characteristics and dynamics of schizoid thinking from a Kleinian perspective (Rey, 1994; Jackson, 2001: 313–316).
8 If the paranoid-schizoid and depressive positions are seen as alternating states, with one tending to predominate over the other in the individual, a link can be seen with the concept of insecure and secure attachment. For a detailed critique of the link between psychoanalysis and attachment theory, see Fonagy (2001).
9 The Arbours Association centre is an outstanding example (Berke, 1989).
10 Training in the 'naturalistic' observation of infants was initiated by Kleinian analyst Esther Bick. Interested in testing Klein's conclusions about the first year of life, her method has become a world-wide requirement for psychoanalytic and dynamic psychotherapeutic training bodies (Magagna et al., 2005).
11 I am indebted to Richard Lucas for these two examples. Since this was written, Lucas has, tragically, died.
12 This 'mafia-style' control was brilliantly represented in the film A Beautiful Mind.

References

Alport, G.F. (1989). *Melanie Klein and Critical Social Theory*. New Haven, CT: Yale University Press.

Bell, D. (ed.) (1997). *Reason and Passion: A Celebration of the Work of Hanna Segal*. London: Duckworth.

Bell, D. (ed.) (1999). *Psychoanalysis and Culture: A Kleinian Perspective*. London: Duckworth.

Berke, J.H. (1989). *The Tyranny of Malice*. London: Simon & Schuster.

Bion, W.R. (1967). *Second Thoughts*. London: Heinemann.

Bléandonu, G. (1994). *Wilfred Bion: His Life and Works*. London: Free Association Books.

Bowlby, J. (1988). *A Secure Base: Clinical Implications of Attachment Theory*. London and New York: Routledge.

Boyer, L.B. (1983). *The Regressed Patient*. New York: Jason Aronson.

Conran, M. (1991). Running on the spot, or can nursing really change? *Psychoanalytic Psychotherapy* 5, 2: 109–114.

Covington, C., Williams, P., Arundale, J. and Knox, J. (eds) (2002). *Terrorism and War: Unconscious Dynamics of Political Violence*. London: Karnac.

De Masi, F. (2003). On the nature of intuitive and delusional thought. *International Journal of Psycho-Analysis* 84: 1149–1170.

Fairbairn, W.R.D. (1952). *Psychoanalytic Studies of the Personality*. London: Tavistock.

Fonagy, P. (2001). *Attachment Theory and Psychoanalysis*. New York: Other Press.

Freeman, T. (1988). *The Psychoanalyst in Psychiatry*. London: Karnac.

Freud, S. (1925). An autobiographical study. *Standard Edition*, 20: 60. London: Hogarth Press.

Garelick, A. and Lucas, R.N. (1996). The role of a psychosis workshop in general psychiatric training. *Psychiatric Bulletin of the Royal College Psychiatrists* 20: 425–429.

Grotstein, J.S. (1985). *Splitting and Projective Identification*. New York: Jason Aronson.

Grotstein, J.S. (2001). A rationale for the psychoanalytically-informed psychotherapy of schizophrenia and other psychoses: towards the concept of 'rehabilitative psychoanalysis'. In P. Williams (ed.) *A Language For Psychosis*. London: Whurr.

Hinshelwood, R.D. (1989). *A Dictionary of Kleinian Thought*. London: Free Association Books.

Jackson, M. (1993). Manic-depressive psychosis: psychopathology and individual psychotherapy within a psychodynamic milieu. *Psychoanalytic Psychotherapy* 7, 2: 103–133.

Jackson, M. (2001). *Weathering the Storms: Psychotherapy for Psychosis*. London: Karnac.

Jackson, M. and Cawley, R. (1992). Psychodynamics and psychotherapy on an acute psychiatric ward: The story of an experimental unit. *British Journal of Psychiatry* 160: 41–50.

Jackson, M. and Williams, P. (1994). *Unimaginable Storms: A Search for Meaning in Psychosis*. London: Karnac.

Klein, M. (1935). A contribution to the psychogenesis of manic-depressive states. In *The Writings of Melanie Klein*, Vol. 1: 262–289.

Klein, M. (1940). Mourning and its relation to manic-depressive states. In *The Writings of Melanie Klein*, Vol. 1: 344–369.

Klein, M. (1946). Notes on some schizoid mechanisms. In *The Writings of Melanie Klein*, Vol. 3: 1–24.

Lucas, R. (2003). Psychoanalytic controversies: the relationship between psycho-analysis and schizophrenia. *International Journal of Psychoanalysis* 84: 3–15.

Magagna, J., Bakalar, N., Cooper, H., Levy, J. and Shank, C. (eds) (2005). *Intimate Transformations: Babies with their Families*. London: Karnac.

Main, T.F. (1957). The ailment. *British Journal of Medical Psychology* 30: 129–145.

Martindale, B. (2007). Psychodynamic contributions to early interventions in psychosis. *Advances in Psychiatric Treatment* 13: 34–42.

Meltzer, D. (1994). *Sincerity and Other Works*. London: Karnac.

Ogden, T.H. (1989). *The Primitive Edge of Experience*. New York: Jason Aronson.

Rey, J.H. (1994). *Universals of Psychoanalysis in the Treatment of Psychotic and Borderline States*. London: Free Association Books.

Rosenfeld, H.A. (1987). *Impasse and Interpretation*. London: Tavistock.

Rustin, M. (1991). *The Good Society and the Inner World*. London: Verso.

Searles, H.F. (1965). *Collected Papers on Schizophrenia and Related Subjects*. London: Hogarth Press and Institute of Psycho-Analysis.

Searles, H.F. (1986). *My Work With Borderline Patients*. New York: Jason Aronson.

Segal, H. (1981). *The Work of Hanna Segal*. New York: Jason Aronson.

Segal, H. (2007). *Yesterday, Today and Tomorrow*. London: Routledge.

Volkan, V. (1995). *The Infantile Psychotic Self and its Fates*. New York: Jason Aronson.

Volkan, V. and Akhtar, S. (eds) (1997). *The Seed of Madness*. Madison, CT: International Universities Press.

Williams, A.H. (1998). *Cruelty, Violence and Murder: Understanding the Criminal Mind*. London: Karnac.

Winnicott, D.W. (1975). *Through Pediatrics to PsychoAnalysis*. London, Hogarth.

Part 2: Psychological therapies for schizophrenic psychoses in the UK

David Kennard

Treatment for schizophrenia in the National Health Service

In the UK psychological treatments for people with a diagnosis of schizo-phrenia have taken a major step forward in the past ten years with the rise of evidence-based practice in the National Health Service (NHS). Cognitive behaviour therapy and family interventions have since 2002 been approved as treatments that should be available to NHS patients and their families. The process by which this was decided was through the National Institute for Health and Clinical Excellence (NICE). NICE was established by the government in 1999 to give advice on the clinical and cost effectiveness of treatments for a variety of conditions, based on the views of panels of experts on the balance of evidence from research trials (highest priority is given to treatments for which there is evidence of effectiveness from a randomised control trial) and recommended good practice. NICE guidelines largely determine what can and cannot be provided by the NHS. In 2002 NICE published its guideline on schizophrenia, which advises:

> Psychological treatments should be an indispensable part of the treat-ment options available for service users and their families in the effort to promote recovery. Those with the best evidence of effectiveness are cognitive behaviour therapy and family interventions. These should be used to prevent relapse, to reduce symptoms, increase insight and promote adherence to medication.

Elsewhere, in relation to the early post-acute period, while recommending cognitive behavioural therapy (CBT) and family work, the guideline states: 'Counselling and supportive psychotherapy are not recommended . . . However service user preferences should be taken into account, especially if other more efficacious psychological treatments are not locally available.' This suggests that the compilers of the guideline, while giving priority to evidence-based treatments, were aware that other factors might be more important, such as what patients wanted and what was actually available. It is a pity that their recommendation of these alternatives appears so half-hearted, and even more so that there is no mention of psychodynamic or group approaches. The omission of psychodynamic approaches may come as no surprise. One of the main differences between psychoanalytic and cognitive behavioural approaches is that, while both claim to be based on evidence, the first takes its evidence from clinical observation in therapeutic settings, while the second takes it from systematic research using quantified observations of comparative samples. It has been argued (Hinshelwood, 2002) that randomised trials are not the most appropriate way to evaluate psychotherapy, which essentially is about relationships rather than techniques. At the time of writing, NICE is undertaking an update of the guideline which is scheduled to be issued in early 2009. Four members of the International Society for the Psychological Treatments of the Schizo-phrenias and other Psychoses (ISPS) UK are on the guideline development group so there may be some hope of influencing the approach to evaluating the evidence for psychological therapies. In the meantime, the fact that NICE recommends some form of psychological treatment for psychosis may be seen as a positive step forward from a purely pharmacological approach.

Cognitive behavioural therapy for psychosis

Cognitive behavioural therapy (CBT) evolved in the UK in the 1980s out of the merging of 1950s behaviour therapy and 1970s cognitive therapy. The initial focus was on the treatment of depression and different types of anxiety including panic attacks, obsessive compulsive disorder (OCD) and post-traumatic stress disorder (PTSD) but the attempt to apply CBT to psychotic symptoms followed quite soon (Fowler and Morley, 1989). By the mid-1990s sufficient work had been done for several major books to be published on CBT for psychosis (Kingdon and Turkington, 1994; Fowler et al., 1995; Chadwick and Trower, 1996).[1]

CBT practitioners identify their approach as one that is concerned with helping the person with psychosis to understand and make sense of their experiences, and one that works to achieve collaboration between patient and therapist rather than in a more didactic, interpretative or confronta-tional style. There is particular emphasis on engaging in detailed discussion of delusions and hallucinations once a therapeutic alliance has been established, with the aim of encouraging the patient to look for alternative explanations that can make hallucinations or delusions understandable and manageable. The general aims of CBT for psychosis have been stated as reducing the distress and disability caused by psychotic symptoms, reducing emotional disturbance, and promoting active participation in managing the risk of relapse and social disability (Fowler *et al.*, 1995).

Family-centred approaches

Interest in working with the families of individuals with a diagnosis of schizophrenia began in the UK in the 1950s, and was associated with a potent mix of psychoanalytic theory (in particular Winnicott), existential philosophy, and a sociological critique of society. The best known pioneer was R.D. Laing, who became an iconic anti-psychiatry figure in the 1960s, and who acknowledged Bowlby, Bateson and Goffman as his chief influences. Laing made his mark on psychological approaches to psychosis in two main ways. He argued eloquently that what psychotic individuals said was meaningful and should be listened to and understood. I do not think I am alone in belonging to a generation of mental health professionals whose interest in madness and its meaning was fired by Laing's inspirational writing. The other way in which Laing made his mark was by propounding the view that the blame for a young person's psychosis belonged with the family and the wider society, whose contradictory messages, mystifying communication and attempts to brainwash their son or daughter into conformity made 'madness' the only way of dealing with the situation. Laing's published evidence was a series of 11 case studies (Laing and Esterson, 1964). Unfortunately this contributed to a widespread rejection of psychological approaches to psychosis by the families of people diagnosed as schizophrenic. Laing's views were also rejected by the establishment, and were used as a basis for treatment in only a few places – for example, at Shenley Hospital and at Kingsley Hall (see below for more details). This pattern of rejection by the psychiatric establishment was later repeated in the USA where Loren Mosher set up the Soteria project (see Chapter 23) based on Laing's ideas, despite high quality evidence of its effectiveness (Mosher and Burti, 1994).

At around the same time a quite different approach to studying the impact of families on the course of illness in people with a diagnosis of schizophrenia was being undertaken at the Medical Research Council's social psychiatry unit in London. It was this work by John Wing, George Brown, Jim Birley, Christine Vaughan and Julian Leff that led to the concept of expressed emotion (EE), which has become the cornerstone of psycho-educational work with families. This work is so well documented that I will only describe it briefly here (Brown *et al.*, 1962, 1972; Leff and Vaughn, 1985). Researchers found an interaction between medication, relapse, amount of time in contact with the family and the level of expressed emotion in the family. For the purposes of the research, expressed emotion was defined by three components: *critical comments* made about the patient during interviews with carers; expressions of *hostility* including intense anger and rejection; and *over-involvement* fuelled by a mixture of anxiety and guilt leading relatives to try to do everything possible to make up for the impact of the illness. Patients who had a lot of direct contact with families with high levels of expressed emotion were more likely to relapse. They could be protected against the risk of relapse by medication and also by educating families on the nature of schizophrenia and on the role of the family in its management.

Proponents of family psycho-education have been strongly influenced by the wish to distance their approach from family therapy models that identified the family as the cause of the psychotic breakdown (see McFarlane, 2000; Kuipers et al., 2002). Thus families are clearly told that schizophrenia has a biological basis, relatives are shown empathy for the burden of caring for someone suffering from schizophrenia, and professionals work in an open, collaborative way with the family, sharing what information they have and helping the family to build on their strengths. Medication is seen a central part of treatment.

This approach to family work has become the basis for psychosocial interventions (see below) but it has its critics. One criticism (Kuipers et al., 2002) is that the concept of high expressed emotion is misleading if it is taken to mean that family members should suppress all emotion. High levels of warmth are good for patients and 'low-EE' relatives do more than simply not emote. To quote Kuipers et al. (2002): 'Whereas high-EE relatives discount the patient's psychotic experiences as "nonsense", "it's just your imagination", or "the doctor says you're mad", low-EE relatives acknowledge the reality of the patient's experiences. However they make it clear that they do not share these experiences.' Instead they have a number of coping strategies – for example 'a father whose son claimed that there were microphones in the door knobs gave him a screwdriver and asked him to dismantle the knob in order to check it'.

Another criticism less easy to resolve is that the attempt to distinguish between the family as a potential contributor to relapse but not a causal influence can be experienced by families as a double message. 'The message can and does come across to some families as, "You are not to blame for your son's/daughter's condition, it's just that people like you seem to provoke more schizophrenia, so you'll need to be taught to behave differently"' (quoted in Johnstone, 1993). Johnstone argues that there is a similarity between the 'blame' model in which relatives were said to give contradictory messages, and the way family management teams behave towards families (Johnstone, 1993).

Psychosocial interventions

In the 1990s psychological treatments for people with 'serious mental health problems'[2] were introduced into the National Health Service primarily through the development of psychosocial interventions (PSI). The term PSI was adopted to refer to a combination of psycho-educational family work and CBT-based psychological management techniques for individuals, within a framework of outcome-oriented assessment, case management and early intervention.

Since 1992 the training of mental health professionals in skills subsumed under the heading PSI has been provided on university courses that aim to teach members of all mental health professions the skills to work with people with serious mental health problems based on research evidence about effective interventions (Brooker, 2001). Initial evaluation of these courses found that the nurses' skills improved and that their clients showed significant reductions in symptom severity and increased social functioning. This created sufficient impetus that by 2001 there were an estimated 27 undergraduate and five postgraduate programmes across the UK. Despite this expansion the numbers trained have been only a drop in the ocean of NHS staff. In 2001 Brooker calculated that 600 mental health professionals had been trained in PSI approaches, and in 2005 an informal 'guesstimate' (A. Brabban – personal communication, 2005) was that one to two per cent of the mental health workforce had sufficient training to be able to offer patients with psychosis a course of CBT.

More recent evaluation of these courses has led to more mixed con-clusions. Brooker and Brabban (2005) identified 37 studies that attempted to evaluate PSI training for work with people with psychosis. They found improved clinical skills and a more positive and hopeful attitude with the adoption of a recovery model. But they also found that the capacity of participants to implement the new skills in their work situation depended on support from managers and other members of the team, on small caseloads and the time necessary to undertake interventions, and on access to good local clinical supervision. They also needed the skills and confidence to engage families and offer meaningful interventions to meet their needs (which may not be easy in the light of the criticism referred to above), and the capacity to integrate behavioural techniques of family work into a broader range of conceptual frameworks within a clinical team.

Group and therapeutic community approaches

In contrast to the evidence-based approaches advocated by NICE and the published data they have generated, what follows is more anecdotal. It is based on my impressions from 30 years working as a clinical psychologist and group analyst, my former role as editor of the journal *Therapeutic Communities*, and my present role as chair of ISPS UK. From these obser-vations it appears that interest in the use of groups to help and support people with psychosis, and more recently their carers and families, has been remarkably strong and persistent but probably under-reported in the UK. Five strands can be identified: the therapeutic community approach;

modified group analysis; psycho-education groups; self-help groups; and the arts therapies – which are both individual and group.

Two quite different kinds of therapeutic communities emerged in the UK for people experiencing psychosis in the 1950s and 1960s (Kennard, 1998). In some of the large mental hospitals medical superintendents developed the 'therapeutic community approach'. This was an attempt to humanise the quality of life of long-term residents, giving them back some control over their lives, with meaningful activity and shared responsibility for aspects of ward life (Clark, 1964, 1965; Mandelbrote, 1965). This approach more or less disappeared with the closure of most of the large mental hospitals. The other type was associated with the anti-psychiatry movement, most notably by R.D. Laing, Joseph Berke and others at Kingsley Hall in London's East End, and David Cooper in Villa 21 at Shenley Hospital. Both projects were small and short-lived but have had a lasting impact, not least through the inspiration they gave Loren Mosher to create Soteria in California. Today one direct offshoot of Kingsley Hall remains in the UK: the Arbours Crisis Centre, established by Joseph Berke, offers up to six guests non-medicated round-the-clock support with psychoanalytic supervision (Berke *et al.*, 1995).

More recently an amalgam of these approaches has been developed for people recovering from psychoses, drawing on the half-way house model of the Richmond Fellowship and the philosophical underpinnings of the anti-psychiatry movement (Tucker, 2000). Community Housing and Therapy (CHT), started in 1994, runs six residential projects in and around London, and Threshold runs four therapeutic communities (TCs) in Belfast.

Two of the pioneers in the seminal therapeutic community experiments in the 1940s, W.R. Bion and S.H. Foulkes, went on to develop group methods that have had an enormous influence on psychotherapeutic approaches to psychosis, in the UK and elsewhere. Although his work with groups was short-lived, Bion's influence on group approaches in mental health services has been pervasive. Both his technique and his writings on basic assumption functioning in small groups (Bion, 1961) have been a constant reference point for group workers, not always to good effect. One of my earliest group experiences was sitting in a group run by a young psychiatrist on a long-stay male ward. Having convened the session with around 20 patients, the group met for an hour in almost total silence. It was only some time later that I was able to understand this rather unhelpful style of group facilitation as being probably the inappropriate use of the method Bion developed as an innovative teaching tool in a quite different context.

Although Foulkes was less known for his writings on psychosis, his method of group analysis has had an increasing influence on mental health practice through the development of an accredited training programme by the Institute of Group Analysis (IGA) founded in 1971. Around 200 professionals a year undertake its one year Introductory courses in England

and Scotland, but perhaps a more salient indicator has been a series of workshops run jointly by the IGA and ISPS UK on working with psychosis in groups. Each workshop drew 50 participants from a range of mental health disciplines and was heavily oversubscribed, indicating an appetite for developing this kind of work.

In practice it is known that analytic techniques require adaptation for working with psychosis, and in the field of group work the most effective model combines elements of educative, psychodynamic and interpersonal approaches (Kanas, 2000). Modified group analytic psychotherapy groups have been developed as slow-open weekly groups in both day hospital and inpatient settings for individuals with long histories of psychosis (Canete and Ezquerro, 1999; Brownbridge, 2006). These groups provide individuals with the opportunity to discuss personal experiences in depth, but use group analytic principles on a flexible basis:

> The model fosters a shared space working towards dialogue, under-standing and integration. This is crucial in groups with psychotic patients. As fellow members know what it is like to be psychotic, their experience is validated and, in turn, it can be redefined and integrated as part of their life experiences. The 'sealing over' defensive strategies are lessened.
>
> (Canete, 2003)

These clinical findings are supported by evidence from the UK's leading researcher in this area, who found a slight negative correlation between transference-oriented interpretations and patient responsiveness in groups for patients with severe mental illness, but that group members valued the therapist's efforts to make them feel accepted and to help them explore the effects of mental illness on their lives as human beings (Kapur, 1999).

Purely psycho-educational groups are also used routinely in a number of psychiatric day hospitals, providing information and support in a time-limited format of eight sessions for individuals with psychosis. These groups have been found to engage individuals when other services have failed to engage, acting in some cases as stepping stones to their pursuing further individual work in relation to issues related to the experience of psychosis or its consequences (J. Smith, personal communication, 2002).

Following the work of Romme and Escher (1989, 1993) on the preval-ence of voice hearing in the general population, groups for people who hear voices and who may or may not have a diagnosis of schizophrenia began to be established in the UK. The first Hearing Voices group was formed in Manchester in 1988 and a national Hearing Voices Network was estab-lished that offers guidance to anyone wanting to set up a group and has a well-used website. A number of Voice Hearers groups, in some cases co-led by a service user and a professional, meet in different parts of the country.

The network places a strong emphasis on respect for the individual's own explanation of voice hearing.

Arts therapies

Grandison (2002) writes that 'the history of art therapy is inextricably linked with the practice of art therapy with psychosis', which began in the large asylums in the 1940s and was formally recognised as a health service profession in 1980. Mental hospital art therapy departments were able to provide a separate creative space away from the ward, and could sometimes offer daily sessions of self-directed activities where people could use the setting and its materials in whatever way they wanted (Killick, 1996). Over time other therapies have emerged using different expressive modalities, and these are reflected in the growing membership of ISPS UK which now includes art therapists, music therapists, drama therapists and dance and movement therapists – collectively known as 'arts therapists'.

With the closure of the large mental hospitals and the move to care in the community, arts therapists have had to adapt to employment in specialist settings (Killick and Schaverin, 1997). These include specialist mental health services for children and adolescents, adults, older adults, autistic spectrum disorders and offenders. Many arts therapists are also trained in verbal psychotherapies, and while most have a psychodynamic orientation there are differences in approach determined partly by the nature of the client group and partly by theoretical models. It is a developing field and new syntheses are still emerging. Recent examples include McNeilly (2006), who has been developing a model of group analytic art therapy that seeks to move beyond the split he identifies between directive and non-directive art therapists; Compton Dickinson (2005) who has developed a synthesis of music therapy and cognitive analytic therapy in her work with ethnic minority offenders; and Casson (2004) who has developed new techniques drawing on dramatherapy, psychodrama and self psychology for people who hear voices.

Early intervention

Over the past few years one of the most energetic and inspiring developments in the treatment of psychosis has been the early intervention (EI) or early psychosis movement. Following on from pioneering work by Falloon in the 1980s, when family doctors in Buckinghamshire were trained to recognise early signs of psychosis and refer to mental health teams (Falloon *et al.*, 1984), and from other pioneers in Scandinavia and Australia (see chapters in Martindale *et al.*, 2000), the movement came together with the founding of the International Early Psychosis Association (IEPA) in Australia in 1998. In the UK early intervention gathered momentum in 2002, the year in which the Newcastle Early Psychosis Declaration was drawn up at the launch of the National Institute for Mental Health in England (NIMHE), and also the year when practitioners and government health advisors from the UK were among the 1000 who attended the third international conference of the IEPA in Copenhagen. Although EI includes the full range of biological and psychological approaches, the five goals of the Early Psychosis Declaration, which was relaunched in 2004 with supporting statements from the UK government and the WHO, are predominantly psychosocial.[3] They are:

1   *Raising community awareness* – overcoming stigma, prejudice and discrimination.
2   *Improving access and engagement by health services* – reducing the duration of untreated psychosis and the use of compulsion for first admissions.
3   *Promoting recovery and regaining a normal life* – overcoming social exclusion.
4   *Promoting family engagement and carer support* – overcoming relatives' feelings of alienation and disempowerment.
5   *Practitioner training* – overcoming pessimism and hopelessness among primary care staff.

Around the country a number of projects have been developed to put these goals into practice. These are some examples.

Raising community awareness

On the Edge is an award-winning mental health education programme that has toured schools and colleges. It is an interactive play developed by the Exstream Theatre Company and rehabilitation psychiatrist Glenn Roberts, showing what happens to a student, his friends and family, as the student begins to experience psychosis. The project is intended to reduce stigma and enable young people to seek help early, and has gained support from the Royal College of Psychiatrists and from the All Party Parliamentary Group on Mental Health.

Improving access and engagement by health services

The Birmingham early intervention service, established in 1995, is providing more acceptable alternatives to traditional hospital admission in small respite houses with 24-hour support by a small staff group (Taylor, 2003); Lambeth Early Onset (LEO) service in South London provides two-year follow-up for young people experiencing their first episode of psychosis, offering CBT for persistent symptoms, vocational, social groups and carer support/family interventions.

Promoting recovery and a normal life

There are a number of projects linking mental health services with services like Connexions and the Youth Enquiry Service that offer advice and information on education, accommodation, careers and personal development.

Promoting family engagement and carer support/practitioner training

In reality these often go together. It has been increasingly recognised that carers need recognition, help and support, in particular at the period of greatest crisis around a first admission to hospital, but that routine clinical practice often ignores the needs – even the presence – of family members (Fadden, 1997; Hardcastle et al., 2007). Meriden, the West Midlands Family Programme, was set up by Fadden in 1998 to provide front line mental health workers with training in how to work with families, with the goal that thinking of the needs of families becomes part of the clinical culture. By 2005 Meriden had provided this training for 2000 people.

In the past decade the tension between the two approaches of family therapy and family intervention (with its commitment not to define the family as being in need of therapy) has been addressed in an attempt to integrate the best of both approaches. Learning from Fadden's evaluation of Falloon's pioneering work (Falloon et al., 1984; Fadden, 1997), Burbach and Stanbridge (1998) developed a training programme for teams providing family support services in the county of Somerset. Recognising that training in manualised treatment approaches does not equip therapists with sufficient flexibility to engage with the wide range of families they encounter, their course combines theories and techniques of CBT, family intervention and basic family therapy to enable trainees to form therapeutic relationships with a wide range of families. Early indications of success have created considerable interest in this work as more family therapists are appointed to early intervention teams around the country. Two other influences on the practice of British family therapists working with psychosis are the Open Dialogue approach of Seikkula and Trimble (2005), and the application to the psychoses of Michael White's Narrative Therapy (J. Webster, personal communication, 2005).

Despite, or perhaps because of, the impressive drive forward by early intervention services, there is also some resistance or cynicism amongst practitioners. Martindale (2002) identified two sources of this. One is a fear that a consequence of EI could be the increasing colonisation of human distress by drug companies. Martindale counters this with the view that unless there is evidence that treatments are dangerous the aim of reducing the duration of untreated psychosis is fully justified on humanitarian grounds, providing it is based on the principles of building an enduring relationship, engaging families as soon as possible, and using the lowest doses of medication needed. The other resistance comes from a concern that as EI gains momentum it will take away resources from other services for enduring mental illness. This is inevitably a concern at a time when many NHS Trusts are cutting services and creates an imperative for service providers to conceive of early intervention, relapse prevention, inpatient services and longer term support as all belonging under the same umbrella of care.

The role of the voluntary sector and mental health charities

This chapter should not end without mention of the important role played by the voluntary sector, which is a vibrant force in the UK. The voluntary sector includes specialist services that often depend for their income on statutory funding but have the independence to develop outside the general framework of the NHS. Examples include The Retreat, Arbours, CHT and Threshold, all of which provide specialist therapeutic living environments for people with psychosis. There are also a number of mental health charities that offer information and support for people suffering from mental distress (a term preferred by service user organisations) and their carers/ family members, and play a major role in campaigning for the rights of people with mental illness and influencing government policy. Foremost in the field for people affected by severe mental illness is Rethink (formerly National Schizophrenia Fellowship). Others include MIND and SANE. All provide telephone helplines, and websites with a wealth of information and links for service users, relatives and for professionals.

Conclusion

Rereading this chapter I was struck by how much I didn't know before I started writing it and only learnt through researching it – reading, 'googling' and talking to people. I consider myself a reasonably well-informed clinical psychologist with a wide range of professional contacts. This suggests that a state of mutual ignorance of each other's work may be a common feature of the UK scene when it comes to psychological approaches to psychosis. This is not too surprising when you consider our affiliations. Most readers probably have at least four affiliations, each of which provides a certain range of vision but also a potential set of blinkers. The four are our profession (psychiatry, psychology, nursing, different arts therapists, etc.); our employment sector (state, private, charitable); our work setting (hospital, community); and our therapeutic orientation (psychodynamic, cognitive behavioural, systemic). These alone generate 72 combinations – and readers may think I have left out some categories. It is little wonder we do not know who inhabits all the other spaces and what they do, which may help to explain why service users and their families find it such a confusing world as they try to make sense of what they are told by different services and professionals.

This fragmentation poses an immediate question and challenge to all of us to be more aware of the range of services on offer, or at least to be aware of how limited our knowledge is. The positive aspect of this situation is the large number of therapeutic initiatives, some of which have been described above. These include the many training courses for staff working with people experiencing psychosis and their families, the number of new service projects, the nationwide development of early intervention teams, the enthusiasm and mutual support of groups of different therapists working with psychosis, and the raised profile given to some psychological therapies (as against none) in the NHS guideline on schizophrenia. But there are also downsides to this plethora of initiatives. There is a risk of disillusion as idealistic hopes of a new initiative begin to fade; of rivalry or mutual misperceptions between professions or therapeutic movements preventing us from learning from each other; and that we avoid the huge but rather less exciting task of reaching out to the majority of mental health staff who continue to work with very little awareness of any of the psychological approaches to psychosis that are available.

For the future to continue to be one we can believe in, we need to keep supporting each other in groups and communities that are developing better ways to be and work with psychosis; but we need to avoid being seen as exclusive holders of the truth in a way that ignores or alienates potential allies in other therapies and disciplines.

Notes

1 The terms cognitive therapy and cognitive behavioural therapy are to some extent used interchangeably. One of the main differences is the extent to which practical behavioural assignments are carried out between therapy sessions.
2 It is interesting how at the same time that family workers are using the terminology of biological condition and illness to reassure carers that they are not to blame, the proponents of PSI are joining with those who hold that illness labels are stigmatising and even the most severe disorders should be described as problems, albeit serious ones.
3 The prime movers of the Early Psychosis Declaration in the UK have been clinical psychologist Jo Smith and GP/carer David Shiers, who have since been appointed as joint leads of a National Early Intervention in Psychosis Programme jointly sponsored by NIMHE and Rethink. The full declaration can be read in pdf format on the Rethink website (www.Rethink.org).

References

Berke, J., Masoliver, C. and Ryan, T. (eds) (1995). *Sanctuary: The Arbours Experience of Alternative Community Care*. London: Process Press.

Bion, W.R. (1961). *Experiences in Groups*. London: Tavistock.

Brooker, C. (2001). A decade of evidence-based training for work with people with serious mental health problems: progress in the development of psychosocial interventions. *Journal of Mental Health* 10: 17–31.

Brooker, C. and Brabban, A. (2005). *Measured Success*. London: National Institute for Mental Health in England.

Brown, G.W., Monck, E.M., Carstairs, G.M. and Wing, J.K. (1962). Influence of family life on the course of schizophrenic illness. *British Journal of Preventative and Social Medicine* 16: 55–68.

Brown, G.W., Birley, J.L.T. and Wing, J.K. (1972). Influence of family life on the course of schizophrenic disorders: a replication. *British Journal of Psychiatry* 121: 241–258.

Brownbridge, G. (2006). Group analysis as psychosocial intervention for psychosis. Paper presented at the 15th International ISPS Conference, Madrid.

Burbach, F.R. and Stanbridge, R.I. (1998). A family intervention in psychosis service integrating the systemic and family management approaches. *Journal of Family Therapy* 20: 311–325.

Cañete, M. and Ezquerro, A. (1999). Group-analytic psychotherapy of psychosis. *Group Analysis* 32: 507–514.

Canete, M. (2003). Day psychotherapy with psychotic patients in the community. Paper presented ISPS UK conference held at Bart's Hospital, London, 26 June 2003.

Casson, J. (2004). *Drama, Psychotherapy and Psychosis: Dramatherapy and Psychodrama with People Who Hear Voices*. London: Brunner-Routledge.

Chadwick, P.D. and Trower, P. (1996). *Cognitive Therapy for Delusions, Voices and Paranoia*. Chichester: Wiley.

Clark, D.H. (1964). *Administrative Therapy*. London: Tavistock.

Clark, D.H. (1965). The therapeutic community – concept, practice and future. *British Journal of Psychiatry* 111: 947–954.

Compton Dickinson, S. (2005). Rapping at the door: songs of innocence and experience with ethnic minority offenders. Paper presented at the 11th World Congress of Music Therapy.

Fadden, G. (1997). Implementation of family interventions in routine clinical practice following staff training programmes: a major cause for concern. *Journal of Mental Health* 6: 599–612.

Falloon, I.R.H., Boyd, J.L. and McGill, C.W. (1984). *Family Care of Schizophrenia*. New York: Guilford Press.

Fowler, D. and Morley, S. (1989). The cognitive-behavioural treatment of hallucinations and delusions: a preliminary study. *Behavioural Psychotherapy* 17: 123–134.

Fowler, D., Garety, P.A. and Kuipers, E. (1995). *Cognitive Behaviour Therapy for Psychosis: Theory and Practice*. Chichester: Wiley.

Grandison, S. (2002). Arts therapies and ISPS UK. *ISPS UK Newsletter*. 3: 8–9.

Hardcastle, M., Kennard, D., Grandison, S. and Fagin, L. (2007). *Experiences of Inpatient Mental Health Care: Narratives from Service Users, Carers and Professionals*. London: Brunner-Routledge.

Hinshelwood, R.D. (2002). Symptoms or relationships. *British Medical Journal* 324: 292–293.

Johnstone, L. (1993). Family management in 'schizophrenia': its assumptions and contradictions. *Journal of Mental Health* 2: 255–269.

Kanas, N. (2000). Group therapy and schizophrenia: an integrative model. In M. Martindale, A. Bateman, M. Crowe and F. Margison (eds) *Psychosis: Psychological Approaches and their Effectivenes.* London: Gaskell.

Kapur, R. (1999). Clinical interventions in group psychotherapy. In V.L. Schermer and M. Pines (eds) *Group Psychotherapy of the Psychoses.* London: Jessica Kingsley Publishers.

Kennard, D. (1998). *An Introduction to Therapeutic Communities.* London: Jessica Kingsley Publishers.

Killick, K. (1996). Unintegration and containment in acute psychosis. *British Journal of Psychotherapy* 13: 232–242.

Killick, K. and Schaverin, J. (1997). *Art, Psychotherapy and Psychosis.* London and New York: Routledge.

Kingdon, D.G. and Turkington, D. (1994). *Cognitive Behaviour Therapy of Schizophrenia.* Hove, UK: Lawrence Erlbaum Associates Ltd.

Kuipers, E., Leff, J. and Lam, D. (2002). *Family Work for Schizophrenia: A Practical Guide.* London: Gaskell.

Laing, R.D. and Esterson, A. (1964). *Sanity, Madness and the Family.* London: Tavistock.

Leff, J. and Vaughn, C.E. (1985). *Expressed Emotion in Families.* New York: Guilford Press.

McFarlane, W.R. (2000). Psychoeducational multi-family groups: adaptations and outcomes. In M. Martindale, A. Bateman, M. Crowe and F. Margison (eds) *Psychosis: Psychological Approaches and their Effectiveness.* London: Gaskell.

McNeilly, G. (2006). *Group Analytic Art Therapy.* London: Jessica Kingsley Publishers.

Mandelbrote, B.M. (1965). The use of psychodynamic and sociodynamic principles in the treatment of psychotics. *Comprehensive Psychiatry* 6: 381–387.

Martindale, B. (2002). Report of the International Early Psychosis Association Conference, Copenhagen, Sept. 2002. *ISPS UK Newsletter* November: 6–7.

Martindale, B., Bateman, A., Crowe, M. and Margison, F. (eds) (2000). *Psychosis: Psychological Approaches and their Effectiveness.* London: Gaskell.

Mosher, L.R. and Burti, L. (1994). *Community Mental Health: A Practical Guide.* New York: Norton.

National Institute for Clinical Excellence (NICE, 2002). *Schizophrenia: Core Interventions in the Treatment and Management of Schizophrenia in Primary and Secondary Care.* London: NICE.

Romme, M. and Escher, S. (1989). Hearing voices. *Schizophrenia Bulletin* 17: 357–359.

Romme, M. and Escher, S. (eds) (1993). *Accepting Voices.* London: MIND Publications.

Seikkula, J. and Trimble, D. (2005). Healing elements of therapeutic conversation: dialogue as an embodiment of love. *Family Process* 44: 461–475.

Taylor, K. (2003). Early intervention in psychosis – local report. *ISPS UK Newsletter* July: 4–6.

Tucker, S. (2000). *A Therapeutic Community Approach to Care in the Community.* London: Jessica Kingsley Publishers.

Websites

Hearing Voices Network. www.hearing-voices.org.
MIND. www.mind.org.uk.
Rethink. www.Rethink.org.
SANE. www.sane.org.

Chapter 9

German-speaking Central Europe

Part 1: The development of psychosis psychotherapy in Switzerland

Klaus Hoffmann

> Precisely by not demanding a cure of the patient, the therapist tacitly gives him the confidence that the possibilities for cure lie within him, the patient, and only thus does he take him fully seriously. . . . Such a rejection of the clinical notion of cure, of statistics of cure and of the therapist's own ambition makes the highest demands of a personal sort on the therapist, which he can only satisfy within a therapeutic group that supports him. This support is often the only satisfaction he can hope for as a reward for his own undertaking for a long time. The rest does not lie in his hands.
>
> (Meerwein, 1957: 253)

Continuity despite the time of National Socialism

The Bellevue Sanatorium in Kreuzlingen and the Burghölzli in Zurich

Ludwig Binswanger's clinical and philosophical principles (shortened version of Hoffmann, 1997)

National Socialism led to the flight and emigration from Germany to the USA of some well-known psychoanalysts who had worked with psychotic patients, above all Frieda Fromm-Reichmann, who had run a sanatorium in Heidelberg in the 1920s. Her work at Chestnut Lodge Sanatorium became well known in Switzerland and the German-speaking world during the 1950s (see Hoffmann and Elrod, 1999).

It was in 1942 during the era of National Socialism that Ludwig Binswanger (see Chapter 4) wrote *Grundformen und Erkenntnis menschlichen Daseins* [Basic Forms] (Binswanger, 1942/1993), in which he formulated the dialogical philosophy of Martin Buber: *through a transformation of the basic I–Thou to the basic Thou–I*, as the foundation of the sciences of psychiatry and psychoanalysis – an approach that is universally accepted today in the realms of psychoanalytic treatment of psychoses, child psychiatry, and object relations theory. Even with seriously mentally ill patients the in-between, the encounter space, can be the subject of verbal and non-verbal therapy. Binswanger remained in contact with both the German emigrant and American psychoanalysts, for example, Leslie Farber, the director of psychotherapy at Chestnut Lodge, Edith Weigert, whose memorial to Fromm-Reichmann appeared in German as the foreword to the working edition of Fromm-Reichmann's writings (Weigert, 1978), and Morris Schwartz, one of the authors of the Chestnut Lodge study (Stanton and Schwartz, 1954). Thus, Binswanger remained familiar with the discussion of psychoanalytically designed therapeutic milieus. He also remained in contact with the neurologist and patron of Fromm-Reichmann, Kurt Goldstein, who had fled from Berlin to New York.

'Der Mensch in der Psychiatrie' [The Person in Psychiatry], originally published in 1957, contains a summary of Binswanger's recommendations for good psychotherapeutic and psychiatric work. The therapist must expose himself or herself existentially. Quoting Kierkegaard: 'The doctor in an asylum for the insane, who is stupid enough to believe that he is sane for all eternity and that his portion of reason is insured against all damages for life, is in a certain sense still cleverer than the psychotics but at the same time stupider than they are and will not get well again' (Binswanger (1957/1994: 57). He supported the intensive psychotherapies of schizophrenic patients carried out in the USA and compared them to his own therapeutic practice:

> In this respect psychiatry has made great progress precisely in the last years by no longer contenting itself with encountering the mental patient – as is still the case today in a standard work of psychiatry – 'with indifferent kindness', nor with just talking to him and systematically going through his life history. Psychiatrists have begun to bring this up actively, as the writer himself did many years ago already in the analysis of a hysterical phobia and also in other cases. . . . The more these attempts – incidentally also as the modern physical and chemical curative methods in psychiatry develop under the sign of existential communication and not only under the sign of psycho- and physico-therapeutic ambition and therapeutic routine – the more likely it is that the mental patient himself turns from the role of the blind struggler and silent sufferer on the stage of madness into an existential partner, i.e. not only a healthy human being but a human being.
>
> (Binswanger, 1957/1994: 71–72)

It is easy to understand why Franco Basaglia, one of the founders of Democratic Psychiatry in Italy, interested himself in the form of psychoanalysis worked out by Binswanger. Established academic psychiatry too opened up in the 1950s and 1960s vis-à-vis the psychoanalysis of psychoses.

Binswanger even received the Kraepelin Medal of the Max Planck Institute in Munich. He remained a full member of the Swiss Psychoanalytic Society (which meant also of the International Psychoanalytic Association, IPA) until his death. Among the psychoanalysts of these years, he had the closest contact with Gustav Bally, who acknowledged that Binswanger brought a philosophical approach into psychoanalysis.

Binswanger retired in 1956. His son Wolfgang Binswanger led the Bellevue Sanatorium until it closed in 1979 for financial and management reasons. Norman Elrod worked there from 1960 to 1968. In the early 1960s, Fabrizio Napolitani (1963) founded a community with patients in the Villa Landegg of the Bellevue Sanatorium, where up to 23 patients lived without nursing care. They had to look after themselves, supported by two therapists who spent a lot of time with them.

Gustav Bally (1893–1966) – an important bridge between the psychoanalytic therapy of psychoses in Switzerland and the international psychoanalytic movement

The Swiss psychoanalyst Gustav Bally started his psychiatric career at Burghölzli in Zurich, received his analytic training in Berlin in the 1920s, and returned to Switzerland at the beginning of the Nazi era. On 27 February 1934, he firmly objected to Jung's presidency of the International General Medical Psychotherapy Association, which was an organisation supporting Nazi ideology, in an article 'Deutschstämmige Psychotherapie' [Psychotherapy of German Descent] in the *Neue Zürcher Zeitung*. In the 1940s and 1950s, he had among others the important schizophrenia therapists Gaetano Benedetti, Martti Siirala, and Johannes Cremerius as training analysands. Bally played an important role in getting the German Psychoanalytic Association back into the IPA, especially by supporting Alexander Mitscherlich and the founding of the journal *Psyche*. Bally was a member of the medical faculty at the University of Zurich from 1956 onwards and president of the Swiss Psychiatric Society from 1956 until 1958.

Bally regarded countertransference and the therapist's action as the central points in psychoanalysis with psychotics. 'This "new technique" consists in giving up the objectivist position and in risking an unconditional partnership with the patient. Expressed in the language of psychoanalysis: the physician must "act" with the psychotic. If he does this, then he addresses his patient not only with his understanding, but with his whole heart. Then he experiences what Sullivan already observed, in contrast to Freud: "The psychotic is not only not incapable of transference, but his transference is of a quite special strength and absoluteness"' (Bally, 1956; also in Elrod, 2002: 858).

Bally's broad interest in propagating the psychoanalytic therapy of psychoses can be seen in his introduction and organisation, together with the existential analyst Medard Boss, of continuing psychotherapeutic education of resident physicians at Burghölzli beginning in 1948. Boss (1941) had interviewed psychiatrist colleagues who carried out shock therapies about their dreams and found that the theme of power stood in the forefront. He qualified in 1947 as a lecturer at the University of Zurich in the field of psychotherapy and the Swiss Society for Existential Analysis. The latter was among the founding organisations of the International Federation of Psychoanalytic Societies (IFPS) in 1962.

For Bally, psychotic experience was a general human phenomenon, having to do with fear of giving meaning to interpersonal relations. He gave a differentiated description of the advantages and disadvantages of psychiatric drugs and of shock treatments:

> The mentioned tools have led to the virtual disappearance of restlessness and aggression from our clinics. But they also have the effect that doctors and staff have become more sensitive toward aggressive behaviour and that the clinic will no longer tolerate the psychotic originality of individual patients. In the process of the social integration tendency they are 'forced into line' . . . But it can only be attributed to psychoanalysis if today the inter-personal relation is recognized as a possible carrier of curative happening and taken seriously scientifically.
>
> (Bally, in Elrod, 2002: 855)

Psychotherapeutic practice, research and training with psychotic patients at the Psychiatric University Hospital Burghölzli in Zurich in the 1950s

The Geneva psychologist and psychoanalyst Marguerite Séchehaye exerted a great influence with her descriptions of the healing of 'Renée' and amongst other things through her method of symbolic wish fulfilment (Séchehaye, 1947; see Chapter 10). On Manfred Bleuler's invitation, Séchehaye presented her concept in lectures at the University Psychiatric Clinic in Zurich and her work that was published in the USA was also well received (Brody and Redlich, 1952).

Like his father 40 years earlier, the leader of the Burghölzli, Professor Manfred Bleuler, took up psychoanalytic concepts, especially the direct analysis of John Rosen (1953), maybe then the best known psychosis therapist, whose method was later, and rightly, abandoned (Masson, 1988; Hoffmann and Elrod, 1999). Less attention was paid to Fromm-Reichmann. Therapists like Benedetti, Elrod, Siirala and Christian Müller treated schizophrenic patients in individual and group therapies and emphasised that the creation and maintenance of a therapeutic relationship making use of all available psychoanalytic knowledge is essential. Twenty-five years later, Bleuler summarised this period as follows:

It became clear that it is always possible to address the health of the schizophrenic and find a personal relation with him, just as it is with a healthy person. Although no possibility emerged to treat the majority of schizophrenics psychoanalytically, there developed at least a powerful motivation to treat them with less demanding means.

(Bleuler, 1979: 7)

In a systematic case study of 94 psychotherapeutically treated patients (Müller, 1961), a clear subjective improvement appeared in many cases, and in individual cases impressive cures were achieved through psychotherapy. Success depended heavily on the knowledge and commitment of the therapist.

Doubt was repeatedly cast on the effectiveness of the psychoanalytic treatment of psychoses with the argument that those treated successfully had not suffered from psychoses at all since they were capable of responding to psychotherapy – which Walter Bräutigam and Müller (1962) disproved, using as examples Mme Séchehaye's case of 'Renée', a case of Benedetti, the Hans Zimmermann case of Elrod, and a chronic schizophrenic patient treated by Müller. Psychoanalytic individual and group therapies in institutions are expensive and must struggle against not only the patients' resistance but often that of professional colleagues and nurses as well. Even inside the psychoanalytic movement, above all in the IPA, the therapy of psychoses remained controversial for a long time (Faugeras, 2000).

Methodological and clinical developments

Gaetano Benedetti (born 1920)

Gaetano Benedetti, born in 1920 in Catania, Sicily, came to the Zurich clinic in 1947 and was sent by Manfred Bleuler in 1950 for a year to John N. Rosen in New York. He was in a training analysis for six years with Bally. In 1953 he qualified as a lecturer in psychiatry at the University of Zurich. In 1956 he was called to the University of Basel as Professor of Psychohygiene and Psychotherapy, where he worked until his retirement in 1985. In his autobiography Benedetti (1994) expresses himself very critically toward Rosen, confirming the criticism that already existed in the USA (Masson 1988):

I was impressed by Rosen's optimism, his participation, the courage of his (often arbitrary and overpowering) interpretations, from the force of his personality, the decisiveness with which he stood behind his patients. But I also quickly noted the power aspects of his 'direct analysis', which attempted to break down resistance mainly by force. When resistance proved to be stubborn, it was countered with (physical) blows. Rosen taught that the destructive super-ego was broken in this way. I followed his example on one single occasion – that was the only deed in my life which fills me with shame even today. Rosen's method left few traces in my later activity, although I was considered in Europe as a 'Rosen student' for a long time.

(Benedetti, 1994: 40)

In Basel Benedetti was unable to continue the intensive psychotherapy of schizophrenics at the university clinic as had been possible in Zurich. The Basel University psychiatry was almost wholly oriented toward psychiatric drugs. Benedetti worked under Raymond Battegay at the outpatient clinic, where he was able not only to develop a fully independent activity, but for almost 30 years through colloquia, seminars, lectures, training analyses could educate a whole generation of young psychiatrists (Benedetti, 1994: 45). In an English paper Benedetti described the outstanding therapeutic results with schizophrenic patients reported by one of his students, Bertha Neumann, working in Milan, Italy (Benedetti, 1969). In the 1970s Benedetti and Johannes Cremerius founded the Assoziazione di Studi Psicoanalitici (ASP), which was taken into the IFPS in 1989.

Dealing with the mentally ill is on the one hand a situation defined by certain learnable and practicable 'technical' rules; on the other hand a situation with a fellow human being in the simplest and most absolute sense. . . . Both are true, the necessity of technique and the openness toward a spirit that breaks through all technical rules.

(Benedetti, in Elrod, 2002: 923)

The ego's fragmentation, disorganisation, disintegration, and loss of ability to differentiate are for Benedetti central aspects of schizophrenic psychopathology: 'the skin is peeling off my face; my arms and legs are not attached to the torso; my blood is changing into water; I'm falling into the void' (Benedetti, 1983: 159). The therapist can respond to this with his or her countertransference. In the therapist's mental rough drafts, dreams and countertransferences, a development can arise in favourable cases that has a structuring effect on the patient's fragmented inner world. Benedetti employed in his dialogical psychotherapeutic thinking concepts like counter-identification, duality, mirroring, transitional subject. The therapist must be able to perceive the deep psychic disruptions of the other person also in his or her own inner ups and downs. In this process the patient can acquire 'a feeling for the indivisibility of suffering and truth'. The therapist's unconscious is an essential factor for the recovery of the patient.

Benedetti presents his concepts of schizophrenia therapy in detail in his work *Todeslandschaften der Seele* [Dead Landscapes of the Mind], which appeared in 1983:

From time to time he (the therapist) can give these not yet delimited processes which he has taken over, after they have been 'filtered' through him, back to the patient; this happens especially in the communication of his own dreams. These psycho-pathological aspects, passed through the psychic metabolism of the therapist in this way, undergo during this process a sublimation and at the same time an opening toward horizons of communication which the patient dares to enter into.

(Benedetti, 1983: 306f)

When we think of the fragility of ego boundaries, about which Federn already wrote decades ago, we can also imagine how the schizophrenic is on the one hand not only much more vulnerable than we who are healthy, but on the other hand also much more open and receptive to all not consciously perceived aspects brought to bear upon him by the therapist, the family and society as such.

(Benedetti, 1983: 179; see also Schelling, 1998)

The emergence of a transference psychosis is seen by Benedetti again and again as an important precondition of recovery: 'Likewise the possibility that the sick person in his relation to the therapist develops, say, persecution ideas is no longer regarded today as the terrible end of the psychotherapy, but rather as an important step in the psychotherapeutic process, indeed even as the condition sine qua non of psychotherapeutic healing' (Benedetti, 1957: 115). Benedetti's method reflects a new identity to the patient through the therapist's own countertransference, in which the psychotic conflicts can better be dealt with.

In 1956 Benedetti and Christian Müller launched the International Symposium for Psychotherapy of Schizophrenia which until 2006 was organised 15 times (see Alanen *et al.*, 2006). In the 1960s he introduced Sullivan's and Fromm-Reichmann's work in Italy and even translated Sullivan's *Conceptions of Modern Psychiatry* into the Italian language.

At the first International Symposium for the Psychotherapy of Schizophrenia (ISPS) in 1956 in Lausanne, Benedetti gave an overview of the sociological, psychological and psychotherapeutic schizophrenia research from 1951 to 1956. Already here the close link between these disciplines and the inclusion of societal and group-oriented questions in psychotherapy is quite clear.

Most authors now bring these early schizophrenic disturbances of self-perception and contact into relation with the lack of an adequate acceptance by other human beings, of a meaningful caring, life-affirming parental model, in terms of which alone the young child can acquire those qualities that later really make a human being out of a newborn child.

(Benedetti, 1957: 109)

In 1979, in *Psychiatrie der Gegenwart* [Psychiatry Today], Benedetti published the chapter 'Psychodynamik als Grundlagenforschung der Psychiatrie' [Psychodynamics as Basic Research in Psychiatry]. Almost 30 years were to pass before his findings here, via the reception of current neurobiology and attachment research, once again came into professional discourse.

Philosophical and clinical developments against the split of therapeutic schools

Norman Elrod (1928–2002)

Norman Elrod, born 1928 in Saint Louis, USA, worked as a psychologist at Burghölzli from 1951 to 1957, at the Basel Hospital with Benedetti from 1957 to 1959, at Binswanger's Bellevue Sanatorium from 1960 to 1968, and afterwards in private practice. In 1979, he founded and thereafter led the Institute for Psychoanalysis (IfP), which became a full member of the IFPS in 1998.

From Elrod's experiences as a psychotherapist in hospital settings, he analysed the different interests involved in psychoanalytic treatment in hospitals. Nurses might be interested in the good everyday functioning of meals, work and ergotherapy; patients might just be interested in being left alone and undisturbed. Administrators and health insurance companies might be interested in quick and effective treatment; patients might just want to be cared for, even for months on end. Psychoanalysis, for Elrod, has to be aware of these conflicts and be a partisan of the patient. In fact, not only academic psychotherapists, but also nurses and even cleaning staff can be very good in encounters with patients. Therapeutic forces in the individual, in the group on the ward, in the institution, and in the social environment have to be discovered and mobilised to this end.

In agreement with the experiences of Fromm-Reichmann and Stanton and Schwartz (1954), Elrod wrote noteworthy theoretical works as well as case studies. He expressed the conviction that the therapy of psychoses must take individual, collective, and social subjectivities seriously, and is not just a matter of individual psychotherapy, but also of group psychotherapy, and of the attitude of all participants in the treatment and the attitude of the institution as a whole (see Rostek, 2003: 290).

In 1957 Elrod published a case study of his patient Hans Zimmermann: *Zur Phänomenologie der Besserung in der Psychotherapie* [Criteria of Improvement in Psychotherapy], from which he had reported in 1956 at the first ISPS symposium in Lausanne (Elrod, 1957/2002). In this monograph he described a course of treatment which he examined again 18 and a half years later as a case study follow-up (Elrod, 2002: 377–424). Elrod went intensively into the patient's world of images and took up its symbols as ways of curing him. In this manner, Zimmermann gradually gained insight into his own biography, what he triggered off for himself and his environment with his symptoms. Crazy thinking and actions have meaning, especially when they occur in a therapeutic encounter. Experiences of boredom, disappointment, saying goodbye to dreamed of and longed for ideas of happiness belong just as much to this as does the courage to confide shameful, crazy, and perverse items in the therapist. The goals formulated by Elrod were 'increased life competence' and social adaptation, including individual, collective, and societal subjectivity. In 1974, 18 and a half years after his treatment, Hans Zimmermann appeared in his own and other people's eyes to be healthy (Elrod, 2002: 377). He 'showed altogether an enormous capacity to make the best of any situation and to be thankful, not in a hackneyed but in a concrete way' (Elrod, 2002: 380). In successful therapies the patient and the therapist can be thankful to each other for the experiences during their work together.

Elrod carried out both individual and group psychotherapies, which he documented extensively, in part with tape recordings. He also published case histories of unsuccessful treatments and analysed the failures. The settings for therapy were arranged individually – face-to-face meetings, walks, meals together, or trips taken in common. Of major importance was the psycho-therapeutic penetration of everyday life on the one hand and philosophical reflection on the other. He took up current concepts of work with counter-transference (Heimann, 1950) and was concerned to anchor therapist and patient in society as presently constituted and historically formed.

In an essay dedicated to Ludwig Binswanger on the latter's eightieth birthday, Elrod formulated four principles for access to the schizophrenic patient's world of feeling and thought, despite the fundamental loneliness of these patients: '(a) ignoring temporarily the causal researches of medical and natural science; (b) non-therapy or encounter; (c) causality and therapy; (d) the paradoxical' (Elrod, 1961/2002: 432ff). The emphasis on the factual does not exclude historical features, characteristic of psychoanalytical access, but puts the existential bond between patient and therapist to the forefront: 'The therapist – and this is a central point of our work in the chronic schizophrenic situation – thus adopts a paradoxical stance. He can raise the question of the cause of the patient's distress as well as pass over this question. He can both treat the patient as well as encounter him as an existing fellow human being' (Elrod, 1961/2002: 435).

Elrod's works can be found in the 1150-page volume *Psychotherapie der Schizophrenie* [Psychotherapy of Schizophrenia], which was published shortly before his death in 2002.

Requirements for hospital settings

Christian Müller (born 1921), Fred Singeisen (1909–1982), Johannes Cremerius (1918–2002)

From 1961 to 1987 Christian Müller was Professor of Psychiatry and director of the psychiatric university hospital in Lausanne. As well as Ludwig Binswanger, he followed a family tradition: his father Max Müller was Professor of Psychiatry in the University of Berne and medical director of a big hospital, and his grandfather had also been a psychiatrist. Christian Müller was a member of Swiss Psychoanalytic Society, a branch of the IPA. In 1979 he was co-publisher of the influential book *Psychiatrie der Gegenwart* (with K.P. Kisker, J.E. Meyer, E. Strömgren). Müller has a great interest in history and was for many years publisher of the *Schweizerische Medizinhistorische Zeitschrift* [Swiss Medical-Historical Magazine] *Gesnerus*.

While working in Burghölzli in the 1950s, Müller published one of the pioneering case reports of successful psychotherapeutic treatment of a patient suffering of severe schizophrenia (Müller, 1955). At the second ISPS symposium he underlined the necessity of a comprehensive therapeutic approach:

> It's not a matter of picking individual sick persons out of the mass of the many institutional patients and of curing them, but we must penetrate the entire atmosphere of the institution, that in the final analysis our work tends toward a transformation of all the conditions of care of the mentally ill . . . It is essential that the schizophrenia therapy be kept in the hands of a homogeneous therapeutically oriented group.
>
> (Müller, 1960: 292–294)

At the fourth ISPS symposium in Turku, Finland, Müller (1972) dealt with the resistances to psychotherapy of schizophrenic patients. He mentioned the general arguments that were often advanced such as the excessive time investment; the fact that only a few schizophrenics can profit from this form of treatment; that the results of treatment do not differ essentially from those with other methods. However, referring to the obviously diminished interest in psychoanalytically oriented treatment of psychotic patients, he also dealt with the unconscious motivations of the therapist:

> I believe that up to the present too little attention has been devoted to the unconscious phantasies of the therapist, satellite to the problem of narcissism. In more concrete terms it seems to me that the current

caution in the application of psychoanalytic methods . . . has its root here. The matter at issue is the fear of frustrations which the therapist has not overcome in himself; the fear of uncontrolled aggressivity as a reaction to narcissistic insults.

(Müller, 1972: 78)

None of the material in this presentation is to be interpreted as an accusation because all of us, myself included, stand as actors in the footlights. *Mea res agitur.* My intention is merely to remind ourselves not to close our eyes against the forces governing within each of us, and within the scope of our continuing self-analysis constantly to test as well our relationship and encounters with the schizophrenic.

(Müller, 1972: 82)

From 1951 to 1974, Fred Singeisen was director of the Cantonal Psychiatric Clinic at Wil. He examined critically the therapeutic community on an analytical basis and promulgated these ideas to the specialist public. On the occasion of the anniversary of Freud's one hundredth birthday in 1956 he paid tribute to the significance of psychoanalysis in the therapy and prevention of psychosis in an essay also published in the nurses' magazine *Praktische Psychiatrie pratique* where he worked actively for more than 20 years (Red, 1992: 8):

The teachings of Freud convey altogether a deeper understanding of the human being, of his mental background, of his relations to the environment. Knowledge of how mental disturbances arise also points the way to their prevention: This must be aimed at by creating conditions as healthy as possible in the way human beings live together and, through spreading corresponding information, by avoiding harmful environmental influences such as errors in education. Psychoanalysis has thus paved the way for *psychohygiene*.

(Singeisen, 1956: 127)

In the early 1960s, the German psychoanalyst Johannes Cremerius was working at Wil; in the 1970s he founded the ASP in Milan together with Benedetti. In one of his papers, dealing with dynamic processes in care personnel, especially resistance and transference, during the psychoanalytic treatment of a schizophrenic patient, Cremerius describes impressively his intensive work in close dialogue with the nurses (Cremerius, 1963). It deals with one of the few psychoanalytic descriptions of an acute psychiatric treatment including the use of force (such as fettering and force feeding) due to the danger that the patient might harm herself. Cremerius tells how the distance of the care personnel toward the patient lessened with growing understanding of their affects: 'As I allowed them to express their old annoyance, the rejection diminished' (Cremerius, 1963: 688). Essential requirements for a qualified inpatient psychotherapy could already be found at that time:

> On the basis of our experiences we come to the conclusion that in-patient psychosis therapy without simultaneous observation of the dynamic field around the patient loses value as a research tool, since the phenomenon to be observed cannot be isolated to a sufficient degree. Under the therapeutic aspect such a neglect of the field is equivalent to an operation where sterility is ignored. Through this, not only the patient but also the care personnel are endangered. . . . The nurses acquire more joy in their work. They feel like real collaborators of the doctor and are happy to be able to give up the role of 'keepers'. The sick persons, heretofore unintelligible to them, become beings with difficulties and problems which, to their astonishment, they find not to be dissimilar to their own.
>
> (Cremerius, 1963: 703–704)

Luc Ciompi, a former co-worker of Müller's, introduced at Berne Psychiatric University Hospital in 1984 the Soteria approach pioneered by Loren S. Mosher – partly following the examples given by H.S. Sullivan in the 1930s. Acutely ill psychotic patients are admitted to a small family-like unit with six to eight patients. This work is described in Chapter 23.

Impacts on other European countries

Beginning in the 1950s, the Swiss psychoanalytically oriented schizophrenia psychotherapists had a great impact in many other European countries, especially in Northern Europe and in Italy. The greatest sources of influence were the seminars led by the dedicated Benedetti, as well as his writings. The Finnish psychiatrist Martti Siirala became a close co-worker of Benedetti, having – as well as his colleagues Kauko Kaila and Allan Johansson – had his psychoanalytic training in Switzerland. In 1958 in Helsinki, Siirala founded the psychoanalytic institute Therapeia, a member of the IFPS. In his home country of Italy Benedetti's influence was strong and long-lasting, reaching from the Milan IFPS institute to the social psychiatrists advocating the democratic psychiatry movement, such as Paolo Tranchina and Paolo Serra (1981). The developments in Italy are described in Chapter 11 and those of the Northern European countries in Chapter 12.

Summary

In Switzerland in the 1950s and 1960s, psychoanalysis, existential analysis, and phenomenology engaged in a lively exchange of ideas precisely because of experiences in psychosis therapy. By the 1980s and 1990s – not least because of conflictual questions in career politics (Hoffmann, 1999) – these approaches were being marginalised in everyday clinical work. Regrettably, group therapy too was supplanted in many places by a form of therapeutic community that puts team interests before patient interests, that overemphasises pedagogical aspects and has a deprofessionalising effect (Hoffmann, 2005). The ever shorter stays of even seriously ill patients in the psychiatric clinics shifted medium and long-term psychotherapeutic tasks to the outpatient situation, where only few appropriately trained psychotherapists are to be found.

In 1983, Benedetti summarised the development of psychosis therapy less sceptically and with more emphasis on the discourse between psychoanalytic groups as follows: 'The development of the psychotherapy of the psychoses in the last two decades shows how very much now the contributions of Freudian psychoanalysis, the analytic psychology of Jung, the existential analysis of Binswanger and the American transaction analysis have merged together' (Benedetti, 1983: 303). This corresponds to the situation in professional politics: at least three institutes that originated from the psychoanalytic treatment of psychoses in Switzerland (ASP, Milan; IfP, Zurich; Therapeia, Helsinki) are members of the IFPS; the important psychoanalysts Binswanger, Bally, Cremerius, Singeisen, and Müller were or are members of the IPA. Perhaps psychoanalytic interest in these treatments can further not only contemporary research (child psychiatry, attachment research, mentalisation concepts) but may also contribute to a more intensive dialogue between the international psychoanalytic groups. This in turn might lead to more professionals becoming interested again in these types of encounters with their patients and with other professionals working in the field.

Acknowledgement

I thank Hans Red for permission to check the documentation 'Psychotherapy of Schizophrenia' in the Institute of Psychoanalysis.

References

Alanen, Y.O., Silver, A.-L.S. and González de Chávez, M. (2006). *Fifty Years of Humanistic Treatment of Psychoses*. Madrid: Fundación para la Investigácion y Tratamiento de la Esquizofrenia y otras Psicosis.

Bally, G. (1956). Gedanken zur psychoanalytisch orientierten Begegnung mit Geisteskranken. *Psyche* 10: 437–447. Reprinted in N. Elrod (ed.) *Psychotherapie der Schizophrenie.* [Psychotherapy of Schizophrenia.] Zurich: Althea, 2002, pp. 853–866.

Benedetti, G. (1957). Die soziologische, psychologische und psychotherapeutische Schizophrenieforschung 1951–1956. In G. Benedetti and C. Müller (ed.) *1. Internationales Symposium über die Psychotherapie der Schizophrenie. Vorträge und Diskussionen*. Basel: Karger, pp. 106–128.

Benedetti, G. (1969). Rehabilitation and psychotherapy with schizophrenic patients. *Psychotherapy and Psychosomatics* 17: 11–19.

Benedetti, G. (1979). Psychodynamik als Grundlagenforschung der Psychiatrie. In K.P. Kisker, J.E. Meyer, C. Müller and E. Strömgren (ed.) *Psychiatrie der Gegenwart. Forschung und Praxis*. Berlin, Heidelberg, New York: Springer, pp. 43–89.

Benedetti, G. (1983). *Todeslandschaften der Seele*. Göttingen: Vandenhoeck & Ruprecht.

Benedetti, G. (1994). Mein Weg zur Psychoanalyse und zur Psychiatrie. In L.M. Hermanns (ed.) *Psychoanalyse in Selbstdarstellungen II*. Tübingen: Edition Diskord.

Binswanger, L. (1942). *Grundformen und Erkenntnis menschlichen Daseins*. Newly issued by Max Herzog and Hans-Jürg Braun. Heidelberg: Asanger, 1993.

Binswanger, L. (1957). Der Mensch in der Psychiatrie. Pfullingen: Neske. In A. Holzhey-Kunz (ed.) (1994) *Ludwig Binswanger. Ausgewählte Werke*. Vol. 4: *Der Mensch in der Psychiatrie*. Heidelberg: Asanger, pp. 57–72.

Bleuler, M. (1979). Einleitung. In M. Bleuler *Beiträge zur Schizophrenielehre der Zürcher Psychiatrischen Universitätsklinik Burghölzli (1902–1971)*. Darmstadt: Wissenschaftliche Buchgesellschaft, pp. 1–10.

Boss, M. (1941). Alte und neue Schocktherapien und Schocktherapeuten [Old and new shock therapies and shock therapists]. *Zeitschrift für die gesamte Neurologie und Psychiarie* 173: 776–782.

Bräutigam, W. and Müller, C. (1962). Zur Kritik der Schizophreniediagnose bei psychotherapeutisch behandelten Kranken. *Nervenarzt* 33: 342–349.

Brody, E.B. and Redlich, F.C. (eds) (1952). *Psychotherapy with Schizophrenics*. New York: International Universities Press.

Cremerius, J. (1963). Beobachtungen dynamischer Prozesse beim Pflegepersonal, insbesondere von Widerstand und Übertragung, während der psychoanalytischen Behandlung einer Schizophrenen. *Psyche* 16: 686–704.

Elrod, N. (1957). *Zur Phänomenologie der Besserung in der Psychotherapie*. Basel: Karger. 2nd edn. Munich: Kindler, 1974. Reprinted in N. Elrod (ed.) *Psychotherapie der Schizophrenie*. Zurich: Althea, 2002, pp. 75–372.

Elrod, N. (1961). Das Problem des Sich-Kennen-Lernens in der chronisch schizophrenen Situation. Für Ludwig Binswanger zu seinem 80. Geburtstag in Verehrung gewidmet. *Jahrbuch für Psychologie, Psychotherapie und medizinische Anthropologie* 8: 90–124. Reprinted in N. Elrod (ed.) *Psychotherapie der Schizophrenie*. Zurich: Althea, 2002, pp. 429–481.

Elrod, N. (ed.) (2002). *Psychotherapie der Schizophrenie*. Zurich: Althea.

Faugeras, P. (2000). Übersetzen als Dimension der Begegnung. In B. Rachel *Die Kunst des Hoffens. Begegnung mit Gaetano Benedetti*. Göttingen: Vandenhoeck & Ruprecht, pp. 28–46.

Heimann, P. (1950). On countertransference. *International Journal of Psychoanalysis* 31: 81–84.

Hoffmann, K. (1997). Ludwig Binswanger's Collected Papers – Introduction and Critical Remarks. *International Forum of Psychoanalysis* 6: 191–201.

Hoffmann, K. (1999). Ludwig Binswangers Einfluß auf die deutsche Psychoanalyse nach 1945. *Jahrbuch der Psychoanalyse* 41: 191–208.

Hoffmann, K. (2005). Grandlagen der forensischen Psychotherapie. In G. Ebner, V. Dittmann, B. Gravier, K. Hoffmann and R. Raggenbass (eds) *Psychiatria und Recht*. Zürich, Basel, Genf: Schulthess, pp. 171–197.

Hoffmann, K. and Elrod, N. (1999). Frieda Fromm-Reichmann: on her contribution to psychoanalysis and psychiatric theory. *International Forum of Psychoanalysis* 8: 13–18.

Kisker, K.P., Lauter, H., Meyer, J.E., Müller, C. and Strömgren, E. (eds) (1979). *Psychiatrie der Gegenwart, 2*. Berlin: Auflage. Heidelberg, New York, Tokyo: Springer.

Masson, J.M. (1988). *Against Therapy*. New York: Atheneum.

Meerwein, F. (1957). Die Bedeutung der Anstalt für die Gegenübertragung des Therapeuten. In G. Benedetti and C. Müller (eds) *1. Internationales Symposium über die Psychotherapie der Schizophrenie. Vorträge und Diskussionen*. Basel: Karger, pp. 248–253.

Müller, C. (1955). Über Psychotherapie bei einem chronischen Schizophrenen. *Psyche* 9: 350–369.

Müller, C. (1960). Die psychiatrische Klinik und die Psychotherapie der Schizophrenen. In G. Benedetti and C. Müller (eds) *2. Internationales Symposium über die Psychotherapie der Schizophrenie*. Basel: Karger, pp. 291–296.

Müller, C. (1961). Die Psychotherapie Schizophrener an der Zürcher Klinik. Versuch einer katamnestischen Übersicht. *Nervenarzt* 32: 354–368.

Müller, C. (1972). The problem of resistance to psychotherapy of schizophrenic patients. In D. Rubinstein and Y.O. Alanen (eds) *Psychotherapy of Schizophrenia*. Amsterdam: Excerpta Medica, pp. 77–82.

Napolitani, F. (1963). Experiment einer Psychotherapie der Psychosen, durchgeführt in einer durch Patienten selbstverwalteten Abteilung. *Bibliotheca Psychiatrica Neurologica* 118: 23–29.

Red, H. (1992). *100 Jahre Psychiatrie in Wil. Einige Überlegungen zu diesem Jubiläum*. Wil: Kantonale Psychiatrische Klinik.

Rosen, J.N. (1953). *Direct Analysis. Selected Papers*. New York: Grune & Stratton.

Rostek, H. (2003). Obituary – Norman Elrod (November 22, 1928 – July 1, 2002). Unity and Conflict of Opposites. *International Forum of Psychoanalysis* 12: 289–295.

Schelling, W.A. (1998). *Das Unbewusste und die Einheit in der Begegnung mit den Todeslandschaften der Seele. Zum Werk von Gaetano Benedetti*. [The Unconscious and the Unity in the Encounter with the Dead Landscapes of the Mind. On the Work of Gaetano Benedetti.] *WzM* 50: 132–143.

Séchehaye, M.-A. (1947). La réalisation symbolique. *Revue Suisse de psychologie et de la psychologie Appliqué Suppl. 12*.

Singeisen, F. (1956). Sigmund Freud und die Psychoanalyse. [Sigmund Freud and psychoanalysis.] *Praktische Psychiatrie pratique* 35: 122–127.

Stanton, A.H. and Schwartz, M.S. (1954). *The Mental Hospital*. New York: Basic Books.

Tranchina, P. and Serra, P. (1981). Community work and participation in the new Italian psychiatric legislation. In H. Stierlin, L.C. Wynne and M. Wirsching (eds) *Psychosocial Intervention in Schizophrenia, An International View*. Berlin, Heidelberg: Springer, pp. 109–120.

Weigert, E. (1978). Foreword. In F. Fromm-Reichmann *Eine Auswahl aus ihren Schriften*. [A Selection from her Writings.] Stuttgart: Klett-Cotta, pp. 7–14.

Part 2: The development of psychosis psychotherapy in Germany and Austria

Stavros Mentzos

GERMANY

Psychodynamic understanding of psychosis: pro and predominantly contra

Many may presume that in German and Austrian psychiatry there is little scope for a psychodynamic understanding of psychosis and even less for a corresponding psychotherapy. The vast majority of psychiatrists are presumed to represent a significantly biological concept, or at least advocate a purely descriptive view even though emphasizing acceptance of a bio-psycho-social model. That is, however, only partially accurate. Already in the first half of the nineteenth century psychiatrists such as Karl-Wilhelm Ideler (1795–1860) intensively examined intrapsychic conflict in cases of psychosis. For example, Ideler speaks of the antagonism of affective drives (*Gemütstriebe*) or of conflicting affectivity (*Gemützustand*) or of logical contradictions of consciousness (Scharfetter, 2006: 26). Surprisingly, Wilhelm Griesinger (1817–1869) – usually only known for equating mental illness with brain illness – also wrote in 1861 of the psychological causes of mental illness: 'They are considered the most frequent and prolific sources of madness' (Scharfetter, 2006: 30), seen as a consequence of previous emotional and affective conditions of a pathogenic nature, not of intellectual exertion. Griesinger anticipated our 'modern' concept of psychosis as psychosomatic disorders of the brain (Mentzos, 2000); according to him such affective states are seldom the direct, but more frequently the indirect results 'derived from deviations from normal organ processes . . . from which the mental disorder has evolved as a secondary result' (Griesinger, 1861: 170–172).

The closer we come to 1900, the turn of the century, and the subsequent period, the more we are confronted with the increasing rarity of positive statements on the role of psychodynamics in both Germany and Austria.

This is primarily due to the all-encompassing influence of Emil Kraepelin (1856–1926), the emphatic protagonist of a somatogenic view.

Greater significance weighs therefore on the discoveries and international influence of Sigmund Freud and psychoanalytical psychosis therapists working here in the beginning of the twentieth century, for example, Paul Federn (see Chapter 5). In the 1920s Ernst Simmel opened the first psychoanalytical clinic in Berlin-Tegel. In the course of the 1930s such and similar attempts and endeavours were destroyed by the Nazis. Many psychosis therapists had to leave Germany or Austria and then achieved international acclaim, e.g. Frieda Fromm-Reichmann (see Happach and Piegler, 2000). Psychoanalytic interest and preoccupation with psychosis arose again after 1945 stemming from the influence of colleagues from Switzerland which had been spared from National Socialism.

Initial post-war steps in Germany

Only gradually throughout the 1950s, psychoanalysts or psychiatrists with psychodynamic leanings took tentative steps to take on psychotherapy treatment of psychosis. However, apart from rare exceptions, the bulk of the German Psychoanalytical Association (DPV) and the German Psychoanalytical Society's (DPG) analysts including other groups such as the followers of Jung and Adler appeared insufficiently motivated or prepared to treat psychosis cases in this way.

Nevertheless there were many 'lone fighters'. As early as 1954, W. Th. Winkler published psychoanalytically oriented articles on schizophrenia and in 1956 gave a paper on psychodynamic factors in the structure of schizophrenia at the first ISPS symposium in Zurich (Winkler, 1954a, 1954b, 1957).

In Munich, Paul Matussek (1919–2003) achieved the first tangible breakthrough: a clear psychodynamic approach to psychosis by a university professor (from 1956 onwards) constituted completely new territory, especially coming from a man who had previously researched in the field of classical psychiatry represented by Kurt Schneider in Heidelberg. Matussek was Director of the Research Department on Psychopathology and Psychotherapy in the Max Planck Society in Munich (see Matussek, 1982). His contributions – dealing not only with schizophrenias but also with depressive psychoses – focus on the psychodynamics of the psychoses that had previously been labelled 'endogenous'. Faced with the alternatives of either continuing research on the psychiatric phenomenology of delusional perception or entry into a method of treating the mentally ill rated in Germany as absurd – namely incipient work in psychotherapy – he chose the latter and assessed his decision as a crucial turning point in his life (Pohlen, 2004).

The initially limited scope of 'psychodynamization' in psychiatry

Hopes that were roused under the personal influence of Matussek – that psychiatry in general and especially the psychiatric university clinics could now be permeated by psychoanalytic or psychodynamic thought – were sadly not fulfilled. Only in the field of social psychiatry, flourishing world-wide in the 1970s, did psychodynamically oriented views win widespread acclaim and recognition in Germany, especially under the influence of the Psychiatry Reform Commission of Inquiry after 1971. However, from this quarter also there was no encouragement of psychodynamic psychosis therapy. Private psychoanalytic institutes that had grown considerably were neither prepared nor interested in teaching or offering psychosis therapy. Behind this reserve the underlying reason was presumably also a considera-tion of professional policy: the psychoanalysts' fear of provoking open controversy between the mighty institution of psychiatry and the uni-versities. The Department of Psychotherapy and Psychosomatics of the University of Frankfurt am Main, directed by the author of this contri-bution from 1971 to 1995, was one of the few exceptions. The development in university psychiatry in Germany was totally different from that in the sphere of university psychosomatics: in the 1970s and 1980s almost all German universities had initiated psychosomatic departments based on psychodynamic principles.

In spite of this large official resistance on the part of traditional academic psychiatry, within the Association of Psychiatrists, e.g. German Society for Neurology and Psychiatry (DPGN), contributions on psychodynamic prin-ciples were occasionally held at conferences or other occasions. Eberhard Jung, director of a large clinical Institute in Berlin-Spandau, successfully performed diagnostic and therapeutic work on analytic principles until his retirement in 2001. During the 1970s and 1980s there were university professors who showed open-mindedness towards psychiatry organized on psychodynamic and psychoanalytic principles such as Kisker in Hannover, Meyer in Göttingen, Haimann in Tübingen (and nowadays Mundt in Heidelberg, Emrich and Machleidt in Hannover, etc.). They were and are, however, in a minority. In the late 1980s the trend to favour biological and descriptive methods of approach and treatment in the university psychiatric departments became intensified, partly under the influence of American psychiatry.

The counter-reaction of the 'outsiders'

Nevertheless the position of psychosis psychotherapy in Germany today need not to be viewed pessimistically. Psychosis therapy based on psycho-dynamic ideas is taught, researched and put into practice in Germany to a greater extent than ever before. How did this come about?

The unsuccessful endeavour to integrate psychodynamic principles into university psychiatry in the 1980s did in fact cause disappointment, and led to a counter-reaction. Many psychotherapeutic centres were formed outside the university settings in which psychosis therapy began to develop. This happened in hospitals (predominantly not university hospitals) in which the director, oriented towards psychodynamics or even a trained psychoanalyst, made such development possible. From the late 1980s and early 1990s training institutes were founded across the nation, designated to perform this project systematically. These initiatives and similar endeavours that now exist at many locations represent an extremely important development in the area of psychosis in the last 20 years in Germany. Clinics are involved such as Tiefenbrunn by Göttingen (Streeck, Dümpelmann), Hamburg-Bergedorf (Piegler), Stuttgart (Weiss), Hamburg-Eppendorf (Aderhold) or Friedberg/Hessen (Putzke), in which psychodynamically oriented psychiatry and corresponding psychosis therapy are partly practised. Also nation-wide training centres have been founded such as in Munich or Frankfurt am Main in which many interested candidates – mostly fully trained psychotherapists and psychoanalysts – receive further training in the field of psychosis therapy.

The current situation

Clinic and ambulatory training and therapy

In Germany today there exists the following paradoxical situation: the majority of university psychiatric clinics that are inclined towards a pre-valently biological-descriptive approach have always tended towards a somewhat hostile attitude towards psychodynamics and psychoanalysis. They have a greater emphasis on behaviour therapy rather than depth psychology or psychoanalytically orientated therapy. On the other hand, however, beyond the universities and the university clinics there have emerged the above-mentioned centres of primarily psychodynamic treatment methods and corresponding training activities. Their priority lies in outpatient treatment. The author of this contribution, for instance, performs supervision in one psychiatric inpatient unit, but does a greater amount of group supervision of psychosis treatments of the outpatients treated in the offices of psychiatrists and psychoanalysts who have undergone this specialized training in psychosis therapy. I shall mention some of these centres, albeit of necessity briefly.

Munich

In Munich in the early 1990s a supraregional study group for training in psychosis therapy was founded, focusing both on theoretical lectures and casuistic and supervision seminars of individual treatment of psychotic outpatients as well as family and group therapy and hospitalized treatment in clinics. Its training is in heavy demand from doctors and psychologists as well as other professionals of psychiatric clinics. Thrice yearly block sessions are visited by many (100–200) therapists who have an opportunity for long-term supervision of their psychotic patients where they live and work – often far removed from Munich.

The North German Working Group for Psychodynamic Psychiatry

The North German Working Group for Psychodynamic Psychiatry (NAPP) has also existed for a number of years. Its members are enrolled from psychiatrists interested in psychodynamics to psychoanalysts and nursing staff from several cities in North Germany. Their predominant endeavour is to enhance the treatment of hospitalized patients with psychodynamic aspects, alongside concurrent group processes. Here the corresponding special training of nursing staff has a relative priority (see e.g. Heltzel, 2006).

Tiefenbrunn

The psychoanalytically oriented psychotherapeutic clinic in Tiefenbrunn (near Göttingen) has achieved acclaim for decades on account of its size and the quality of the specialized training it has offered and still offers. Initially under the influence of Heigl and Heigl-Evers, later under Streeck, who is still Director of the Clinic, and in important collaboration with Dümpelmann, crucial concepts evolved to modify psychoanalytically based psychotherapy for treatment of serious disturbances. The principles of an 'answer' instead of directing interpretation to the unconscious and the Göttingen model of group therapy must be mentioned in this context (see below). In the early stages, only small numbers of psychotic patients were treated. Since inauguration of a ward with 43 beds in 1991, functions and specialized programmes for inpatient psychiatric and psychoanalytical treatment of psychotic patients have been developed, directed by Dümpelmann. Research on traumatic etiological factors in psychotic states is going on – a topic that is not receiving adequate consideration in the international literature so far.

Kassel

Significant collaboration of psychoanalysts under the auspices of the German Psychoanalytical Association's Institute (DPV) in Kassel (including Kipp, Georgios and Sybille Styllos) led to the introduction of psychodynamic principles in the treatment of psychotic patients in the city of Kassel's psychiatric hospital.

Hamburg-Bergedorf

Similarly methods on psychodynamic principles in the treatment of psychiatric and psychotic patients have commenced in the General Hospital of Hamburg-Bergedorf whose Director is Piegler.

Frankfurt Psychosis Project

Since the early 1980s our own endeavours within the framework of the Department of Psychotherapy and Psychosomatics of the University of Frankfurt ultimately led to the emergence of the Frankfurt Psychosis Project elaborating the concept of 'dilemmatic' structure of psychosis dynamics. The activities and results of the Frankfurt Psychosis Project have been reported in several publications (e.g. Mentzos, 1991, 1992, 1995). After the director's retirement, however, the university department was cut back radically and the project could no longer be conducted there. But through the private initiative of the former director and many of the trained former employees, who had entered private practice, a society was founded in its place with the identical name (Frankfurt Psychosis Project) that since 1998 has published a series under the title *FORUM of Psychoanalytical Psychosis Therapy* (two volumes yearly). Regular conferences and occasional congresses are organized by the secretary of the FPP (Gudrun Liehr-Völker) as well as supervision of psychosis treatments of outpatients in the Rhein-Main area. There is close cooperation with the Munich training group.

The concept of the 'dilemmatic' structure of psychotic dynamics developed in this Frankfurt Psychosis Project has frequently been positively assessed in Germany and other German-speaking areas in Europe and partly integrated (see Mentzos, 2002). From this Frankfurt circle, psychoanalytically oriented psychosis psychotherapists have emerged and they will be able to develop them further both in theory and in practice: Günter Lempa (1992, 1995, 2005; now in Munich); Heinz Böker (*Psychoanalyse und Psychiatrie*, 2006; in Burghölzli in Zurich); Thomas Müller (Hanau by Frankfurt am Main); Norbert Matejek, Elisabeth Troje, Alois Münch, Franziska Lorenz-Franzen. Most of them have also participated actively in the editorial work of *FORUM*.

Berlin

The positive echo and positive theoretical and practical results of the Munich and Frankfurt programmes culminated in the introduction of a similar programme in Berlin, in the Charité clinic of the Medical University in autumn 2005 – initially directed by Juckel, now under the leadership of Dorothea von Haebler – in which two training blocks are offered annually, finding wide resonance and general approval from a large number of psychiatric and other colleagues (see von Haebler *et al.*, 2007). The Charité psychiatric department is focused on the research of prodromal stages of schizophrenia in adolescents.

Frankfurt-Höchst, Friedberg/Hessen, Würzburg, Hamburg-Eppendorf

Among other centres representing a psychodynamic approach to the treatment of psychotic patients I will mention the psychiatric department of the city clinics in Frankfurt-Höchst, directed by Peter Hartwich; Friedberg/Hessen (Michael Putzke); the University Psychology Institute in Würzburg (Lang); and Schultze-Jena in Hamburg. Volkmar Aderhold (earlier Assistant Medical Director of the Psychiatric University Clinic in Hamburg-Eppendorf) has tried to implement the Scandinavian integrated treatment approach in Germany (see Aderhold *et al.*, 2003).

Stuttgart

Psychotherapy oriented towards the school of Melanie Klein has been favourably accepted by some psychoanalytic colleagues in Germany, especially in the individual treatment of outpatients. Neo-Kleinian methods have also been practised in hospitalized settings, for example, in the department of psychosomatic medicine of the Robert-Bosch-Hospital in Stuttgart (Heinz Weiss and Claudia Frank). The Kleinian influence is related to the intensive supervisory activity of Rosenfeld, Britton, Meltzer and other British Neo-Kleinian psychoanalysts.

Beyond these centres there are numerous individual colleagues and also clinics nationwide from Bremen to Reichenau (Hoffmann) and from Cologne (e.g. Matakas, 1991; Meyer) to Dresden that have similarly attempted to introduce psychodynamic principles in psychiatric treatment.

Theoretical considerations

Concept of the dilemmatic structure of psychotic dynamics

Freud assumed that conflict lay at the roots of psychosis, although not as in cases of neurosis lying between the structural instances ego–id–superego. Psychotic symptoms were therefore to be viewed as an expression of an attempt to 'resolve' this conflict (see Chapter 3). This recalls our concept of the dilemmatic structure of psychotic dynamics (Mentzos, 1992, 2002), and also other psychoanalytical concepts as formulated by Racamier or Melanie Klein. Even if the psychic antagonisms postulated in these concepts differ (Freud's view: 'ego versus reality'; Racamier's view: 'narcissism versus anti-narcissism'; Melanie Klein's view: 'destructive or death drive versus libido'), yet they share the common concept of conflict or dilemma – a fact of not only theoretical, but also practical importance. Moreover, our view of the contrast 'self identity versus unifying binding to a degree of total merging' (normally a temporary situation that is dialectically surmountable, but in unfavourable circumstances becomes rigid and psychotic; see Mentzos 1992, 2002) seem closest to Freud's hypothesis that in Schreber's case paranoia was a function of resistance to homosexual love. Today we no longer believe that psychosis may have this particular function of resistance to homo-sexuality, but Freud obviously grasped the central point of the intrapsychic antagonism of schizophrenia, when he recognized the problem of endangering the self through an attractive, desirable but simultaneously dangerous object.

Family and group therapies

Family therapy concepts began to be applied to psychotic disturbances from the 1960s corresponding to psychosocial priorities, and the results were deemed successful. In the ensuing decades family therapy as well as group therapy did in fact spread, especially in outpatient settings more than in hospitalized patient treatment of psychosis patients. There were different directions and schools of thought as regards both theory and practice. Systemic and psychoanalytically oriented methods were initially given priority, whereas later on cognitive behavioural therapy was increasingly employed in psychiatric clinics and has today become the most dominant direction.

Helm Stierlin and the group that emerged around him in Heidelberg had a definitive influence for the establishment and spread of systemically oriented family therapy e.g., Stierlin, 1975; Retzer, 1994). There were doubtless also other family and group therapists before Stierlin, but he was the figurehead from the USA in the 1970s responsible for importing the well-known procedures developed there and he himself developed the theory and practice for psychosis treatment. Through countless publications, lectures, seminars, etc. he has achieved a large influence that still prevails in German-speaking countries today. Following in his footsteps, Fritz B. Simon and Arnold Retzer have intensified, advanced and specialized systemic family therapy in both theory and practice. Even though Stierlin and even more emphatically the subsequent representatives of systemic theory and practice have mostly distanced themselves from psychoanalysis, yet they have retained many basic insights and ideas of psychoanalysis either directly or indirectly (see Chapter 17 by Helm Stierlin).

Parallel to the family therapy in cases of psychosis as developed by Stierlin and his colleagues as well as other independent spirits and dissidents, there has always been definite psychoanalytically oriented family and group therapy. I indicate especially the extensive family and group therapy work performed in the Munich area by Frank Schwarz, previously Matussek's colleague (Schwarz, 1983, 2000; Schwarz and Maier, 2001) and the book edited by Sandner (1986). In the vicinity of Horst Eberhard Richter in Giessen many family and group therapies were performed, albeit to treat primarily neurotic and psychosomatic cases. The same is true of the University Psychotherapy Clinic in Mainz directed until recently by S.O. Hoffmann. In Giessen, Terje Neraal implemented psychoanalytically oriented family psychosis therapy, which he is still performing intensively today and – as in the Frankfurt Psychosis Project – its starting point is a similar model of bipolarity and dilemma. In various publications (e.g. Neraal, 2001) he shows in what way this model can be implemented in the analysis of family dynamics. It reveals, for example, bipolar theme structures such as working out specific differences contrasted with demonstrating similarities, or treating fear of isolation versus fear of autonomy loss.

Psychoanalytically oriented group therapy was and still is being offered in Berlin today, for example, over many years by Greve, who does not use interpretations but by emphasizing his acceptance of the patients and their problems and by awaiting a spontaneous development of dynamics within the group does in fact and per se follow a psychodynamic course that has achieved many a therapeutic success. Within the framework of his clinical activity, Eberhard Jung too has provided intensive analytically oriented but similarly modified technique in group therapy.

AUSTRIA

Psychoanalytically oriented psychosis therapy until 1938

In nineteenth-century Austria, long before the emergence of psychoanalysis, as in Germany, there had also been psychiatrists prepared to contemplate psychogenic and psychodynamic aspects in cases of psychosis. The first genuine psychoanalytic consideration occurred with Sigmund Freud. Freud himself was extremely reserved as far as the possibilities of psychoanalytic technique with psychotic patients, yet he did occupy himself intensively with psychoses on a theoretical level.

In spite of Freud's pronounced reserve in implementing psychoanalytical methods in cases of psychosis, several of his followers in Austria did later on perform therapy in such cases, for instance, Paul Federn (see Chapter 5), Otto Tausk, Karl Landauer, Paul Schilder and Edward Bibring. The latter two were successive directors of the outpatients department for the treatment of psychoses of the Viennese Psychoanalytical Association. Ms Rößler-Schülein has recalled in a personal message that Schilder recorded in 1925 how one individual, who had regressed to a lower level, in spite of that retained patterns of higher development, and even in the deepest phase of regression the mature individual did not drop to the psychological organization comparable to a child. At that time Schilder was engaged in writing his *Psychiatrie auf psychoanalytischer Grundlage* (in English, c.f. Schilder, 1928) and holder of an assistant professorship in the University Psychiatric and Neurological Clinic in Vienna under the directorship of Wagner-Jauregg. Federn treated psychotic patients within his private practice and in close cooperation with the Viennese University Clinic. Meißel is of the assumption that Helene Deutsch's important theoretical work on human relationships may have been particularly inspired by work in psychiatric wards and with psychotic patients.

Later development

This altogether positive and promising development was abruptly halted and destroyed at the time of the annexation of Austria by Nazi Germany in 1938. In the subsequent post-war phase only few of the most renowned analysts were engaged in the treatment of psychosis, for example, Hans Strotzka, who has, however, predominantly been active in the field of social psychiatry, and Raoul Schindler who introduced analytical concepts of psychosis in the 1950s and collaborated with Benedetti and Christian Müller in Switzerland (Meißel, personal information; see e.g. Schindler, 1960). Since the 1970s there have been various psychiatric institutions in which analysts have endeavoured to consider and integrate psychodynamic aspects in their psychiatric casework. First and foremost the efforts of the large psychiatric hospital in Gugging (north of Vienna) are to be named, supported by its directors, first Alois Marksteiner and later Gerd Eichberger (see Meissel and Eichberger, 2002). Within this clinic, Leo Navratil was active with his long-term endeavours in the field of art therapy (*Gestaltung*) and the large collection of art by schizophrenic patients has been acclaimed worldwide. Rainer Danzinger came from Graz to Gugging, later to Salzburg and ultimately returned to Graz where he was given responsibility to be director of the large Sigmund Freud Hospital for several years. There Gert Lyon has directed the important outpatient pilot department since the 1970s.

A traditional attitude of animosity was perpetuated within the university level of psychiatry until the 1980s. (Quotes that follow in this paragraph are from personal communications from Rößler-Schülein.) 'It is entirely the merit of individual analysts active in social psychiatry, e.g. Otto Hartmann, who propagated the implementation of psychoanalytical concepts in regular clinic procedure, to establish a long-term institution with multifunctional teams and attempt psychoanalytically oriented psychotherapy with psychotic patients.' It was not until the 1980s that 'within the Viennese Psychoanalytical Association the developments of the previous 50 years such as the object relation theories of the Anglo-American school were integrated'. After the passing of the Psychotherapy Law in 1991, psychotherapy in Austria became part of the public health system, granting committed analysts in private practice the opportunity to treat psychotic patients in their practices by psychoanalytical methods. For example, in 2004 Daphne Stock published a case study of a young psychotic patient. Rößler-Schülein has witnessed a tendency of many analysts in Vienna in the last few years towards modern Kleinian techniques 'as these provide a consistent technical procedure for the treatment of psychosis and serious personality disorders'. On the basis of other contacts with Austrian colleagues, the author of this contribution was given the impression that other directions, such as the concepts of Frankfurt or Munich, are increasingly gaining influence.

Many of the colleagues who are active in Austria have participated in the cross-country training in psychosis therapy in Munich that was briefly outlined in the section on Germany. There is reciprocal benefit in this continual exchange. In the area of family and group therapy in Austria, as in Germany, there are many promising endeavours which could not be discussed more precisely in this chapter.

Concluding remarks

The clinical and ambulatory institutions as well as the psychotherapists in private practice named above represent merely a partly random selection within the scope of therapeutic work with psychotic patients in Germany and Austria. Apart from the brief outline of the initial stages in the first half of the twentieth century, the purpose has been to depict the currently prevalent orientation, endeavours and concrete ongoing programmes in order possibly to foresee future developments.

The extent and consolidation of psychodynamically or even psychoanalytically oriented therapy of patients with psychotic disorders came to an abrupt and violent disruption through the National Socialist regime, leaving a gap which could only be filled painstakingly. Today, however, those negative consequences of National Socialism have not only finally worn off but also recuperated, and one may even assume an advance in certain respects, e.g. in comparison with North America. One must admit that, with few exceptions, in the university clinics and psychiatric hospitals of Germany and Austria the approach is rather one-sidedly biologically oriented (as in North America today). Yet countless non-university, clinical and particularly outpatient treatments have gained very much ground in the last 20 years.

The following must also be taken into account: not only a sceptical and sometimes even hostile attitude of academic psychiatry has stood in the way of more extensive psychosis therapy until recently (partly even today), but also a certain rigid dogmatism of psychoanalysis itself. One gets the impression that it is not only resistances and challenges from without, but also negative effects from unfavourable and unproductive struggles between different schools of psychoanalysis have had an adverse effect. There is still no general consensus as regards aetiopathogenetics, psychodynamics and psychotherapy of psychoses within and between different schools of psychoanalysis. But it seems to me that this is now changing. Even where theoretical concepts may officially have hardly changed, one gets the impression that the result of therapeutic experiences in this difficult task of psychotherapy with psychotic patients has been a compelling force towards the development and practice of astoundingly similar procedures. The great advances in this field and the increasing tendency to cooperation is clearly indicating an altogether positive and promising future.

Acknowledgements

The author is deeply indebted to Austrian colleagues for kind, personal information, particularly to Theodor Meissel (Gugging, Nord Donau Psychiatric Clinic, Vienna) and Hemma Rössler-Schülein (Viennese Psychoanalytic Association) to whom I here express my sincere gratitude. I would also like to thank Eberhard Gabriel for the information I have been given.

References

Aderhold, V., Alanen, Y.O., Hess, G. and Hohn, P. (eds) (2003). *Psychotherapie der Psychosen. Integrative Behandlungsansätze aus Skandinavien*. Giessen: Psychosozial-Verlag.

Böker, H. (ed.) (2006). *Psychoanalyse und Psychiatrie*. Heidelberg: Springer.

Griesinger, W. (1861). *Die Pathologie und Therapie der psychischen Krankheiten. 2. Auflage*. Stuttgart: Krabbe.

von Haebler, D., Müller, T. and Matejek, N. (eds) (2007). *Perspektiven unxd Ergebnisse der psychoanalytischen Psychosentherapie. Forum der psychoanalytischen Psychosentherpie, Band 17*. Giessen: Vandenhoeck & Ruprecht.

Happach, C. and Piegler, T. (2000). Zur Geschichte der psychoanalytischen Behandlung von Psychosen. *Psychotherapeut* 45: 39–43.

Heltzel, R. (2006). Psychodynamische Aspekte in der stationären Behandlung psychotischer Patienten. In H. Böker (ed.) *Psychoanalyse und Psychiatrie*. Heidelberg: Springer, pp. 265–278.

Lempa, G. (1992). *Zur psychoanalytischen Theorie der psychotischen Symprombildung*. Göttingen: Vandenhoeck & Ruprecht.

Lempa, G. (1995). Zur psychioanalytschen Behandlungstechnik bei schizophrenen Psychosen. *Forum der Psychoanalyse* II: 133–149.

Lempa, G. (2005). Schizophrenie-Screening und anschließende Frühintervention. Kritische Überlegungen aus psychodynamischer Sicht. In G. Juckel and E. Troje *Psychodynamische Therapie von Patienten im schizophrenen prodromalzustand.*

Forum der psychoanalytischen Psychosengtherapie, Band 13. Göttingen: Vandenhoeck & Ruprecht.

Matakas, F. (1991). *Neue Psychiatrie.* Göttingen: Vandenhoeck & Ruprecht.

Matussek, P. (1982). Geschichte und Entwicklung der Forschungsstelle Psychotherapie und Psychodynamik von Schizophrenen. *Bericht des Max-Planck-Instituts München* 4: 82.

Meissel, T. and Eichberger, G. (eds) (2002). *Perspektiven einer künftigen Psychiatrie.* Linz: Edition Pro Mente.

Mentzos, S. (1991). *Psychodynamische Modelle in der Psychiarie.* Göttingen: Vandenhoeck & Ruprecht.

Mentzos, S. (1992). *Psychose und Konflikt.* Göttingen: Vandenhoeck & Ruprecht.

Mentzos, S. (1995). *Depression und Manie. Psychodynamik und Therapie affektiver Störungen.* Göttingen: Vandenhoeck & Ruprecht.

Mentzos, S. (2000). Die 'endogenen' Psychosen als die Psychosomatosen der Gehirns. *Forum der psychoanalytischen Psychosentherapie* 3: 13–32.

Mentzos, S. (2002). Psychoanalyse der Psychosen. *Psychotherapie im Dialog* 3: 223–229.

Neraal, T. (2001). Familiendynamik and psychoanalytische Familienpraxis bei Psychosen. In F. Schwarz and C. Maier (eds) *Psychotherapie der Psychosen.* Stuttgart: Georg Thieme, pp. 136–145.

Pohlen, M. (2004). Im Memorium Paul Matussek. *Der Nervenarzt* 75, 5: 496–498.

Retzer, A. (1994). *Familie und Psychose. Zum Zusammenhang von Familieninteraktione und Psychopathologie bei schizophrenen, schizoaffektiven und manisch-depressiven Psychosen.* Stuttgart: Fischer.

Sandner, D. (ed.) (1986). *Analytische Gruppentherapie mit Schizophrenen.* Göttingen: Vandenhoeck & Ruprecht.

Scharfetter, C. (2006). Psychodynamik vor Freud. In H. Böker (ed.) *Psychoanalyse und Psychiatrie.* Heidelberg: Springer, pp. 23–32.

Schilder, P. (1928). *Introduction to a Psychoanalytic Psychiatry.* New York: Nervous and Mental Disease Publishing Company.

Schindler, R. (1960). Das psychodynamjsche Problem beim sogenannten schizophrenen Defekt. In G. Benedetti and C. Müller (eds) *2. Internationale Symposium über die Psychotherapie der Schizophrenie.* Basel: Karger, pp. 276–288.

Schwarz, F. (1983). Psychoanalytische Familientherapie bei schizophrenen Psychosen. *Praxis der Psychotherapie und Psychosomatik* 28: 73–79.

Schwarz, F. (2000). Empirische Studien zur psychodynamischen Psychosentherapie. *Forum der Psychoanalyse* 8: 123–129.

Schwarz, F. and Maier, C. (ed.) (2001). *Psychotherapie der Psychosen.* Stuttgart: Georg Thieme.

Stierlin, H. (1975). *Von der Psychoanalyse zur Familientherapie.* Stuttgart: Klett.

Winkler, W.T. (1954a). Krisensituationen und Schizophrenie. *Nervenarzt* 25: 500–501.

Winkler, W.T. (1954b). Zum Begriff der Ich-Anachorese beim schizophrenen Erleben. *Archives of Psychiatry and Neurology* 192: 234–240.

Winkler, W.T. (1957). Bericht über den Verlauf einer psychotherapeutischen Behandlung bei einer katatonen Schizophrenie. In G. Benedetti and C. Müller (eds) *Internationales. Symposium über die Psychotherapie der Schizophrenie,* Lausanne, Oktober 1956. Basel: Karger, pp. 162–193.

Chapter 10

France

The contribution of some French psychoanalysts to the clinical and theoretical approaches to transference in the psychodynamic treatment of psychosis

Jean-Max Gaudillière and Françoise Davoine

This chapter is dedicated to a survey of the work of certain French clinicians and theoreticians concerned with the psychoanalytical approach to psychosis during the last 50 years. This particular history is strongly marked by the political outcomes of World War II in France. We are not attempting to record an exhaustive list of all French authors in this field, and we take upon ourselves the responsibility for our partiality and for our choice to ignore chronological order. Rather, we are following the path of our own training, in the course of which we met Gaetano Benedetti, invited him to speak in France in 1988, and then participated in almost all the symposia organized by the International Society for the Psychological Treatments of the Schizophrenias and other Psychoses (ISPS) before we formally joined the association.

We first met Gaetano Benedetti at the beginning of the 1980s in the United States, at the jubilee of the late Otto Will. It is already an interesting point, with regard to the specificity of psychoanalysis in France at that time, that there was no French translation of Benedetti's work, and that it was necessary to cross the Atlantic in order to meet such a prominent psychoanalyst, even though he lived less than six hours drive from Paris. Deeply impressed by his talk at the Austen Riggs Center in Massachusetts, we decided to invite him to Paris at the beginning of 1985, and we discovered that this was his first professional invitation to France. After that, we held a yearly seminar on his work and began the editing and translation of some of his articles into French; we also initiated the translation of his books. (For more on Benedetti, see Chapter 9.)

When we invited Gaetano Benedetti in 1985, we organized several seminars: one was at Paul Guiraud, a public psychiatric hospital in Villejuif (in the suburbs of Paris). We also invited certain psychoanalytic colleagues, who shared the same kind of clinical experience as Benedetti's. One of them, Françoise Dolto, immediately became involved and entered into direct dialogue with Benedetti following his clinical presentation.

M.-A. Séchehaye and Françoise Dolto

Before entering into an account of the development of the psychoanalysis of schizophrenia in France, our focus on the French language for once gives us the opportunity to look beyond our borders, to Switzerland and the time when the work of Marguerite Séchehaye (1887–1964) was first published there in French. We also recall that the first ISPS meetings, organized by Gaetano Benedetti and Christian Müller in Lausanne and Zürich, were held in both German and French before switching to the universal English.

Séchehaye's major theoretical book, *La Réalisation Symbolique*, was published in 1947. Three years later, *Le Journal d'une Schizophrène* (Séchehaye, 1950) was published; subsequent editions were illustrated with stills from the film made in 1968 based on the memoirs of Renée (the patient), with a commentary by her therapist.

What is striking is Madame Séchehaye's extraordinary courage and freedom. She was never frightened of the powerful regression and delusion of her young patient. As a therapist, she responded directly to every significant moment of the psychotic transference, even to the level of fetal regression. She managed to impose her will to cure Renée, although sometimes the patient had to be hospitalized. Dr. Séchehaye did not hesitate to share aspects of everyday life with her patient, at times actually feeding Renée in order to stay in touch with her. The analyst was greatly helped by her studies of Jean Piaget's descriptions of the psychic development of children (1951). In the last chapter of her book, containing her conclusions about Renée's memoirs, she wrote (our translation):

> A dynamic conceptualisation of the process of disaggregation in Schizophrenia: When we are in the presence of a patient who, like Renée, has moved to the point of deep regression to the primitive states of his/her evolution, one can consider these phenomena in the light of Piaget's theory. From this comparison, we could conclude (and this is particularly important) that what appears to us as a disaggregative process can under certain conditions become a reconstructive process.
>
> (Séchehaye, 1950: 131–132)

Here we are not so far from some of the formulations of Benedetti. Certainly we recognize the same approach in the work of Christian Müller (1982).

Séchehaye's work can be seen as a prelude to subsequent research and clinical interventions in France. Even her approach anticipates the work and personality of Françoise Dolto, who began her practice of psychoanalysis with disturbed children in 1938 and together with Jacques Lacan founded the Ecole Freudienne de Paris.

In France, Françoise Dolto (1908–1988) holds a place similar to that of D.W. Winnicott in England. Her family (her maiden name was Marette) had participated actively in the Resistance. She began working with children at the beginning of World War II. From then on she would show a consistent genius in working psychoanalytically, even with babies who were in the greatest of difficulties, seemingly beyond the reach of any family member or professional. She was efficient and rigorous, and expressed a true commitment to working with transference; but at the same time she also clearly admonished anyone who attacked the 'children's cause', a phrase that she coined (Dolto, 1971a, 1971b). She expressed herself in clear language, without any jargon. Like Winnicott during the war, in the 1970s Dolto gave a regular and widely known live radio broadcast, in which she also responded as an analyst to the questions of anxious parents, but without becoming demagogic or weak in her words. Her voice quickly became a reference point for many people, mostly far from the field of psychoanalysis.

Françoise Dolto was also accustomed to basing her theory on the direct experience of transference, as the following example shows. In another working conference we had invited some Sioux medicine men to Paris, having worked clinically with them for several summers in South Dakota. We had asked Françoise Dolto to hear Joe Eagle Elk, with the help of his friend Stanley Red Bird, describe a very difficult case he had treated in the state hospital at the request of the regular doctors. Within the framework of his own cultural background, and of the healing ceremony that he performed with the young boy, who was nearly dying, Joe described how he saw the boy's body becoming luminous in the darkness of the hospital room, and how he gave him some water to drink after the ceremony. The boy began to recover, and the same evening was even able to eat something, after several days of wasting away. We already knew the story, and we wondered how Parisian analysts would react. Françoise Dolto answered the medicine man:

> I'm not surprised by what you told us concerning your own feelings during the healing ceremony, dedicated to a young boy unable to express anything with words or even with his eyes. I have exactly the same experience with suffering babies, who can be seen as almost catatonic in certain circumstances. When such a patient is unable to express his own feelings, let alone feel them, I am feeling them in his place, through my body, the very primary oppositions, such as light/ dark, cold/warm, etc, and I express them back to him.

Jacques Lacan

Almost from the beginning of her professional commitment with children, Françoise Dolto was in touch with the teaching of Jacques Lacan (1901– 1981). She was one of the few to address him with the French familiar *tu*.

Their lives covered the same decades of the twentieth century, and we can see them as the two major French predecessors in our field of work.

Lacan never formulated clear theories concerning psychotic transference. He preferred to stop his research at the very limit before 'the question of the possible maneuver of transference in psychosis' (for this 'question', see his *Ecrits*; Lacan, 1966). He considered that his work in rereading Freud was a huge task dedicated to rediscovering the roots of the Freudian discoveries: for example, the unconscious and repression, linked with a theory of language. The issue of psychosis in psychoanalysis was to be explored afterwards. He used to joke about his experience with psychosis as a psychoanalyst: 'Clearly I had some psychotic patients in psychoanalysis. I cured some of them; I'm not able to say how.'

Perhaps his training as a psychiatrist, in which field he had already achieved a high reputation prior to World War II, together with his activities as a member of a Surrealist group for a while, were the keys to his approach to madness. For years he constantly presented patients in public, in the setting of Sainte Anne's psychiatric hospital in Paris, as did Gaetan Gatien de Clérambaut, the only master he would ever recognize. On the other hand, in line with a psychoanalytic approach, he organized several working conferences dedicated to the analysis of psychoses in the institute he had created, the Ecole Freudienne de Paris. The greater part of his teaching concerning psychosis, however, comes from his oral seminars, especially two of them: *The Psychoses*, where he comments on Freud's Schreber case, and *The Ethics of Psychoanalysis* (Lacan, 1986), where he reflects profoundly upon the texts of classic Greek tragedies and anthropology.

Rereading Freud and Schreber, Lacan gave rise to key concepts, which are useful for the analyst in determining where he is in the transferential journey with madness. As a translation of the Freudian '*Verwerfung*', Lacan coined the 'foreclosure of the Name of the Father'. The famous triad, *Symbolic, Imaginary and Real*, ended in Lacan's teaching with the mysterious and provocative Borromean knot: when one of the three circles representing these three domains is cut, the other two are loosened, and there it is: madness itself. The concept of the Real is particularly interesting in our field, in that it designates an order without any name, word, or image. In transference, we certainly have to be very precise to recognize what happens at the borders of these three categories.

Lacan helps us go deeper by commenting on the Sophoclean tragedies *Antigone* and *Œdipus at Colonus*. These masterpieces open up an important field for us, which Lacan calls 'the space in between two deaths'; a space and time we can approach between the moment of biological death and the moment when the name can be ritually written on a grave. If we are concerned with the evident links between madness and trauma, how can we refuse this elementary lesson, taught to us by war veterans or by survivors of attacks or natural disasters?

Naturally, all these concepts are highly demanding and complex, and cannot be simplified or separated out from the whole of Lacanian theory. Considering for instance, the 'foreclosure of the Name of the Father' as a semiotic trait in order to establish a diagnosis of psychosis is simply ludicrous.

Gisela Pankow and Piera Aulagnier

Lacan's style was frequently provocative. We sometimes saw him being ferocious with people he didn't respect, even among his own students. But one of the most important psychoanalysts in our field was, in another way, even fiercer. Françoise Davoine, who spent some years under Gisela Pankow's mentorship, used to say jokingly: 'After experiencing the personality and commitment of Gisela Pankow (1914–1998), I was never again made fearful by any psychotic patient.' Pankow was of German origin: after her medical studies in Germany, she began to work as a psychoanalyst in Paris in the early 1950s. Until the end of her life, she also led a clinical seminar at Sainte Anne public psychiatric hospital. For quite a few years she was probably the only person in Paris who was actually able to undertake the challenge of treating the most severely disturbed patients by psychoanalysis, including the overtly psychotic, against the injunctions of classical analysis (Pankow, 1969). She carried this out in her private practice. Although she was hardly an easygoing person, she supervised many practitioners, including psychiatrists working in the public hospitals, who at that period in the history of the treatment of psychosis in France were often also psychoanalysts. The medical director of our ward, Edmond Sanquer, was one such supervisee. They had a great respect for each other. Clearly the landscape changed radically after this period, as evidenced by the fact that at the beginning of the 1970s 80 per cent of psychiatrists were in analysis; today that is probably true of less than 5 per cent. Perhaps we need the strength and courage of another Gisela Pankow.

One story will illustrate how Pankow used to deal with psychotic transference, in immediacy and in proximity (following Thomas Salmon's principles of 'forward psychiatry'). One day, she was entering her waiting room to fetch the next patient, who already had one leg over her balcony (on the seventh story of the building). Calmly, in her strong German accent, she asked him: 'What shall I do with your corpse?' He came back, and in the session they discussed this important issue. With respect to suicide attempts, she would say to her colleagues and to her patients that in trying to kill themselves patients clearly have something they need to kill in themselves, rather than needing to take their own lives.

To both evoke and explain a key idea within the transference, Pankow was keen on the use of clay modelling. She would place the monstrous figures produced by her patients on a little table between her and her client, saying, 'Bring me some monsters! I am a monster dealer.' Her general theoretical frame dealt with the image of the body, but she also used it as a readable representation of the accidents that had occurred in the history of the lineage. In the transference, she was probably able to intervene with such effectiveness because she was speaking from her own history, deeply marked by the two world wars. This brings to mind another German psychoanalyst in exile, Frieda Fromm-Reichmann, when she declared at Chestnut Lodge: 'Even in the case of the most regressed catatonia, when one says that there is no transference, in fact everything is transference.' On the same path, Gisela Pankow coined the formula of the 'graft of trans-ference'. Pankow kept her independence until her death and transmitted her knowledge in several books and numerous articles, which give a good idea of her style and effectiveness.

We now speak of a third female psychoanalyst, Piera Aulagnier (1923–1990). It is remarkable that, like Gisela Pankow, Aulagnier too was born abroad (in Italy under Mussolini) and also began to work in France as a psychoanalyst. Having been a member of the first institute created by Jacques Lacan, she left it because she questioned the methods used in training analysts. But she continued to be inspired by Lacan's teaching in the elaboration of her own psychotherapeutic position with psychosis. Aulagnier's books give a good view of her demanding precision in present-ing her clinical work. In *The Violence of the Interpretation* (Aulagnier, 1975) she focused on the part of transference that was not totally mediated by ordinary means of representation. Thus she was able to differentiate between the classic Lacanian 'signifier', accessible to the formations of the repressed unconscious, and the 'pictogram' in use when the chain of lan-guage and transmission is broken. When she separated from Lacan, Aulagnier created the 'Quatrième Groupe', the Fourth Group. Unfortu-nately she died before she was able to work further with this group.

P.-C. Racamier, Claude Barrois and others

Paul-Claude Racamier (1924–1996) participated actively at an early stage in the ISPS symposia initiated by Gaetano Benedetti and Christian Müller. He directed several psychiatric services in France and Switzerland, and published an impressive number of books and articles dedicated to the psychoanalysis of psychosis. In one of the best known, *Le Psychoanalyste sans divan* [The Psychoanalyst without a Couch], he explores the specificity and possibility of psychoanalytical work in a hospital setting (Racamier, 1970). He also published a book about schizophrenic patients (Racamier, 1980). Importantly, in his last book, *Le Génie des origines* (1992), he stresses the malignant efficacy of cognitive distortions, and how madness works as a touchstone revealing these manipulations of the mind, the soul and the body.

Racamier does not give many details concerning his personal way of working in this field, but he does give us enough to demonstrate the strength of his involvement in the transferential process. He himself would never use any such descriptions in reference to etiology, and we know that this attitude is probably the only possible basis for any psychoanalytical intervention in this domain, consisting as it does to a powerful degree of such traits as violence, withdrawal, foreclosure, denial and eradication.

We might also mention the work of Claude Barrois. For many years, until his retirement, he was head of psychiatry at the Military Hospital of Val de Grâce in Paris. As well as being a highly sensitive psychoanalyst, he was one of the few practitioners able to treat and explore war traumas as an analyst, and to explain their connections with madness (Barrois, 1993, 1998).

Sidney Stewart (1920–1998) spent his entire career as an analyst in Paris, one of the few survivors of the hell of the Bataan March and the Japanese camps during World War II (Stewart, 1980). Here we also have an opportunity to mention the role of his wife, Joyce MacDougall, who in addition to her own outstanding work also played the role of an important *passeur* or mediator, helping French psychoanalysts cross international boundaries and stay in touch with British, American and Northern European clinicians and theoreticians. Also worth mentioning is the psychiatrist Georges Daumezon (1912–1980), who was responsible for a service at Sainte Anne Hospital until his death. He was a mentor to many young psychiatrists who were receptive to psychoanalysis in the setting of a public psychiatric hospital.

Clearly, there are many other important figures, whom we cannot refer to in this brief presentation. We have focused on those who have given us indispensable tools in achieving the purposes of the ISPS, and who are in accord with Benedetti's principles – or at least are not in contradiction with them. After more than 30 years in psychiatric hospitals and in private practice, in our own work (Davoine and Gaudillière, 2004) we aspire to continue along the lines opened up by our predecessors, who considered transference in the psychodynamic treatment of psychosis as a process of co-research with the patient, exploring the 'death areas' (Benedetti, 1983) that represent ruptures in the social fabric, in order to regenerate lost capacities for speech and history (Freud, 1939a).

References

Aulagnier, P. (1975). *La violence de l'interprétation: du pictogramme à l'énoncé.* Paris: Presses Universitaires de France.

Barrois, C. (1993). *Psychanalyse du guerrier*. Paris: Hachette.

Barrois, C. (1998). *Les Névroses traumatiques*. Paris: Dunod.

Benedetti, G. (1983). *Todeslandschaften der Seele*. Göttingen: Vandenhoeck und Ruprecht.
Davoine, F. and Gaudillière, J.-M. (2004). *History beyond Trauma*. New York: Other Press.
Dolto, F. (1971a). *Psychanalyse et Pédiatrie*. Paris: Editions du Seuil.
Dolto, F. (1971b). *Le cas Dominique*. Paris: Editions du Seuil.
Freud, S. (1939a). Moses and monotheism. *Standard Edition* XXIII. London: Hogarth Press.
Lacan, J. (1966). *Ecrits*. Paris: Editions du Seuil. In English: *Ecrits, A Selection*. New York: Norton 1959–1960.
Lacan, J. (1986). *Séminaire VII: L'éthique de la psychanalyse*, 1959–1960. Paris: Editions du Seuil. [English edn *The Seminar of Jacques Lacan Book VII: The Ethics of Psychoanalysis*, trans. D. Porter. New York: Norton, 1977.]
Müller, C. (1982). *Etudes sur la psychothérapie des psychoses*. Toulouse: Privat.
Pankow, G. (1969). *L'Homme et sa psychose*. Paris: Editions Flammarion.
Piaget, J. (1951). *Play, Dreams and Imitation in Childhood*, trans. C. Gattegno and F.M. Hodgson. New York: Norton.
Racamier, P.-C. (1970). *Le Psychoanalyste sans divan*. Paris: Payot.
Racamier, P.-C. (1980). *Les Schizophrènes*. Paris: Payot.
Racamier, P.-C. (1992). *Le Génie des origines. Psychanalyse et psychoses*. Paris: Payot.
Séchehaye, M.-A. (1947). La Réalisation symbolique. *Revue de psychanalyse et de psychanalyse appliquée* 12. [English edn *Symbolic Realization: A New Method of Psychotherapy Applied to a Case of Schizophrenia*. New York: International Universities Press, 1951.]
Séchehaye, M.-A. (1950). *Le journal d'une Schizophrène*, Paris: Presses Universitaires de France.
Stewart, S. (1980). *Give Us This Day*. New York: Avon.

Chapter 11

Italy

The psychiatric care reform bill and the
development of psychotherapeutic approaches

Marco Alessandrini and Massimo di Giannantonio

The legislative reforms

In May 1978, the Italian parliament passed a Psychiatric Care Reform Bill
(Law 13 May 1978, nr. 180). In the same year, on 23 December, the law was
incorporated into a more comprehensive Health Care Legislation (Law nr.
833). The only difference between the two is that law 180 set a 15-bed
ceiling for each psychiatric ward, whereas law 833 entrusts the social health
plan, as established by each region, with the task of setting the number of
beds (Cazzullo, 2000).

These major reforms resulted from a long series of innovations and ideas
that originated particularly in specific cities, like Gorizia, Arezzo and
Perugia. Unquestionably, the name of Franco Basaglia (1924–1980) is well
known to many: in 1962 he ran the Psychiatric Hospital of Gorizia; it was
he who sparked off a renewal process that reached its peak with the
establishment of the first Italian 'therapeutic community', inspired by the
therapeutic community of Maxwell Jones in the UK (Basaglia, 1982;
Colucci and Di Vittorio, 2001).

At that time, the focus of those experiences was based on a communism-
driven political ideology. The idea was to replace the only existing facilities,
the mental hospitals, with a large network of 'centri territoriali' (territorial
centres). Today, such centres are called by many different names depending
on the Italian regions, although the most common name is 'Centro di
Salute Mentale' (mental health centre). While patients used to be hospitalized in mental hospitals for an unspecified period of time, without receiving
any true treatment or rehabilitation (which contributed to them falling into
complete social isolation), now they can only be hospitalized in the psychiatric wards of public hospitals, and only for a couple of days. Law 180
revolutionized Italian psychiatry.

Mental health centres are now located everywhere across the country and
are often separate and distant from public hospitals. Their mission is to
deliver therapy, rehabilitation procedures or to conduct activities aimed
at the patient's social inclusion, either from the patient's home or within

their own outpatient setting. Psychiatric patients have to be exactly like any other medical patient, receiving an intensive therapeutic effort both on an outpatient and a territorial basis, the ultimate goal being their return to a normal life in society. The mental hospital based psychiatry has been substituted by a 'territory-based' psychiatry (Berti Ceroni and Correale (eds), 1999).

The operating centres

Since 1978 to date, the history of Italian psychiatry has been characterized by a harsh debate and political-cultural argument over the enforcement of law 180. Mental hospitals have been closed down and no longer exist. However, the network of 'centri territoriali' has been only partially established. This is why such networks show many deficiencies and some room has been created for highly inconsistent, non-homogeneous therapeutic rehabilitation practices (Rossi Monti, 1994).

Basically, each azienda pubblica ospedaliera (public hospital) has its own 'dipartimento di salute mentale' (department of mental health) and its own director. In its turn, the department accommodates a number of therapeutic centres to which patients are referred according to their current acute condition. The first of such centres, albeit not the most important, is the psychiatric emergency ward ('Servizio psichiatrico di diagnosi e cura'); it is physically located inside the public hospital and is used to hospitalize acutely ill patients for short periods of time. Hospitalization can also be statutory; however, in these specific cases, according to law 180, it cannot last for more than seven days. The second type of centre is the mental health centre (referred to above) which consists of several 'unità operative' (operating units) and is generally located, as noted above, away from the public hospital. The idea is to allow inpatients to stay in an environment as different as possible from a conventional hospital.

Of the operating units which are part of the mental health centre, the 'unità territoriale' (territorial unit) is by far the most important and the core of the department. The territorial unit employs psychiatrists, psychologists and social workers, and offers outpatient visits, psychotherapy, home-based activities, vocational training and workplace integration activities. These professionals assist patients to explore their life and psychic and relational dynamics in depth to put together a personalized therapeutic project. If necessary, the unit arranges a short stay at the psychiatric emergency ward to overcome a temporary acute condition or can refer the patient to the other operating units of the mental health centre, if required, for the personalized therapeutic project established for each individual patient.

The other operating units are generally located in the same building as the mental health centre (or in its vicinity) and mostly include the day hospital to manage any sub-acute state and avoid hospitalizing acutely ill patients; and the day centre to rehabilitate more chronically ill patients. Finally, the other therapy centres belonging to the mental health department, to which a patient can be referred from the territorial unit, include: the therapeutic community where patients voluntarily decide to live for a number of months or for as long as two or three years, in order to receive a more intensive, community-based treatment; family houses for long-term residential guests, i.e. patients with more limited chances of social inclusion in a short time span. In essence, family houses offer a residential setting that is integrated with the urban and social context; in this setting, patients receive more gradual rehabilitation activities. The so-called 'gruppi appartamento' (apartment groups) have a similar purpose. In these apartments, patients, still followed by the territorial unit, can spend short or even fairly long periods of time in order to help them separate themselves from their families, as soon as they are ready for this, and to get a job. Since patients live in these apartments with others, a mutual solidarity often develops. Finally, in some regions, e.g. in Piedmont, patients may go to live for a temporary period with a family other than their own, to activate a detachment and new identification process supported in a better improved relational context than before (Aluffi, 2001).

Thus, the current Italian model is entirely focused on the patient's therapy and rehabilitation through multiple therapy centres, coordinated by the same department, mostly employing individual projects established by the territorial unit of the mental health centre. In most instances, a territorial unit psychiatrist develops an ongoing therapeutic and personal relationship with the individual patient. He or she becomes the doctor of reference and, most importantly, the one who prepares, in collaboration with the patient, the different steps of the therapeutic project.

Current difficulties

While this model looks highly innovative on paper, it has been implemented in an incomplete manner. There are two major weaknesses. First of all, therapy centres do not exist in every department of mental health; and some of them are not run by a public (government-operated) hospital but by private companies. Therefore, it can happen that a patient is unduly 'parked' in day centres or family houses that do not have any real interest in the patient's social inclusion. Second, this situation may occur when the staff members of the territorial units of mental health centres lack an adequate psychotherapeutic and professional background; or, even when the staff member does have a proper background but does not work as a member of a team. This is why psychoanalytic, systemic-relational, cognitive, group interventions and other 'spontaneous' techniques may coexist without the staff having any dialogue and, ultimately, without using such techniques in an integrated manner.

In summary, if one looks at the Italian situation in the different departments of mental health within the same region and even more so if one considers departments across different regions, it appears quite fragmented and heterogeneous. In fact, the entire range of therapy centres does not always exist, and when they do, they do not necessarily comply with the legal requirements, maybe because they are located in inadequate buildings or more simply because they are understaffed. More often than not, no individual department adopts the same psychotherapeutic model to amalgamate the various therapeutic techniques delivered by the staff. In addition, the use of psychoactive agents has become the rule. Hence, a large number of psychiatrists in the territorial units of mental health centres do not develop any psychotherapeutic project for their individual patients; they simply try to control symptoms by means of drugs.

The role of psychotherapies

The psychotherapy of schizophrenic patients is mostly delivered, albeit to an insufficient extent, by public therapy centres, most commonly at the territorial units of mental health centres. However, all too often psychotherapy cannot be adequately delivered in the latter centres, either because the staff are too busy or because the way the various activities are organized is just too chaotic (Bonfiglio, 1999). This explains why psychotherapy is often delivered by specialists in private practice, where they can offer more accurate and continuous therapies. Sometimes, a specialist accepting a patient with schizophrenia in his private practice for a psychotherapeutic treatment may also work in a public therapy centre and when a patient is financially well off the therapist may suggest a private treatment. Public medical care in Italy is offered almost for free. Specialists working in a private practice charge their clients for services.

As to the psychotherapy of schizophrenic patients, at present no region has therapy centres where this is particularly well developed or where a research project is in place. It is practised just about everywhere, but in a scattered, fragmented manner, largely thanks to the efforts made by individual therapists. There exist, e.g. in Rome, psychiatric hospital wards or entire mental health centres where, thanks to the skills of individual psychiatrists-managers, all staff members, including nurses, receive a psychodynamically oriented psychotherapeutic training (or, at times, systemic-relational). In these cases, teamwork is common and everybody follows a homogeneous psychotherapeutic model (Ferruta, 2000).

In Trieste, where over time the initial approach set by Franco Basaglia has become deeply rooted, the overall 'territorial' model looks quite original, with a psychotherapeutic activity entirely focused on social inclusion. In essence, according to the Trieste model, the focus of psychotherapy does not emphasize the intrapsychic change of the schizophrenic patient but the possibility of inducing the patient to 'adapt' his psychotic functioning to the social context, playing a critical, self-affirmative, transformation role vis-à-vis the context. In fact, according to this model, psychotherapy has no definite orientation – psychodynamic, systemic-relational, etc. – but is aimed at promoting the patients' self-esteem, their capacity for empathy, improving their decision-making skills and enhancing their positive characteristics. As a consequence, patients acquire the ability to adjust themselves to the social reality despite their being 'different', so as to stimulate society itself to recognize and accept, and indeed to help them.

Elsewhere, for example, in Milan – and as noted above in Rome – and in some other cities, the psychotherapy of schizophrenic patients follows a 'classical' approach, mostly psychodynamic (Correale and Rinaldi, 1997) or systemic-relational (Covini et al., 1984). The integration between these two approaches is, however, uncommon. Group therapy is less common, although present, and is mostly based on the approach of Foulkes (Di Maria and Lo Verso, 1995) or on strictly rehabilitative procedures, like in the Spivak model. Gaetano Benedetti's, as well as, partly, Cremerius's experiences have become popular mostly in Milan and in Lombardy, and to some extent in Perugia (Benedetti, 1980, 1991, 1992). A true research effort, however, with the elaboration of tested procedures and the subsequent proposal of operational models, has never been carried out in these cities, or only to a partial extent.

In particular, two prevailing models can still be mentioned; they are especially common in Lombardy and elsewhere in Northern Italy and, more sporadically, in other cities. The first model is that followed by public (government-operated) therapy centres: it is focused on psychotherapy delivered by a team. The mental health centre, and particularly the territorial unit staff, holds regular weekly meetings and discuss individual patients, so as to 'contain' and 'transform', through a kind of group rêverie, the 'unthinkable' psychic contents conveyed to the staff by patients. Clearly, this approach draws upon psychodynamic theories, with special emphasis on Bion's work. Bion is in fact much studied in Italy, also thanks to the Società Psicoanalitica Italiana (SIP), the members of which include many mental health centre psychiatrists. This model provides patients with both a psychodynamic individual psychotherapy and a psychodynamic or systemic-relational family psychotherapy, or the complete set of additional rehabilitation resources made available by the various therapy centres of the mental health centre (day hospital, day centre, etc.). Finally, group therapies inspired by Foulkes or by psychoanalysis are all but rare, and they generally make reference to Salomon Resnik (often present in the area of Venice for training workshops); even expressive techniques, such as psychodrama (Morenian, Jungian, etc.), theatre therapy, art therapy using plasticine figures, are commonly employed.

The second model concerns private therapy centres. These operate outside public (government-operated) therapy centres and present themselves as a different 'option', i.e. by offering a set of activities that public centres cannot always provide. For example, they offer the mother–child couple the possibility to spend some time in special apartments where, with the therapists' support, they re-create a temporary, although intense, symbiotic phase to 'repair' their previous unsatisfactory symbiotic experiences (Ferrero, 1999). Here, the psychodynamic models of reference include Klein, Mahler, Kohut and Benedetti, as well as Zapparoli (1987, 2002) and many more authors, including the French school represented by Lacan, Racamier and Sassolas. Phenomenological psychiatry has equally been quite successful and is largely employed in territorial therapy centres (Rossi Monti, 1994).

Some experiences are inspired by cognitive therapy approaches and are followed by the cognitive-oriented residential therapeutic communities, in line with Carlo Perris' approach (Perris, 1989). Finally, a number of residential therapeutic communities adopt a dual approach: psychodynamic (mainly inspired by Kernberg) and systemic-relational (Cancrini, 1999).

Conclusions

In Italy the psychotherapy of schizophrenic patients does not follow a single model, nor has it founded a truly innovative, specific approach. What we see is a highly contradictory picture, undoubtedly brought about by the partial enforcement of law 180 and by the lack of systematic staff training programmes. However, by the same token, it is also a dynamic and changing reality, where the most advanced international proposals are welcomed and re-elaborated in very original ways.

Aside from the highly original Trieste model, which has now been quite stable over time, other models, largely based on authors like Mahler, Bion, Benedetti, Kohut and Lacan, are also original and innovative; yet, they have not gained enough stability and popularity to be proposed as proper 'models'. Perhaps in the near future we shall see the emergence of more structured and strong Italian models for the psychotherapy of schizophrenic patients. Already the first model described above, i.e. the model followed by the public (government-operated) therapy centres, despite differences across the various contexts, shows consistent traits wherever it has been adopted. We may note especially the high degree of attention in providing individual psychotherapeutic treatment (psychodynamically oriented) along with the weekly team meetings, equally conducted according to psychodynamic modalities.

Another common trait is the provision of work which the team of staff does on themselves – a whole set of therapeutic-rehabilitative interventions available within public therapy centres. In fact, such therapeutic-rehabilitative interventions make individual psychodynamic modalities richer. They provide patients with a large number of concrete opportunities in terms of vocational training, job tutoring, independent living and social fulfilment. Moreover, these interventions offer a true group setting, making them open to an ongoing testing.

A third trait is the growing attention to the family. If the family is available to go through some form of therapy, a systemic-relational or psychodynamically oriented family therapy is arranged, depending on the circumstances. Even when the family refuses to participate in this therapeutic path, self-help groups, including patients' families, are presented as an option.

The true challenge for the psychotherapy of schizophrenic patients in Italy at present, however, is not the elaboration of 'original' models. As a matter of fact, such models already exist, mostly thanks to the intersection, probably the only one in Europe, between the 'territorial' model inaugurated by law 180 and the dissemination of psychotherapeutic practices. Combining these latter with the network of territorial centres enables psychotherapy, especially the psychodynamically oriented psychotherapy, never to limit itself to the individual treatment only. All the staff members, in fact – be they psychiatrists, psychologists, nurses or social workers – become a sort of a treating 'extended family' for the patient, offering actual work, living circumstances, social inclusion and integration. The true challenge is whether such experiences can effectively counter the increasingly massive penetration of a reductionistic neurobiological approach. This latter is largely advocated by pharmaceutical companies that, in turn, fund university research institutions. In fact, it is important to note that several public (government-operated) therapy centres in Italy belong to the local university (also owned by the government).

References

Aluffi, G. (2001). *Dal manicomio alla famiglia*. Milano: Franco Angeli.

Basaglia, F. (1982). *Scritti, Vol. I (1953–1968)*. Vol. II (1968–1980). Torino: Einaudi.

Benedetti, G. (1980). *Alienazione e personazione nella psicoterapia della malattia mentale*. Torino: Einaudi.

Benedetti, G. (1991). *Paziente e terapeuta nell'esperienza psicotica*. Torino: Bollati Boringhieri.

Benedetti, G. (1992). *Psychotherapie als exsistentielle Herausforderung*. Göttingen: Vandenhoeck & Ruprecht. [Italian edn *La psicoterapia come sfida esistenziale*. Milano: Raffaello Cortina, 1997.]

Berti Ceroni, G. and Correale, A. (eds) (1999). *Psicoanalisi e psichiatria*. Milano: Raffaello Cortina.

Bonfiglio, B. (1999). *Uno psicoanalista al 'servizio'. Psicoanalisi nei Centri di Salute Mentale*. Roma: Borla.

Cancrini, L. (1999). *La luna nel pozzo. Famiglie, comunità terapeutiche, contro-transfert e decorso della schizofrenia*. Milano: Raffaello Cortina.

Cazzullo, C.L. (2000). *Storia breve della psichiatria italiana*. Milano: Masson.

Colucci, M. and Di Vittorio, P. (2001). *Franco Basaglia*. Milano: Bruno Mondadori.

Correale, A. and Rinaldi, L. (eds) (1997). *Quale psicoanalisi per le psicosi?* Milano: Raffaello Cortina.

Covini, A., Fiocchi, E., Pasquino, R. and Sellini, M. (1984). *Alla conquista del territorio. Processo di trasformazione sistemica di un centro psichiatrico*. Roma: La Nuova Italia Scientifica.

Di Maria, F. and Lo Verso, G. (eds) (1995). *La psicodinamica dei gruppi*. Milano: Raffaello Cortina.

Ferrero, P. (1999). *Psicosi. Programma di trattamento, percorso di vita*. Milano: Franco Angeli.

Ferruta, A. (2000). *Un lavoro terapeutico. L'infermiere in psichiatria*. Milano: Franco Angeli.

Perris, C. (1989). *Cognitive Therapy with Schizophrenic Patients*. New York: Guilford Press. [Italian edn *Terapia cognitiva con i pazienti schizofrenici*. Torino: Bollati Boringhieri, 1996.]

Rossi Monti, M. (ed.) (1994). *Manuale di psichiatria nel territorio*. Firenze: La Nuova Italia.

Zapparoli, G.C. (1987). *La psicosi e il segreto*. Torino: Bollati Boringhieri.

Zapparoli, G.C. (2002). *La follia e l'intermediario*. Bergamo: Dialogos.

Chapter 12

Northern Europe

Developments in the Scandinavian countries

Jukka Aaltonen, Yrjö O. Alanen, Johan Cullberg,
Svein Haugsgjerd, Sonja Levander and Bent Rosenbaum

The Scandinavian countries – Denmark, Finland, Iceland, Norway and Sweden – have common cultural features permeating psychiatric activities by way of congresses, journals, exchange visits and research projects. The Nordic welfare states have particularly supported the development of community psychiatry, However, each country has its own developmental history. We will therefore describe the psychotherapeutically oriented schizophrenia research and practices in each country except for the smaller Iceland (well known for its tradition of psychiatric epidemiology initiated by Helgason, 1964). We finish with a joint overview.

SWEDEN – FROM BJERRE TO THE PARACHUTE PROJECT

Sonja Levander and Johan Cullberg

Pioneers of psychodynamic treatment of psychoses

In Sweden the early development of psychotherapy for psychotic patients followed growing knowledge from the psychoanalytic movement. Poul Bjerre (1876–1964) was the first to introduce psychoanalysis in Sweden. In 1910 he became acquainted with Freud, and in 1911 he lectured on psychoanalysis to the Swedish Medical Association. His rich and accessible authorship, including eight volumes of *Collected Psychotherapeutic Papers* (Bjerre, 1933–1944), contributed considerably to the growing Swedish interest in psychotherapy. He formulated a psychotherapeutic/psycho-analytic model, 'psychosynthesis', emphasizing the self-healing process of the psyche and its innate striving for completeness. He understood psychotic symptoms as a provisional solution related to the healing process.

Bjerre's best known case was a paranoid female patient who consulted him in 1909 with persecutory symptoms going back ten years (Bjerre, 1911). A crucial element in her problems was a 20-year correspondence with a man she had never met, but with whom she was completely obsessed. When she accidentally met her fantasized lover the spell was broken – the idealized person did not exist in reality. The patient received 40 sessions, one session every other day. Bjerre wrote that he spared no effort to try to persuade her to accept the reality of the situation. She experienced great relief as her symptoms disappeared and 'her contact with the outer world became completely realistic'. Bjerre was asked by the patient to publish her case.

Following Bjerre, several Swedish psychotherapists published their work with psychotic patients arousing interest and lively debate in both professional and non-scientific literature. In the 1950s Torsten Herner (1908–1996), who participated in the first International Society for the Psychological Treatments of the Schizophrenias and other Psychoses (ISPS) symposium in Switzerland, developed a theoretical model based on his view of man's existential situation, 'existential dialectics', and his therapeutic work with a female patient. He presented his model in *The Challenge of Schizophrenia* (Herner, 1982).

Palle Villemoes's treatment model, 'ego-structuring psychotherapy' (Villemoes, 2002), is based on Lacan's definition of psychosis: As humans the symbolic order of language ties us into a network of time, rules, generations and gender, all expressed in our personal history. Like Herner, he describes a method to help psychotic patients to relive early periods of their lives, in Villemoes's terms 'try to subordinate themselves to the castration complex by entering into the linguistic symbolic order with time as the basic structure'.

Barbro Sandin is an important pioneer in psychotherapy for psychotic patients. In the mid-1970s she started her clinical work as a social worker at a mental hospital in Säter, Sweden, without any formal training in psychotherapy. Her first patient, who had received a schizophrenia diagnosis at the age of 14, met Sandin after nine years in the hospital. He is now working as a psychologist after 12 years of therapy with her.

Sandin became the head of a small hospital unit primarily treating patients with chronic schizophrenia. Later she started a private unit for similar patients. In books and papers she has presented her view that psychosis results from a blocking or obstruction of normal development by unpredictable and menacing childhood experiences. Sandin's work was much debated in the Swedish media and remains controversial among psychiatrists.

Johan Cullberg and Sonja Levander studied seven cases with a clear schizophrenia diagnosis treated with intensive psychotherapy by Sandin or her co-workers (Cullberg, 1991; Cullberg and Levander, 1991). Patients who were not fully recovered were interviewed and compared with the recovered group. The former had more negative symptoms and more longstanding hallucinations in their clinical histories prior to therapy.

In another study (Levander and Cullberg, 1994) Barbro Sandin and five of her former patients were interviewed about the way she worked as a therapist and about therapeutic processes. Generally she was described as an affirmative psychodynamic psychotherapist. The former patients talked of her as strong and convincing. In a straightforward way she had confronted them with facts about their childhood that they had had difficulties in accepting and made them see the relationship between these experiences and their psychosis. The patients also told about 'sinking therapy', a kind of unguided imagery. With just a few questions they opened up to feelings that they had not realized before and these were later integrated with a verbal understanding.

Sandin informed us that she saw herself as having 'strong male aspects' requiring responsibility and endurance from the patients for the anxiety reactions in the therapeutic process. She thought that these functions were particularly important for male patients who lacked a strong or adequate father in the early home situation. The maternal functions in the psychotherapy had to be provided by the rest of the staff.

Sandin has completed 30 to 35 long psychotherapies with deeply disturbed schizophrenic patients and been responsible for the education of complete therapeutic teams working in different parts of Sweden. Her ideas are published (in Swedish) in *Den zebrarandiga pudelkärnan* (Sandin, 1986). Rolf Sjöström (1985, 1990) has published follow-up studies on patients treated by Sandin and her co-workers.

Cognitive psychotherapy

Carlo Perris (1928–2000) introduced cognitive psychotherapy in Sweden and developed approaches especially suitable for psychotic patients. He wrote several books including *Cognitive Therapy with Schizophrenic Patients* (Perris, 1989) and *Cognitive Psychotherapy of Psychotic and Personality Disorders: Handbook of Theory and Practice* (Perris and McGorry, 1998). Perris was active over many years in educating cognitive psychotherapists and started several treatment centres with a cognitive approach that included psychotic patients.

Giacomo d'Elia also works in the cognitive field but is more oriented toward psychopedagogical interventions (PPI). He teaches, consults and supports psychiatric units in different parts of the country.

The Soteria Nacka

'Nacka Soteria' was started in 1993. It is a small home-like unit outside the hospital area for first episode psychotic patients and was inspired by Swiss psychiatrist Luc Ciompi (see Chapter 23). Staff members work to establish trustful and healing relationships with patients and antipsychotic medication is kept to a minimum. The treatment's theoretical base is the assumption that the psychotic experience forms an existential crisis for the patient who therefore needs a psychotherapeutic crisis intervention. Another assumption is that the psychotic person in his thinking, behaviour and symptoms is conveying important aspects of his problems. In the early phase of the psychosis staff help the patients describe their problems in words that can also be understood by the environment – the 'work of formulating the problem' (Levander, 2002). This description results from close cooperation with the patient – and his family if possible – and forms the basis for the individual treatment plan. In most cases this leads to a better understanding of what is central in the problems experienced.

'Nacka Soteria' is available to all first episode psychotic patients in the area and is run flexibly to adapt to the particular patients' needs during their individual course of recovery, offering different kinds of support, psychotherapy and rehabilitation. Evaluation after five years (Lindgren *et al.*, 2006) demonstrated success in terms of both recovery and patient satisfaction. Unfortunately, economic cutbacks during recent years have greatly reduced the possibilities to offer this kind of inpatient care and continuity, of vital importance for psychotic patients.

The Parachute Project

The Parachute Project is a multicentre study covering 175 first episode patients from the catchment areas of one-fifth of the Swedish population, and was led by Johan Cullberg and Sonja Levander. Repeated assessments have been made over five years, covering a considerable variety of bio-logical and psychosocial factors (Cullberg *et al.*, 2002, 2006.) Its main purpose is to develop psychiatric care at the different centres, making them better adapted to the individual needs of the psychotic patients. Six guidelines or principles led the care and treatment:

1   Easy access without referrals or waiting time for those in need of treatment.
2   Crisis intervention and psychotherapeutic approach aimed at making the experience of psychosis more comprehensible. The formulation involving clarification of the problem(s) together with the patient forms the basis for the treatment plan.
3   Cooperation with the family, especially during the first months.
4   No change of staff or treatment philosophy during the five years of the project. Integration of treatment into different phases of the course of illness.
5   Medication – if needed, in low doses.
6   Crisis homes for 24-hour care in a small home-like setting without strict hospital routines and with time for individual attention and support.

The need for hospitalization and antipsychotic medication has been significantly reduced compared with the treatment-as-usual-group. However, no significant differences were found in comparison with a highly quality social-psychiatric university unit, but the parachute group had significantly lower treatment costs (Cullberg *et al.*, 2006). Similar community units have now started in other parts of Sweden and the need-adapted treatment of psychotic patients is growing. The focus of research seems to shift from individual psychotherapy outcome to the total treatment situation; perhaps focusing less on cure and more on finding ways of facilitating the patient's own potential for recovery.

Cullberg's (2000) book *Psykoser – ett humanistiskt och biologiskt perspektiv* [in English *Psychoses: An Integrated Perspective*, 2006] offers an integrated and influential view on the psychoses and their treatment.

ISPS in Sweden

In 1991 Stockholm was host to the tenth ISPS symposium with the theme 'Facilitating and Obstructing Factors in treating Schizophrenia'. Experts from a broad range of approaches were invited. There were about 700 participants. Barbro Sandin (1997) and Johan Cullberg (2003) have become Life Honorary Members of the ISPS. In 2002 ISPS Sweden was formed in Stockholm.

Closing remarks

The psychodynamic therapists mentioned were strong and gifted pioneers in mental illness and inspired many with the hope of finding a solution to the mystery of schizophrenia (see Cullberg, 1991; Werbart and Cullberg, 1992). However, current results do not differ much from other recent projects in different parts of the world: they are better than treatment as usual, but a number of patients with schizophrenia still do not recover. The methods of the pioneers are rarely applied in general psychiatric work, although they have generated lively discussions in wide circles and their interesting hypotheses have invited further investigation. However, they have largely remained unconfirmed by other groups than those started by the originators. As in other countries, current discussion about the optimal treatment for psychotic patients has two main debates:

- between those advocating biological science (supported by pharmacological establishments) and those advocating psychological treatments – the climate has been harsh with heated discussions
- within those advocating psychological treatment – the debate between psychodynamic and cognitive/behaviouristic lines of thinking.

The most serious hindrance to the use of psychodynamic treatment of psychosis has probably been the demands for evidence-based results which are difficult to apply to psychodynamic research questions. Cognitive frameworks seem better suited to the Cochrane standards (2006).

This polarized way of understanding psychosis has been detrimental. Fortunately today's trend is towards a more comprehensive 'need-adapted treatment' – a concept in accordance with Alanen *et al.* (1991), using traditional methods with close consideration of the patient's family and overall social situation.

The reduction of polarization can indirectly be seen in a growing interest amongst psychoanalysts to supervise both individual therapists and complete teams involved with psychotic patients. Research projects have been started by psychodynamic/psychoanalytic groups working with psychotic patients and during the last decade a number of national and regional courses have started to teach the psychotherapy of psychosis.

NORWAY – WARDS FOR INTENSIVE PSYCHOTHERAPY

Svein Haugsgjerd

Psychoanalysis was introduced in Norway during the 1930s by people who trained in Vienna and Berlin, most notably by the philosopher and first professor of psychology at the University of Oslo, Harald Schjelderup. After World War II relations between the small Norwegian psychoanalytic milieu and the International Psychoanalytic Association were strained for almost two decades because of the supposed influence of Wilhelm Reich who lived in Oslo from 1935 to 1939.

The idea of applying psychoanalytically informed psychotherapy to psychotic patients was probably the result of psychiatrist and psychoanalyst Trygve Braatøy's study period at the Menninger Clinic, Topeka, Kansas from 1949 to 1951, and Braatøy's invitation of Milton Wexler to Oslo for several months in 1952 and their influence on younger psychiatrists and psychologists.

This trend was also championed by Braatøy's successor at the psychiatric department, Ullevål University Hospital in Oslo, Herluf Thomstad, who was strongly influenced by Tom Main and Maxwell Jones, and who organized his psychiatric service as a therapeutic community from 1961, and by Harald Frøshaug at Dikemark Mental Hospital near Oslo, one of a handful of Christian, humanistic leaders in psychiatry who were followers of Adolf Meyer's bio-psycho-social approach, and favourable to psychoanalysis as well as to the existentialism increasingly influential during the 1960s.

Endre Ugelstad and Jarl Jørstad

Among the next generation of psychiatrists interested in the psychotherapy of schizophrenia, the most influential were Endre Ugelstad and Jarl Jørstad. Endre Ugelstad (1920–1996) was one of the three young psychoanalysts who broke with the IPA-affiliated Norwegian Psychoanalytic Society (which he later rejoined) to form the Institute of Psychotherapy, a successively very influential training institution affiliated with the William Alanson White Institute and the International Federation of Psychoanalysis. He pioneered psychotherapy and group psychotherapy with schizophrenic inpatients at Gaustad Mental Hospital in Oslo and attended the ISPS international symposia from the 1950s forming close personal ties with leading international contributors (Benedetti, Müller, Lidz, Alanen, Freeman and Stierlin), including also colleagues influenced by Reich and Dasein concepts, e.g. Medard Boss, Luc Ciompi, as well as the English Anna Freud Psychoanalytic Study group.

Jarl Jørstad (1922–2006) was chief psychiatrist at the psychotherapeutically oriented ward Lien at Dikemark Hospital and influenced many younger colleagues to train in the psychotherapy of schizophrenia, such as Per Vaglum, Eivind Haga and Bjørn Østberg. Later Jørstad became Thomstad's successor at the Ullevål Psychiatric Department. The influential annual Dikemark conferences invited guests such as Benedetti, Szalita, Otto Will, Ruth and Theodore Lidz, Alanen, Stierlin, Wynne, VandenBos, Gunderson, Vaillant and McGlashan.

The 1975 ISPS symposium took place in Oslo with Jørstad and Ugelstad as joint presidents (Jørstad and Ugelstad, 1976). Representatives of groups new to the ISPS were invited: the Milan family therapy group (Selvini Palazzoli), the Italian Democratic Psychiatry movement from Perugia, the new psycho-educational treatment (Carol Anderson), and the neo-Kleinian psychoanalytic group (Donald Meltzer). Meltzer subsequently was a biannual guest for the next 20 years to different Norwegian groups.

Wards for intensive psychotherapy, development of research and training

Three important developments followed from the upsurge of interest in the psychotherapy of schizophrenia created by the 1975 conference:

1   The creation of small wards for intensive psychotherapy with schizophrenic patients.
2   Research into psychosocial treatment of psychotic states.
3   The creation of formal training programmes for this kind of work.

The small wards flowered for a limited period, between the end of the 1970s until around 1990. Lien, in Dikemark Sykehus, led by Jørstad was the first specialized ward started in the late 1960s. Per Vaglum initiated scientific research looking at the differences in treatment response by the ward patients (a mixture of patients with schizophrenia and drug addicts).

Endre Ugelstad pioneered a time-limited intensive psychosocial treatment programme for younger (upper age limit 40 years) chronic schizophrenic patients at Gaustad Hospital. This three-year programme marked the beginning of Ugelstad's research projects (Ugelstad, 1978; Ugelstad and Gilbert, 1994). In 1977 Ugelstad was succeeded by Svein Haugsgjerd, then a training candidate in psychoanalysis. With other colleagues training in psychoanalysis and psychotherapy, like Per Anthi, Anne Kristin Rustad, Marie Hulleberg, Sidsel Gilbert and Sigrid Næss, he created a small intensive psychotherapy treatment unit, Kastanjebakken, at Gaustad Hospital. The treatment philosophy was influenced by Bion's and Meltzer's ideas as well as the work of Swedish and Danish treatment centres, especially those connected with Barbro Sandin. This unit existed for about 15 years (see Haugsgjerd, 1983). After ten years psychoanalyst Sverre Varvin's (1991) outcome study showed that one-third of the patients, all younger chronic schizophrenics, improved considerably. This unit was the first of about a dozen special units in Norway that developed during the 1980s but closed during the 1990s, partly due to:

- results failing to match high expectations
- the influence of research-based treatment ideas like psycho-education
- a greater focus on cost-benefit considerations
- a shift in professional interests to neuropsychiatry and psychopharmacology.

The lasting impact of this era was a generation of young psychotherapists and psychoanalysts interested in object relations theory and neo-Kleinian theories. A non-training association was formed in 1980, the H.W. Major Association (named after the founder of psychiatry in Norway) for The Advancement of the Psychoanalysis of Psychotic Conditions. Many French, British and South American psychoanalysts lectured to this association and it made pioneering contact with psychoanalysts from eastern Europe, the Baltic States and Russia.

Endre Ugelstad, together with Alanen in Finland, Sjöström in Sweden and Rosenbaum in Denmark started the Nordic multicentre study (NIPS) of the development and results from psychotherapeutic treatment with first-admitted psychotic patients (Alanen *et al.*, 1994). Ugelstad was very active in the further development of the ISPS that had begun in the 1950s (see Alanen *et al.*, 2006). In Norway he also founded the Centre for Rehabilitation and Psychosocial Treatment of Psychotic Conditions (SEPREP) which became an important Norwegian-wide organization, providing a multidisciplinary training programme. The current leading persons in SEPREP are Torleif Odland, Sidsel Gilbert, Torleif Ruud, Tore Sørlie and Jan Olav Johannessen. Sørlie and Johannessen with many others have also been central in the Norwegian branch of ISPS.

A significant achievement was the establishment of the large research project, Early Intervention in Psychosis (TIPS), founded in Stavanger by Johannessen, Tor Ketil Larsen and Gerd Ragna Bloch Thorsen, assisted by Vaglum and MacGlashan ((Larsen and Opjordsmoen, 1996; Larsen *et al.*, 1996, 2006; described in detail by Larsen in Chapter 21). Components of the TIPS project are also in Roskilde, Denmark and the Lien Treatment Center, Oslo. The Stavanger group arranges the annual 'Schizophrenia Days' conference, drawing big audiences.

Other important research projects have been Paul Møller's (2000) study of prodromal symptoms in schizophrenia and Håvard Bentsen's (1998) study of psychoeducational family treatment. Interesting contributions are Tom Andersen's (1995) and Jaakko Seikkula's (see the Finnish part) systems oriented network treatment, Oddbjörg Haram's work with voice hearing analysis, and Reidar Kjær's application of Hogarty's personal therapy and cognitive behavioural therapy (CBT) treatment with schizophrenic patients.

Professor Björn Rishovd Rund and collaborators (2005) have made important studies on the cognitive defects in schizophrenia and their significance for treatment.

In 2000, the very successful thirteenth ISPS symposium was arranged in Stavanger, led by Johannessen and Bloch Thorsen.

DENMARK – PROGRESS BY MEANS OF PROJECT WORK

Bent Rosenbaum

Vanggaard's pioneering work

In the 1950s, Thorkil Vanggaard (1910–1998) returned to Denmark from the USA after completing his psychoanalytic training. He wrote (Vanggaard, 1955) on the psychoanalytically oriented psychotherapy of schizophrenia discussing – with references to Knight, Bak, Eissler, Federn, Fromm-Reichmann, Rosen, Séchehaye and Wexler – the following topics:

1 Establishing contact with affectionate and aggressive responses.
2 Interpretations of dynamics and content.
3 The therapist's personal qualifications.
4 The prospect of full cure.

He concluded that although cure was questionable, the possibility of social adjustment of schizophrenic patients by psychoanalytic psychotherapy seemed established beyond doubt.

Vanggaard did not himself treat people with schizophrenia but was interested in the phenomenology of borderline schizophrenia; his preferred label was 'schizophreniform pseudoneurosis' (Vanggaard, 1958, 1978). He clarified its phenomenology, the method of psychotherapy applicable to this category of persons, and the pitfalls which therapists would unavoidably meet. Vanggard underlined that the creation of emotional contact with the patient had to be on a narcissistic basis. Making the patient feel that 'he (the therapist) understands me, so he must be like me' is an important step. This relationship becomes strongly personal and cannot easily be transferred to other therapists. It is through understanding in itself (conveyed by discrete signs) and not by expressing one's understanding through interpretation that the path of narcissistic identification and contact can be opened up for the patient. Interpretation of psychosexual content should be avoided as it meant telling the patient what he or she already knew, or as inducing guilt and shame in the patient.

Other psychiatrists trained in the USA returned to Denmark with an analytic approach. Risskov Hospital in Aarhus, led by Professor Erik Strömgren, established a psychoanalytically informed outpatient psychotherapy centre for long-term schizophrenic patients.

Regional development and inspirations from abroad from 1970 onwards

Copenhagen, Roskilde and Aarhus were the epicentres for upheavals and developments in psychosis psychotherapy.

Individual psychotherapy and group analytic approaches

Optimism developed towards individual psychotherapy with people with psychosis. For ten years from the mid-1970s, English group analysts conducted regular theoretical courses and supervision. Although the teaching was not directed towards psychotic patients, their Kleinian and Winnicottian foundations gave support and inspiration to the psychotherapy of psychotics and in such a small country the influence quickly spread to several psychiatric departments. The emphasis remained on the creation of emotional contact with the patient mainly on a narcissistic basis and on non-interpreting attitude. But these principles were now discussed in the light of concepts like projective identification, containment, holding environment and therapist's reverie. The insights of Murray Cox (Cox and Theilgaard, 1987), inspired by his experiences with psychotic criminals in Broadmoor in England became part of the Danish heritage.

Associations and educational activities

Contact with the psychoanalyst Donald Meltzer by the Norwegian Major-Forening led to supervision courses twice a year and during the following two decades a sister organization, called Psychosis and Psychotherapy was established in Denmark. From 1983 to 1996, seminars occurred three to five times per year and became the most important discussion and supervision forum for psychoses psychotherapy with approximately 100 members, the organization being chaired by Bent Rosenbaum. A great number of cases were supervised in large group settings and newsletters with short papers were signs of intensive activity. Of numerous foreign visitors, Murray Jackson and Meltzer probably had the most influence. Niels Ernst, a psychoanalytically oriented director of a small homelike institution for autistic children in Denmark, contributed in important ways to supervision seminars.

In 1979 Benedetti was invited to Denmark by Lars Thorgaard and conducted an important seminar with lectures and case supervision subsequently published in Danish. Benedetti returned in the 1990s to Aarhus which by now had a longstanding tradition of treating psychotic patients with psychotherapy. The charismatic and persevering psychotherapist Torben Bendix had had a big influence demanding that supervision was conducted with audiotaped psychotherapy sessions, becoming a common tradition in western Denmark. Bendix's book *Give Me a Thought on which I Can Concentrate* (not available in English) gave public evidence that psychotherapy with psychotics was possible.

Contemporaneously, resulting from close links with Norwegian psychosis psychotherapists, Jens Bolvig Hansen arranged seminars on psychosis psychotherapy in the northern part of Jutland, the so-called Brønderslev Psychotherapy workshop (starting in 1984). In Sct. Hans Hospital in Roskilde, chief psychologist Birgitte Brun was the principal organizer of psychotherapy for chronically disturbed patients and for adults with psychosis since childhood (Brun *et al.*, 1993).

The NIPS project in Denmark

In the 1980s two major research projects were established influencing the atmosphere and learning connected with the psychotherapy of psychosis. In 1981, during the ISPS symposium in Heidelberg, a meeting between leading Nordic psychotherapy researchers took place in a cosy 'Wein- und Bierstube', that led to NIPS, the Nordic Investigation of the Psychotherapy of Psychosis. The patients studied were aged between 18 and 45, newly diagnosed with schizophrenia, schizophreniform psychosis or schizoaffective psychosis (*DSM-III*). Under Bent Rosenbaum's leadership,

Roskilde became the Danish participant, and eight therapists[1] met for almost ten years to discuss and evaluate the results (Bechgaard and Winther, 1989; Lauritsen, 1989; Rosenbaum, 1989; Alanen *et al.*, 1994; Rosenbaum and Burgaard, 1993; Rosenbaum *et al.*, 1994). The Danish group had several unique features. First, manualizing the psychotherapy giving strict paradigms for writing up each session, so that their investigation could be more easily summarized and sessions compared. Second, individual sessions and the complete course of therapy could also be investigated through the supervision process (Rosenbaum, 1989; Bechgaard and Winther, 1989).

The Danish National Schizophrenia Project

The organization 'Psychotherapy and Psychosis' and other initiatives led to the idea of a Danish educational platform where psychosis psychotherapy could be taught. The Aarhus Department of Psychotherapy established a two-year educational course, with supervision and theory as part of the programme. Some years later a similar initiative was taken in Copenhagen.

  Those who participated in the 1996 Hilleröd meetings were professionals devoted to psychosis psychotherapy from different hospitals throughout Denmark. The NIPS project had published its results, and it was agreed that a network of many psychiatric units had to be built if there was to be a larger scale investigation of first episode psychotic breakdown and to strengthen the foundation of psychosis psychotherapy. The Danish National Schizophrenia Project (DNS) was established with the following aims:

1   Establishing a network of psychiatric services offering systematic early interventions for first episode patients with schizophrenia.
2   Developing quality research instruments and forms of treatment for these patients and to ensure an effective integrated treatment strategy, involving collaboration with the primary care health services, including the development and integration of many treatment elements, which constitute 'treatment as usual'.
3   To perform scientific research and investigate:
    • where and how the mental health care system meets the persons suffering from a first episode psychosis of the schizophrenic type
    • the characteristics of patients with their first episode of schizophrenic psychosis and whether different treatment methods lead to different outcomes.

  The study was a prospective, longitudinal, multicentre investigation (16 centres, covering 45 per cent of the population in Denmark).[2] It included 562 patients, consecutively referred over two years, with a first episode psychosis of *ICD-10* F-2 type, and treated with:

1   Supportive psychodynamic psychotherapy supplementing 'treatment as usual'.
2   Integrated, assertive, psychosocial and psycho-educational treatment programme. (cf. the Opus study)[3]
3   'Treatment as usual'.

The supportive psychodynamic psychotherapy group comprised of 119 patients participating in a scheduled and manualized supportive individual psychotherapy (one session of 45 minutes per week, for a period of one to three years) and/or group psychotherapy (one session of 60 minutes per week for a period of one to three years).

The integrated treatment group comprised 139 patients participating in a two-year programme consisting of assertive community treatment, psycho-educational multifamily treatment using McFarlane's method in which four to six families (including the patients) meet for one and a half hours fortnightly for one and a half years, social skills training, medication management, care of themselves, coping with symptoms, developing skills in conversation, and in solving problems and resolving conflicts.

At both one- and two-year follow-up the two specific interventions did better than treatment as usual, and generally the integrated treatment showed the best results (Rosenbaum et al., 2005, 2006). But an equally interesting outcome was the enormous activity that the whole project has led to. Twice a year, 30 to 50 therapists and raters meet to improve the validity and reliability of the ratings, and to exchange knowledge and experiences in relation to psychosis psychotherapy. Therapists are guided by a manual for psychosis for individual psychotherapy and group psychotherapy (not yet translated).

A small sample from the DNS became part of the TIPS study (linking New Haven, Stavanger and Roskilde), and a larger part of the sample was from the Danish OPUS study (encompassing Copenhagen and Aarhus). The significance of this linkage is of importance. McFarlane's ideas involving long-term multifamily work became known, and supplemented the existing short-term (eight sessions) educational programme for relatives (Buksti et al., 2006). In particular, the OPUS study documented benefits from assertive approaches to first episode schizophrenic patients, especially in suicide prevention, reduction in hospital admissions and symptoms (Petersen et al., 2005; Thorup et al., 2006).

Milieu therapy

Interest in milieu therapy for psychosis began in the 1970s. Birgitte Brun's project combined psychodynamic milieu therapy with pedagogical/educational methods for adults who had been psychotic since childhood.

Even though hospitalized for many years, some remarkable results led to some patients getting their own apartments and leaving hospital.

Milieu therapy was increasingly promoted by the old state hospitals with special units becoming established for its development and for psychotherapy for long-term psychotic patients. Munke Wulff was taken by the ideas of Maxwell Jones and Yalom and staff and patients worked together on the daily jobs of cleaning, buying and making food for themselves and the visiting guests. The unit had its own economy and strict rules for participation in duties and meetings.

ISPS networking

The DNS network led to the first Danish ISPS initiative. In 1999 a Nordic ISPS workshop had the title 'Subjectivity and the Treatment of Psychosis' with more than 100 participants. Speakers included Josef Parnas, Johan Cullberg, Anne Stefenson, Paul Møller, Klaus Lehtinen and Svein Haugsgjerd. Subjectivity as part of both the psychotic's psychopathology and creative expressions and of therapist functioning featured centrally in the inauguration of the Danish ISPS (March, 2006, Copenhagen (see www.isps.org. homepage).

Bent Rosenbaum, a longstanding member of ISPS, is now on the international board of ISPS and with colleagues will organize the sixteenth ISPS Congress in Copenhagen in 2009.

Acknowledgements

Thanks to Per Knudsen, Anne Køster, Kristian Valbak, Gerda Winther, Birgitte Bechgaard and Lars Thorgaard for expanding my memory with additional historical facts and information.

FINLAND – CONTINUOUS EFFORTS TO A SHARED SPACE OF UNDERSTANDING

Jukka Aaltonen and Yrjö O. Alanen

Beginnings

In Finland, the history of psychotherapy with psychotic patients began during the 1950s. The interest grew rapidly and became quite active during subsequent decades. A key initial factor was the leadership of the psychiatric department of the University of Helsinki (Lapinlahti Hospital) by Professor Martti Kaila between 1948 and 1968. Contrary to most university departments in Scandinavia, he supported psychodynamic endeavours including the study and treatment of schizophrenia. For two decades from

the late 1960s, the chairmen of three Finnish university psychiatric departments (K.A. Achte, Yrjö O. Alanen, Veikko Tähkä) had psychoanalytic
training and the other two (Erik E. Anttinen and Pekka Tienari) were
psychodynamically oriented. All had 'grown up' in the Lapinlahti environment and schizophrenic disorders were amongst their interests. Alanen,
Tähkä and Tienari – internationally well known for his extensive adoption study (see Chapter 1) – replenished their training with fellowships in
the USA.

An even more important factor was the development of psychoanalytic
training communities. In 1951, the Association for the Promotion of
Psychoanalysis in Finland was established by young psychiatrists and
psychologists, organizing clinical meetings, highlighted by seminars led by
visiting foreign psychoanalysts. For schizophrenia psychotherapy, that of
Gaetano Benedetti in 1954 had a remarkable and inspiring influence.

A core group of the founders of this association went for psychoanalytic
training in Stockholm and then returned to Finland. With Veikko Tähkä's
leadership (see his major work, *Mind and Its Treatment*, 1993), the Finnish
psychoanalytic training programme began in Helsinki and by 1967 the
rapidly growing Finnish Psychoanalytic Association was officially established as a member of the International Psychoanalytic Association (IPA).
The training programmes focused on classical psychoanalytic theory
and method and the therapy of psychotic disorders was not included for a
long time.

Outside of the IPA, another psychoanalytic training institute, the
Therapeia Foundation, was established in Helsinki in 1957 by Martti
Siirala, a psychiatrist returned to Finland after training in Switzerland (see
Chapter 9). Two other Swiss-trained psychoanalysts, Kauko Kaila and
Allan Johansson, soon joined him. The Therapeia training programme was
initially rather informal: Siirala, Kaila, Johansson and the psychiatrist and
author Oscar Parland (a senior psychiatrist from Nikkilä Hospital near
Helsinki) led the psychosis seminars together and these were experienced as
very lively and interesting (Pirkko Siltala, personal communication, 2006).
Therapeia gradually organized a more formal psychotherapeutic training
including a six-year psychoanalytic training, and in 1973 was accepted into
the International Federation of Psychoanalytic Societies (IFPS).

Relations between the two organizations were strained but the two
training institutes complemented each other: the IPA training gave a solid
and thorough psychoanalytic education centred on neurotic and narcissistic
disorders while Therapeia trainees also learnt psychoanalytically oriented
psychotherapy with psychotic patients as well as with psychosomatic disorders. However, there was cooperation between some members of these
associations, especially in the fields of psychosis psychotherapy and family
therapy. During the 1970s a group of 20 to 30 psychotherapists from Turku
and Helsinki arranged twice yearly two days of closed workshops, in which

they intensively discussed even the most personal aspects connected with individual psychotherapy of schizophrenic patients.

The Therapeia psychosis therapists

Martti Siirala became internationally known as a psychoanalytically oriented philosopher and social pathologist, while Kauko Kaila and Allan Johansson were explicitly clinically oriented psychoanalysts. Siirala (1922–2008) describes how his experience of treating three schizophrenic patients in Zurich under the supervision of Gaetano Benedetti 'led me, actually forced me to let a most generally human, on that sense "anthropological" articulation of therapy emerge. Its first materialization was a passionate report of encounter within schizophrenia as one basic human situation' (Siirala, 2000). Siirala's therapeutic anthropology was present in his early book on schizophrenia (1961). Quotations from a later lecture may give in a nutshell a picture of some crucial features of Siirala's thinking (2000):

- Psychoanalysis means refinding the core region of therapy in general.
- Psychoanalysis signifies restitution of the lost contact with the message contained in illness.
- The contact implies listening faithfully to the message that opens up gradually only where a readiness to *sharing* that process is found between men. Here, what is most naturally human proves to be an exception. The realization that such a listening process and signs of solidarity meets with the most manifold resistances within the human community, not least from the side of medicine, psychiatry and, alas, often also psychoanalysis.
- What is to be shared are the burdens that have been transferred to the shoulders of an individual patient – once he or she has found the way to such a readiness to share, then this deserves the name 'therapy'. Becoming a patient in this sense means entering one's own suffering as a passage of emerging hope – from a faceless, repeated, painful dead end – to a wandering through something.

A more comprehensive idea of Siirala's thinking can be found in his book, *From Transfer to Transference* (Siirala, 1983).

Kaila's (1920–1987) considerable influence was as an astute clinician and supervisor of individual psychotherapies with psychotic patients and also his leadership of a therapeutic community for psychotic patients in Lapinlahti Hospital.

Johansson (1921–1987) had a natural talent for work with psychotic patients. His early work (before the Swiss training) with the psychotherapy of schizophrenic patients in Kupittaa Hospital, Turku was practised alone and in a mistrustful environment. One of these treatments was published in the German journal *Psyche* (Johansson, 1956). During the 1980s, he published (in Finnish) a book of his experiences, with follow-up information about many of his patients, some of them treated 30 years previously (Johansson, 1985). Besides Benedetti, his teacher, he was influenced by American psychosis therapists, especially Fromm-Reichmann and Searles. Johansson had a significant impact on the development of psychoanalytic psychotherapy of patients with schizophrenia in Finland.

Among the later generation of Therapeia psychosis psychotherapists, especially Pirkko Siltala (see Siltala, 1971), Marja-Leena Heinonen and the family therapists Heimo Salminen and Katriina Kuusi should be mentioned here. Besides Parland, other Therapeia-trained hospital psychiatrists promoted psychodynamic activities in their field (Esko Orma in Helsinki; Mikko Roine in Espoo; Heikki Majava in Imatra).

The Turku group and the beginnings of the need-adapted treatment model

In 1968, Yrjö O. Alanen, an IPA-trained psychoanalyst and researcher of the family environment of schizophrenic patients (Alanen, 1958, 1980), became professor of psychiatry at Turku University and medical director of the Turku Psychiatry Clinic, part of the community psychiatric system of Turku (population 170,000). He led a long-term effort to bring the psychotherapy of psychoses into the academic culture and establish systematic training in both psychodynamic individual and family psychotherapy of schizophrenia. He also led the development of research into schizophrenia and its psychotherapeutically oriented treatment systems as part of public health organizations including the municipal inpatient and outpatient centres. A social dimension close to the patient's everyday setting has been historically characteristic of almost all Finnish psychotherapeutic approaches to schizophrenia.

Alanen started supervision meetings of psychosis psychotherapy with the residents and psychologists and established the Turku Schizophrenia Project with his co-workers (to begin with Viljo Räkköläinen, Simo Salonen, Aira Laine, Ville Lehtinen; later Jukka Aaltonen, Raimo Salokangas, Klaus Lehtinen, Riitta Rasimus, Juhani Laakso, Anneli Larmo, Ritva Järvi, Tapio Aaku, Hilkka Virtanen, Matti Keinänen). The foundation of the project was built on two goals:

1 The great variability of therapeutic needs meant it was necessary to develop a treatment system that was sufficiently comprehensive.
2 The psychotherapeutically oriented treatment should be developed so that it could be applied more generally to public psychiatric health care.

On-the-job training and supervision brought out the capacities of individual members of the multiprofessional staff. Both individual and family work and therapeutic relationships were developed and hospital wards were gradually turned into 'psychotherapeutic communities' (Alanen, 1997). Pharmacotherapy in small or moderate doses was regarded as an auxiliary treatment mode supporting psychosocial therapies. Follow-up cohort studies of all first-admitted schizophrenia patients allowed outcomes to be evaluated.

During the 1970s, the focus was clearly on psychodynamic individual therapy carried out at many levels depending on the training and capacities of the therapists. It was found that psychiatric nurses – with warm personalities and awareness of schizophrenic patients' problems – constituted a therapeutic reserve not often adequately utilized (see the follow-up study by Aaku *et al.*, 1980). The variation of the patients' therapeutic needs was confirmed (Alanen *et al.*, 1986).

Systemic family therapy training established in 1978 led to remarkable innovations in therapeutic practices. Inspired by training, psychiatrists Räkköläinen, K. Lehtinen, Virtanen and the ward nurse Rasimus began in 1981 to arrange joint meetings for all newly admitted psychotic patients with their family members or other persons close to them and the therapeutic team. It was soon noticed that besides the considerable amount of significant information acquired that helped guide therapeutic planning, the meetings themselves had a remarkable therapeutic function, often leading to rapid improvement of the patient's psychotic state. These meetings were soon called 'therapy meetings' and were also carried out in later phases of the therapy. Besides this great increase of family-centred work, individual psychotherapies were continued where indicated and with motivated patients (see the figure in Alanen *et al.*, 2000: 240).

Klaus Lehtinen's (1993a) study clearly revealed the improved prognosis. Compared with the 1976–7 cohort, the percentage of all first-admission patients with *DSM III* diagnoses of schizophrenic, schizophreniform or schizoaffective disorder who at five-year follow-up were without manifest psychotic symptoms and able to work increased within the 1982–3 cohort from 40 per cent to 60 per cent and the average number of hospital days per patient diminished from 272 days to 132 days. With these developments, the main principles of the need-adapted approach were specified as follows (Alanen *et al.*, 1991; Alanen, 1997):

1   Therapeutic activities are planned and carried out flexibly and individually in each case so that they meet the real, changing needs of the patients and the people in their personal networks (usually the family). The family-centred approach is important both in order to alleviate strains on family members caused by the psychosis; and because the outcome of schizophrenic psychoses is especially dependent on family

interrelations and attitudes of family members (and/or other important people) to the patients.

2   Treatment is dominated by a psychotherapeutic attitude and open dialogue.

3   The different therapeutic activities should supplement each other rather than constitute an either/or approach.

4   The treatment should attain and maintain the quality of a continuing process.

5   Follow-up evaluation of both individual patients and the development of treating units and the treatment system as a whole is important.

The most important concrete developmental achievement were the therapy meetings, in which the staff members, patient and his or her family members from the very beginning of the treatment process together try to find psychological and relational understanding of the illness, and together find the most feasible treatment plans. These meetings were crucial for different therapeutic understandings. Here there is something that is at the essence of the Finnish approach in different levels: a culture-based continuous effort towards a shared understanding, first between therapists, and now between various staff members, patient and family members together. Aaltonen and Räkköläinen (1994) have described this (in a hospital ward) as 'The shared image guiding the treatment process'.

Alanen's major work, *Schizophrenia – Its Origins and Need-Adapted Treatment* (1997), has been translated into four other European languages. Räkköläinen had a very important part in developing the approach. He also studied psychodynamic factors influencing the onset of psychosis and protective factors influencing its outcome (Räkköläinen 1977; Räkköläinen *et al.*, 1979). K. Lehtinen (1993b) widened his exploration to a general examination of the importance of family therapy in schizophrenia and Salokangas (1978; Salokangas *et al.*, 1991) extended the follow-up studies from Turku cohorts to the National Schizophrenia Project. Aaltonen (1982) began his studies examining the basis for a family-centred treatment process in psychiatric outpatient care. Salonen (1979, 1989, 2002) followed a more classic psychoanalytic line studying the inner psychodynamics of schizophrenic patients and the primary identification process. Larmo (1992) studied the impact of parental psychosis on family and children, based on psychoanalytic object relation theories.

The National Schizophrenia Project 1981–1987

Multiprofessional psychosis teams

A national programme for developing the study, treatment, and rehabilitation of schizophrenic patients was carried out in Finland between 1981 and 1987 (State Medical Board in Finland, 1988; Alanen *et al.*, 1990; Tuori *et al.*, 1998). Alanen chaired the leading task force group. There were two major subprojects. The first was the New Schizophrenic Patients (NSP) Project, led by the Turku team, in which the need-adapted approach described above was applied in several other community psychiatric contexts. The establishment of multiprofessional acute psychosis teams was the most important tool to put the need-adapted approach into effect. The teams consist of psychiatrist, psychologist and a social worker or nurses and were created in more than half of all mental health districts in Finland during the 1980s and 1990s (Tuori *et al.*, 1998).

The second subproject, led by Professor Erik E. Anttinen and psychologist Markku Ojanen, focused on developing rehabilitation of long-term schizophrenic patients outside of hospitals. Anttinen and co-workers, in particular nurse Leena Salmijärvi, had developed during 1970s the Sopimusvuori therapeutic communities for psychiatric long-term hospital patients in the Tampere region (Anttinen, 1983). Activities were based on a humanistic and psychodynamic spirit, with a special appreciation of peer relationships. This approach had considerable influence in Finland and also in Sweden.

Psychotherapy training programmes

The fourth ISPS Symposium in Turku in 1971 (Rubinstein and Alanen, 1972; see Alanen *et al.*, 2006), Otto Will's psychotherapy seminar in 1971 and Helm Stierlin's family therapy seminar in 1972 were important learning experiences for Finnish psychosis psychotherapists. Otto Will's deep commitment to the psychotic patients' internal and external world and Stierlin's innovative way of integrating psychoanalytic concepts with his transactional modes greatly deepened our understanding of schizophrenic patients and their treatment.

However, the need for systematic training programmes became apparent. A three-year multiprofessional family therapy training programme began in 1978 in Helsinki and Turku, established by the Finnish Association for Mental Health, with a one-year training of future trainers through seminars led by well-known family therapists invited to Finland (Stierlin and Michael Wirsching from Heidelberg, Arnon Bentovim and Alan Cooklin from London); to be continued later with other seminar leaders from both sides of the Atlantic. The training was systemic (combined with psychodynamic understanding) and training soon spread to different parts of Finland with families of schizophrenic patients remaining one of the main focuses. By 1988, an advanced multiprofessional six-year training programme was established. The psychoanalyst and family therapist Aaltonen became professor in family therapy in Jyväskylä University where he promoted psychotherapy training programmes in both family therapy and psychodynamic individual therapy, focusing on psychotic disorders. Together with many other experienced trainers he carried out extensive national supervision activities with psychosis teams.

In 1993, Aaltonen, Räkköläinen and Alanen established an advanced special level training in individual psychotherapy of severe (psychotic or borderline level) mental disorders (see Aaltonen *et al.*, 2002), leading to a special association for this purpose. Other trainers have been psycho-analysts Gustav Schulman (representing the Kleinian orientation) and Matti Keinänen (see his innovative book *Psychosemiosis as a Key to Body–Mind Continuum*, 2005).

The API project

The National Research and Development Centre for Welfare and Health (STAKES) organized a multicentre research and development project – Acute Psychosis Integrated Treatment (API) – carried out between 1992 and 1998 (Lehtinen *et al.*, 1996, 2000; Aaltonen *et al.*, 2000) to test the feasibility of the need-adapted approach. Another objective was to evaluate the role of neuroleptic drug treatment when psychosocial and psychother-apeutic measures are applied maximally in the treatment of first episode psychoses. The following elements were included in the initial treatment of all patients:

1   The patients were regularly included in all situations involving treat-ment planning as were their families and other significant others.
2   With all patients, the multidisciplinary case specific psychosis team started within a few days of referral an intensive, family and network centred examination of the situation and provided continuity of therapy as long as it was needed. A staff member was assigned to each patient who was responsible for individual interviews, crisis therapy and sometimes a more intensive and longer individual psychotherapy.
3   An important element in the treatment process were therapy meetings which were initially held several times a week, but later at longer intervals. The patient and, usually, his family participated regularly and others significant for the patient took part when indicated.

Two new psychotherapeutic principles of the need-adapted approach were defined on the basis of these findings (Aaltonen *et al.*, 2000):

•   An emphasis on horizontal expertise that seeks consciously to cross professional boundaries and barriers between different sectors of expertise.

- Deritualization of treatment and the use of 'open dialogue'. The expertise of all staff members is best utilized in a setting in which rituals are minimalized and patients have considerable freedom of choice over treatment; often the treatment process is carried out in the patient's home.

In family therapy we aim to break the multigenerational chain of disorders and to help the family to begin a chain of better understanding. Family therapy is important both in improving prognosis as an independent psychotherapeutic method and when integrated into other modes of psychotherapy improved the efficiency of those treatments (V. Lehtinen *et al.*, 2000). The experiences with neuroleptic-free approach are examined in Chapter 20.

The API project resulted in over 40 recommendations as to how to create the need-adapted approach and keep it psychotherapeutically alive (Aaltonen *et al.*, 2000). One was that staff should have ongoing training in different psychotherapeutic methods arising from the needs of clinical work. The capacity for a shared understanding must be guaranteed from one staff generation to another – just as the multigenerational chain of mutual understanding in the families.

Other projects

The Western Lapland Project (WLP 1)[4]

The most innovative of the local projects took place in a catchment area of 75,000 inhabitants. WLP was established in 1987 in cooperation with the University of Jyväskylä (Professor Aaltonen) and the local leaders, including medical director Jyrki Keränen and the psychologist Jaakko Seikkula. A modification of the framework of the need-adapted approach was developed and named the Open-Dialogue Approach (ODA) (Seikkula *et al.*, 1995, 2003; Aaltonen *et al.*, 1997; see Chapter 17).

The aim of the WLP was to develop a comprehensive family and network centred psychiatric treatment model on the boundary between the outpatient and inpatient treatment systems:

- giving all local multiprofessional psychiatric staff members in outpatient and inpatient care a three-year, on-the-job training in systemic and network oriented family therapy – that is, to saturate municipal psychiatric system of treatment with family therapeutic skills
- subsequently starting a two-year psychodynamically oriented individual therapy on-the-job training

- establishing mobile, multidisciplinary acute psychosis teams and case-specific teams (including both outpatient and inpatient staff) for both psychotic and other severe psychiatric crises in all psychiatric treatment centres.

The main results of the WLP project can be summarized as follows:

- Altogether 70 to 80 per cent of all the inpatient and outpatient staff (psychiatrists, psychologists, psychiatric nurses and mental health nurses) have received a specialist level training in some form of psychotherapy.
- The number of new long-term schizophrenic hospital patients soon fell to zero as the only psychiatric catchment area in Finland (Tuori, 1994).
- A radical decline in the indications for hospital treatment (Keränen, 1992).
- Decline in involuntary hospital treatment (Seikkula, 1991).
- A shift of schizophrenia disorders towards the less severe end.
- The possibilities for psychotherapeutic treatments have increased.

Other projects

Mauno Saari (2002) studied the outcome of psychiatric care in another small psychiatric catchment area in Kainuu before and after the establishment of acute psychosis teams (1992–1996) in the treatment of severe acute mental disorders. The work of the psychosis team was more profitable and economical than conventional psychiatric treatment. A new subproject largely following the lines of the WLP (above) has been started.

Amongst the research done in the psychology department of Jyväskylä University, those into the narrative approach in family therapy of acute psychoses of Holma and Aaltonen (1995, 1997, 1998; Holma 1999) are of special interest. Family therapeutic research and activities will continue under the leadership of Professor Jaakko Seikkula, Aaltonen's workmate and successor.

In Finland, cognitive-behavioural orientation has been little utilized in psychotic disorders, except for some projects connected with the rehabilitation of long-term hospitalized patients. However, K. Lehtinen, now in Tampere, has included behavioural elements in his new project dealing with first-admitted patients. Eeva Iso-Koivisto (2004) studied the subjective experience of first psychotic episodes. Based on Kleinian terminology, she concluded that patients and families with attitudes predominated by a paranoid-schizoid position, i.e. a tendency to attribute causes of their disturbances to external factors, benefit from a psycho-educational approach; whereas psychodynamic therapy suits best those with the Kleinian depressive position. However, internal exploration corresponding to the depressive position often only becomes possible when an empathic therapeutic relationship has been established.

Closing remarks

In Finland the history of psychotherapies with psychotic patients has, from its beginning, been characterized by continuous efforts to share understanding of different aspects and dimensions of psychosis involving psychotherapists from different psychoanalytic traditions, family therapists and recently all staff members in psychiatric catchment areas.

From the 1970s the crucial central influence on development has been the need-adapted approach and its various applications in the public mental health systems. These developments in the psychotherapeutic culture are not imported wholesale to the area; they are created from its own resources – thereby being need adapted from the very beginning. This overall approach has led to wider positive developments, including the rise of social capital and a more positive attitude towards psychiatric care in the local population with the role of patients and their families in this development changing from objects to subjects in defining their needs.

The use of multiprofessional teams has proved efficient aid in all kinds of acute psychiatric crises in centres in which different psychotherapeutic practices have a deep-seated role as part of their treatment culture. A psychotherapeutic treatment system for the most severe disorders can thus have a positive influence on treatment of milder psychiatric disorders as well as preventive activities.

There have also been setbacks. The National Schizophrenia Project succeeded well in its targets over the ten years from 1982 to 1992; the number of new and old long-term schizophrenic patients in Finnish hospitals declined by 60 per cent and the number of staff in outpatient care rose from 2.7 to 5.1 per 10,000 inhabitants, leading to a considerable increase of activity (Tuori et al., 1998). However, at that point a difficult economic depression in Finland led to a disastrous outcome: the reduction of hospital beds continued, but the development of outpatient care stopped and even declined. Psychotherapeutically trained staff found that maintaining their work to correspond to their abilities is difficult in rushed and stressed therapeutic environments. This is especially a problem in bigger towns. In smaller and more sparsely populated catchment areas the situation has been easier to control.

Another problem is the decrease of psychotherapeutically trained teachers in psychiatric university departments. Retrograde steps may also occur in the leadership of the community-based districts: psychotherapeutically trained staff have had to defend well-developed ways of doing therapy due to new leaders that lack understanding of their work. There are now positive signs resulting from increasing integration of international psychiatric

research. The best guarantee for further development may be the popularity
and increase of multiprofessional psychotherapy training programmes
focusing on patients with schizophrenia and those close to them.

DEVELOPMENT IN NORTHERN EUROPE – A SUMMARY

Jukka Aaltonen, Yrjö O. Alanen, Johan Cullberg,
Svein Haugsgjerd, Sonja Levander and Bent Rosenbaum

Despite variations of emphasis, the development of schizophrenia psychotherapy in Scandinavian countries has followed the same basic lines: the
interest in psychotherapeutic treatment of schizophrenic patients increased
after World War II, and knowledge was acquired from other countries with
more advanced traditions – USA, Great Britain, Switzerland – through
study trips combined with long training periods, and by domestic seminars
led by foreign experts. The predominant approach was a psychoanalytic,
psychotherapeutic orientation aiming at understanding the patients' problems. This has remained central, though other orientations also exist.

Initially, individual psychotherapeutic treatments had a dominant position. Subsequently the areas of family, group and milieu therapies developed with group therapy being particularly practised in Denmark, systemic-
psychodynamic family therapy in Finland, hospital wards suitable for
intensive psychotherapy being most characteristic of Norway, and treatment homes outside of hospital being characteristic of Sweden. There have
been disagreements about schizophrenia and its treatment between biologically and psychotherapeutically oriented researchers and therapists,
most so in Sweden. These disputes have mainly settled with low dose
neuroleptic treatment being usual practice; and in Sweden crisis homes are
now even officially recommended as a treatment milieu of choice for young
people with psychosis.

The greatest factor in common that has influenced change has been the
development of psychotherapeutic approaches within the framework of
community psychiatry, corresponding to the growing demands of the
Scandinavian welfare society to secure the equality of citizens in their social
needs and medical care. With regard to psychosis psychotherapy, the
project work has had a central influence. Psychotherapeutically oriented
projects have been established in all Nordic countries, some having even
included the whole country – such as the national projects in Finland and
Denmark – or involved centres in more than one country. Besides their
formal results, these projects have had a powerful stimulating effect on the
multiprofessional mental health staff, due both to innovatory activities and
to a feeling of appreciation in work that is often not acknowledged.

Enlarging the therapeutic capacities of especially nursing staff has been a central goal and multiprofessional psychotherapy training programmes have been developed, especially in Finland.

The main focus has been the development of the treatment of first episode psychosis patients, based on the great importance of early treatment for the outcome of the patients. Recently, multicountry studies directed at improving the early detection of psychoses have been established, especially in the Stavanger centre in Norway (see Chapter 21).

Whole catchment area projects highlight the differences in the therapeutic needs of different patients: a particular treatment may not best suit the needs of every patient and this experience has led to the need-adapted approach, developed first in Finland. The importance of an initial – and also continuing – family and environment centred intervention for the outcome was strengthened by the findings of several Finnish projects and is often also the precondition for a successful individual psychotherapy. The Swedish Parachute Project followed the same lines, with a special attention to treatment homes becoming established outside of hospitals, as pioneered in northern Europe by Soteria Nacka near Stockholm.

We began our summary by referring to the influences on the Scandinavian psychotherapists who, some 50 years ago, searched for knowledge and skills in other countries and were then able to establish their work. Is it now the turn of Northern European experiences to stimulate development in the global framework?

Notes

1 Bent Rosenbaum (project leader), Birgitte Bechgaard, Steen Borberg, Lars Burgaard, Anne Lindhardt, Laurits Lauritsen, Haakon Lærum, Jørgen Nystrup, Gerda Winther.
2 The research steering group consisted of: Bent Rosenbaum (project leader), Lars Burgaard (later substituted by Anne Køster), Susanne Harder, Per Knudsen, Matilde Lajer, Anne Lindhardt, Kristian Valbak, Gerda Winther.
3 **The Opus Study**. A small sample from the DNS became part of the TIPS study (linking New Haven, Stavanger and Roskilde) and a larger part of the sample was from the Danish OPUS study (encompassing Copenhagen and Aarhus). The OPUS study (the integrated treatment group above) comprised 139 patients participating in a two-year programme consisting of assertive community treatment, psycho-educational multi-family treatment using McFarlane's (2000) method (in which four to six families, including the patients, meet for one and a half hours fortnightly for one and a half years), social skills training, medication management, care of themselves, coping with symptoms, developing skills in conversation and solving problems and resolving conflicts. In particular, and separate from the DNS project, the OPUS study documented benefits from assertive approaches to first-episode schizophrenic patients especially in suicide prevention, reduction in hospital admissions and symptoms (Peterson et al., 2005). The OPUS concept for patients with a first episode psychosis has now been

implemented in all our regions of Denmark, and has become the standard treatment for that group.

4 It is not Arctic Lapland but an area around the northern end of the Gulf of Bothnia, including two small towns and the lower course of the Tornio river, forming the south western part of the province of Lapland.

References

Aaku, T., Rasimus, R. and Alanen, Y.O. (1980). Nursing staff as individual therapists in the psychotherapeutic community. In *Yearbook Psychiatria Fennica*. Helsinki: Foundation for Psychiatric Research in Finland, pp. 9–31.

Aaltonen, J. (1982). *Basis for Family-centred Treatment Process in Psychiatric Outpatient Care* [in Finnish, with English summary]. Turku: Annales Universitatis Turkuensis.

Aaltonen, J. and Räkköläinen, V. (1994). The shared image guiding the treatment process. A precondition for integration of the treatment of schizophrenia. *British Journal of Psychiatry* 164 (Suppl. 23): 97–102.

Aaltonen, J., Seikkula, J., Alakare, B. and Keränen, J. (1997). Western Lapland Project: a comprehensive family- and network-centred community-psychiatric project. Paper presented at the Twelfth International Symposium for the Psychotherapy of Schizophrenia, London.

Aaltonen, J., Koffert, T., Ahonen, J. and Lehtinen, V. (2000). *Skitsofrenian hoito on ryhmätyötä* [The treatment of schizophrenia is team work, in Finnish with English summary]. Helsinki: Stakes.

Aaltonen, J., Keinänen, M., Räkköläinen, V. and Alanen, Y. (2002). An advanced specialist-level training programme in psychodynamic individual psychotherapy of psychotic and borderline patients: The Finnish approach. *European Journal of Psychotherapy, Counselling and Health* 5: 13–30.

Alanen, Y.O. (1958). The mothers of schizophrenic patients. *Acta Psychiatrica et Neurologica Scandinavica* 33 (Suppl. 124).

Alanen, Y.O. (1980). In search of the interactional origin of schizophrenia. The Stanley R. Dean Award Lecture. In C.K. Hofling and J.M. Lewis (eds) *The Family, Evaluation and Treatment*. New York: Brunner/Mazel, pp. 285–313.

Alanen, Y.O. (1997). *Schizophrenia – Its Origins and Need-Adapted Treatment*. London: Karnac.

Alanen, Y.O., Räkköläinen, V., Laakso, J., Rasimus, R. and Kaljonen, A. (1986). *Towards Need-specific Treatment of Schizophrenic Psychoses*. Heidelberg: Springer-Verlag.

Alanen, Y.O., Anttinen, E.E., Kokkola, A., Lehtinen, V., Ojanen, M., Pylkkänen, K. and Räkköläinen, V. (1990). Treatment and rehabilitation of schizophrenic psychoses. The Finnish treatment model. *Nordic Journal of Psychiatry* 44.

Alanen, Y.O., Lehtinen, K., Räkköläinen, V. and Aaltonen, J. (1991). Need-adapted treatment of new schizophrenic patients: experiences and results of the Turku project. *Acta Psychiatrica Scandinavica* 83: 363–372.

Alanen, Y.O., Ugelstad, E., Armelius, B.-Å., Lehtinen, K., Rosenbaum, B. and Sjöström, R. (1994). *Early Treatment for Schizophrenic Patients. Scandinavian Psychotherapeutic Appproaches*. Oslo: Scandinavian University Press.

Alanen, Y.O., Lehtinen, V., Lehtinen, K., Aaltonen, J. and Räkköläinen, V. (2000).

The Finnish integrated model for early treatment of schizophrenia and related psychoses. In B. Martindale, A. Bateman, M. Crowe and F. Margison (eds) *Psychosis: Psychological Approaches and their Effectiveness*. Glasgow: Gaskell (ISPS), pp. 235–265.

Alanen, Y.O., Silver, A.-L.S. and González de Chávez, M. (2006). *Fifty Years of Humanistic Treatment of Psychoses*. Madrid: Fundácion para la Investigación y Tratamiento de la Esquizofrenia y otras Psycosis.

Andersen, T. (1995). Reflecting processes. Acts of informing and forming. In S. Friedman (ed.) *The Reflective Team in Action. Collaborative Practice in Family Therapy*. New York: Guilford Press, pp. 11–35.

Anttinen, E.E. (1983). Can the vicious circle of chronicity and institutionalization be broken? In *Yearbook Psychiatria Fennica*. Helsinki: Foundation for Psychiatric Research in Finland, pp. 21–31.

Bechgaard, B. and Winther, G. (1989). *Group supervision*: The group process as research instrument. *Nordic Journal of Psychiatry* 43, 1: 69–74.

Bentsen, H. (1998). Predictors of expressed emotion in relatives of patients with schizophrenia and related psychoses. Doctoral thesis, Oslo.

Bjerre, P. (1911). Zur Radikalbehandlung der chronischen Paranoia. In *Jahrbuch fuer Psychoanalytische Forschungen*, Vol. 3. Liepzig: Deuticke.

Bjerre, P. (1933–1944). *Samlade Psykoterapeutiska Skrifter* [Collected Psychotherapeutic Papers]. Stockholm: Bonniers.

Brun, B., Pedersen, E.W. and Runberg, M. (1993). *Symbols of the Soul: Therapy and Guidance through Fairy Tales*. London: Jessica Kingsley Publishers.

Cochrane Standards (2006). Updated software. www.cochrane.org. 10 August 2006.

Cox, M. and Theilgaard, A. (1987). *Mutative Metaphors in Psychotherapy*. London: Tavistock.

Cullberg, J. (1991). Recovered versus non-recovered schizophrenic patients among those who have had intensive psychotherapy. *Acta Psychiatrica Scandinavica* 84: 242–245.

Cullberg, J. (2000). *Psykosr – ett humanistiskt och biologiskt perspektiv*. Stockholm: Natur och Kultur. [English edn *Psychoses – An Integrated Perspective*. London and New York: Routledge, 2006.]

Cullberg, J. and Levander, S. (1991). Fully recovered schizophrenic patients who received intensive psychotherapy. A Swedish case-fining study. *Nordic Journal of Psychiatry* 45: 253–262.

Cullberg, J., Levander, S., Holmqvist, R., Mattsson, M. and Wieselgren, I.-M. (2002). One-year outcome in first episode psychotic patients in the Swedish Parachute project. *Acta Psychiatrica Scandinavica* 106: 276–285.

Cullberg, J., Mattsson, M., Levander, S., Holmqvist, R., Tomsmark, L., Elingfors, C. *et al.* (2006). Treatment costs and clinical outcome for first episode schizophrenic patients – a three-year follow-up of the Swedish 'Parachute project' and two comparison groups. *Acta Psychiatrica Scandinavica* 114: 274–281.

Haugsgjerd, S. (1983). *Psykoterapi og miljoterapi ved psykoser I–II*. Oslo: Pax.

Helgason, T. (1964). *Epidemiology of Mental Disorders in Iceland*. Copenhagen: Munksgaard.

Herner, T. (1982). *The Challenge of Schizophrenia*. Stockholm: Almqvist & Wiksell.

Holma, J. (1999). The search for a narrative – investigating acute psychosis and the need-adapted treatment model from the narrative viewpoint. *Jyväskylä Studies in Education, Psychology and Social Research* 150.

Holma, J. and Aaltonen, J. (1995). The self-narrative and acute psychosis. *Contemporary Family Therapy* 17: 307–316.

Holma, J. and Aaltonen, J. (1997). The sense of agency and acute psychosis. *Contemporary Family Therapy* 19: 463–477.

Holma, J. and Aaltonen, J. (1998). Narrative understanding in acute psychosis. *Contemporary Family Therapy* 20: 253–263.

Iso-Koivisto, E. (2004). *'Pois sieltä, ylös.takaisin'* – *ensimmäinen psykoosi kokemuksena.* ['Away from there, upwards, back again' – meaning given to the experience of first psychotic episode. In Finnish with English summary.] Turku: Annales Universitatis Turkuensis.

Johansson, A. (1956). Psychotherapeutische Behandlung eines Falles von Schizophrenie. *Psyche* 10: 568–587.

Johansson, A. (1985). *Skitsofrenian analyyttisen psykoterapian ongelma.* [The problem of the psychoanalytical psychotherapy of schizophrenia, in Finnish.] Turku: Annales Universitatis Turkuensis.

Jørstad, J. and Ugelstad, E. (eds) (1976). *Schizophrenia 1975. Psychotherapy, Family Studies, Research.* Oslo: Universitetsforlaget.

Keinänen, M. (2005). *Psychosemiosis as a Key to Body–Mind Continuum. The Reinforcement of Symbolization-Reflectiveness in Psychotherapy.* New York: Nova Science.

Keränen, J. (1992). *The choice between outpatient and inpatient treatment in a family-centred psychiatric system.* [In Finnish, with English summary.] *Jyväskylä Studies in Education, Psychology and Social Research* 80: 227–232.

Larmo, A. (1992). *The parent's psychosis: impact on family and children.* Turku: Annales Universitatis Turkuensis.

Larsen, T.K. and Opjordsmoen, B.R. (1996). Early identification and treatment of schizophrenia: conceptual and ethical considerations. *Psychiatry* 59: 371–380.

Larsen, T.K., McGlashan, T.H. and Moe, L.C. (1996). First episode schizophrenia: I. Early course parameters. *Schizophrenia Bulletin* 22: 241–256.

Larsen, T.K., Melle, I., Auestad, B. *et al.* (2006). Early detection of first-episode psychosis: the effect on one-year outcome. *Schizophrenia Bulletin* 32: 758–764.

Lauritsen, L. (1989). Conditions for psychotherapy with schizophrenics. *Nordic Journal of Psychiatry* 43: 57–67.

Lehtinen, K. (1993a). Need-adapted treatment of schizophrenia: a five-year follow-up study from the Turku project. *Acta Psychiatrica Scandinavica* 87: 96–101.

Lehtinen, K. (1993b). *Family therapy and schizophrenia in public mental health.* Turku: Annales Universitatis Turkuensis.

Lehtinen, V., Aaltonen, J., Koffert, T., Räkköläinen, V., Syvälahti, E. and Vuorio, K. (1996). Integrated treatment model for first-contact patients with a schizophrenia-type psychosis. The Finnish API project. *Nordic Journal of Psychiatry* 50: 281–287.

Lehtinen, V., Aaltonen, J., Koffert, T., Räkköläinen, V. and Syvälahti, E. (2000). Two-year outcome in first-episode psychosis treated according to an integrated model. Is immediate neuroleptisation always needed? *European Psychiatry* 15: 312–320.

Levander, S. (2002). *Problemformuleringsarbete – ett identitets- och jagstärkande arbetssätt med förstagångspsykotiska patienter. [Problem formulation work – an identity – and ego strengthening work with first time psychotic patients.]* Stockholm: Samhällsmedicin.

Levander, S. and Cullberg, J. (1994). Psychotherapy in retrospect. Accounts of experiences in psychotherapy obtained from five former schizophrenic patients. *Nordic Journal of Psychiatry* 48: 263–269.

Lindgren, I., Falk Hogstedt, M. and Cullberg, J. (2006). Outpatient vs. comprehensive first-episode services, a five-year follow-up of Soteria Nacka. *Nordic Journal of Psychiatry* 60: 405–409.

McFarlane, W.R. (2000). Psychoeducational multi-family groups: adaptation and outcomes. In B. Martindale, A. Bateman, M. Crowe and F. Margison (eds) *Psychosis: Psychological Approaches and their Effectiveness*. Glasgow: Gaskell (ISPS), pp. 68–95.

Møller, P. and Husby, R. (2000). The initial prodrome in schizophrenia: searching for the naturalistic core dimensions experience and behaviour. *Schizophrenia Bulletin* 26: 217–232.

Perris, C. (1989). *Cognitive Therapy with Schizophrenic Patients*. New York: Guilford.

Perris, C. and McGorry, P. (eds) (1998). *Cognitive Psychotherapy of Psychotic and Personality Disorders: Handbook of Theory and Practice*. New York: Wiley.

Petersen, L., Nordentoft, M., Jeppesen, P., Öhlenschläger, J., Thorup, A., Christensen, T.Ö. et al. (2005). Improving one-year outcome in first-episode psychosis: OPUS trial. *British Journal of Psychiatry* 87 (Suppl. 48): 98–103.

Räkköläinen, V. (1977). *Onset of Psychosis: A Clinical Study of 68 Cases*. Turku: Annales Universitatis Turkuensis.

Räkköläinen, V., Salokangas, R. and Lehtinen, P. (1979). Protective constructions in the course of psychosis. In C. Müller (ed.) *Psychotherapy of Schizophrenia*. Amsterdam: Excerpta Medica, pp. 233–243.

Rosenbaum, B. (1989). Individual psychotherapy with psychotic patients: the Danish NIPS design. *Nordic Journal of Psychiatry* 43: 75–78.

Rosenbaum, B. and Burgaard, L. (1993). Psychotherapy of schizophrenia: aspects of the therapist's position. In G. Benedetti and P.M. Furlan (eds) *The Psychotherapy of Schizophrenia*. Frankfurt am Main: Springer Verlag, pp. 125–129.

Rosenbaum, B., Bechgaard, B., Borberg, S. et al. (1994). The Danish project. In Y. Alanen, E. Ugelstad, B. Armelius, K. Lehtinen, B. Rosenbaum and R. Sjöström (eds) *Early Treatment for Schizophrenic Patients*. Oslo: Scandinavian University Press, pp. 33–44.

Rosenbaum, B., Valbak, K., Harder, S. et al. (2005). The Danish National Schizophrenia Project: prospective, comparative, longitudinal treatment study of first-episode psychosis. *British Journal of Psychiatry* 186: 394–399.

Rosenbaum, B., Valbak, K., Harder, S. et al. (2006). Treatment of patients with first episode psychosis: two-year outcome data from the Danish National Schizophrenia Project. *World Psychiatry* 5: 100–103.

Rubinstein, C. and Alanen, Y.O. (eds) (1972). *Psychotherapy of Schizophrenia*. Amsterdam: Excerpta Medica.

Rund, B.R., Melle, I., Friis, S., Larsen, T.K., Midbøe, L.J., Opjord-Smoen, S. et al. (2005). Neurocognitive dysfunction in first-episode psychosis: correlates with symptoms, premorbid functioning and duration of untreated psychosis. *American Journal of Psychiatry* 161: 466–472.

Saari, M. (2002). *Psychosis Team in Treatment of Severe Mental Disorders in Kainuu in 1992–1996*. [In Finnish with English summary.] Oulu: Acta Universitatis Ouluensis.

Salokangas, K.R.K. (1978). *Psychosocial Prognosis in Schizophrenia*. Turku: Annales Universitatis Turkuensis.

Salokangas, R.K.R., Stengård, E., Räkköläinen, V. and Alanen, Y.O. (1991). *Uusien skitsofreniapotilaiden hoito ja ennuste. Viiden vuoden seuranta. USP-projekti V.* [Treatment and Prognosis of New Schizophrenic Patients: A Five-year Follow-up. NSP Project V. In Finnish with English summary.] Helsinki: Foundation for Psychiatric Research in Finland.

Salonen, S. (1979). On the metapsychology of schizophrenia. *International Journal of Psycho-Analysis* 60: 73–81. Also in: S. Salonen *Psychotherapeutic Studies in Schizophrenia*. Turku: Annales Universitatis Turkuensis.

Salonen, S. (1989). The restitution of primary identification in psychoanalysis. *Scandinavian Psychoanalytic Review* 12: 102–115.

Salonen, S. (2002). Understanding psychotic disorder. *Scandinavian Psychoanalytic Review* 25: 143–146.

Sandin, B. (1986). *Den zebrarandiga pudelkärnan*. Stockholm: Rabén & Sjögren.

Seikkula, J. (1991). The family-hospital boundary system in the social network [In Finnish, with English summary.] *Jyväskylä Studies in Education, Psychology and Social Research* 80.

Seikkula, J., Aaltonen, J., Alakare, B., Keränen, J. and Sutela, M. (1995). Treating psychosis by means of open dialogue. In S. Friedman (ed.) *The Reflective Team in Action*. New York: Guilford Press, pp. 62–80.

Seikkula, J., Alakare, B., Aaltonen, J., Holma, J., Rasinkangas, A. and Lehtinen, V. (2003). Open dialogue approach: treatment principles and preliminary results of a two-year follow-up on first episode schizophrenia. *Ethical Human Sciences et Services* 5: 163–182.

Siirala, M. (1961). *Die Schizophrenie des Einzelnen und der Allgemainheit*. Göttingen: Vanderhoeck und Ruprecht.

Siirala, M. (1983). *From Transfer to Transference – Recovery from the Effects of Disordered Trans-generational Interactions through Therapeutic Relationships*. Helsinki: Therapeia Foundation.

Siirala, M. (2000). Psychoanalysis will succeed by failing. Waiting for Godot? Paper presented at the Ninth Forum, IFPS, Florence.

Siltala, P. (1971). Psychotherapy of a chronic schizophrenic patient. Case history. In D. Rubinstein and Y.O. Alanen (eds) *Psychotherapy of Schizophrenia, Proceedings of the IVth International Symposium*. Amsterdam: Excerpta Medica, pp. 107–121.

Sjöström, R. (1985). Effects of psychotherapy in schizophrenia. *Acta Psychiatrica Scandinavica* 71: 513–522.

Sjöström, R. (1990). Psykoterapi vid schizofreni – en prospektiv studie. *Svenska Läkartidningen* 87: 3279–3282.

State Medical Board in Finland (1988). *The Schizophrenia Project 1981–87. Final Report of the National Programme for the Study, Treatment and Rehabilitation of*

Schizophrenic Patients in Finland. [In Finnish with English summary.] Helsinki: Valtion Painatuskeskus.

Tähkä, V. (1993). *Mind and Its Treatment: Psychoanalytic Approach.* New York: International Universities Press.

Thorup, A., Petersen, L., Jeppesen, P., Öhlenschläger, J., Christensen, T., Krarup, G. *et al.* (2006). Integrated treatment ameliorates negative symptoms in first-episode psychosis – results from the Danish OPUS-trial. *Schizophrenia Research* 78: 95–105.

Tuori, T. (1994). *The Treatment of Schizophrenia is Profitable. Report of Ten-year Follow-up of the Finnish National Schizophrenia Project.* [In Finnish with English summary.] Helsinki: Stakes.

Tuori, T., Lehtinen, V., Hakkarainen, A., Jääskeläinen, J., Kokkola, A., Ojanen, M. *et al.* (1998). The Finnish National Schizophrenia Project 1981–1987: ten-year evaluation of its results. *Acta Psychiatrica Scandinavica* 97: 10–17.

Ugelstad, E. (1978). *Psykotiske langtidspsiegter i psykiatriske sykehus – Nye behandlingsforsok.* Oslo: Universitetsforlaget.

Ugelstad, E. and Gilbert, S. (1994). The Norwegian project. In Y.O. Alanen, E. Ugelstad, *et al. Early Treatment for Schizophrenic Patients.* Oslo: Universitets-forlaget, pp. 57–68.

Vanggaard, T. (1955). A discussion of the basic principles of the psychoanalytically oriented psychotherapy of schizophrenia. *Acta Psychiatrica et Neurologica Scandinavica* 30, 3: 507–527.

Vanggaard, T. (1958). Neurosis and pseudoneurosis. *Acta Psychiatrica et Neurologica Scandinavica* 33: 251–254.

Vanggaard, T. (1978). The diagnosis of schizophrenic borderline state. *Acta Psychiatrica Scandinavica* 58: 213–230.

Varvin, S. (1991). A retrospective follow-up investigation of a group of schizophrenic patients treated in a psychotherapeutic unit: the Kastanjebakken study. *Psychopathology* 24: 335–344.

Villemoes, P. (2002). Ego-structuring psychotherapy. *Journal of the American Academy of Psychoanalysis* 30: 645–656.

Werbart, A. and Cullberg, J. (eds) (1992). *Psychotherapy of Schizophrenia. Facilitating and Obstructive Factors.* Oslo: Scandinavian University Press.

Chapter 13

Eastern Europe

Did the Iron Curtain influence the use of psychotherapy in treatment of people diagnosed with a schizophrenic disorder?

Jacek Bomba

As a consequence of political solutions following World War II, Europe was divided into two parts: its large Central Eastern part was isolated from the Central Western one. For more than four decades, exchanges of people and ideas between East and West were intentionally blocked. Psychiatry in Central Eastern Europe is thought to have existed under the strong influence of a specific Soviet orientation, including psychiatry's abuse for political purposes. At the time of the falling of the Berlin Wall, a symbol of the lifting of the Iron Curtain, the popular assessment of mental health care in the East described it as being 50 years behind the West. This opinion placed Eastern European psychiatry in a position somewhat like that of the mental patient for decades isolated from social life and in an asylum, and diagnosed as suffering from hospitalism. Certainly a feeling of isolation was predominant amongst psychiatrists in Central Eastern European countries and this generated a strong orientation towards knowledge and skills coming from the West. Some have assumed that the approach to schizophrenia treatment had developed in Eastern European countries in a single specific way, forgetting the number of countries and the many language differences.

The end of World War II left mental health care in the majority of Eastern European countries with a seriously limited number of professionals. Some of the pre-war psychiatrists-psychotherapists had left Europe already during the 1930s for the United States, thereby often saving their lives. Many others died in the Holocaust, and the intellectuals in societies were put into slavery.

It should be mentioned here that in many Eastern European countries the Nazi Action T4 programme was put into practice. 'Euthanasia' of psychiatric hospital inmates had been performed in such a way that extermination is a much more adequate term. In many hospitals the whole population of patients was killed. For example, the patients of Kraków-Kobierzyn were sent to gas chambers in Auschwitz (Jaroszewski, 1993).

The shadow of loss had seriously influenced the efforts to solve problems of mental health care in tough post-war conditions. The goal to

implementing post-war tendencies to utilize psychotherapy in the treatment
of patients with schizophrenia could be achieved by collecting information
from those psychiatrists who could remember psychotherapy teaching and
practice, and from searching the literature. Unfortunately the first way
brought only limited data. The most important information concerns the St
Petersburg School of Soviet Psychiatry, namely the approach developed in
the Bechkterev Institute that stayed clear of the abuse of mental patients
practised by Soviet forensic psychiatry. According to Stefan Leder, who
was a postdoctoral student at the Institute in the 1950s, psychiatrists there
had full access to current psychiatric and psychotherapeutic literature.
Leder himself brought to Poland the idea of group psychotherapy and his
team's presentation is among the first in post-war Polish literature on the
psychotherapeutic treatment of schizophrenic patients (Leder and Wolska,
1961). At the same time, group psychotherapy was also introduced by
Antoni Kępiński (Kępiński and Orwid, 1960), who brought this approach
back having acquired it during his postdoctoral studies at the London
Institute of Psychiatry.

Further development of the St Petersburg School has been concerned
with rehabilitation of patients with schizophrenia and it placed psychotherapy among the methods of rehabilitation. Kabanov *et al.* (1976) wrote
that psychotherapy should be subdued to rehabilitation tasks. The goal of
psychotherapy in schizophrenia is, according to them, the reconstruction of
'patients' personality and social status' (Kabanov *et al.*, 1976: 30). The
theoretical basis for the use of psychotherapy and the delineation of its
tasks was a conceptualization of personality-psychological factors as having
triggered the illness, and of the illness itself as having a negative impact on
the patient's relations with his or her environment. This approach still
characterizes psychiatry in Russia (Makarov, 2002, 2006). It strongly
influenced the therapeutic strategies used in GDR, but can also be traced
among professionals in Kosova, which used to be a part of former
Yugoslavia where relations with the Soviet Union were quite different from
other Iron Curtain countries (Cesko, 2002, 2006).

Psychotherapeutic thought and practice, based on psychoanalysis, has
been developing as the continuation of classical psychoanalysis in Hungary
and the Czech Republic, which had first originated during the time when
they were part of the Austro-Hungarian Empire. Many Polish psychoanalysts and analytically oriented psychotherapists acquired training in
Budapest or Prague. Nevertheless, information on psychotherapy for
schizophrenic patients both in the Czech Republic and Hungary was
extremely scarce. Dosužkov (1975), for example, supported the Freudian
opinion on the treatment resistance of narcissistic neuroses, but admitted
that some psychotherapists were continuing such efforts. Such an attitude
can be traced today. During the 1950s and 1960s, the Czech Ferdinand
Knobloch (e.g. Knobloch and Sofrnova, 1954) published studies on family

therapy with schizophrenic patients. A recent report does not enlist psychotherapy as a method used in the treatment of schizophrenic patients, but quotes a patient's book on her experience of psychotherapy (Vybiral, 2002). An account of the present situation in Hungarian psychotherapy (Harmatta, 2002) does not mention the treatment of patients with schizophrenia. Twenty years earlier, Füredi and Palffy (1980) discussing rehabilitation of the mentally ill emphasized the role of individual psychotherapy, the importance of its supervision and the need for family therapy. Family therapy was successfully introduced in the 1980s – for example, in Estonia it was suggested to be one of the standard treatments in those with schizophrenia (Mikkin, 2002).

Unfortunately, information collected by Pritz (2002), including the authors mentioned above, seems to be incomplete with regard to the field of psychotherapy for patients with schizophrenia. Psychotherapy in the treatment of schizophrenia is not mentioned in accounts from Croatia, Slovenia and Slovakia. Personal contacts (Ivesic, 2005) however, as well as the papers by Ivesic *et al.* (2001; Ivesic, 2003) prove that there are mental health centres employing psychodynamic psychotherapy, cognitive behavioural therapy (CBT), family therapy and eclectic approach with patients with schizophrenia.

It is difficult to assess whether the development in the psychotherapeutic approach to treatment of people diagnosed as suffering from schizophrenia in Poland is characteristic for the region. Publications in *Psychoterapia*, the only psychotherapeutic journal in Eastern Europe until the 1980s, reveal a series of papers on the experience of psychotherapeutic treatment in various modalities, and with varying goals. The majority concern group psychotherapy (e.g. Gołebiewska-Popielarska *et al.*, 1973; Orwid *et al.*, 1975; Kostecka, 1978) used both in inpatient and outpatient settings. In a textbook on group treatment in psychiatry by Wardaszko-Lyskowska (1973) two chapters deal exclusively with group psychotherapy for schizophrenic patients. There is a delineation of group therapy and group work in therapeutic community settings, as well as employment of group therapy in rehabilitation. Therapists were also sharing their experience in individual, analytically oriented psychotherapy with schizophrenic patients (e.g. Jakubczyk, 1974). Efforts to assess the effects of group psychotherapy with patients diagnosed having schizophrenia were performed in the 1970s (Orwid *et al.*, 1976).

Since the 1970s family therapy has been introduced to the treatment of patients with schizophrenia (Orwid 1975; Namysłowska, 1973, 1983; de Barbaro, 1992). Changes in the theoretical background and in the methods of family therapy employed have been parallel to the development of family approaches both in Europe and the USA, including a tendency to introduce family psycho-education based on studies of expressed emotion (EE; Rostworowska, 1991).

Changes in whole systems of mental health care have been started, at least in Poland, during the 1970s, with a strong tendency to dismantle regional psychiatric hospitals and to develop easy access to outpatient services. The programme emphasized the importance of continuity of care. The changes, however, missed the psychotherapeutic part of treatment. Two decades later, the next systemic changes in the whole health care system wiped out a network of outpatient services almost completely. The new situation, paradoxically, created a chance for the building of new services, based on the ideas of community psychiatry and the introduction of various services more adequate to the varying needs of patients themselves.

It seems that the present tendency abandons the differentiation between therapy and rehabilitation, which was so important in the past. More emphasis is being put on what is called early rehabilitation. That means a use of various therapeutic modalities, depending on the context and assessment of the individual patient's needs right at the beginning of her or his psychiatric pathway, to meet these needs, prevent withdrawal and to support her or him in their individual development. The Krakow team is a good example of developing a model of an integrative treatment system for schizophrenic patients (de Barbaro et al., 1979a, 1979b; Cechnicki et al., 1979). The team carries on with prospective follow-up studies assessing the effectiveness of the treatment model measured in psychopathological and social dimensions (Cechnicki, 2003).

Every other year, for the last eight years, the Krakow group has been organizing a series of conferences under the title 'Schizophrenia: Various Contexts – Various Therapies'. The position of the psychotherapeutic approach in the integrated treatment of patients diagnosed with schizophrenic disorders is discussed from various theoretical points of view, and also, a matter that we think is most important, with the participation of the patients themselves. These discussions bring us toward a position that takes into account the complexity of disturbances in people diagnosed as suffering from schizophrenia, and the very varied needs of people suffering from these disturbances, as well as their families. There is a place for almost every psychotherapeutic approach, providing the therapy is suggested when needed and skilfully applied. The same approach can be found in the recent textbook on psychotherapy in schizophrenia (Meder and Sawicka, 2006).

References

de Barbaro, B. (1992). *Brzemie rodziny w schizofrenii. Próba ujecia systemowego*. Krakow: SP PTP.

de Barbaro, B., Cechnicki, A., Zawadzka, K. and Zadęcki, J. (1979a). Model terapii i rehabilitacji w schizofrenii. *Psychoterapia* 28: 6–9.

de Barbaro, B., Hodura, E., Śliwa, K. and Zadęcki, J. (1979b). Obraz społeczności leczniczej w świetle badań ankietowych. *Psychoterapia* 28: 11–15.

Cechnicki, A. (2003). The quality of life of schizophrenic patients. Part one: research results of the psychosocial treatment programme. *Archives of Psychiatry and Psychotherapy* 5: 45–57.

Cechnicki, A., Drozdowski, P., Kurgan, A. and Zadęcki J. (1979). Terapia bifokalna w leczeniu schizofrenii. Bilans dwuletnich doświadczeń z grup rodzinnych. *Psychoterapia* 28: 21–27.

Cesko, E. (2002). Kosova. In A. Pritz (ed.) *Globalized Psychotherapy*. Vienna: Facultas Universitaetasverlag, pp. 196–199.

Cesko, E. (2006). Personal communication.

Dosużkov, B. (1975). O istocie psychoterapii. *Psychoterapia* 12: 14–17.

Füredi, J. and Palffy, J. (1980). Psychologiczne problemy rehabilitacji psychicznie chorych. *Psychotherapia* 35: 15–22.

Gołebiewska-Popielarska, M., Jankowska, H. and Rzewuska, M. (1973). Psychoterapia grupowa w psychozach. *Psychoterapia* 6: 3–16.

Harmatta, J. (2002). Hungary. In A. Pritz (ed.) *Globalized Psychotherapy*. Vienna: Facultas Universitaetasverlag, pp. 165–168.

Ivesic, S. (2003). Types of transference studied in a group of schizophrenic patients. *Medicinski Arhiv* 57: 241–246.

Ivesic, S. (2005). Personal communication.

Ivesic, S., Ljubimir, V. and Urlic, I. (2001). Therapist–patient relationship in treatment of chronic schizophrenic patients. *Medicinski Arhiv* 55 (Supp. 1): 39–46.

Jakubczyk, A. (1974). Przebieg psychoterapii pacjenta psychotycznego. *Psychoterapia* 8: 29–32.

Jaroszewski, Z. (ed.) (1993). *Zagłada chorych psychicznie w Polsce 1939–1945. Die Ermordung der Geisteskranken in Polen 1939–1945*. Warszawa: PWN.

Kabanov, M.M., Karwasarskij, B.D., Murzenko, W.A. and Tupicyn, J.A. (1976). Optymalne formy stosowania psychoterapii specjalistycznej. *Psychoterapia* 18: 29–32.

Kępiński, A. and Orwid, M. (1960). Dalsze uwagi praktyczne o stosowaniu psychoterapii grupowej. *Neurol Neurochir Psychiat Pol* 10: 697.

Knobloch, F. and Sofrnova, M. (1954). Notes on the technique of family psychotherapy. [In Czech.] *Neurologia a psychiatria czeskolovenska* 17: 217–224.

Kostecka, M. (1978). Krótkoterminova psychoterapia grupowa pacjentów z rozpoznaniem schizofrenii. *Psychotherapia* 6: 20–25.

Leder, S. and Wolska, H. (1961). *O stosowaniu grupowej psychoterapii u chorych z psychozami. Pamiętnik XXV Zjazdu Naukowego Psychiatrów Polskich*. Warszawa: PZWL, p. 111.

Makarov, V.V. (2002). Russian Federation. In A. Pritz (ed.) *Globalized Psychotherapy* Vienna: Facultas Universitaetasverlag, pp. 266–282.

Makarov, V.V. (2006). Personal communication.

Meder, J. and Sawicka, M. (eds) (2006). *Psychoterapia schizofrenii*. Kraków: Biblioteka Psychiatrii Polskiej.

Mikkin, H. (2002). Estonia. In A. Pritz (ed.) *Globalized Psychotherapy*. Vienna: Facultas Universitaetasverlag, pp. 95–112.

Namysłowska, I. (1973). Psychoterapia grupowa schizofrenii. In H. Wardaszko-Łyskowska (ed.) *Terapia grupowa w psychiatrii*. Warszawa: PZWL, pp. 115–133.

Namysłowska, I. (1983). *Społeczna i emocjonalna adaptacja rodzin pacjentów chorych na schizofrenię*. Warszawie: Wydawnictwo AM.

Orwid, M. (1975). Zasadnicze wskazania i kierunki psychoterapii oraz terapii rodziny w zaburzeniach psychicznych u młodzieży dojrzewającej. *Psychoterapia* 14: 19–22.

Orwid, M., Badura, W., Bomba, J., Mellibruda, L. and Pajor, Z. (1975). Trudności w stosowaniu grupowych form leczenia w psychiatrycznym oddziale młodzieżowym. *Psychoterapia* 14: 15–19.

Orwid, M., Bomba, J., Badura, W., Pajor, Z. and Mellibruda, L. (1976). Five-year follow-up study of adolescent schizophrenics. Psychopathological dynamics and results of group psychotherapy. In J. Jørstad and E. Ugelstad (eds) *Schizophrenia 75*. Oslo: Universitatsforlaget, pp. 373–386.

Pritz, A. (ed.) (2002). *Globalized Psychotherapy*. Vienna: Facultas Universitaetasverlag.

Rostworowska, M. (1991). *Wpływ wskaźnika Ujawnionych Uczuć na przebieg schizofrenii – 18 miesięczna katamneza*. Krakow: Biblioteka Collegium Medicum UJ.

Vybiral, Z.S. (2002). Czech Republik. In A. Pritz (ed.) *Globalized Psychotherapy*. Vienna: Facultas Universitaetasverlag, pp. 89–94.

Wardaszko-Łyskowska, H. (ed.) (1973). *Terapia grupowa w psychiatrii*. Warszawa: PZWL.

Chapter 14

Eastern Asia

Part 1: Developments in Eastern Asia – a focus on Singapore

Lyn Chua

The practice of Western psychiatry in the treatment of mental disorders is relatively young in Eastern Asia. It was gradually introduced to the East sometime in the early nineteenth century when the West started trading in the region and colonized some of these Far East and South-East Asian countries. It appears, however, that psychotherapy in the treatment of mental illness, and in particular schizophrenia, has not been emphasized. The approach seems to have remained predominantly biomedical until today.

The Far East countries include China, Japan, Korea and Hong Kong. South-East Asia comprises countries such as Malaysia, Thailand, Indonesia, Singapore and the Philippines. Numerous epidemiological studies have demonstrated that the incidence of schizophrenia in Asian countries is very similar to that of countries in the West; that is about 1 per cent of the total population of each of the countries studied (Jablensky *et al.*, 1992).

Prior to the introduction of antipsychotic medication, various culturally influenced approaches, for example, exorcism and religious rituals (Razali *et al.*, 1996), acupuncture and moxibustion (Wiseman, 2000) were used by witch doctors and traditional healers to deal with some of the bizarre behaviours and disruptive symptoms of schizophrenia. The methods of witch doctors in China were pluralistic, combining aspects of Taoist, Buddhist and animistic beliefs (Lin, 1981). They explained illnesses in terms of spirits and ghosts, and stated that they treat patients by intervening in the spirit world on their behalf.

Psychological treatment and psychotherapeutic approaches were later considered useful as an adjunct to the antipsychotic medication. These bio-psychosocial methods are, however, not widespread in many East Asian countries for numerous reasons, including the shortage of skilled man-power, economic constraints and the strong inclination towards a biomedical treatment approach, as well as due to cultural and religious influences.

Recent studies have demonstrated that certain psychotherapeutic approaches have been effective and efficacious in preventing relapses and in helping patients cope and function better in life. Jackson *et al.*'s (1998)

Cognitively Oriented Psychotherapy for Early Psychosis (COPE) has been shown to be effective in dealing with patients' delusions and hallucinations, and the distress caused by these symptoms was reduced through better understanding and more rational explanations for their occurrence.

Logically, psychotherapy would be similarly effective for Asian patients. However, Lin (1981) has suggested that in order to practise modern psychiatry in different cultures, it is of the utmost importance to have an adequate understanding of each culture's medical and folk religious beliefs and treatment approaches. Hence, the psychotherapist needs to be cognizant of the underlying cultural and religious influence on the etiology of the delusions and hallucinations. Societal values, cultural values, superstitions and religious beliefs play a prominent role in providing the themes for the delusions and hallucinations and in culturally shaping these symptoms. Awareness of these underlying influences in psychotherapy is paramount in engaging the patients in meaningful psychotherapy. When patients feel that their beliefs are understood, acknowledged and respected, not dismissed or devalued, the process of psychotherapeutic interventions would be meaningful and effective.

A focus on Singapore

Singapore is an island state with a total land area of 648 sq km and a multi-ethnic population of 3.6 million, of which 77 per cent are Chinese, 14 per cent Malays, 8 per cent Indians and the remaining 1 per cent of other races. There is a dual system of health care – the public sector and the private sector. There are 87 psychiatrists with the majority working in the public sector. The Institute of Mental Health and Woodbridge Hospital is the only state psychiatric hospital and it is the principal treatment centre in Singapore for those with severe mental illnesses like schizophrenia.

Primary health care is usually provided by family doctors, doctors in the policlinics, and practitioners of Traditional Chinese Medicine (TCM); there are approximately 1300 registered TCM practitioners in Singapore. Other traditional healers include spiritual healers like the *bomohs* (Malay traditional medicine men), *tang-kis* (Chinese temple mediums) and temple priests and religious persons affiliated to churches, mosques and temples. These traditional healers are often the first choice for treatment and the first point of contact for many patients and their family members. The *bomoh* is popular among the Malays who believe that these traditional healers are well equipped to handle all aspects of mental illness (Razali, 1989). In fact, the *bomoh* is considered a good psychotherapist who can communicate with the patient more effectively than the medical practitioner (Razali *et al.*, 1996). The Chinese temple medium is often sought to exorcize the evil spirits that have entered to cause disturbances within the body of the patient. Patients sometimes turn to TCM practitioners and also to Ayurvedic medicine and homeopathic healers. Dialogues have been carried out with the TCM practitioners in an attempt to streamline the management of patients with schizophrenia (Chua and Tan, 2004).

Before the 1940s, the treatment of psychiatric patients in Singapore was rather primitive, as documented by Ng (2001). Shortly after World War II ended in Asia, the Mental Disorders and Treatment Ordinance was introduced in Singapore under British rule, but even so the mental hospital was considered an asylum and the approach was still very custodial in nature. About 75 per cent of the patients were suffering from schizophrenia. In 1947, electroconvulsive therapy was introduced, followed by insulin coma treatment and carbon dioxide therapy; prefrontal leucotomy was recommended for chronic cases who were distressed by their symptoms and was performed on three patients in the early 1950s (Colony of Singapore, Department of Health report, 1953). In 1956, occupational therapy, social work and psychological services were started. Psychometric testing was carried out when required and behaviour therapy including the token economy programme was introduced. The psychosocial intervention that resembled psychotherapy seemed more like counselling and was offered to only about 6 per cent of the patient population. Pharmacotherapy became the mainstay in the treatment of mental illness, with atypical antipsychotic medication being included recently. The overall approach in the treatment of schizophrenia today remains very biological in orientation; it was very noticeable that psychotherapy was not emphasized. Group therapy dealt mainly with social and communication skills; training in the activities of daily living was provided within the rehabilitation programme.

Mainly owing to the stigma attached to the psychiatric services and also because of longstanding cultural and religious beliefs, most patients preferred to seek treatment from traditional and religious healers, temple mediums and witch doctors rather than from psychiatrists. To convince patients with schizophrenia that they needed psychiatric treatment, psycho-education aimed at impressing upon patients that they had a biological illness and, as in other physical illness, they would benefit from taking medication. Despite that, resistance and denial of being affected by any mental illness remained prevalent and by the time these patients came into contact with the psychiatric services they had been ill for a long duration and had deteriorated considerably.

A recent study in Singapore showed that the mean duration of untreated psychosis (DUP) of patients with schizophrenia is 32.6 months (Chong *et al.*, 2005). The study also revealed that 24 per cent of the patients with first episode psychosis had sought the help of traditional healers at the onset of the illness. When it was evident that the long DUP was detrimental to the patients, resulting in poor prognosis and higher health care costs in the long run, the Early Psychosis Intervention Programme (EPIP) was developed under the auspices of the Ministry of Health (Chong and Chua, 2002). The main thrust of the programme is early detection and intervention. It advocates a truly bio-psychosocial approach in that the multidisciplinary team of psychiatrists, psychologists, social workers, occupational therapists, nurses and case managers addresses all aspects of needs of the patients. The concept of case management was the first to be introduced to the health care system in Singapore. There is a strong emphasis on psychotherapy as it became obvious that patients needed to talk about their thoughts and feelings concerning their psychotic experiences, to deal with their losses in the wake of the illness, and to work through and come to terms with the reality of the illness to enable them to 'move on' in life.

A culturally relevant and culturally sensitive form of psychotherapy was developed specifically for EPIP patients. The Personal and Strategic Coping Therapy for Early Psychosis (PASTE) is a psychotherapy 'package' developed in Singapore with cultural perspectives in mind (Chua and Choo, 2004). Considering that the mind is 'torn asunder' (Bleuler, 1950), PASTE is the 'glue' that 'pastes' the fragmented parts of the mind together. The goal of this psychotherapy package is to help individuals make sense of what has happened and is happening to them, to enable them to deal with the cognitive and emotional aspects of the illness, to develop a more rational attitude towards the illness and to cope better with life in the wake of the illness. It incorporates various psychotherapeutic concepts and approaches but its unique quality is that it takes into account the prevailing social, cultural and religious influences.

The main components of PASTE are supportive therapy, personal therapy, psycho-education, cognitive therapy and strategic coping therapy. The sequence in which these components are delivered to the patient may change or be repeated, depending on the needs of the patient. Supportive therapy involves active listening and providing a listening ear to the experiences which the individual has gone through. The supportive psychotherapy component of PASTE should be implemented at an early stage of the psychotic episode as Jackson (Jackson *et al.*, 2000) had shown that psychotherapy delivered at an earlier stage of the psychotic episode resulted in a better outcome.

Personal therapy allows the individual to come up with a personal explanation or understanding of what he has gone through. This personal explanation is often influenced by the individual's cultural and religious background. However unlikely, 'faulty' and even bizarre the individual's explanations may sound to the therapist, they should not be challenged at this point in time.

Arthur Kleinman, the American psychiatrist and social anthropologist, proposed that people use 'explanatory models' to make sense of illnesses (1978). The facilitation of an 'explanatory model' enables the individual to come to terms with the occurrence of the traumatic experiences, which may later help him to accept and adapt to the illness with less resistance. It is this facilitation of a personal explanation and understanding that makes PASTE an individualized form of psychotherapeutic intervention as it takes into account the cultural and/or religious background of that individual.

Psycho-education provided by an independent nurse educator (to preserve the therapeutic alliance) complements PASTE with the 'scientific' facts of the illness. Areas covered include a broad overview of the psychotic and schizophrenic illnesses, types of treatment available, patterns of recovery and future prospects. Reasons for the need for medication, the types of medication available, the dosages and possible side effects, the relevance of psychotherapy, group and occupational therapy will be discussed and the importance of compliance with treatment emphasized. Patients are also taught how to monitor for signs and symptoms of an impending relapse and where to seek help.

A cognitively oriented approach is then used to help the patient arrive at a more reasonable or acceptable explanation for the illness that will enable them to come to terms with it and facilitate better compliance with the proposed treatment. Using a systematic and structured approach to reality testing, the patient is encouraged to test alternative explanations in an unchallenging manner. The ultimate goal is to assist the patient to form new beliefs for causes of symptoms through cognitive therapy and belief modification that will enhance compliance with treatment. The focus is on positive and negative symptoms, illogical thoughts and cultural beliefs that will result in refusal of treatment.

Strategic coping therapy moves on to explore the difficulties that the patient may have in coping with the illness and returning to optimal functioning. He may need help to overcome the traumatic episode, regain his self-confidence and reintegrate into the community. At this point in therapy, the psychotherapist will be on the look-out for co-morbid disorders like panic attacks, general anxiety disorder, social anxiety or post-traumatic stress disorder. When there is some insight and realization that he is suffering from a mental illness, he may become depressed, and even contemplate suicide. Strategic coping therapy also encourages patients to take stock of their current life situations, examining how the illness has affected their lives, adapting to the changes, building new coping skills and considering the options for the future. The application of PASTE is illustrated in the following case.

Case example

A 20-year-old university student was referred to the EPIP clinic by his GP when he reported that he was experiencing a great deal of distress as he believed that his classmates were planning to harm him. He could hear them talking about him and ridiculing him even in the middle of the night when he was alone in bed. After an assessment by the psychiatrist, he was referred for PASTE. At first he felt rather embarrassed talking about his feelings, but when reassured by his therapist he opened up and talked about the fear, confusion and terror he was experiencing; he felt so alone in his predicament. His mother had brought him several times to consult the temple medium as she believed that he had been possessed by spirits. The patient himself agreed with his mother as he believed he had offended a spirit one evening a few weeks ago while he was on his way home from the university. He had accidentally stepped on an ancestral altar that had been placed at the foot of a tree near the bus stop. The temple medium had performed rituals and given him 'holy water' to drink but he did not get better. He was relieved that he could express his fears and beliefs as his therapist could validate his feelings and took into account his religious beliefs.

A few weeks later, his symptoms faded after he took the medication prescribed by the psychiatrist. The nurse then talked to him about the various causes of such symptoms. At first he was unconvinced he had a psychotic illness, adamant that he had been possessed. However, he agreed to continue with the treatment. He attended the clinic and psychotherapy sessions regularly; he was keen to discuss what had actually happened to him. He felt that the therapy enabled him to understand and make sense of what had happened to him. Subsequently he came to terms and accepted that he did have an illness. He felt that his traumatic experiences could have been triggered by the extremely stressful period just before his last exams. He wondered if he was capable of continuing with his studies. He also felt anxious occasionally, fearful that he may start hearing those hostile voices again. After several sessions talking about his fear and depression, he decided that he felt confident enough to resume his studies, mindful that he would need to monitor himself and continue with treatment at the EPIP clinic.

Psychotherapy within EPIP plays a major role in the treatment of patients with early psychosis and those diagnosed with schizophrenia. Research is ongoing to demonstrate that such a culturally relevant form of psychotherapy is effective, more readily accepted by patients and helps the patient to return to optimal functioning at the social, occupational and psychological level and to move on in life.

Conclusion

Psychotherapy for patients with schizophrenia in East Asia has lagged far behind that in the West. At present, much of the focus is still on the biomedical model. However, with the realization of the need for a more holistic bio-psychosocial approach, countries in the Far East and South-East Asia, and in particular Singapore, have taken steps to incorporate a psychotherapy component as a necessary modality in the treatment of schizophrenia. However, the psychotherapy has to be sensitive to the cultural and religious background of the patient. Anthropologists of the earlier era like Murphy (1973) and Henderson and Primeaux (1981) have emphasized the importance of understanding the cultural background of patients to engage them meaningfully and to avoid emotional conflicts and cognitive dissonance. Acceptance of the patients' personal explanations or interpretations of their symptoms will strengthen the therapeutic relationship. Mental health care professionals can work with traditional healers, not preventing patients from consulting them as long as this does not interfere with the psychiatric treatment. These professionals should also learn about the belief system of the various cultures and religions. There seems to be a paucity of published studies and accounts of psychotherapy in this part of the world in the extant literature. With greater awareness of the benefits of psychotherapy in the treatment of schizophrenia and a movement towards a more balanced bio-psychosocial approach, it is hoped that psychotherapy will play a more prominent role in East Asia.

References

Bleuler, E. (1950). *Dementia Praecox or the Group of Schizophrenias*. (trans. J. Zinkin). New York: International Universities Press.

Chong, S.A. and Chua, L. (2002). Evolution of the early psychosis intervention programme in Singapore. *Acta Psychiatrica Scandinavica* (Suppl. 106): 69.

Chong, S.A., Mythily, Lum, A., Chan, Y.H. and McGorry, P. (2005). Determinants of duration of untreated psychosis and the pathway to care in Singapore. *International Journal of Social Psychiatry* 51: 55–62.

Chua, L. and Choo, L. (2004). Psychotherapy for early psychosis in an Asian culture of exorcism and superstitions. *Schizophrenia Research* 70 (Suppl. 1).

Chua, L. and Tan, P.I. (2004). In partnership with Traditional Chinese Medicine (TCM) practitioners in the treatment of early psychosis in Singapore. *Schizophrenia Research* 70 (Suppl. 1).

Henderson, G. and Primeaux, M. (1981). *Transcultural Health Care. Introduction*. Menlo Park, CA: Addison-Wesley.

Jablensky, A., Sartorius, N., Ernberg, G., Anker, M., Korten, A., Cooper, J.E. *et al.* (1992). *Schizophrenia: Manifestations, Incidence and Course in Different Cultures*. New York: Cambridge University Press.

Jackson, H.J., McGorry, P.D., Edwards, J., Hulbert, C., Henry, L., Francey, A. *et al.* (1998). Cognitively-oriented Psychotherapy for Early Psychosis (COPE): Preliminary results. *British Journal of Psychiatry* 172: 93–100.

Jackson, H.J., Hulbert, C. and Henry, L. (2000). The treatment of secondary morbidity in first episode psychosis. In M. Birchwood, D. Fowler and C. Jackson (eds) *Early Intervention in Psychosis: Guide to Concepts, Evidence and Intervention*. Chichester: Wiley.

Kleinman, A.J. (1978). Concepts and a model for the comparison of medical systems as cultural systems. *Social Science and Medicine* 12: 85–93.

Lin, K.M. (1981). Traditional Chinese medical beliefs and their relevance for mental illness and psychiatry. In A. Kleinman and T.Y. Lin (eds) *Normal and Abnormal Behaviours in Chinese Culture: Culture, Illness and Healing, Vol. 2*. Dordrecht: Reidel.

Murphy, H.B.M. (1973). Current trends in transcultural psychiatry. *Proceedings of the Royal Society of Medicine* 66: 711–716.

Ng, B.Y. (2001). *Till the Break of Day: A History of Mental Health Services in Singapore 1841–1993*. Singapore: Singapore University Press.

Razali, S.M. (1989). The consultation of traditional healers by Malay patients. *Medical Journal of Malaysia* 44: 3–12.

Razali, S.M., Khan, U.A. and Hasanah, C.I. (1996). Belief in supernatural causes of mental illness among Malay patients: impact on treatment. *Acta Psychiatrica Scandinavica*. 94: 229–233.

Wiseman, N. (2000). *Soothing the Troubled Mind: Treatment and Prevention of Schizophrenia with Acupuncture and Moxibustion*. Boulder, CO: Paradigm.

Part 2: Taopsychotherapy in Korea

Chan Hee Huh

To describe what Taopsychotherapy encompasses – in the ways it has been originated and founded by Professor Rhee Dongshick – we could quite simply state that Taopsychotherapy is Professor Rhee's psychotherapy of fusing the Tao with the essence of Western psychotherapy. He has worked for 64 years as a psychiatrist and 53 years as a psychotherapist. He has conducted numerous psychotherapy sessions on a weekly basis throughout most of his lifetime and at one stage was seeing patients for up to 79 hours per week.

Professor Rhee's experience and influences as a psychotherapist

Professor Rhee began studying psychiatry in 1942 at Seoul (then Keijo Imperial) University, when World War II was under way. At that time the Japanese occupied every leading position in every area; psychiatry was no exception. The Japanese psychiatry being practised was organic psychiatry of the Kraepelinian tradition. Rhee was exposed to German literature along with taking a personal interest in British, American and French psychiatry. At the beginning, he was influenced by Eugen Bleuler, Ernst Kretschmer and Kurt Kolle. Later on, as a result of the influences of Sigmund Freud, Pierre Janet and Jean-Martin Charcot, he came to believe in the emotional origins of most mental disorders which further confirmed the personal insights he had formed during late childhood. He then came across Ludwig Binswanger's (1928) paper on 'inner life history'. After three or four years study of psychiatry, he began to understand the inner world of his patients. As a medical student he was exposed to Hermann Hesse's novels which depict the inner world and loneliness. He also read Arthur Schopenhauer and much of Friedrich Nietzsche, Soeren Kierkegaard and Max Scheler. In the first years of his psychiatric studies he was also introduced to Martin

Heidegger's (1928) *Sein und Zeit* [Being and Time]. He read almost all of the books written by Bertrand Russell except *Principia Mathematica* (1910–1913), and studied linguistics, psychology and cultural anthropology, and was interested in the American philosophers William James and John Dewey, plus the study of shamans and shamanism.

In 1953, he worked with a case of psychogenic headaches which he successfully treated over a period of 12 sessions without supervision. In 1954, he went to New York to study psychoanalysis on the strong recommendation and urging of an American military psychiatrist. Here, he was exposed to North American psychiatry and was analysed for six months, also attending the William Alanson White Institute as a general student for one year. After four years of study at various other US institutions, he visited Europe and attended four international congresses, including the World Philosophers' Congress.

Upon his return to Korea at the end of 1958, he introduced dynamic psychiatry, psychotherapy and interview techniques, as well as existential psychiatry to Korea. Since 1965, he has been studying the Eastern Tao including Buddhism, Confucianism, Laotzu and Chuangtzu with prominent Buddhist monks and scholars.

In 1974, Rhee founded the Korean Psychotherapy Case Study Group, which then developed into the Korean Psychotherapy Study Group in 1976 and became the present Korean Academy of Psychotherapists (KAP) after 1979. It is at this academy that Rhee has been teaching Taopsychotherapy for more than 30 years. His professional activities encompass broad areas such as psychotherapy, problems of identity and subjectivity in and of Koreans, fusion of the Tao and Western psychotherapy, significance of the Tao in contemporary times, relationship between the Tao and science as well as psychotherapy and traditional culture within Korea.

Lately, Rhee was elected honorary member of International Federation for Psychotherapy (IFP). As early as 1958 he attended the International Congress of Medical Psychotherapy (IFMP) in Barcelona. In 1988 he became an IFP council member. In 1994 he was Congress President and Chairman of the Organizing Committee of the sixteenth IFP World congress of Psychotherapy, which was held in Seoul, Korea, under the theme 'Psychotherapy: East and West', and gave a plenary lecture on 'Tao and Western Psychotherapy'. During this congress, he also acted as co-founder of the Asian chapter of IFP, the Asia Pacific Association of Psychotherapists (APAP) of which he became Honorary President in 1996. At the thirteenth meeting of IFMP in Yugoslavia in 1985 and the fourteenth meeting of IFMP in Switzerland in 1988, he organized some symposia about 'Psychotherapy in East and West', which made a significant contribution to integration of the Eastern Tao and Western psychotherapy; these were both co-chaired with Medard Boss (c.f. Boss and Rhee, 1992).

The essence of Taopsychotherapy

One of the most important considerations in Taopsychotherapy is to empathize with the patient's feelings (Huh, 2004). Rhee insisted that the feelings of the psychotherapist cure the patient's feelings. According to Rhee, the principles of Taopsychotherapy can be applied to neurosis, psychosis and psychosomatic disease quite irrespective of the diagnosis of the mental disorder. The only differences in application of the therapeutic response relate directly to the period of the identified developmental stage during which the patient experienced the trauma. This reflects a need to pay deliberate attention to the differing levels of consonant ego strength in the patient, as is similarly recognized in Western psychotherapy. In Taopsychotherapy, it is critical to empathize with the patient's feelings in all types of mental disorders. Rhee has repeatedly stated his perception that even very severely psychotic patients suddenly improved as soon as they felt they were understood. In 2003 he led the symposium titled 'Taopsychotherapy of Psychoses' at the fourteenth International Symposium of the Psychological Treatments of Schizophrenias and Other Psychoses (ISPS) in Melbourne, Australia.

In one of his papers Rhee (1970) pointed out the primary importance of grasping and overcoming the patient's 'nuclear feelings' which hold such sway over the patient's mind and behaviour throughout his or her life at every moment. He argued that nuclear feelings are the same as 'something stuck in the chest' which Tahui (the great Suhn [Zen] master of Song dynasty in China) spoke of 1000 years ago.

Second, one of the most important things in Taopsychotherapy is the issue of how a therapist can attain perfect empathy so as to empathize with the patient's feelings. For this purpose, therapists should resolve (remove) their own nuclear feelings (neurotic desires) through purification of their minds. This is one of the distinctively different issues worked with in Taopsychotherapy. This question of how well the therapist understands the patient's feelings is very seriously attended to in Taopsychotherapy, as compared with Western psychotherapy (depth of empathy).

Rhee always says that 'the therapist should treat a patient with his/her own compassion or, the therapist should have compassion and the patient will be cured by it', and that 'a therapist's mind must be in a state of "fasting" in order to empathize with the feelings of others'.

Taopsychotherapy and Western psychotherapy: similarities and differences

In Rhee's paper 'The Tao, Psychoanalysis and Existential Thought' (1990) he speaks of both the common elements and differences between Eastern

Tao, psychoanalysis and existential thought. He compares the goal of the Eastern Tao with that of Western psychoanalysis and psychotherapy. He concludes that the goal of Western psychoanalysis/psychotherapy and Eastern Tao is the same and the only difference is one of degree or level. He also compares the processes of psychoanalysis and Suhn practice and concludes that both of the processes are the same, but only up to a particular point.

One of the most commonly asked questions by Western psychoanalysts about Rhee's Taopsychotherapy is: In Western psychoanalysis, one of the most important aspects is understanding and solving the patient's transference feelings. In Taopsychotherapy, how is this aspect of treatment carried out? Rhee maintains that Taopsychotherapy literally attends to the transference of nuclear feelings. In other words, the transference of the nuclear feelings tends to be considerably more focused upon and in particular the core aspect of these feelings in Taopsychotherapy.

In Taopsychotherapy, interpretations are viewed as 'directly pointing at the patient's mind' and the therapist is viewed as expressing perfect empathy, in the state of subject–object congruence. In the paper 'Integration of East and West Psychotherapy: Prof. Rhee Dongshick's Case', Kang Suk-Hun explained some of the characteristics of Rhee's interpretation. He described Rhee's interpretations as a form of 'killing and making alive' or 'taking life and giving life' nature (Kang, 1996). In Suhn dialogue, masters usually use this type of interpretation to cut through their disciples' delusions or discriminating thoughts. In addition, Kang described another characteristic interpretation of Rhee's as 'cutting away the roots of the patient's dependency and hostility'.

In Taopsychotherapy, Rhee stresses the importance of active involvement of the therapist's mature personality. As to the concept of the patient's 'resistance' within psychoanalysis, the viewpoint of Taopsychotherapy is that this interpretation can actually represent a lack of empathy in the therapist. Rhee argues that this concept is a therapist-centred idea, and that the subjective, experiential aspect of the patient is the only reality for consideration.

Summary

In summary, the essence of Taopsychotherapy is to bring spring to the patient who is shivering in a frozen land. In other words, Taopsychotherapy is empathizing with the patient's nuclear feelings, which hold sway over the patient's mind and behaviour, from the gesture of a hand to the peculiarity of breathing, throughout his or her life at every moment. In order to achieve perfect empathic capacity, the therapist should both have and develop compassion which can be attained by resolution of the therapist's nuclear feelings through purification of the mind. Nuclear feelings, purification of the mind (elimination of nuclear feelings) and compassion (empathy) are the three key words of Taopsychotherapy (Rhee, 2004).

References

Binswanger, L. (1928). 'Lebensfunktion und innere Lebensgeschichte' [Life Function and Inner Life History]. *European Neurology* 68: 1–6.

Boss, Medard and Rhee, Dongshick (1992). Dialogue between Prof. Medard Boss and Prof. Rhee Dongshick. *Psychotherapy* 6: 30–43.

Huh, Chan Hee (2004). Introduction to Taopsychotherapy. In *Proceedings of the International Forum on Taopsychotherapy and Western Psychotherapy*, Seoul, Korea, pp. 6–18.

Kang, Suk-Hun (1996). Integration of east and west psychotherapy: Professor Rhee Dongshick's case. Paper presented to First Meeting of the Asia Pacific Association of Psychotherapy, Bali, Indonesia, 27 October.

Rhee, Dongshick (1970). Research on psychotherapy of Korean patients. *New Medical Journal* 1: 77–101.

Rhee, Dongshick (1990). The Tao, psychoanalysis and existential thought. *Psychotherapy and Psychosomatics* 53: 21–27.

Rhee, Dongshick (2004). The essence of Taopsychotherapy in comparison with western psychotherapy/psychoanalysis. *Proceedings of the International Forum on Taopsychotherapy and Western Psychotherapy*, Seoul, Korea, pp. 19–28.

Chapter 15

New Zealand

A history of treatment approaches to psychosis

J. Geekie, M. Taitimu, P. Randal, D. Rook, M. Ang and J. Read

Introduction

Contemporary New Zealand (NZ) is a dynamic society, with a diverse population and a broad cultural mix. An appreciation of crucial aspects of NZ history and culture will help to facilitate an understanding of our discussion of the range and nature of psychotherapeutic interventions for psychosis provided to clients of mental health services.

Aotearoa/New Zealand was formally established with the signing in 1840 of the Treaty of Waitangi (TOW), a document endorsed by the British Crown and most of the Mäori chiefs of the time. This treaty delineates the nature of the relationship between the two parties, Pakeha (those of European descent) and Mäori, and recognises the rights of the indigenous people of NZ. The treaty remains an important 'live' document today, expressing a commitment to uphold its spirit in service delivery, including mental health services, which are bicultural in nature, catering to the needs of both Mäori and Pakeha (Kawharu, 1989).

Although NZ occupies a unique geographical and cultural position, the history of mental health services subsequent to colonization shares much with other Western nations. NZ, like all Western countries, historically housed large numbers of people deemed mentally ill in long-stay custodial care hospitals, such as Carrington Hospital in Auckland, which at its peak housed over 2000 patients. The medical model of care dominated in these institutions, with opportunities for psychological interventions being rare. Though mainstream public mental health services continue to operate within a largely medical model of care, there have been significant changes in the range of services now available to clients who have psychotic experiences. In this chapter we chart some of these changes, focusing on the psychotherapeutic and psychosocial interventions offered to those who have such experiences.

In common with other Western countries, NZ mental health services have changed in response to the growing influence of the consumer movement, now well established in NZ in all levels of mental health service planning, with the demand that services are more responsive to the needs of consumers. Other factors which have influenced the range of services offered to psychotic clients include the development of early intervention services (EISs), loosely following the model of the Early Psychosis Prevention and Intervention Centre (EPPIC) in Melbourne (see Gleeson and McGorry, 2004), and the more general impact of the growing body of literature which demonstrates the importance and value of psychotherapeutic interventions for psychosis. In addition to these broad Western influences on mental health services, within NZ there has also been the unique impact of the policy of 'biculturalism', which outlines the rights of Māori to receive services which are sensitive to and concordant with Māori cultural values.

In accordance with the Treaty of Waitingi, NZ public mental health services include 'mainstream' services and Kaupapa Māori services. Mainstream services are, by and large, designed and delivered along similar lines to other Western countries, whereas Kaupapa Māori services aim to provide a service that embodies Māori cultural principles and practices such as 'whanaungatanga' (family dynamics) and 'whakapapa' (genealogy). These services differ from mainstream services in a number of important ways, including the use of 'kaumatua' (elders) in providing guidance, and facilitating access to traditional forms of healing. In addition to Kaupapa Māori services, the past decade has also witnessed the development of mental health services for Pacific Island peoples within the main cities. In practice, cultural services and mainstream services work alongside each other and have a reciprocal impact on each other.

Māori mental health

Subsequent to the rapid urbanization of Māori in the 1970s, Māori have been disproportionately represented in admission rates (and, to an even greater extent, readmission rates) to inpatient units, and these admissions have been predominantly compulsory or forensic and at acute stages of psychosis (Mental Health Commission, 1998). Such statistics point quite clearly to the need to provide services which are congruent with Māori culture and values. To address these issues, an understanding of Māori well-being is essential for service development and delivery (Mental Health Commission, 1998, 2004). While many models of Māori health exist, all represent the holistic nature of Māori perspectives. Durie (1994) outlines the 'Whare Tapa Wha' framework (also referred to in English as 'four walls of the house') which is utilized extensively in the health sector today and proposes that mental wellness is a combination of four dimensions of the self: 'wairua' (spirituality); 'whanau' (family); 'hinengaro' (mental); and 'tinana' (physical). Just as four walls hold up a house, the four dimensions of a person interact collectively to contribute to wellness, with the spiritual dimension arguably being the most important. The Whare Tapa Wha framework has been incorporated into an outcome measure that can potentially be utilized within other services and which has been piloted across a number of sites in NZ (Kingi and Durie, 2001).

One model which is consistent with the Whare Tapa Wha framework and has been applied both within Kaupapa Mäori mental health services and within early intervention for psychosis services is the Pounamu model. This model was developed by Peta Ruha and introduced into a Mäori mental health service, Te Whare Marie, in 1999 (Manna, 2002). The Pounamu model stresses the importance of beginning clinical sessions with 'karakia' (prayer) and 'mihimihi' (introducing familial background), and incorporates a cultural and clinical assessment process based on the four walls of the Whare Tapa Wha model outlined above. Clients (or, in Mäori, 'tangata whaiora' – people seeking wellness) and 'whanau' (family) are presented with a visual representation of the Whare Tapa Wha model in which the various aspects of one's self fill out each dimension, collaboratively with the clinician and a cultural advisor (see Figure 15.1). The Pounamu model has been incorporated into the Wellington EIS and was delivered as a training workshop at a national conference in 2005.

Another vital aspect of Mäori approaches to mental health has been to stress the importance of cultural factors in understanding clinical presentations. This is particularly relevant in the area of psychosis, where certain experiences that may be construed as pathological from a conventional Western psychiatric position are deemed normative by Mäori (Taitimu, 2007). For example, the experience of hallucinations may be a normal, understandable and sometimes positive aspect of Mäori spirituality. In addition, oratory for Mäori is often metaphorical and it is common for Mäori to talk around a topic, a tendency that may be misinterpreted as tangential thinking or thought disorder. Of note for younger Mäori ('rangatahi') is 'whakama', a culture-bound experience including shame, self-abasement, feeling inferior or withdrawal, which is considered a normal and appropriate reaction to unfamiliar processes or environments, but could be misinterpreted as negative symptoms (Sachdev, 1990) – these environments might include, for example a clinical assessment room at a mental health service, or a new classroom at school, environments with mostly Pakeha, or when 'rangatahi' are asked to speak in front of others they do not know. To reduce the likelihood that misdiagnosis is contributing to the overrepresentation of Mäori using inpatient units for psychotic disorders, it is imperative that clinical staff are educated regarding cultural presentations. Education in New Zealand is currently very limited in this regard.

Mäori clinical services and the commitment to bicultural policy within mainstream services in NZ have arguably helped foster an atmosphere conducive to the survival of holistic, rather than narrow biomedical

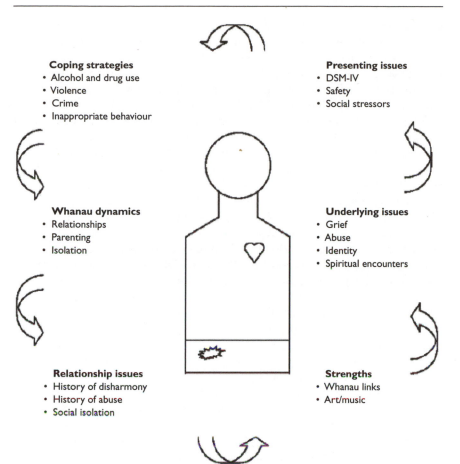

Coping strategies
- Alcohol and drug use
- Violence
- Crime
- Inappropriate behaviour

Presenting issues
- DSM-IV
- Safety
- Social stressors

Whanau dynamics
- Relationships
- Parenting
- Isolation

Underlying issues
- Grief
- Abuse
- Identity
- Spiritual encounters

Relationship issues
- History of disharmony
- History of abuse
- Social isolation

Strengths
- Whanau links
- Art/music

Figure 15.1 The Pounamu model

understandings of and approaches to mental health difficulties, including psychosis. The emphasis within the Māori framework on a holistic approach to psychosis, which recognizes the importance of factors such as family dynamics and history, as well as cultural and spiritual values, is congruent with certain aspects of psychological interventions for psychosis. We may see elements of this in some of the psychological innovations which have been developed in mainstream services.

Mainstream services

Although many of the recent innovations in psychological interventions for psychosis have taken place within EISs, the work of Randal *et al.* (2003), carried out in a residential rehabilitation centre in Auckland, demonstrates the value of 'late intervention' for those with so-called 'treatment resistant' psychotic disorders, and the centrality of the psychotherapeutic relationship in achieving positive outcomes for those clients. This approach is based on the notion of 'building a bridge of trust' with the people we serve, in the context of a hope-inducing spiral developmental model of 'recovery', whereby it is possible to create victorious (as opposed to vicious) cycles using a psychological skills approach to building strengths and reducing vulnerabilities, including those acquired by trauma (see Figure 15.2). This work has led to the development of a multimodal skills training package (Randal, 2004) for mental health staff which aims, among other things, to broaden the range of psychotherapeutic interventions that staff are able to offer to clients of mental health services. An important aspect of this work, which reflects a growing interest within NZ, is the emphasis given to the client's spirituality, and spiritual understandings of distressing experiences.

Predating the proliferation of EPPIC style early intervention services, the work of the local psychiatrist Ian Falloon (Falloon and Fadden, 1993) also had an impact on mainstream mental health services, particularly within Auckland where in the early 1990s it was embraced as the preferred model of care by community mental health services. Falloon's model of integrated mental health care emphasizes the importance of including psychotherapeutic and family interventions within standard mental health care, albeit within a predominantly medical paradigm.

At the time of writing, other psychotherapeutic innovations within mainstream mental health services with EISs include a joint consumer–clinician run Hearing Voices group (Lampshire and Loretto, 2004) offered to long-term clients of community mental health services in Auckland. This group is currently being evaluated, with initial results being encouraging.

Early intervention services (EISs)

EISs developed in NZ from the mid-1990s. They were given a particular impetus following an International Early Psychosis Association (IEPA) conference in Melbourne in 1996. Early intervention services have developed considerably throughout NZ since that time. By 2000, there were 18 statutory mental health services that worked wholly or partly in this area (Turner et al., 2004). At least three further services have been set up since then. Psychotherapeutic interventions are a core component of these services. Individual psychotherapies offered within EISs generally have a cognitively oriented flavour (Jackson et al., 1996), although inevitably individual inclinations of the practitioner mean that other psychotherapeutic approaches (including psychodynamic, personal construct theory, narrative, etc.) are also aspects of the work within EISs. These various approaches all emphasize the importance of helping clients construct personally meaningful

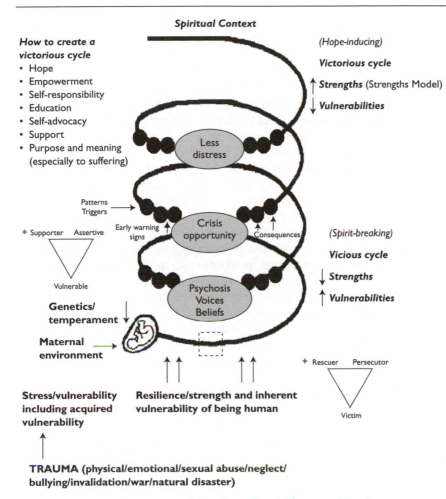

Spiritual Context

How to create a
victorious cycle
• Hope
• Empowerment
• Self-responsibility
• Education
• Self-advocacy
• Support
• Purpose and meaning
(especially to suffering)

(Hope-inducing)

Victorious cycle

↑ **Strengths** (Strengths Model)

↓ **Vulnerabilities**

Less
distress

Patterns
Triggers

* Supporter   Assertive

Early warning
signs

Crisis
opportunity

Consequences

Vulnerable

Psychosis
Voices
Beliefs

(Spirit-breaking)

Vicious cycle

↓ **Strengths**

↑ **Vulnerabilities**

**Genetics/
temperament**

**Maternal
environment**

+ Rescuer   Persecutor

Victim

**Stress/vulnerability
including acquired
vulnerability**

**Resilience/strength and inherent
vulnerability of being human**

**TRAUMA (physical/emotional/sexual abuse/neglect/
bullying/invalidation/war/natural disaster)**

* Quinby Durability Triangle   + Karpman Drama Triangle (Stewart and Jones)

As we go through life, we tend to re-cover the same old ground in our journey of
recovery. We are all born with some resilience and some vulnerability. The traumas
of life can sometimes make us more vulnerable and we can get into vicious cycles,
repeating old patterns which increase our vulnerability. However, with each new life
crisis we have the opportunity to increase our strengths and decrease our vulnerabilities
and create a victorious cycle.

Figure 15.2 Map of the journey of recovery

understandings of psychotic experiences and the need for flexibility in interventions.

Groups

EISs also offer a range of groups, many of which have psychotherapeutic aspects. While many such groups are a standard component of EISs worldwide (such as psycho-education and activity-based groups), in NZ they are imbued with a particular NZ flavour which recognizes the influence of factors such as culture on psychotic experiences. Examples of innovations within this field include philosophy groups (Burdett, 2001) and storytelling groups (Rook and Geekie, 2004), both offered by an EIS in Auckland. The philosophy group is a joint consumer–clinician facilitated group, which to date has been offered only to clients of EISs. Though more philosophical than psychotherapeutic in its orientation, it does have some overlap with psychotherapeutic interventions. In this group, clients are encouraged to explore issues of a philosophical nature (such as 'What is the nature of mind?' and 'Does medication change your personality?'). Provisional qualitative evaluations (Burdett and Geekie, 2003) suggest that clients feel they derive benefit from the group, and are clear about how it differs from other groups they have participated in: that is, they comment that it encourages them to think and question rather than providing them with information.

Also within an Auckland EIS, a storytelling group was initiated in response to requests by clients that they should be given more time to share their stories of psychosis with other clients. This group focuses on clients first developing their own unique story of psychosis (with no expectation that this ought to fit within any particular model of psychosis) and then sharing this with the group. The group endeavours to promote authoring of one's story, integration of this story, and reflection on the meaning of one's own – and others' – stories of psychosis and is also very well received by clients (Rook and Geekie, 2004).

Residential options

Recent years have witnessed developments within inpatient facilities that have helped promote psychotherapeutic interventions. In particular, in Auckland, a non-governmental organization (NGO), Mind Matters Trust, has established a five-bedded unit which offers brief focused interventions for younger clients (up to age 30). These interventions include, where appropriate, psychological support for psychotic experiences. Within the clinical community there is also support for establishing a Soteria House (Mosher et al., 2005) facility within NZ, although this remains at the proposal stage, awaiting funding at the time of writing.

Recovery through meaningful occupation

Enabling people to lead purposeful and satisfying lives by supporting them to engage in occupations – the things they want, need or are expected to do – has been increasingly recognized as essential in recovery from psychosis. Many EISs offer groups that provide opportunities for skill and role development to build personal strengths, confidence and identity. Clinical work can explore the meaning made of psychosis and the impact on occupational performance. This in turn fosters the ability to engage in a personally meaningful way with occupations and integrate into a community of choice. Vocational officers embedded within early intervention teams have also been shown to improve employment outcomes for clients.

Research

New Zealand also contributes to the international research effort. Recent years have seen NZ studies of: Māori understandings of what Pakeha call psychosis (Taitimu, 2007); the explanatory models used by service users who experience psychosis (Geekie and Read, 2009) and by voice hearers in the general population (Beavan, 2005); the relationship of psychosis to childhood trauma (Read *et al.*, 2003) and to substance abuse (Fergusson *et al.*, 2005); the relationship between psychosis in childhood and adulthood (Poulton *et al.*, 2000; Read *et al.*, 2008); evaluation of one of New Zealand's EISs (Theuma *et al.*, 2007); the views of service users and staff regarding alternatives to hospitalisation (Agar-Jacomb and Read, in press); the role of drug companies in influencing public opinion about psychosis (Read, 2008) and the origins of prejudice against people diagnosed 'schizophrenic' (Read and Harre, 2001; Read, 2007).

National support and development structures

In addition to and running alongside the clinical services described, there are a number of regional and national organizations which have a strong emphasis on psychotherapeutic and psychosocial approaches to psychosis. These include the National Steering Group for Early Intervention Services, a body which promotes EISs generally throughout the country. Since 1998 there has been an annual two- or three-day national training forum for clinicians working in the area of EISs and this generally has a strong psychotherapeutic representation. For the past few years, the recently formed NZ branch of ISPS has organized an annual 'Making Sense of Psychosis' (MSOP) conference. Consumer input is highly valued at both the national training forum and the MSOP conference, which have a tradition of offering a range of presenters, including both local and international experts. Both these conferences are well attended with around 200 delegates from around NZ. There are also local groups such as the Regional

Auckland Psychosis Group, which meets monthly to discuss theoretical and clinical approaches to psychosis.

These national and local initiatives both reflect and create a great energy and commitment within NZ to clinical approaches to psychoses, including but not limited to psychotherapeutic approaches. Indeed, they provide a platform for debate and discussion regarding the various understandings of and interventions for psychoses, and involve contributions from clients and a broad range of clinicians, with various cultural perspectives (Mäori, Pacific Island and Pakeha) represented. We conclude that while not free of difficulties or tensions, psychotherapeutic interventions for psychoses are in reasonably good health in NZ. There is increasing recognition of the value of such interventions and opportunities for working in innovative ways are encouraged.

References

Agar-Jacomb, K. and Read, J. (in press). Mental health crisis services: What do service users need when in crisis? *Journal of Mental Health*.

Beavan, V. (2007). *Angels at Our Tables: New Zealanders' experiences of hearing voices*. Unpublished doctoral dissertation, University of Aukland.

Burdett, J. (2001). Using group philosophical inquiry as a means of promoting recovery for people who experience mental illness. Unpublished Masters thesis, Deakin University, Australia.

Burdett, J. and Geekie, J. (2003). Philosophial inquiry groups for clients of a first episode psychosis service. Paper presented at 14th ISPS Symposium, Melbourne, September.

Durie, M.H. (1994). *Whaiora*. Auckland: Oxford University Press.

Falloon, I. and Fadden, G. (1993). *Integrated Mental Health Care*. Cambridge: Cambridge University Press.

Fergusson, D., Horwood, J. and Rideer, E. (2005). Tests of causal linkages between cannabis use and psychotic symptoms. *Addiction* 100: 35466.

Geekie, J. and Read, J. (2009). *Making Sense of Madness: Contesting the Meaning of Schizophrenia*. London: Routledge.

Gleeson, J.F.M. and McGorry, P.D. (eds) (2004). *Psychological Interventions in Early Psychosis: A Treatment Handbook*. Chichester: Wiley.

Jackson, H.J., McGorry, P.D., Edwards, J. and Hulbert, C.A. (1996). Cognitively-oriented psychotherapy for early psychosis. In P. Cotten and H.J. Jackson (eds) *Early Intervention and Prevention in Mental Health*. Melbourne: Australian Psychological Society, pp. 131–154.

Kawharu, H. (1989). *Waitangi: Mäori and Pakeha Perspectives of the Treaty of Waitangi*. Auckland: Oxford University Press.

Kingi, T.K.R. and Durie, M.H. (2001). Hua Oranga: a Mäori measure of mental health outcome, mental health outcomes research in Aotearoa. Mental health research and development strategy. In *Proceedings of the September 2000 Conference*. Auckland: Health Research Council.

Lampshire, D. and Loretto, M. (2004). A hearing voices group. Paper presented at

ISPS – NZ 2nd Annual Making Sense of Psychosis Conference, Auckland, October.

Manna, L. (2002). Biculturalism in practice.Te Pounamu: integration of a Mäori model with traditional clinical assessment processes. In L.W. Nikora, M. Levy, B. Masters, W. Waitoki, N. Te Awekotuku and R.J.M. Etheredge (eds) *Proceedings of the National Mäori Graduates of Psychology Symposium 2002*, University of Waikato, 29–30 November.

Mental Health Commission (1998). *Blueprint for Mental Health Services in New Zealand: How Things Need To Be*. Wellington: Mental Health Commission.

Mental Health Commission (2004). *Early Intervention in Psychosis*. Wellington: Mental Health Commission.

Mosher, L., Hendrix, V. and Fort, D. (2005). *Soteria: Through Madness to Deliverance*. Philadelphia: Xlibris.

Poulton, R., Caspi, A., Moffitt, T., Cannon, M., Murray, R. and Harrington, H. (2000). Children's self-reported psychotic symptoms and adult schizophreniform disorder: a 15-year longitudinal study. *Archives of General Psychiatry* 57, 1053–1058.

Randal, P. (2004). Multimodal therapy for facilitating recovery and addressing barriers to a life worth living: a twelve weeks skills-based course. Paper presented at ISPS Conference, Manchester.

Randal, P., Simpson, A. and Laidlaw, T. (2003). Can recovery-focused multimodal psychotherapy facilitate symptom and function improvement in people with treatment-resistant psychotic illness? A comparison study. *Australian and New Zealand Journal of Psychiatry* 37: 720–727.

Read, J. (2008). Schizophrenia, drug companies and the internet. *Social Science & Medicine* 66: 99–109.

Read, J. and Harre, N. (2001). The role of biological and genetic causal beliefs in the stigmatisation of 'mental patients'. *Journal of Mental Health* 10: 223–235.

Read, J., Agar, K., Argyle, N. and Aderhold, V. (2003). Sexual and physical assault during childhood and adulthood as predictors of hallucinations, delusions and thought disorder. *Psychology and Psychotherapy: Theory Research and Practice* 76: 1–22.

Rook, D. and Geekie, J. (2004). A storytelling group. Paper presented at ISPS – NZ 2nd Annual Making Sense of Psychosis Conference, Auckland, October.

Sachdev, P. (1990). Whakama: culturally determined behaviour in the New Zealand Mäori. *Psychological Medicine* 20: 433–444.

Taitimu, M. (2005). Ngä Whakawhitinga – Standing at the Crossroads: Mäori ways of understanding extra-ordinary experiences and schizophrenia. Unpublished doctoral dissertation. University of Aukland.

Theuma, M., Read, J., Moskowitz, A. and Stewart, A. (2007). Evaluation of a New Zealand early intervention service for psychosis. *New Zealand Journal of Psychiatry* 36: 119–128.

Turner, M., Nightingale, S., Smith-Hamel, C. and Mulder, R. (2004). Early intervention for psychosis in New Zealand. *New Zealand Medical Journal* 117: U1001.

Part III

From present to future

Different modalities of treatment and interventions

Chapter 16

Psychodynamic treatment of psychosis in the USA

Promoting development beyond biological reductionism

Brian Koehler and Ann-Louise S. Silver

Reductionism versus integration between biological and psychosocial

We in the US Chapter of the International Society for the Psychological Treatments of the Schizophrenias and other Psychoses (ISPS-US), since we began in 1998, have felt locked in an exhaustingly chronic wrestling match with biological reductionism. We bristle at each pharmaceutical advertisement and educational offering that begins, 'Schizophrenia is a brain disease', as if top-down processing, i.e. the effect of the mind and social experience on the brain, did not exist, or was largely, by agreement, irrelevant. We draw back from *The Guidelines for the Treatment of Schizophrenia*, issued by the American Psychiatric Association that promote the use of various medications singly and in combination, while giving only a passing nod to the role of human interaction. As noted by Yrjö Alanen (1997; Koehler, 2007), integrated psychiatry includes interactionality with other persons as part of human biology. We protest against recommendations that would have psychodynamic therapy ruled outside of 'appropriate' treatment for psychotic conditions. (Don't talk with 'them' in any depth. It can only upset them; and besides, you have no 'evidence' that your approach has ever worked.) As Adolf Meyer (1908) taught us a century ago:

> In the little instruction the [medical] student gets, he is apt to be made to understand that it is unscientific to think of mental disorders in any other terms than disorders of the brain itself, or cerebral disorders induced by disease of various internal organs. . . . [However,] to be helpful . . . we must have a good history with special attention to the early developments, and to the possibilities of early management . . . Psychiatry consists in what we have learned to do with the patient.
>
> (Meyer, 1908: 5–8)

This century-old quote still applies today in our pharmaceutically driven environment.

We often feel that ISPS-US is a beleaguered band of Hortons, as depicted in Dr. Seuss's classic, *Horton Hears a Who!* (1954). Jungle animals jeer at Horton the elephant who, with his great floppy ears, can hear the cries for help of the microscopic inhabitants of a town located on a speck of dust. The inhabitants all cry out together, unheard by the animals until a shirker named Jo-Jo finally joins the community's shouts. We have heard our patients' cries of alarm, and are trying to persuade the larger mental health community not to forget Martin Buber's statement: 'All real living is meeting.' We want people to rediscover Sullivan's (1962) *Schizophrenia as a Human Process*, Fromm-Reichmann's (1950) *Principles of Intensive Psychotherapy* and *Semrad: The Heart of a Therapist* (Rako and Mazer, 1984).

We and the sufferers of psychosis all need time together, regular dependable time, to build our relationships and our bridges back to manageable emotions and everyday living. We struggle against the ever more forceful trend supporting evidence-based medicine, with its disdain for the anecdotal. We quote Grace Jackson's comments on the listserve of the International Center for the Study of Psychiatry and Psychology, posted on 24 February 2004:

Evidence Based Medicine is a Postmodern phenomenon that encompasses aspects of a unique ontology (worldview) and epistemology (way of knowing) – since the 1970s, a dependence upon the Randomized Controlled Trial. A cultural historian might suggest to us that Evidence Based Medicine has been the predictable outgrowth of Postmodernism – that phase of human development associated with the confluence of logical positivism, biostatistics, digital technologies, and the nihilism that has arisen from the continuing tragedies of the nuclear age. What few physicians seem to contemplate is the possibility that the 'acceptance' of EBM is inherently a philosophical (ontological) act. It rests upon the assumptions that Evidence *can* be determined, and that Evidence *should* be determined (and applied) as a basis for medical decision making.

. . . In the Postmodern landscape, Evidence has come to be based upon quantities, similarities, populations, and averages – rather than qualities, idiosyncrasies, individual narratives, and specifics. This medical epistemology might not be so critical, were it not for the ethical crises which now denude the integrity of the prevailing Evidence: 1) publication bias; 2) concealment of negative findings (file drawer effect); 3) manipulations in clinical research designs (placebo washouts, non-comparative dosing strategies, underpowered studies, paltry effect sizes).

Recognizing the dubious reliability of the Evidence upon which clinical practice has increasingly come to depend (e.g. the information presented by journals, textbooks, government agencies, the news

media), the time has come for physicians to contemplate the ramifi-
cations of Postmodern philosophy within their profession. It is time for
providers to reassess the value of direct observation, and to trust more
readily both the empirical and intuitive discoveries they make each day
in their personal experience (even if those discoveries are contradicted
by the 'best available Evidence'). (Jackson, 2004)

That is, we should value 'practice-based evidence.'

For an elaboration of the ethical crises and their long history, we
recommend McGovern (1985), and Whitaker (2002), as well as David
Brendel's (2006) *Healing Psychiatry: Bridging the Science/Humanism Divide*.

We believe that in the not so distant future, once the limitations of
radical reductionism have been fully understood, there may occur a shift in
our psychiatric-neuroscientific models of the human being, which follows
the shifts taking place in some other sciences, e.g. post-quantum physics, a
shift from reductionism to emergence-complex organizational structures
which cannot be reduced to the more basic structural processes which
initiated them. Laughlin (2005), professor of physics at Stanford University
and Nobel Laureate for his work on the fractional quantum Hall effect,
pointed out that: 'There are two conflicting primal impulses of the human
mind – one to simplify a thing to its essentials, the other to see through the
essentials to the greater implications' (p. ix). Laughlin notes that 'the
natural world is regulated by the essentials and by the powerful principles
of organization that flow out of them' (p. ix). This organization can acquire
meaning and a life of its own, and begin to transcend the parts from which
it is made. At higher levels of complexity, such as are found in human
beings and their relational and cultural contexts, cause-and-effect relationships are more difficult to document. The reductionistic ideal, that nature
will be revealed and understood through division into smaller and smaller
component parts, needs to be supplemented by the study and understanding of how nature organizes itself, i.e. reductionism giving way to emergence. Philosopher of science Karl Popper (Mayr, 2007) pointed out that 'as
a philosophy, reductionism is a failure . . . we live in a universe of emergent
novelty which, as a rule, is not completely reducible to any of the preceding
stages' (p. 79). As much as we might want to reduce psychosis to specific
abnormalities in genetic coding and in neurotransmission, it is far more
complex and individualistic than that; it reflects a life story, its calamities
and its victories.

Harvard evolutionary biologist Ernst Mayr (2007) offers us a critique of
the failure of reductionism in accounting for complex biological systems.
For a comprehensive understanding of complex systems one also needs to
understand the interaction among the component parts, e.g. partitioning
water into hydrogen gas and oxygen tells us nothing of the liquidity of water.
As pointed out by neuroscientist Steven Rose (2005), life is not a static thing

but a dynamic process. Throughout the organism's development, life is a dynamic relationship between homeostasis (stability) and homeodynamics (change). Rose argues that living beings are continuously constructing themselves, analogous to rebuilding an airplane in mid-flight. This process of self-creation, a process emerging from gene–environment interactions, Rose calls 'autopoiesis', a process in which the organism becomes an active player in its own destiny. We believe that along with the emphasis on gene–environment interactions 'and the role of random processes in development, we must take autopoietic processes into account in order to encompass the richness and complexity of the human being in general, and the human being suffering from severe mental illness in particular.

Taylor and Gonzaga (2007) point to the significant importance of social relationships and their role in survival because relationships provide the protection needed to maintain one's sense of safety and that of one's offspring. They reviewed research data which demonstrates that social contacts protect against the adverse effects of stress partly through oxytocin-induced suppression of the limbic-hypothalamic-pituitary-adrenal axis (LHPA). Uchino and colleagues (2007) reported that both the quality and quantity of one's social relationships predict lower all-cause mortality. The associations between social relationships and health are most evident for cardiovascular mortality, but also with cancer and HIV mortality. Carter (2007) noted that the benefits of social bonds and social support have been demonstrated in epidemiological studies: 'Perceived social support is often negatively correlated with various illnesses, ranging from mental illness to heart disease and cancer' (p. 425). He also underscores the role of oxytocin as a putative social neuropeptide as a buffering agent to stressful experience through its down-regulating effect on the limbic-thalamic-pituitary-adrenal axis.

The intergenerational transmission of inducible defenses against threats to safety and survival and the role of gene–environment interaction have also been documented at the biological level by Meaney (2004), Suomi (2004) and Sapolsky (2005). Holmes (1993) has proposed that attachment may be the biological basis for psychotherapy. Cozolino (2002) adds to this concept that attachment, at its core, may be a means of survival and thus a means of controlling anxiety. The association between attachment and affect regulation has been recently documented by Carter and colleagues (2005).

Cozolino (2002) reported on the early primate studies by Harry Harlow involving monkeys raised in social isolation and the subsequent attempts to resocialize them. Harlow used younger monkeys who persistently initiated contact despite the isolates' defensive reactions, e.g. withdrawal, freezing, etc. These younger 'therapist' monkeys continued to approach and cling to the social isolates. Gradually, the isolates 'thawed' out and learned to initiate play and positive social behaviors. Cozolino (2002) suggests that these younger monkeys connected to their isolate counterparts on a very basic physical, visceral and emotional level. In addition, they were persistent, refusing to stop despite the defensive behaviors of the isolates. In referring to these younger 'therapists' Cozolino concluded:

> Their clinging, cuddling, and soothing behaviors interrupted the isolates' autistic behaviors, allowing them to engage in movement, exploration, and social interactions. Whereas human therapists take years to learn how to facilitate these healing changes, these little monkeys did it reflexively. This small but eloquent study demonstrates that learning not to fear and learning to love are biologically interwoven.
>
> (Cozolino, 2002: 314)

Many of us in ISPS-US feel that the work of the therapist has been made overly elitist, requiring years of very expensive training (college, medical school, psychiatric training, psychoanalytic training; or college, PhD training, internship, psychoanalytic training, etc.). But there are many people who have chosen to work with those with mental disorders, who work as case managers and psychiatric technicians, who should be supported with additional training and supervision, so that they could work more confidently and in greater depth with their clients. Those of us who choose this work very often began our 'training' as toddlers (Fromm-Reichmann, 1989: 470). Cozolino (2002) noted:

> There is no doubt that evolution has shaped us to love one another . . . Loving relationships help our brains to develop, integrate, and remain flexible. Through love we regulate each other's brain chemistry, sense of well-being, and immunological functioning. And when the drive to love is thwarted – when we are frightened, abused, or neglected – our mental health is compromised.
>
> (Cozolino, 2002: 314)

Perhaps, the World Health Organization's consistent finding that persons diagnosed with schizophrenia in 'developing' countries do significantly better than their counterparts in the 'developed' world could be attributed to the importance of sociocultural factors (Hopper, 2004). Small (2006) laments the marginalization of a cultural and medical anthropological perspective on psychiatric illnesses in Western societies. She interviewed Harvard psychiatrist-medical anthropologist Arthur Kleinman on the role of culture in psychiatric disorders. Small noted:

> What is missing from . . . diagnoses, Kleinman feels, is an understanding of how the human mind is entwined with the whole experience of being an individual embedded in a family, a culture, and a society.

Mind and body cannot be separated, and both are affected by everything else in life. He believes strongly that all human experiences are
social, and that to understand someone's mental state you must know
everything about that person's relationships.

Surprisingly, Kleinman thinks that what is absent from health care
practice is anthropology . . . being a careful observer and a good
listener, and interested in the details of human relationships. After
decades of observing thousands of psychiatric interviews in both
Western and Chinese cultures he believes that patients are missing what
they need most: compassionate understanding not just of their symptoms but also of their lives.

(Small, 2006: 149)

We in ISPS aim to reverse this trend. Small (2006: 150) observed that when
clinicians and researchers ignore the very personal and cultural aspects of
illness 'they turn a blind eye to how deeply we are all affected by forces
other than viruses, genes and biochemistry'. Our perspective at ISPS-US is
that mind and culture are intimately involved in gene expression through
the dynamic bridge of transcription factors which are important in the link
between social experience and gene expression. This has been demonstrated
in the schizophrenia spectrum disorders by the adoption research of Tienari
and colleagues (2004) in which the results pointed to genetic control of
sensitivity to the environment or environmental control of gene expression.

Otto Will (see Sacksleder *et al.*, 1987) reminds us that we not only inherit
our genes, but also our cultures. Harvard social psychiatrist Leon Eisenberg
(2004) reiterates this theme and points out that although genes set the
boundaries for what is possible, it is the environment which parses out the
actual. Genes, as noted by Linden (2007), cannot specify the complete
development of the complex structure of the human brain. Linden, a
neuroscientist at the Johns Hopkins University School of Medicine, informs
us: 'The precise specification and wiring of the brain depends upon factors
not encoded in the genes (called epigenetic factors), including the effects of
the environment' (p. 52). Many biochemical factors, including transcription
factors, enable experience to influence gene expression, i.e. the activation
(e.g. acetylation, demethylation) or suppression of gene expression (e.g.
methylation of DNA). The neurodevelopment of the brain is influenced by
a host of factors, including prenatal stress, social isolation, various kinds of
psychosocial trauma (e.g. sexual, physical and emotional abuse), profound
and chronic stress, etc. Indeed, many of the neuroscience findings in
schizophrenia and bipolar research overlap substantially with the neuroscience of stress/fear/trauma and social isolation/defeat (Cotter and
Pariante, 2002; Pariante and Cotter, 2004; Koehler, 2007).

Culture and genes must be part of our language which takes on the
ethical responsibility of describing and treating the variety of mental

disorders. The models of belief to explain mental disorders which incorporate biology and culture, as well as the complexity of the interaction between the wider history of the culture into which the individual has been inserted and the 'smaller' history of the unique individual and family (Davoine and Gaudillière, 2004), are testaments of hope, as Small (2006) points out, and that hope is an antidote to the human misery often associated with mental illness.

A reason for hope, as opposed to therapeutic nihilism, are the findings of recovery patterns across countries. In regard to ten long-term follow-up studies of schizophrenia that had average follow-up periods of 15 years or more, Calabrese and Corrigan (2005) conclude:

> Each of these studies found that, rather than having a progressively deteriorating course, schizophrenia has a heterogeneous range of courses from severe cases requiring repeated or continuous hospitalization to cases in which a single illness episode is followed by complete remission of symptoms. The findings reported in these studies as a whole indicate that roughly half of the participants recovered or significantly improved over the long-term, suggesting that remission or recovery is much more common than originally thought.
>
> (Calabrese and Corrigan, 2005: 71)

In a recent review of the relevant psychosocial research in schizophrenia, Boydell *et al.*, (2004), conclude:

> It is now clear, however, that, in order to understand the causes of schizophrenia, the role of the social environment cannot be continued to be ignored. In saying this, we are not proposing an oppositional social *instead of* biological approach, which we consider as futile as arguing whether poverty or mycobacteria cause tuberculosis! Rather, we suggest that both social and biological factors need to be studied, as well as their interaction. We need to recognize that (i) social factors can impact on brain development, (ii) some social factors give rise to psychological vulnerabilities, and (iii) many social factors act over the life course, creating developmental liabilities . . . It is possible that the social environment creates psychological vulnerabilities that act additively to the risk function in combination with genetic or non-genetic neurodevelopmental impairments. The challenge for schizophrenia researchers in the coming decades is first to distinguish those candidate social factors that do contribute to schizophrenia risk from those that do not and second, to identify the interplay between these factors, genetic susceptibility, and their respective effects on, and interactions with, brain development.
>
> (Boydell *et al.*, 2004: 239–240)

The tide is turning

The tide seems to be turning: evidence of the devastating physiological side effects of the newer antipsychotic medications, the statistics regarding the vast numbers of severely mentally ill housed in jails and prisons, and the statistics on the low average number of mental health visits per year per patient, combine to make the broken mental health system in the United States an embarrassment. Those attending the 2007 American Psychiatric Association's annual meeting in San Diego were pleased and surprised by the frequent emphasis on the importance of psychodynamic work, the need to really get to know one's patient, and to form a real working alliance. We hope that some of the money being poured into very expensive pharmaceuticals will be redirected towards interpersonal approaches, and that the need-adapted approaches developed in Scandinavia will become the model for a US revitalization. Neurobiology is beginning to provide the convincing evidence that the psychoses are responses to severe stress; teamwork and trust are the best treatments for this lonely stress.

Despite the hegemony of reductionistic approaches to mental illness in the United States, psychotherapeutic and psychosocial treatments continue to thrive and be developed. Psychosocial therapies have recently been described in neuropsychiatric textbooks devoted to schizophrenia (Swartz *et al.*, 2006). Psychosocial approaches are wide ranging, including, but not limited to: peer socialization (Davidson, 2003); relapse prevention models (Davidson *et al.*, 2000); identification of the role of the person and healing processes (Strauss, 1997); integrative psychoeducational models (Hogarty, 2002); social skills training (Pratt and Mueser, 2002); person-centered (Prouty, 1994) and pre-therapy models (Prouty, 2003); home-based alternatives to hospitalization (Podvoll, 2003); crisis residential care (Fenton and Mosher, 2000); group psychotherapeutic approaches (Stone, 1996; Kanas, 2000); multiple family therapy (McFarlane, 2004); group cognitive behavioral therapy (CBT) approaches (Landa *et al.*, 2006); CBT/educational programs (Gallagher and Nazarian, 1995); integration of psychoanalysis and psychoneurobiology (Sarwer-Foner, 1997; Koehler, 2007); investigating the role of dissociation in psychosis (Vermetten *et al.*, 2007); psychoanalysis and psychoanalytic therapy (Feinsilver, 1986; Waugaman and Searles, 1990; Marcus, 1992; Eigen, 1993; Robbins, 1993; Blatt and Ford, 1994; Garfield, 1995; Volkan, 1995; Lotterman, 1996; Mitrani and Mitrani, 1997; Volkan and Akhtar, 1997; Bergman, 1999; Spotnitz, 1999; Appel, 2000; Havens, 2000; Karon, 2003; Koehler, 2003; Ver Eecke, 2003; Dorman, 2004; Silver, Koehler and Karon, 2004). Psychoanalysts in the USA are incorporating new developments in the American Relational school, particularly the work of Philip Bromberg (2006). Recent studies in Europe have demonstrated the efficacy of psychodynamic therapy in psychosis (Alanen, 1997; Siani and Siciliani, 2000). Phenomenological approaches to psychosis have been having an influence on psychological models and treatment (Sass, 1994; Davidson, 2003; Kircher and David, 2003). This list is by no means exhaustive.

Psychodynamic psychotherapy and psychoanalysis in the USA continue to benefit from emergent integrative approaches. These include the integration of infant research (Beebe and Lachmann, 2002; Beebe et al., 2005) and neuroscience (Mancia, 2006; Doidge, 2007). Psychoanalysts are incorporating new developments in attachment research (Carter et al., 2005). We hope to establish an integration of new developments in cognitive behavioral approaches to psychosis as well as an ongoing dialogue with cognitive therapists working in the field of psychosis psychotherapy (Bentall, 2003; Freeman and Garety, 2004; Kingdon and Turkington, 2005).

Psychoanalysts affiliated with ISPS-US, have been sensitizing us to the role of the broader social history and culture in psychosis, particularly the effects of transgenerational transmission of trauma from social catastrophes (Davoine and Gaudillière, 2004). We are becoming much more attuned to the role of trauma in psychotic disorders thanks to the research of our ISPS colleague in New Zealand, John Read and his associates (Read et al., 2004). The role of traumatic dissociation in mental disorders is being examined and incorporated in treatment approaches (Vermetten et al., 2007). We are studying the variables and processes in psychosis which lead to recovery from a research perspective (Ralph and Corrigan, 2005), as well as from narratives of persons suffering from the illnesses, e.g. from the National Empowerment Center (www.power2u.org). We are hoping to have much more of a dialogue with and active participation in our proceedings by persons identified as having a mental illness without the 'us' versus 'them' barriers. We in the United States are learning from our ISPS colleagues in other countries, particularly in Scandinavia (Alanen, 1997; Cullberg, 2006).

Cognitive neuropsychiatrists, as psychoanalysts, have been emphasizing the important role of emotions in mental illness (Lane and Nadel, 2000; Aleman et al., 2006). Some believe that the neuroscience of severe mental illness overlaps significantly with the neuroscience findings in profound stress/fear/anxiety/trauma as well as social isolation and social defeat (Koehler, 2007). Anxiety, many psychoanalysts believe, is central to mental disorder. There are encouraging signs of an integration of neuropsychiatric/neuroimaging models and psychodynamic models of mental illness/disorder (David Silbersweig, personal communication).[1] Recent research in neuroplasticity (Begley, 2007; Doidge, 2007) and its relevance to psychotherapetic change and action has been an exciting development in our field. The effects of psychotherapy on the brain is another related new development and we are hoping that the trickle of research studies soon become a flowing stream of positive evidence for its effectiveness in persons with mental illness. Psychologists (Kagan, 2006) and neuroscientists (Freeman, 2001; Edelman,

2004; Sanguineti, 2007) have been demonstrating the limitations of neurobiological reductionism. An integration of neuroscience, including exciting
developments in developmental psychobiology and social neuroscience
(Cacioppo and Berntson, 2004; Hofer, 2004; Sapolsky, 2005; Cacioppo *et al.*, 2006) and mirror-neuron research, particularly as applied to schizophrenia (Gallese, 2007; Maurizio Peciccia, personal communication), cog-
nitive behavioral therapies and psychoanalysis, is what many of us in the US
Chapter of ISPS are striving for.

Perhaps our sociocultural milieu regarding the psychosocial and
psychodynamic treatment of psychosis is depicted in the opening lines
from Charles Dickens' *A Tale of Two Cities*: 'It was the best of times, it was
the worst of times.' We in the United States, patients and clinicians alike,
are struggling against the detrimental and corrosive effects of reductionistic
trends in psychiatric understanding and practice. At the same time, we have
reason to hope as the human need for meaning and relation cannot be
silenced, even when the need for relationship ushers in terrifying fears of
abandonment and loss. I (BK) am reminded here of what Manfred Bleuler,
son of Eugen Bleuler who gave us the term 'the schizophrenias', told ISPS
co-founder Gaetano Benedetti: 'Psychotherapy is the soul of psychiatry'
(Benedetti, personal communication). Cancro (2005: 247), in addressing the
need for relationship in the treatment of even the most psychiatrically ill of
patients, concluded:

> The abandonment of the doctor–patient relationship can only be
> injurious to both the doctor and the patient. Even the most regressed
> patient forms a relationship and can be influenced by that relationship.
> There is nothing more important in a psychotherapeutic relationship
> than the evolution of the relationship, which (as such) is in fact more
> psychotherapeutic then the interpretations. Ultimately, we are social
> creatures, and depend upon relationships to sustain us. This is as true
> for the psychotic individual as it is for those of us who are not.

We in ISPS-US refuse to turn a blind eye to the dynamic living person
embedded within multiple relational and sociocultural contexts. Rather
than assume that mind and social experience are relatively non-significant,
as many contemporary researchers and theorists do, we are attempting to
plumb the depths of human experience and its relationship to human
psychiatric disorders. We believe that the cornerstone of all treatment is the
psychotherapeutic relationship and that the sidelining of that relationship
by whatever theory or practice of contemporary psychiatry, or by whatever
social and personal resistances to engaging in such relationships with more
disturbed individuals, deprives us and our patients of our full humanity and
opportunities for a more lasting recovery.

Note

1 David Silbersweig, M.D. is Co-Director of the Functional Neuroimaging Laboratory at Weill Medical College of Cornell University.

References

Alanen, Y.O. (1997). *Schizophrenia: Its Origins and Need-Adapted Treatment*. London: Karnac.

Aleman, A., Medford, N. and David, A.S. (eds) (2006). *The Cognitive Neuropsychiatry of Emotion and Emotional Disorders*. New York: Psychology Press.

Appel, J.W. (2000). *Who's in Charge? Autonomy and Mental Disorder*. Danbury, CT: Rutledge Books.

Beebe, B. and Lachmann, F.M. (2002). *Infant Research and Adult Treatment: Co-Constructing Interactions*. Hillsdale, NJ: Analytic Press.

Beebe, B., Knoblauch, S., Rustin, J. and Sorter, D. (2005). *Forms of Intersubjectivity in Infant Research and Adult Treatment*. New York: Other Press.

Begley, S. (2007). *Train Your Mind Change Your Brain: How a New Science Reveals Our Extraordinary Potential to Transform Ourselves*. New York: Ballantine Books.

Bentall, R.P. (2003). *Madness Explained: Psychosis and Human Nature*. Harmondsworth: Penguin.

Bergman, A. (1999). *Ours, Yours, Mine: Mutuality and the Emergence of the Separate Self*. Northvale, NJ: Jason Aronson.

Blatt, S.J. and Ford, R.Q. (1994). *Therapeutic Change: An Object Relations Perspective*. New York: Plenum Press.

Boydell, J., van Os, J. and Murray, R.M. (2004). Is there a role for social factors in a comprehensive development model for schizophrenia? In M.S. Keshavan, J.L. Kennedy and R.M. Murray (eds) *Neurodevelopment and Schizophrenia*. New York: Cambridge University Press, pp. 224–247.

Brendel, D. (2006). *Healing Psychiatry: Bridging the Science/Humanism Divide*. Cambridge, MA: MIT Press.

Bromberg, P.M. (2006). *Awakening the Dreamer: Clinical Journeys*. Mahwah, NJ: Analytic Press.

Cacioppo, J.T. and Berntson, G.C. (eds) (2004). *Essays in Social Neuroscience*. Cambridge, MA: MIT Press.

Cacioppo, J.T., Visser, P.S. and Pickett, C.L. (eds) (2006). *Social Neuroscience: People Thinking about Thinking People*. Cambridge, MA: MIT Press.

Calabrese, J.D. and Corrigan, P.W. (2005). Beyond dementia praecox: findings from long-term follow-up studies of schizophrenia. In R.O. Ralph and P.W. Corrigan (eds) *Recovery in Mental Illness: Broadening Our Understanding of Wellness*. Washington, DC: American Psychological Association, pp. 63–84.

Cancro, R. (2005). Frontline: a review of the concept of the schizophrenic disorders. *Journal of the American Academy of Psychoanalysis and Dynamic Psychiatry* 33, 2: 241–247.

Carter, C.S. (2007). Neuropeptides and the protective effects of social bonds. In E. Harmon-Jones and P. Winkielman (eds) *Social Neuroscience: Integrating*

Biological and Psychological Explanations of Social Behavior. New York: Guilford Press, pp. 425–438.

Carter, C.S., Anhert, L., Grossman, K.E. *et al.* (eds) (2005). *Attachment and Bonding: A New Synthesis*. Cambridge, MA: MIT Press.

Cotter, D. and Pariante, C.M. (2002). Stress and the progression of the developmental hypothesis of schizophrenia. *British Journal of Psychiatry* 181: 363–365.

Cozolino, L.J. (2002). *The Neuroscience of Psychotherapy: Building and Rebuilding the Human Brain*. New York: Norton.

Cullberg, J. (2006). *Psychoses: An Integrative Perspective*. London and New York: Routledge.

Davidson, L. (2003). *Living Outside Mental Illness: Qualitative Studies of Recovery in Schizophrenia*. New York: New York University Press.

Davidson, L., Stayner, D.A., Chinman, M.J., Lambert, S. and Sledge, W.H. (2000). Preventing relapse and readmission in psychosis: Using patients' subjective experience in designing clinical interventions. In B. Martindale, A. Bateman, M. Crowe and F. Margison (eds) *Psychosis: Psychological Approaches and their Effectiveness*. London: Gaskell, pp. 134–156.

Davoine, F. and Gaudillière, J.-M. (2004). *History Beyond Trauma: Whereof One Cannot Speak, Thereof One Cannot Stay Silent*. New York: Other Press.

Doidge, N. (2007). *The Brain that Changes Itself*. New York: Viking.

Dorman, D. (2004). *Dante's Cure: A Journey Out of Madness*. New York: Other Press.

Edelman, G.M. (2004). *Wider than the Sky: The Phenomenal Gift of Consciousness*. New Haven, CT: Yale University Press.

Eigen, M. (1993). *The Psychotic Core*. Northvale, NJ: Jason Aronson.

Eisenberg, L. (2004). Social psychiatry and the human genome: Contextualizing heritability. *British Journal of Psychiatry* 184: 101–103.

Feinsilver, D.B. (ed.) (1986). *Towards a Comprehensive Model for Schizophrenic Disorders: Psychoanalytic Essays in Memory of Ping-Nie Pao, M.D.* Hillsdale, NJ: Analytic Press.

Fenton, W.S. and Mosher, L.R. (2000). Crisis residential care for patients with serious mental illness. In B. Martindale, A. Bateman, M. Crowe and F. Margison (eds) *Psychosis: Psychological Approaches and their Effectiveness*. London: Gaskell, pp. 157–176.

Freeman, D. and Garety, P. (2004). *Paranoia: The Psychology of Persecutory Delusions*. New York: Psychology Press.

Freeman, W.J. (2001). *How Brains Make Up Their Minds*. New York: Columbia University Press.

Fromm-Reichmann, F. (1950). *Principles of Intensive Psychotherapy*. Chicago: University of Chicago Press.

Fromm-Reichmann, F. (1989). Reminiscences of Europe. In A.-L. Silver (ed.) *Psychoanalysis and Psychosis*. Madison, CT: International Universities Press, pp. 469–481.

Gallagher, R.E. and Nazarian, J. (1995). A comprehensive cognitive-behavioral/educational program for schizophrenic patients. *Bulletin of the Menninger Clinic* 59, 3: 357–371.

Gallese, V. (2007). The shared manifold hypothesis: embodied simulation and its role in empathy and social cognition. In T. Farrow and P. Woodruff (eds) *Empathy in Mental Illness*. Cambridge: Cambridge University Press, pp. 448–472.

Garfield, D. (1995). *Unbearable Affect: A Guide to the Psychotherapy of Psychosis*. New York: Wiley.

Havens, L. (2000). Treating psychoses. In A.N. Sabo and L. Havens (eds) *The Real World Guide to Psychotherapy Practice*. Cambridge, MA: Harvard University Press, pp. 149–162.

Hofer, M.A. (2004). Developmental psychobiology of early attachment. In B.J. Casey (ed.) *Developmental Psychobiology*. Washington, DC: American Psychiatric Publishing, pp. 1–28.

Holmes, J. (1993). Attachment theory: A biological basis for psychotherapy? *British Journal of Psychiatry* 163: 430–438.

Hogarty, G.E. (2002). *Personal Therapy for Schizophrenia and Related Disorders: A Guide to Individualized Treatment*. New York: Guilford Press.

Hopper, K. (2004). Interrogating the meaning of 'culture' in the WHO international studies of schizophrenia. In J.H. Jenkins and R.J. Barret (eds) *Schizophrenia, Culture, and Subjectivity: The Edge of Experience*. New York: Cambridge University Press, pp. 62–86.

Jackson, G. (Feb. 24, 2004) listserve posting of www.ICSPP.org, the International Center for the Study of Psychiatry and Psychology. (Reprint permission granted by author.)

Kagan, J. (2006). *An Argument for Mind*. New Haven, CT: Yale University Press.

Kanas, N. (2000). Group therapy and schizophrenia: an integrative model. In B. Martindale, A. Bateman, M. Crowe and F. Margison (eds) *Psychosis: Psychological Approaches and their Effectiveness*. London: Gaskell, pp. 120–133.

Karon, B. (2003). The tragedy of schizophrenia without psychotherapy. *Journal of the American Academy of Psychoanalysis and Dynamic Psychiatry* 31, 1: 89–118.

Kingdon, D.G. and Turkington, D. (2005). *Cognitive Therapy of Schizophrenia*. New York: Guilford Press.

Kircher, T. and David, A. (eds) (2003). *The Self in Neuroscience and Psychiatry*. Cambridge: Cambridge University Press.

Koehler, B. (2003). Interview with Gaetano Benedetti, M.D. *Journal of the American Academy of Psychoanalysis and Dynamic Psychiatry* 31, 1: 75–87.

Koehler, B. (2007). The schizophrenias: brain, mind and culture. Paper presented at ISPS Norway, Hamar, Norway, 8 February.

Lane, R.D. and Nadel, L. (eds) (2000). *Cognitive Neuroscience of Emotion*. Oxford: Oxford University Press.

Landa, Y., Silverstein, S.M., Schwartz, F. and Savitz, A. (2006). Group cognitive behavioral therapy for delusions: helping patients improve reality testing. *Journal of Contemporary Psychotherapy* 36, 1: 9–17.

Laughlin, R.B. (2005). *A Different Universe: Reinventing Physics from the Bottom Down*. New York: Basic Books.

Lehman, A. (2004). *Practice Guideline for the Treatment of Patients with Schizophrenia*, 2nd edn. Washington, DC: American Psychiatric Association.

Linden, D.J. (2007). *The Accidental Mind*. Cambridge, MA: Harvard University Press.

Lotterman, A. (1996). *Specific Techniques for the Psychotherapy of Schizophrenic Patients*. Madison, CT: International Universities Press, pp. 69–114.

McFarlane, W.R. (2004). Family intervention in first episode psychosis. In T. Ehmann, G.W. MacEwan and W.G. Honer (eds) *Best Care in Early Psychosis Intervention: Global Perspectives*. New York: Taylor & Francis, pp. 213–220.

McGovern, C. (1985). *Masters of Madness: Social Origins of the American Psychiatric Profession*. Hanover and London: University Press of New England, for the University of Vermont.

Mancia, M. (ed.) (2006). *Psychoanalysis and Neuroscience*. New York: Springer.

Marcus, E.R. (1992). *Psychosis and Near Psychosis: Ego Function, Symbol Structure, Treatment*. New York: Springer-Verlag.

Mayr, E. (2007). *What Makes Biology Unique? Considerations on the Anatomy of a Scientific Discipline*. Cambridge: Cambridge University Press.

Meaney, M.J. (2004). The nature of nurture: maternal effects and chromatin remodeling. In J.T. Cacioppo and G.G. Berntson (eds) *Essays in Social Neuroscience*. Cambridge, MA: MIT Press, pp. 1–14.

Meyer, A. (1908). How can our state hospitals promote a practical interest in psychiatry among the practitioners? *State of New York, State Hospitals Bulletin* 1, 1: 5–20.

Mitrani, T. and Mitrani, J.L. (eds) (1997). *Encounters with Autistic States: A Memorial Tribute to Frances Tustin*. Northvale, NJ: Jason Aronson.

Pariante, C.M. and Cotter, D. (2004). Do degenerative changes operate across diagnostic boundaries? The case for glucocorticoid involvement in major psychiatric disorders. In M.S. Keshavan, J.L. Kennedy and R.M. Murray (eds) *Neurodevelopment and Schizophrenia*. Cambridge: Cambridge University Press, pp. 111–120.

Podvoll, E.M. (2003). *Recovering Sanity: A Compassionate Approach to Understanding and Treating Psychosis*. London: Shambhala.

Pratt, S. and Mueser, K.T. (2002). Social skills training for schizophrenia. In S.G. Hofman and M.C. Tompson (eds) *Treating Chronic and Severe Mental Disorders: A Handbook of Empirically Supported Interventions*. New York: Guilford Press, pp. 18–52.

Prouty, G. (1994). *Theoretical Evolutions in Person-Centered/Experiential Therapy: Applications to Schizophrenic and Retarded Psychoses*. Westwood, CT: Praeger.

Prouty, G. (2003). Pre-therapy: a newer development in the psychotherapy of schizophrenia. *Journal of the American Academy of Psychoanalysis and Dynamic Psychiatry* 31, 1: 59–73.

Rako, S. and Mazer, H. (eds) (1984). *Semrad: The Heart of a Therapist*. New York: Jason Aronson.

Ralph, R.O. and Corrigan, P.W. (eds) (2005). *Recovery in Mental Illness: Broadening Our Understanding of Wellness*. Washington, DC: American Psychological Association.

Read, J., Mosher, L.R. and Bentall, R.P. (eds) (2004). *Models of Madness: Psychological, Social and Biological Approaches to Schizophrenia*. New York: Brunner-Routledge.

Robbins, M. (1993). *Experiences of Schizophrenia: An Integration of the Personal, Scientific and Therapeutic*. New York: Guilford Press.

Rose, S. (2005). *The Future of the Brain: The Promise and Perils of Tomorrow's Neuroscience*. Oxford: Oxford University Press.

Sacksleder, J.L., Schwartz, D.P. and Akabane, Y. (eds) (1987). *Attachment and the*

Therapeutic Process: Essays in Honor of Otto Allen Will, Jr., M.D. Madison, CT: International Universities Press.

Sanguineti, V. (2007). *The Rosetta Stone of the Human Mind: Three Languages to Integrate Neurobiology and Psychology.* New York: Springer.

Sapolsky, R.M. (2005). *Monkeyluv: And Other Essays on Our Lives as Animals.* New York: Scribner.

Sarwer-Foner, G.J. (1997). The humanity of the schizophrenic patient. In H.D. Brenner, W. Böker and R. Genner (eds) *Towards a Comprehensive Therapy for Schizophrenia.* Seattle, WA: Hogrefe & Huber, pp. 262–272.

Sass, L.A. (1994). *The Paradoxes of Delusion: Wittgenstein, Schreber, and the Schizophrenic Mind.* Ithaca, NY: Cornell University Press.

Seuss, Dr. (1954) *Horton Hears a Who!* New York: Random House.

Siani, R. and Siciliani, O. (2000). Patients with psychosis, psychotherapy and reorganization of 'the self.' One model of individual therapy: description and pilot study. In B. Martindale, A. Bateman, M. Crowe and F. Margison (eds) *Psychosis: Psychological Approaches and their Effectiveness.* London: Gaskell, pp. 177–199.

Silver, A.-L., Koehler, B. and Karon, B. (2004). Psychodynamic psychotherapy of schizophrenia: its history and development. In J. Read, L.R. Mosher and R.P. Bentall (eds) *Models of Madness: Psychological, Social and Biological Approaches to Schizophrenia.* London and New York: Brunner-Routledge, pp. 209–222.

Small, M.F. (2006). *The Culture of Our Discontent: Beyond the Medical Model of Mental Illness.* Washington, DC: Joseph Henry Press.

Spotnitz, H. (1999). *Modern Psychoanalysis of the Schizophrenic Patient.* Northvale, NJ: Jason Aronson.

Stone, W.N. (1996). *Group Psychotherapy for People with Chronic Mental Illness.* New York: Guilford Press.

Strauss, J.S. (1997). Processes of healing and the nature of schizophrenia. In H.D. Brenner, W. Böker and R. Genner (eds) *Towards a Comprehensive Therapy for Schizophrenia.* Seattle, WA: Hogrefe & Huber, pp. 252–261.

Sullivan, H.S. (1962). *Schizophrenia as a Human Process.* New York: Norton.

Suomi, S.J. (2004). Aggression, serotonin, and gene-environment interactions in rhesus monkeys. In J.T. Cacioppo and G.G. Berntson (eds) *Essays in Social Neuroscience.* Cambridge, MA: MIT Press, pp. 15–27.

Swartz, M.S., Lauriello, J. and Drake, R.E. (2006). Psychosocial therapies. In J.A. Lieberman, T.S. Stroup and D.O. Perkins (eds) *Textbook of Schizophrenia.* Washington, DC: American Psychiatric Publishing, pp. 327–340.

Taylor, S.E. and Gonzaga, G.C. (2007). Affiliative responses to stress: a social neuroscience model. In E. Harmon-Jones and P. Winkelman (eds) *Social Neuroscience: Integrating Biological and Psychological Explanations of Social Behavior.* New York: Guilford Press, pp. 454–473.

Tienari, P., Wynne, L.C., Sorri, A., Lahti, I. *et al.* (2004). Genotype-environment interaction in schizophrenia spectrum disorder: Long-term follow-up study of Finnish adoptees. *British Journal of Psychiatry* 184: 216–222.

Uchino, B.N., Holt-Lunstad, J., Uno, D. *et al.* (2007). The social neuroscience of relationships: an examination of health-relevant pathways. In E. Harmon-Jones and P. Winkielman (eds) *Social Neuroscience: Integrating Biological and Psychological Explanations of Social Behavior.* New York: Guilford Press, pp. 474–492.

Ver Eecke, W. (2003). The role of psychoanalytic theory and practice in schizophrenia. *Journal of the American Academy of Psychoanalysis and Dynamic Psychiatry* 31, 1: 11–29.

Vermetten, E., Dorahy, M.J. and Spiegel, D. (2007). *Traumatic Dissociation: Neurobiology and Treatment*. Washington, DC: American Psychiatric Publishing.

Volkan, V. (1995). *The Infantile Psychotic Self and Its Fates: Understanding and Treating Schizophrenics and Other Difficult Patients*. Northvale, NJ: Jason Aronson.

Volkan, V. and Akhtar, S. (eds) (1997). *The Seed of Madness: Constitution, Environment, and Fantasy in the Organization of the Psychotic Core*. Madison, CT: International Universities Press.

Waugaman, R. and Searles, H. (1990). Infinite reflections: the opening phases of intensive psychotherapy of a chronically schizophrenic patient. *Journal of the American Academy of Psychoanalysis* 18: 99–114.

Whitaker, R. (2002). *Mad in America: Bad Science, Bad Medicine, and the Enduring Mistreatment of the Mentally Ill*. Cambridge, MA: Perseus.

Chapter 17

The family in schizophrenic disorder
Systemic approaches

Helm Stierlin

During the last half century a variety of models has shaped psychiatric approaches to schizophrenic disorders. As time went on, these models became – more or less – discarded, altered and/or integrated into new (and frequently more complex) models.

With the philosopher Hegel we can speak of a dialectical process or a dialectical flux which evolves by negating, altering as well as conserving preceding models. Despite the obvious differences in what was of concern to Hegel and what was and is of concern to psychiatrists we can discern a similar dialectic flux of models in the field of psychiatry. This flux finally caused not a few psychiatrists, myself included, to pay ever more attention also to the schizophrenic's family.

In trying to put this flux into a historical perspective I begin with two authors whom I got to know in person while still a student at Heidelberg University – Karl Jaspers and Kurt Schneider. In those years – from 1946 till 1948 – Jaspers was already renowned as one of the great philosophers of the time. But it was his voluminous book *General Psychopathology*, originally published in 1913, that shaped my early views on schizophrenia as it shaped the views of many psychiatrists of that time (Jaspers, 1953). And Jaspers did this chiefly by asserting that the schizophrenic's behavior and thinking were in essence incomprehensible – in contrast to the behavior and thinking of ordinary people and that of those with 'neurotic' disorders. Thus Jaspers seemed to confirm what most lay people were – and still are – thinking: the schizophrenic's productions do not make sense. They are abnormal and crazy and bar him or her from meaningful human discourse. And they are evidently caused – such was the most sensible explanation – by some as yet undetected disorder of the brain as this had also been the opinion of Emil Kraepelin when he spoke of 'dementia praecox' as an endogenous affliction.

Jaspers' view was also shared by Kurt Schneider (1962) who during my student years taught psychiatry at Heidelberg. But soon I became inspired by Harry Stack Sullivan's book *Conceptions of Modern Psychiatry* (1940). In stark contrast to Jaspers and Schneider, he suggested that the schizophrenic's productions were – more or less – accessible to empathic understanding. Subsequently I sought and found work in two psychiatric hospitals in which Sullivan had left his mark: Sheppard Enoch Pratt and Chestnut Lodge, both seated in the state of Maryland, USA. I worked in them from 1955 till 1962.

In Sheppard Enoch Pratt I was supervised by Lewis B. Hill who had been strongly influenced by Sullivan (Hill, 1955). In Chestnut Lodge, where I worked for five years as a staff psychiatrist, Frieda Fromm-Reichmann was the dominant figure. In her book *Principles of Intensive Psychotherapy* she had viewed schizophrenic symptoms very much like neurotic symptoms (Fromm-Reichmann, 1950). The positions which Jaspers, Schneider – and to some extent Eugen Bleuler – had held were here negated, altered and/or supplanted by psychiatric authors with a strong psychoanalytic bent.

But Frieda became not only a shining light for psychoanalytically oriented psychotherapists. She also directed psychiatric attention to the schizophrenic's family. This she did by introducing the term 'schizophreno-genic mother'. Frieda's psychoanalytic background had not predisposed her to this feat. For Freud, her revered teacher, had written:

> The external resistances which arise from the patient's circumstances, from his environment, are of small theoretical interest, but of the greatest practical importance . . . For anyone who knows about the splits that tear families apart will as an analyst not be surprised that those closest to the patient will tend to have less interest in his recovering than in his remaining as he is.
>
> (Freud, 1915)

In any way, theoretical interest in the schizophrenic's family began now to boom. And this was not the least due to Gregory Bateson who was then probably most influential in directing psychiatric attention to these families or, perhaps more correctly, to the communication prevailing therein (Bateson, 1972). Bateson's concept of the 'double-bind' became widely known and discussed. Ronald D. Laing, another influential thinker in the 1960s and 1970s, described schizophrenic individuals as victims of a parent-induced 'mystification' (Laing and Esterson, 1964). Theodore Lidz and his associates at Yale University described varieties of mystification and crazy-making in 17 'schizophrenogenic' families with whom they had conducted numerous research interviews (Lidz *et al.*, 1965). They spoke of schisms and skews as features that made it difficult, if not impossible, for growing up children to develop stable inner signposts as preconditions for successful communication with the parties of their inner parliaments and with their family members as well. Lidz's many observations made him speak of a 'transmission of irrationality' and caused him to conclude that if there were no such entity as schizophrenia we would have to postulate it as an expectable outcome of the vicissitudes of human socialization. Mara Selvini Palazzoli and her Milan team also pointed to such vicissitudes when the family members they treated failed to define their relationships and thus facilitated misunderstandings and irrationality (Selvini Palazzoli *et al.*, 1977).

But – in my view – the most significant contributions pointing to the importance of the schizophrenic's family in general and its communication in particular came from the research conducted by Lyman Wynne and Margaret Singer mainly in the 1960s and 1970s (Wynne and Singer 1963a, 1963b; Singer and Wynne, 1965a, 1965b). These two authors, particularly by developing and testing their concept of communication deviances, caused many psychiatrists, myself included, to focus their observing lenses with new alertness on what went on in the schizophrenic's family. And on account of their clinical observations, their conceptual distinctions and their original and stringent research they too appeared to confirm that an unclear, odd, confusing or strange way to communicate was the most noteworthy feature of the schizophrenic's family. That finding was then bound to have a massive impact on how therapy of schizophrenic disorders was to be conducted.

For this meant above all: such therapy could/should no longer be exclusively geared to the schizophrenic's intrapsychic dynamics (or his or her inner parliament). Rather, it had to address itself to the 'games' or perhaps more correctly: to the 'language and communication games' played in the here and now in his or her family. One could speak of a paradigm shift or of a dialectic turn-about opening up a new vista.

Differences that make a difference?

Some 30 or 40 years have gone by since the pioneers of family theory and family therapy left their mark and in these years much has happened in various fields of research and clinical practice which gives us cause to reflect, to qualify and even to question what the pioneers initiated.

In what follows I shall turn to some recent developments in family theory and family therapy in cases of schizophrenia. And I shall ask which features therein may open up pathways for integration and reconciliation of differing models and approaches and which features alert us to – seeming or real – theoretical differences as to whether, how long and in which context the family should or could become involved in the schizophrenic's treatment.

I shall begin with the crucial question raised by the above-mentioned findings concerning the parents' odd and confusing communication: Is such odd and confusing parental communication possibly a reaction to their offspring's odd, confusing or even crazy behavior and communication? And if so, has this behavior a genetic base? Has possibly also the parents' mystifying communication a genetic base? Or is this communication the expression or outcome of relational vicissitudes?

These questions have spurred numerous research projects trying to disentangle in schizophrenia the roles of genetics and heredity on the one side and of the human environment on the other. And so far the probably most significant answers have come from the Finnish Adoption Study of schizophrenia. This study was initiated by Pekka Tienari and his co-workers during the 1960s; later Lyman Wynne joined the project (for references, see Chapter 1 and Wynne *et al.*, 2006a, 2006b). Over time many researchers have contributed to the study which uses an 'adoptee design'. Its sample consisted of adoptive families whose children had been adopted away by women hospitalized because of schizophrenia and of families who had an adoptee whose biological mother had not been schizophrenic. So far this has been the longest lasting, most extensive and most detailed study of possible genotype-family environment interaction in schizoprenia. In what follows, I shall briefly summarize my view of the present state of this kind of research.

There can be little doubt that there exists such interaction. But it is complex and needs to be much better understood. And perhaps most important: about 63 per cent of schizophrenic patients have no family history of the disorder. Therefore one can say with Karl-Erik Wahlberg, a member of the team conducting the Finnish Adoption Study, that 'genotypes do not directly control the onset of schizophrenia, but they may control sensitivity to the risk-increasing or risk-reducing aspects of the environment' (Wahlberg, 2003). One could even say that persons prone to become schizophrenic are more than other people genetically disposed to react sensitively to what transpires in intimate relationships and particularly to what transpires in early intimate family relationships. And this reminds me of something which Frieda Fromm-Reichmann once told me almost half a century ago: 'I believe that schizophrenic individuals can give more love and need more love than other individuals.' The book *I Never Promised You a Rose Garden*, written by her ex-patient Hannah Green (1964), could be seen as giving evidence of such heightened sensitivity.

If we share this view it will not stand in the way of a family therapy of schizophrenics which tries to understand and influence intrapsychic as well as interpersonal processes. Rather the opposite is the case. For it challenges therapists to see and use this sensitivity as a resource in this endeavor – despite the fact that risks, upheavals, complicated communication and suffering are part of the picture.

But things begin to look different when such sensitivity or disposition, instead of being viewed as a resource (albeit combined with heightened risk), becomes viewed and emphasized as resulting from a genetically caused pathology, defect or illness. For the treatment model growing out of such a view is now bound to make a difference for family therapists and clients alike. And this is not least due to the fact that the issue of responsibility and guilt now takes center stage, as it were.

The issue of responsibility and guilt

In order to realize the importance of this issue we need to remind ourselves that a model which emphasizes illness and/or pathology will typically tend to relieve guilt in affected individuals and family members: The schizophrenic and also his or her close relatives are seen as passive victims or bystanders suffering from vicissitudes out of their control. But, again in typical cases, this view is also likely to paralyze personal initiative and decision making in the 'victims'. At best, it may stimulate actions and decisions that enable them to live more comfortably with their undeserved predicament and to make the best of their handicap.

With the above in mind, we can distinguish between several models or views on how a therapy with the schizophrenic's family should or could be conducted. These views can be seen as ideal types in the sense elaborated by the sociologist Max Weber: They can help us to orient ourselves even though in clinical practice they tend to occur (more or less) as mixtures and may never be found in pure form. In each view the therapeutic approach is shaped by certain basic assumptions which direct a therapist's attention. These may cause him to be attentive to – and to single out as central – certain chains of causality while neglecting others, this bearing then also on how guilt and responsibility are perceived or constructed. The view may change or may not change as time goes by and as therapeutic measures show effects. Whatever happens, therapists are faced with a complex situation challenging them to be cautious and yet to take action.

A problematical view

With this in mind I would like to single out a first view which was widely shared when the earlier mentioned pioneers called attention to the confusing communication they observed in parents of a schizophrenic offspring. This view implied a chain of causality in which parents played a major and mostly destructive role. Thus even a pioneer like Selvini Palazzoli came to speak of the parents' 'dirty games' in which their children were bound to be the losers and prone to develop schizophrenic symptoms. This view then called for therapeutic measures such as the once popular – and in quite a few cases effective – paradoxical interventions as means to stop such destructive game playing. Yet even though this view and the interventions derived from it often showed results and were inspired by systems theory, they can hardly be called systemic. For such views tended to reflect a linear thinking with linear attribution of causes and effects and in many cases also with linear attribution of intent and guilt particularly to parents as 'dirty players'.

This, however, had serious consequences: In the United States it made it increasingly difficult to view and to recruit parents as partners in therapy and to use them as a resource. While family therapy for schizophrenia became publicly more known and advocated, there spread also the picture not merely of a schizophrenogenic mother but also of a schizophrenogenic family.

Another view

Another ideal type of viewing family functioning and family therapy in schizophrenia appears shaped by the assumption that the disorder in essence results from a disorder of brain functions. We can speak of a return of the illness model as upheld by early psychiatrists such as Jaspers and Schneider, but now apparently supported – albeit not conclusively proven – by findings of modern brain research. These findings suggest that the brain dysfunction may be due to a genetic disposition, to environmental influences such as a virus infection during a child's early development, yet most probably to the interaction of these and other as yet unknown factors. But they also suggest that various kinds of stress may hasten a schizophrenic breakdown.

Where this view prevails, the thrust of any family therapy – if the term 'family therapy' is at all applicable – will be to empathically support the patient and his family members in their undeserved predicament, to help them to accept it, to mitigate its consequences, to avoid stress which could trigger or exacerbate symptoms, to rely on psychopharmacology to curb the painful and disorganizing impact, particularly of positive symptoms such as delusions, hallucinations and massive thought disorders, and to make the best of the patient's predicament. Here sometimes the comparison with diabetes is invoked: the cause of the disease cannot be removed but its consequences can be held in check by careful attention to one's food intake and, if necessary, by carefully administered medication.

This view has – more or less – bolstered the psycho-educational approach as it has come to be known particularly through the work of Ian Falloon and his team (1984). Presently this appears to be the most widely used and most widely taught approach in the Western world. In this approach it makes sense to recruit the schizophrenic's family – even at a prodromal stage of the disorder – as a resource. This is particularly the case when sessions with multifamily groups are held (see McFarlane, 2000). For it can be an enormous relief for such families when they experience that they are not alone in their plight, that they can share their problems with similarly afflicted families and can give and receive helpful tips. And perhaps most important: the notion of schizophrenia as an illness that overwhelms its victims tends to push into the background the troublesome issue of personal autonomy, guilt and responsibility.

Central is here the meaning which Falloon and those who follow him attribute to the concept 'psycho-education'. Falloon elucidated this meaning for our Heidelberg group a number of years ago when he took part in a conference organized by our Heidelberg team and subsequently recorded by Arnold Retzer (1991). He described psycho-education as a procedure in which family members are educated and informed about 'schizophrenia' as a clearly defined syndrome (described in the diagnostic manuals *DSM-III* and *DSM-IV*) which 'most probably is a biological disorder associated with abnormalities in brain metabolism and genetic dispositions'. In addition they are educated and informed about measures they can take to reduce or avoid stress and about the possibility and/or necessity of neuroleptic medication. In order to make such education and information effective, Falloon could mobilize a team of dedicated professional helpers including members of local health services, nurses and general medical practitioners. In the English community of Buckinghamshire he taught them to recognize possible prodromal symptoms of schizophrenia, to intervene in situations of crisis and to observe and accompany afflicted families in follow-ups.

The results of such efforts are remarkable indeed. In the two years preceding Falloon's project, the rate of new cases of schizophrenia in the catchment area amounted to 7.4 in 100,000. In the following four years – the period during which the project ran – this rate was reduced to 0.75 in 100,000, i.e. by 90 per cent. The only person clearly diagnosed as schizophrenic during this period was treated with a rather small dose of a neuroleptic medication and simultaneous stress management (Falloon and Kydd, 1984).

Given such results it can hardly astonish that the psycho-educational model found wide acceptance. Yet the question remains: Can these results cause us to disregard or at least to marginalize the observations of the pioneers which alerted psychiatrists to confusing communication and disturbing interaction in many families with schizophrenic members? Or, to put this differently: Can a therapeutic approach also be fruitful which primarily tries to understand and possibly influence the intrapsychic as well as the interpersonal processes which here come into play? And can we perhaps construct an ideal type in which these processes become the central issue – despite or because of the questions of guilt and personal responsibility thereby raised?

A third view

With this question in mind I would like to turn to a psychotherapist and researcher who can be seen as coming close to representing this third ideal type: Jaakko Seikkula who works in Northern Finland and was in close geographic and professional contact with the deceased Tom Andersen

(1990), best known for his work with reflecting teams. He exemplifies also essential aspects of the 'need-adapted treatment' developed and described by Yrjö Alanen and his co-workers (Alanen, 1997).

Ian Falloon and Jaakko Seikkula have a few things in common: both operate in catchment areas of relatively small size (72,000 inhabitants in the case of Seikkula); both work with a dedicated team of professionals who maintain close contact with individuals who have become schizophrenic or appear in danger of becoming schizophrenic; both are involved in taking responsibility for their clients' treatment when inpatients or outpatients, including the responsibility for ordering or discontinuing medication; both stay in close contact also with these patients' families; and both have reported excellent results with regard to diminished amount and seriousness of new cases of schizophrenia.

But there are also differences that make a difference. From my present vantage the most significant difference comes across in the terms by which their approaches have come to be known. In the case of Falloon this is 'psycho-education' and in the case of Seikkula this is 'dialogue'.

In a number of writings Seikkula has elaborated the significance and quality of dialogue as practised and fostered by him and his team. He illustrated this with transcripts of interviews held with clients and their family members (Seikkula, 1996, 2002; Seikkula and Trimble, 2005). In what follows I shall limit myself to pointing out some features relevant for my topic. Dialogue, as conceived by Seikkula, becomes important in different realms of interaction in which different types of discourses prevail:

- in an individual's discourse with his or her intrapsychic world (or, as I prefer to call it, with the parties in his or her inner parliament)
- in the discourse that the afflicted family members have with each other
- in the discourse unfolding between the members of the professional team – here Tom Andersen's reflecting team serves as a model
- in the discourse evolving between the professional team and their patients, including family members.

Such dialogue lets stories evolve that can be understood and shared by all participants. These stories should make sense of what at first sight may appear senseless, and, if at all possible, they should make sense of a schizophenic's 'crazy' thoughts and behaviors. Also, they should be more than intellectual exercises and should embrace and convey what is emotionally relevant. Issues of guilt and responsibility should likewise be dealt with.

Seikkula's case examples and transcripts convey how such dialogue can unfold. But they also convey how the dialogue may become blocked in the various types of discourse mentioned earlier – in the intrapsychic discourse, in the discourse between family members, in the discourse between professionals and clients, and in the discourse between members of the professional team.

In many schizophrenic clients a blockage of their inner dialogues can make us think of an inner monotony, a rigid dissociation of certain affects and thoughts from each other – a kind of dissociation which fails to keep inner tensions in check, and fails to prevent explosive outbursts of the dissociated affects and also outbursts of an – for outsiders – incomprehensible and unacceptable irrationality.

In family relations a blockage of dialogue may mirror the members' efforts to avoid any meaningful talk at all, to retreat into a secretive reclusiveness and/or – important in my present context – to resort to a confusing and mystifying communication that may disguise or may help to bypass deep-seated conflicts experienced as catastrophic and irresolvable. And – no less important – blockages of dialogue between the parties in individual inner parliaments and between family members may become intertwined and may reinforce each other.

Published excerpts from two of Seikkula's interviews give us hints of how an intrafamilial dialogue may either become and stay blocked or may evolve in a manner which clarifies matters. They also convey the impact both scenarios – the intrapsychic scenario and the intersubjective scenario – can have on a schizophrenic member. In one family the blockage of the dialogue appears to mire this member ever more in his schizophrenic predicament. In the other family the evolving dialogue evidently helps this member to find his way out of such predicament.

In both cases the schizophrenic member was an adolescent boy in his late teens. This is an age at which the first schizophrenic episode often erupts with dramatically displayed positive symptoms. But it is also an age when the prospects for a succesful therapeutic intervention are favorable. The negative consequences of a (more or less) chronic course such as loss of jobs and loss of friends with subsequent passivity and lasting demoralization are not yet present. Here even a short therapeutic intervention can make this episode appear as a crisis of adolescence or of young adulthood that can be mastered successfully. But if not mastered, such crisis may entail enduring impediments and a diagnosis of chronic schizophrenia. In either case the crisis typically mirrors the adolescent's or young adult's difficulties in his efforts to disentangle himself from his family or, as I would like to describe it, in his efforts to achieve a higher level of related individuation. Since this crisis is typically also a family crisis, it makes eminent sense to involve the family in the treatment.

The excerpts from the two family scenarios supplied by Seikkula allow us to fathom some of the reasons why the crisis smoldered on in one case and could be mastered in the other within a relatively short time span. In the first family there was evidence of massive and enduring conflict between family members and particularly between the parents. There were also hints of the father's problems with alcohol and of his attempts to leave the family altogether. But this was not openly discussed. Instead, there was evidence of mystification and of confusing communication as earlier described. This contrasted with the other family where confusing communication was less apparent and there was also evidence that the family members wanted to do everything possible they could to help their schizophrenic member.

The Heidelberg approach

This lets me turn to our Heidelberg approach that I believe comes close to fit the last mentioned ideal type which pays attention to intrapsychic as well as to intrafamilial conflicts, to possibly confusing communication, to issues of guilt and responsibility and, last but not least, to resources inherent in what at first sight can appear as mere pathology and defect. This approach is described in the book *Die Demokratisierung der Psychotherapie* (Stierlin, 2003) and in a number of papers which compare families with schizophrenic psychoses with families with members diagnosed as manic-depressive or schizo-affective (Stierlin *et al.*, 1985, 1986). Seikkula evidently tried to detect and utilize such hidden resources and so did we in Heidelberg.

When our Heidelberg team began to work with families with schizophrenic members in the 1980s we were in a good position to make use of several resources. The psychiatrists who referred families to us tended to instill in them the belief and hope that family therapy would be helpful. Throughout the subsequent family therapy these psychiatrists continued to handle decisions as to when hospitalization might be needed and about medication. And they agreed with us that they would stay in charge of these matters while we were in charge of the family therapy.

Typically the sessions with the family took place with shorter or longer intervals in between – the intervals lasting typically from two to three months and thus could provide time for 'homework', i.e. for the members reflecting and possibly heeding the recommendations we usually make at the end of the sessions. On average we conducted seven sessions with a family. Hence our approach came to be known as 'long term brief therapy' (*langzeitige Kurztherapie*).

At first sight this approach can seem much less intense and effective than the one employed by Seikkula and his team. We were obviously much less involved with various aspects of the patients' lives, treatment and human environment. But what at first sight may appear as a disadvantage, in our view amounted to an advantage. This can become clearer when we consider the goals as well as the main features of our Heidelberg approach.

Like Seikkula's work our approach appears to best fit the heading 'dialogue'. We try to engage the family members in a dialogue with us and with each other in which possible causes and functions of the schizophrenic's troubling behaviors – such as his 'crazy' speech, his hearing of voices, his withdrawal from family members and friends – can begin to make sense and, hopefully, can be discontinued. Thus we try to end the schizophrenic member's excommunication, that is, try to convey that he too is 'much more human than otherwise'. At the same time, we try to facilitate a dialogue in the two other domains of discourse mentioned earlier: in the discourse that goes on (or is blocked) between the fractions in the inner parliaments of individual members and particularly in the inner parliament of the member diagnosed as schizophrenic, and in the discourse going on (or is blocked) between the family members.

This has the effect that the participants become more able to share a common focus of attention; that is, to pay attention to what the partner means and tries to communicate while they, at the same time, learn and try to communicate as clearly as possible – and this especially in situations where conflictual and emotionally charged issues of guilt and responsibility come to the fore.

However, and this applies mainly to the family member diagnosed as schizophrenic, in order to become a partner in a constructive dialogue he must also manage a constructive intrapsychic dialogue with the parties in his inner parliament; that is, he must come to grips with his own wishes and needs whenever these are in conflict with each other, and he must be able and willing to express, as clearly as possible, what he stands for and what he wants from others. And in doing all this he must learn to live with a 'healthy ambivalence'.

In order to facilitate a constructive dialogue between and with members of a schizophrenic's family our Heidelberg team came to view some features of our approach as most useful. To these belong the early clarification of the therapeutic setting and mandate. Therapists need to ask: What do the different members want and expect from family therapy? Do their motivations differ? And if they differ how will this affect the therapists mandate? Also, we pay special attention to how the referral came about and which overt and covert messages the clients may have picked up from their referring psychiatrist. For it typically makes a difference whether this psychiatrist conveys hope and confidence that the family therapy will be helpful or whether he conveys scepticism by saying 'If you think you need family therapy in addition to the ongoing neuroleptic medication I shall certainly not stand in your way.' Conflicts of loyalties and delegations may then stall the family therapy from the outset unless they are addressed at once. Also, the therapist's neutrality is of special importance and so are an attitude and behavior that avoid, as much as possible, an implicit or explicit blaming of family members. Essentially, whatever has come to be seen as his psychotic and incomprehensible symptoms should thus, if at all possible, begin to make sense for himself and his family members. Or, again in the words of Sullivan, the therapeutic task should now consist in letting him become 'much more human than otherwise'.

This then requires therapists to take note of the many differences in the behaviors, expectations and experiences of the prospective partners in dialogue. Thus, it can make a difference whether the patient's excommunication is of long or short duration. It can make a difference whether he experiences his psychosis as a hell from which he desperately wants to escape or as a state which relieves him from real or imagined burdens. And it can make a difference how and how far affects shape the clinical picture. Thus we came to view a schizo-affective psychosis as much more approachable than a longstanding thought disorder with mainly paranoid features.

In our work with families we rely strongly on (often circularly posed) questions in order to facilitate dialogue(s). These questions should make sense not only for the addressee but for the listening family members as well. And this should be particularly so when the addressee is the patient. As our project unfolded, the questions addressed to him and the ensuing talk with him took up an ever increasing amount of the available time, frequently up to 90 per cent. These questions are not only intended to bring to the fore, to elucidate and discuss the patient's inner world and motivations; they are also intended to convey to his attending family members that his psychotic symptoms can make sense.

To give an example of our approach I refer to a woman of about 40 years whom I shall call Birgit. Before attending our family meetings she had been hospitalized several times because of her psychotic symptomatology and now seemed close to becoming hospitalized again. Central in her symptomatology was the delusional idea that the world was soon to end in an apocalyptic battle taking place in North Africa between the forces of good and evil. She spoke of an 'Endzeit' or apocalypse she believed was near. Given this scenario the therapist asked all attending family members what such 'Endzeit' could possibly mean for some or all of them, and in particular for Birgit's role and function in her family. The ensuing conversation – triggered and guided mainly by hypothetical questions – then turned to vicissitudes and possibly disastrous conflicts which in her family might have been experienced as heralding a similar 'Endzeit'. Birgit remembered such vicissitudes and conflicts as occurring at a time when she felt greatly misunderstood by and estranged from her parents and siblings. And this brought up the question of whether and how her concern with the 'Endzeit' could have something to do not only with what had been going on then but also with what was going on now in her family relations. As the discourse took this turn the images of an apocalypse and 'Endzeit' softened up. They became more and more metaphors or dreamlike visions to which the family members could relate. And – no less important – Birgit felt less and less overwhelmed by voices and ideas hitting her from the outside but instead came to view such voices and ideas as arising from within herself – voices and ideas which she, if we again use the picture of an inner parliament, now could begin to see as messengers from its various fractions. With Wittgenstein one could speak of a 'turning around of the whole perspective' which in Birgit fostered a sense of inner coherence and increased her autonomy.

However, not all the schizophrenic patients seen by our Heidelberg team opened up an avenue for a discourse which sooner or later could undermine or 'soften up' their psychotic symptomatology as happened in the case of Birgit. One could say their inner parliaments were too much out of joint or too chaotic for giving such discourse a chance. And in some of these cases it made sense – for the patient and his family members – to use externalization as a first step on the road to dialogues in the meaning described earlier.

Michael White in Australia was, to my knowledge, the first therapist to describe and practice externalization (White and Epston, 1990). His patients were mainly encopretic childen. One can say that he too invited these patients and their family members to turn around their whole perspective on the problem at hand. Instead of viewing the problem as evincing intrapsychic and or interpersonal conflicts and vicissitudes – conflicts and vicissitudes which could not but raise questions of causality, guilt and responsibility – White asserted that the problem was the problem, i.e. that the problem was the encopresis. Thus he avoided all talk and thought about intrapsychic and interpersonal dynamics which so far had been merely confusing, frustrating and guilt inducing. Instead he invited parents and children to band together in fighting the problem, i.e. in fighting the child's encopresis (now also called the 'little stinker') like an enemy. And this often led to astonishing success.

In Heidelberg my colleague Arnold Retzer has described in detail how also a schizophrenic psychosis can be externalized in a way which makes sense to the patient and his family (Retzer, 1991). He would even ask the patient to give the externalized psychosis a place in the room and then follow this up with questions such as 'Does it make more sense for you to locate the psychosis in the left rather than in the right corner of this room? Which location feels more comfortable to you? What would be the right distance for you?', etc. This kind of externalization can be seen as an intervention that sidesteps issues of causality, guilt and responsibility which so far had only contributed to confusion and frustration in the patient and in those close to him. It could even suggest a comparison with how Ian Falloon and others used the notion of a mental illness to reduce confusion and the blaming of self and/or others.

But there is also a difference. The notion of a mental illness can easily evoke images of defect and pathology that foster passivity and resignation.

In contrast, the externalization of the psychosis as here described can be seen as a first step in facilitating more autonomy and thus can help all concerned to look more closely at what the psychosis might mean in terms of a functioning or not functioning inner parliament and in terms of a functioning or not functioning communication in the family. Accordingly, such externalization of the psychosis can be viewed as a first step on the road to dialogues in the sense earlier mentioned.

In what follows I shall point out a few other features of our Heidelberg approach which we found helpful. One such feature is our position vis-à-vis neuroleptic medication: There can nowadays be little doubt that such medication can be helpful, particularly in cases of distressing positive symptoms (even though there is the risk of irreversible side effects). But the prescription of neuroleptic medication very likely also signals to client and family members that the psychosis is due to a sick or disturbed brain and has little or nothing to do with intrapsychic or interpersonal vicissitudes. Therefore it follows that the main goal of therapy must be to control this sickness or disturbance rather than to focus on such possible vicissitudes, as these might interfere with a facilitation of dialogue and of personal autonomy in the meanings described above.

When faced with this problem we came to appreciate the fact that we were not in charge of the client's medication. For this made it possible for us to pose circular and hypothetical questions such as 'Do you think Bert's subdued state, his silence and evasiveness as shown in particular vis-à-vis his father are more an effect of his neuroleptic medication or are more attributable to a strategy to avoid a possibly disastrous battle between the two men?' and 'If such battle were to occur what would be the conflictual issues and what would be the consequences for father and son?' 'Could the two of them possibly be guided by the assumption that such battle would never end and would leave them estranged from each other for ever?', etc., etc.

This scenario allowed us to take a new look at the unclear, confusing and mystifying communication which authors such as Lyman Wynne, Margaret Singer and Theodore Lidz observed in many families with schizophrenic offspring. For in Bert's family as well as in a good many other families with a young adult diagnosed as schizophrenic we observed such unclear communication. And we were also inclined to view Bert's evasiveness as part and parcel of a family-wide evasive and disqualifying communication that hampered a dialogue as earlier described. But we came to view and describe this unclear communication not as evincing pathology or defect but as something that could make sense and be functional in the light of the (mostly covert) conflicts and apprehensions in these families. As we got to know these families better, we found that many of these conflicts and apprehensions grew out of overt or covert conflicts of loyalties and delegations, sometimes affecting three generations, that gave rise to misunderstandings

and double-binds which in turn could lead to a schizophrenic symptomatology. In such drama also a genetic vulnerability or disposition to become
schizophrenic may play a role. In not a few cases the schizophrenic's plight
can thus be viewed as being co-determined by a particular sensitivity to
signals and to contradictions of signals conveyed in intimate, existentially
important and freqently quite early relationships.

Thus there remains the challenge: How to deal with a confusing communication when our goal is to facilitate dialogue and autonomy? In our
search for answers we came to heed several lessons taught us by the families
seen by us. The first lesson we learned was that it is no use demanding or
recommending a clearer communication as long as the functions of the
unclear communication are not understood. For this will only promote
overt or covert defiance. Therefore, to the extent that we were still lacking
such understanding in a given family we tended to express ourselves even
more unclearly than our clients – up to a point when they (often with smiles
on their faces) admonished us to please express ourselves more clearly.

The second lesson learned was neither to intimate a linear causality, nor
to use any kind of description or evaluation that could amount to a
blaming of parents or other family members for playing dirty games at the
expense of other members. This meant that conflictual issues and in
particular conflicts of loyalties and delegations should be addressed in ways
that can stimulate reflection and recognition of fateful life experiences
without assignment of guilt. At the same time any efforts to cope with and/
or to endure fateful hardships should be appreciated.

The third lesson learned was to help all concerned to accept and utilize
healthy ambivalence (or the coexistence of different fractions in one's inner
parliament) as a precondition for autonomous and responsible action as
mentioned earlier. This meant that in cases where two therapists were
involved, at the end of the session, they would often practise a splitting as
to the desirability of, for example, sticking to a confusing communication
or risking a discourse about conflictual issues with the danger of escalating
conflicts. The task to ponder such a split message can then be part of the
homework to be carried out in the intervals between sessions. In this way
we give back to the clients the responsibility for coping with their ambivalence and for making the best of it. (In cases where only one therapist is
in charge he has to split himself, as it were.)

The fourth lessen learned was to appreciate differences in the psychotic
symptomatology presented to us and to heed their implications for how to
proceed in therapy. In particular we came to appreciate differences in
clients diagnosed as either schizophrenic, as schizo-affective or as manic-
depressive according to *DSM-III* criteria.

Important differences showed up when three years after the end of family
therapy our colleague Arnold Retzer conducted a follow-up study on 60
families treated by us (Retzer *et al.*, 1991). In order to assess results he used

Table 17.1 Relapse rates: medium values before and after family therapy

	Relapse rate		%-reduction	Significance of differences
	Before	*after*		
MDP (n = 20):	1.23	0.40	67.47	*
SAP (n = 20):	1.81	0.25	86.18	***
SCH (n = 20):	0.84	0.34	59.52	***
Total (n = 60):	1.29	0.33	74.41	***

Note: Significance measured by t-Test, testing different medium values in two dependent samples. MDP = manic depressive. SAP = schizo-affective. SCH = schizophrenia.

the clients' and the family members' judgements as to changes they had perceived and he used also criteria applied by an external observer such as quantity and quality of medication taken.

Most striking turned out to be the changes in relapse rates. Retzer defined a relapse as any psychiatric hospitalization without consideration of length of diagnosed psychopathology. Thus the relapse rate is defined as the quotient of the number of hospitalizations divided by the respective periods of observation: The period before family therapy stretched from the first show of symptoms to the first therapeutic interview with the family, and the period following therapy stretched from the last interview to the date of the follow-up. In this way altogether 60 families were evaluated. On average they were seen for 6.5 sessions spaced over 17 months. Patients diagnosed as manic-depressive, schizo-affective and schizophrenic showed a distinct reduction of relapse rates representing an improvement in 75 per cent of all cases. In 13 per cent of the cases there was a deterioration, in 10 per cent no change. All in all the patients' job situation improved and their medication was reduced. Table 17.1 shows the relapse rates before and after family therapy.

References

Alanen, Y.O. (1997). *Schizophrenia. Its Origins and Need-Adapted Treatment.* London: Karnac.

Andersen, T. (1990). The reflective team. In T. Andersen (ed.) *The Reflective Teams: Dialogues and Dialogues about the Dialogues.* Kent: Bormann, pp. 18–107.

Bateson, G. (1972). *Steps to an Ecology of Mind: Collected Essays in Anthropology, Psychiatry, Evolution and Epistemology.* San Francisco: Chandler.

Falloon, I. and Kydd, P.R. (1984). Early detection and intervention for invited episodes of schizophrenia. *Schizophrenia Bulletin* 22: 271–282.

Falloon, I.R.H, Boyd, J.L. and McGill, C.W. (1984). *Family Care of Schizophrenia: A Problem-Solving Approach to the Treatment of Mental Illness.* New York: Guilford Press.

Freud, S. (1915). *Bemerkungen über die Übertragungsliebe. GW Bd.* XVI. Frankfurt: Fischer.

Fromm-Reichmann, F. (1950). *Principles of Intensive Psychotherapy*. Chicago: University of Chicago Press.

Green, H. (1964). *I Never Promised You a Rose Garden*. New York: Signet.

Hill, L.B. (1955). *Psychotherapeutic Intervention in Schizophrenia*. Chicago: University of Chicago Press.

Jaspers, K. (1953). *Allgemeine Psychopathologie* [General Psychopathology]. Berlin: Springer.

Laing, R.D. and Esterson, A. (1964). *Sanity, Madness and the Family*. London: Tavistock.

Lidz, T., Fleck, S. and Cornelison, A.R. (1965). *Schizophrenia and the Family*. New York: International Universities Press.

McFarlane, W.R. (2000). Psychoeducational multi-family groups: adaptations and outcomes. In B. Martindale *et al. Psychosis: Psychological Approaches and their Effectiveness*. London: Gaskell, pp. 68–95.

Retzer, A. (1991). *Die Behandlung psychotischen Verhaltens/Psychoedukative versus systemische Ansätze*. Heidelberg: Carl-Auer-Systeme.

Retzer, A., Simon, F.B., Weber, G., Stierlin, H. and Schmidt, G. (1991). A follow-up study of manic-depressive and schizoaffective psychoses after systemic family therapy. *Family Process* 30: 139–153.

Schneider, K. (1962). *Klinische Psychopathologie*, 6th edn. Stuttgart: Thieme.

Seikkula, J. (1996). Psychotisches Verhalten als eine Geschichte der gegenwärtigen Interaktion: Ein sozial-konstruktivistisches Verständnis der Psychose. [Psychotic behavior as one story of the actual interaction. Social constructionism in understanding psychosis.] *Zeitschrift für systemische Therapie* 14: 25–38.

Seikkula, J. (2002). Open dialogues of good and poor outcome in psychotic crisis. *Journal of Marital and Family Therapy* 28: 263–274.

Seikkula, J. and Trimble, D. (2005). Healing elements of therapeutic conversation: dialogue as an embodiment to love. *Family Process* 44: 461–475.

Selvini Palazzoli, M., Boscolo, L., Cecchin, G. and Prata, G. (1977). *Paradox and Counterparadox: A New Model in the Therapy of the Family in Schizophrenic Transaction*. New York: Jason Aronson.

Singer, M.T. and Wynne, L.C. (1965a). Thought disorder and family relations of schizophrenics: III. Methodology using projective techniques. *Archives of General Psychiatry* 12: 187–200.

Singer, M.T. and Wynne, L.C. (1965b). Thought disorder and family relations of schizophrenics: IV. Results and implications. *Archives of General Psychiatry* 12: 201–212.

Stierlin, H. (2003). *Die Demokratisierung der Psychotherapie/Anstöße und Herausforderungen*. Stuttgart: Klett-Cotta.

Stierlin, H., Weber, G., Schmidt, G. and Simon, F.B. (1985). Why some patients prefer to become manic-depressive rather than schizophrenic. *Yale Journal of Biology and Medicine* 58: 255–263.

Stierlin, H., Weber, G., Schmidt, G. and Simon, F.B. (1986). Features of families with major affective disorders. *Family Process* 25: 325–336.

Sullivan, H.S. (1940). *Concepts of Modern Psychiatry*. New York: Norton.

Wahlberg, K.-E. (2003). Meaning of and possibilities for familial prevention of schizophrenia. In A. Grispini (ed.) *Preventive Strategies for Schizophrenic*

Disorders. Basic Principles, Opportunities and Limits. Rome: Giovanni Fioriti Editore.

White, M.D. and Epston, D. (1990). *Narrative Means to Therapeutic Ends*. New York: Norton.

Wynne, L.C. and Singer, M.T. (1963a). Thought disorder and family relations of schizophrenics: I. A research strategy. *Archives of General Psychiatry* 9: 191–198.

Wynne, L.C. and Singer, M.T. (1963b). Thought disorder and family relations of schizophrenics: II. A classification of forms of thinking. *Archives of General Psychiatry* 9: 199–206.

Wynne, L.C., Tienari, P., Nieminen, P., Sorri, A., Lahti, I., Moring, J. *et al.* (2006a). I. Genotype-environment interaction in the schizophrenia spectrum: genetic liability and global family ratings in the Finnish Adoption Study. *Family Process* 45: 419–434.

Wynne, L.C., Tienari, P., Sorri, A., Lahti, I., Moring, J. and Wahlberg, K.-E. (2006b). II. Genotype-environment interaction in the schizophrenia spectrum: qualitative observations. *Family Process* 45: 435–447.

Chapter 18

Group psychotherapy and schizophrenia

Manuel González de Chávez

Introduction

Group psychotherapy for patients with psychosis is increasingly commonly used as it is very feasible, flexible and adaptable to all institutions and health care facilities. However, amongst psychotherapy interventions for these patients, group psychotherapy continues to be one of the most unknown and least systematized for its adequate use, choice and indication.

Although almost 90 years have passed since the first article was published on group psychotherapy for patients with schizophrenia (Lazelle, 1921) up to the present date, there is a proportionally small amount of scientific literature compared with that of other individual or family therapies in these patients. The 'ambiguity' of the concept of psychosis, the hetero-geneity of the patients (Hummelen, 1994), the difficulties of research in group psychotherapies (Dies and Mackenzie, 1983), issues of the theory and conceptualization of the complexity of groups (Scheidlinger *et al.*, 1997), the great variety of types of groups and the unavoidable uniqueness of each of them and the group therapy processes themselves may be found among the reasons why there is so little research work published.

In spite of this thinness of publications, the effectiveness of group psychotherapy in schizophrenia combined with neuroleptic treatment seems to have been demonstrated repeatedly over the years by different meta-analyses (Gifford and Mackenzie, 1948; Stotsky and Zolik, 1965; Parloff and Dies, 1977; Mosher and Keith, 1980; Scott and Giffith, 1982; Kanas, 1986). In one of the meta-analyses of more than 40 studies, group therapy was significantly better than treatment without this therapy in 67 per cent of the studies with inpatients and in 77 per cent of studies with outpatients (Kanas, 1986, 1996).

Comparative studies have also been made between group psychotherapy and individual psychotherapy in the treatment of schizophrenia. In these studies, similar results (Levene *et al.*, 1970; Herz *et al.*, 1974; Mintz *et al.*, 1976), or even somewhat more favorable ones have been observed for group psychotherapy, with more enthusiasm by the patients and therapists, fewer drop-outs, better treatment compliance, fewer rehospitalizations, better socialization and better functioning of the patients (Purvis and Mismikis, 1970; O'Brien *et al.*, 1972; Donlon *et al.*, 1973). These data do not differ from general comparisons between individual and group therapies – also with non-psychotic disorders – (Toseland and Siporin, 1986) and similar results are found when group therapy has been compared with family interventions (Pilkonis *et al.*, 1984).

In one review 'interpersonal oriented' groups were shown to be more effective than 'insight oriented' approaches in schizophrenic patients (Kanas, 1986). The objectives of the 'interpersonal oriented' groups were to improve the patients' ability to relate to the here and now of interaction with the group members and/or the discussion of their personal problems and possible solutions. The 'insight oriented' ones were aimed at improving the patient's self-knowledge by means of examining evolutional and dynamic aspects and by techniques to uncover and interpret the transference. This was an operational classification in which it was not easy, nor even possible, to include most of the groups of patients.

At present, there is a general trend towards an eclectic integration of all psychotherapies. Except for the recent development of cognitive behavioral groups (Lawrence *et al.*, 2006; Free, 2007), group psychotherapy is also moving towards integrating and forming eclectic approaches including those for psychotic disorders. These groups have different formats and more specific therapeutic objectives that are adapted to the patients' characteristics. More and more, these group formats increasingly serve as a setting for support and aids to self-knowledge, depending on the situation of the patients and the stages of the therapeutic process. Insight oriented groups can now be simultaneously focused on favoring support and interaction between patients (Kanas, 1996; Schermer and Pines, 1999).

Usually group psychotherapies form a part of therapeutic programs and are combined with individual or family psychotherapies. Group psychotherapies facilitate or strengthen the therapeutic activity in schizophrenic patients who generally also receive some neuroleptic treatment (Mosher and Keith, 1980; Alanen *et al.*, 1986). The combined therapies should not compete with each other, but rather are mutually beneficial, synergic and complementary. What is important is the choice, indication and suitability in each case to the overall treatment needs or characteristics of different patients (Alanen, 1997).

In the therapeutic programs and combined therapies mainly used in schizophrenia, we believe that group psychotherapy should occupy a more important place. This is not only because they are easy to carry out, are very viable in any health care facility and have a synergic action in the overall treatment, but also and mainly because group psychotherapy has specific features with great therapeutic potential.

Specific features of group psychotherapy

Group psychotherapy has characteristics that differentiate it from other psychotherapies. It has a combination of therapeutic elements that are completely particular to a group format that may favorably affect the experiences and behaviors of patients with schizophrenia. Special mention must be made of the various active therapeutic consequences of the group context, such as 'mirroring'.

Group therapeutic context

The group context is characterized by being a realistic and egalitarian one that offers different persons with common disorders and problems an opportunity that is not provided by other psychotherapy modalities to know each other, communicate and learn from the interpersonal relationships they mutually establish. The therapy group context is completely different from the dyadic relationship of individual psychotherapy and the family therapy group of members who already know one another (Anthony, 1971; Fleck, 1982). It allows the patients to share experiences and directly meet with other persons who have disorders similar to theirs, to free themselves from the experience of uniqueness and acquire a more realistic view of themselves and become more aware of their own problems.

The group may be a safe context for the patients as they overcome their attitudes and behaviours based on distrust with consequent isolation or defensive withdrawal. When there is adequate guidance to promote and maintain cohesion in a therapeutic setting and a group culture of respect, listening, help and reciprocity, an empathic and receptive audience is created that facilitates self-disclosure and communication. It is also a place where patients can express themselves with sincerity, slowly overcoming their insecurity and improving their self-esteem.

It is a therapeutic context with horizontality, neutrality and greater independence for the patients. It is less dependent and unequal than the family and individual therapies and it does not have the special implications or complicated transactions of family therapy. The patient may establish more independent and balanced relationships with the therapists and other group members. The group facilitates the therapeutic relationship on more realistic bases because the transferences are multiplied and diluted, thus correcting distortions and idealizations and decreasing symbiotic dependencies (González de Chávez and Garcia-Ordás, 1992).

It is also an active, productive, multifocal and multi-intersubjective context that differs from individual therapy (Anthony, 1971). The group is very productive and rich in observations and self-disclosure and disclosures of others, with the possibility for contrasting with the reality, associations, perspectives, information, learning, recognition and redefinitions coming from the other group members, thus allowing for an increase in self-awareness. The multiplicity and multifocality of the group communications aid the cognitive decentering of the patient. This is of great importance in the patient with schizophrenia, who is especially vulnerable to cognitive regression and perceptive egocentrism (Lidz, 1973).

Group therapy is also a socializing and stimulating reality that encourages active participation, therapeutic compliance and group functioning with similar values, rules and objectives. It encourages members to make an effort to confront the adaptations and make changes to their difficulties and conflicts, combat negations, amnesias and self-deceptions and often counters resistances and regressive or evasive patterns.

Finally, it becomes a reference group for its members (Kelman, 1963). This makes it possible to overcome a rigid image of oneself and acquire a more dynamic view of oneself, of one's own life and of therapeutic progress. It gives participants a sense of reality, of time and of the gradual evolution of achievements in both personal and collective objectives. The testimony and improvement of the others increase hope in one's own improvement and encourages the person to overcome relapses and periods of demoralization. Therapeutic help and the perspective that the group members receive form a basic reference in the therapeutic process and a realistic base for the reconstruction of one's own identity.

Group mirroring

Group mirroring is probably the most specific phenomenon of group psychotherapy, differentiating it clearly from other psychotherapy modalities and bestowing on it a large part of its specific therapeutic potentiality. Group mirroring is the intersubjective process of multiple, simultaneous, reciprocal and empathic mirroring reactions based on observation, examination, disclosure, reflection and mutual knowledge between group members.

Every patient is a mirror for the others and the other group members are mirrors for the patient. Every patient sees in others himself or herself or parts of himself or herself. Often these have previously been rejected and repressed and are now reflected back through other members of the group, who are going to react in the same way to these warded off aspects of themselves. The patients may then see their own reactions and behaviors in others, and see the effect that their behavior has on the group. They can become familiar with the images of themselves that the group members return to them. Each one reveals himself or herself to the others, sees oneself in the others and reflects and is reflected in the group, as well as reflecting on the others and on oneself. The patient thereby begins a process of discovering himself or herself through the others, confronting or questioning, validating, confirming or rectifying, and through the mirroring reconstructs and redefines himself or herself (Foulkes, 1964; Cox, 1973; Pines, 1982; González de Chávez and Capilla, 1993).

As a starting point, group therapy with people who have schizophrenia takes advantage of the capacity for insight in the other patients. A capacity develops to observe and recognize in others that which one still cannot observe and recognize in oneself. This is because it is psychologically more feasible to distinguish objective and subjective realities in others. The incapacity to differentiate the external from the internal world of one's own blocks insight in patients. Thanks to the feedback from group mirroring it becomes possible to differentiate between the objective and subjective in the others and patients can begin to question themselves.

Group therapeutic factors

Specific group therapeutic factors are the basic components of change and are inherent to group interaction and not specifically associated with the actions of the therapist. Group interactions are not isolated but rather combined and depend on each subject, the type of group and even on each stage of the group process (Yalom, 1985). Different authors list and classify them somewhat differently and also have a different research methodology (Corsini and Rosenberg, 1955; Bloch et al., 1979, 1981; Bloch and Crouch, 1985; Yalom, 1985; Mackenzie, 1987; Kapur et al., 1988; Sadock and Kaplan, 1993; Scheidlinger et al., 1997). We can distinguish the following:

- *supportive factors* (acceptance or cohesion, universality, hope, altruism)
- *self-disclosure* (catharsis, self-disclosure)
- *learning from other members of the group* (imitation, identification, guidance or advice, information, education, vicarious learning)
- *insight or related factors* (self-understanding and interpersonal learning).

The study of the therapeutic factors that are common to all psychotherapies and those that differentiate them represents research of great value for the training of therapists and the advance and progress of psychotherapies. Group psychotherapy has some therapeutic factors in common to other psychotherapies and others that are specific to group therapy, such as interpersonal learning, universality, cohesion or acceptance and altruism. However, even the factors that are similar to those of other therapeutic modalities acquire different connotations when multiplied horizontally and reciprocally strengthened in the group context. The same occurs with vicarious learning from others through imitations and identifications, information and advice. This is also true of self-disclosures and catharsis that may be about oneself or other members of the group, thus extending their effects, associations and impacts, and affecting the interpersonal learning and insight of each and every one of the group members.

Further discussion now follows of group therapeutic factors that play key roles in the group psychotherapy of schizophrenia. Supportive aspects (universality, acceptance or cohesion, hope and altruism) are generally important in the first stages of a group, in self-help groups and in short-term therapy groups with inpatients and still have an important place in outpatient groups during the entire therapeutic process (Bloch and Crouch, 1985; Yalom, 1985; Kapur *et al.*, 1988; González de Chávez *et al.*, 2000). These qualities promote a working alliance or climate and group cohesion. Groups relieve the anxiety caused by patients feeling unwelcome uniqueness when they discover that others have or have had similar experiences. This facilitates their own self-acceptance and acceptance of other group members. This motivates and involves the patients further in the therapy, instilling expectations of improvement and making them take an active role against demoralization and low self-esteem. In addition, the group gives the patients the possibility, capacity and desire to help others, to recognize and value their own feelings and their positive characteristics in their altruism, leading to being valued and appreciated by the others.

Advice, information, education and vicarious learning from others by imitation or identification are inherent to the group therapy process and work on an elemental level. For many more discreet or passive patients, these are their principal learning strategies and are of great importance in didactic or psycho-educational groups, in cognitive behavioral groups and in supportive groups.

Self-disclosure is essential because without this there are no psychotherapeutic possibilities. Self-disclosure is a precondition of self-knowledge: it may be more cognitive and informative, or more cathartic, emotional and affective; it may be voluntary or involuntary. Furthermore, in the group both patients and therapists have direct observation of many other dimensions or behaviors, such as egocentrism, withdrawal, passiveness, intolerance, hostility, fears and distrust or arrogance and dependence (Anthony, 1971). Interpersonal learning and self-knowledge or intrapersonal learning are the most relevant factors towards insight in groups with a dynamic orientation which last longer within more advanced stages of psychotherapy. Both make up two inseparable aspects of one change mechanism because self-knowledge cannot be acquired without having knowledge of others.

Psychosis, group dynamics and the therapeutic process

We believe that a comprehensive psychological, biological and social view of the patient with a psychosis must utilize broad approaches such as those developed by some authors in recent years (Ciompi, 1988; Alanen, 1997;

Cullberg, 2006). From comprehensive perspectives such as those of the authors just listed, we can easily consider the psychotic episode as an identity crisis of the subject, considering identity as the self in a biographic continuity.

Identity, or the self-view of a subject, is the product of a biological substrate and biographic history in both a familial and social context each with their own dynamics that gives rise to a personality shaped by habitual behavior patterns, defense mechanisms and coping strategies, with tasks adjustments, maladjustments, achievements and failures in multiple aspects: social, political, religious, racial, group or class, cultural, educational, work roles or subidentities as well as those connected with the family, the body, affective and sexual life, and so on (Honest and Yardley, 1987; Lapsley and Power, 1988).

For the purposes of trying to understand the psychotic crisis, identity is also the combination of more or less different subidentities: accepted, public, private, intimate, hidden, rejected or denied in addition to ideal and grandiose identities and others that are introjected from childhood in relationship with parental figures and significant persons.

As a general statement, all the biographic processes of the conception and evolution of the identity are guided by the principles of uniqueness, continuity, independence and self-esteem, and the capacity to assimilate, adapt and evaluate reality (Breakwell, 1986). Biographic episodes that suppose qualitative changes of a negative nature are crises that lead to reflection and questioning of reality and of one's own identity. There are painful processes of resistance, self-deception and coping strategies to save the identity and achieve its adaptation to the new reality. They entail dynamics of a readjustment of the subidentities that make the identity more vulnerable.

When coping strategies fail to defend one's identity involving uniqueness, continuity, independence and self-esteem, breakdown occurs. Psychotic episodes are identity breakdowns (Sullivan, 1962; Mullay, 1970) with splitting and fragmentation of its structure, a resort to paranoid mechanisms and a process of cognitive regression in the inverse direction from that of normal cognitive development, which now carries the patient from formal logic to that of the operational and preoperational, to perceptive egocentrism and finally to magical thinking, where all solutions are possible (Lidz, 1973, 1975).

In the fragmentation of the vulnerable identity, grandiose or feared subidentities acquire predominance in the patient and are transformed into psychotic identities. The hidden, rejected or denied subidentities could be experienced in a paranoid way as delusions of being observed, known, transparent, watched, persecuted, discredited or insulted. Those introjects from significant object relationships which are, at these times, alien and unrecognizable as one's own, can appear in the mind of the psychotic subject as hallucinations of being controlled and criticized or alternatively of support and consolation.

In the recovery process of the psychotic episode, we observe the following *evolution of identity:*

1   *A psychotic identity* exists at the heart of the episode, with a subjective transformation of the ideas about oneself and the experience of reality.
2   Many become aware of the disturbance and accept the psychopatho-logical character of the experiences. They can then be said to have an *identity of being a patient.*
3   At a later time in the psychotherapeutic process they may acquire knowledge of the aspects of themselves and their reality that makes them more vulnerable to psychotic experiences. This is what we call *a vulnerable identity.*
4   The purpose of psychotherapy is for the patient to be able to under-stand the sense or meaning of their disorders and the integration of their experiences and subidentities, to achieve *an integrating identity.*

The pathways that a patient may take after a psychotic episode vary greatly. These range from a lasting continuation of their psychotic identity to a more or less opposite state of accepting with insight that they have a disturbance. During the psychotherapy process, many patients acquire self-knowledge of some psychological and biographical aspects that underly and influence their disorders. A few, barely 13 per cent, in some studies of psychotherapy follow-up (Alanen *et al.*, 1986), achieve a good integration of identity with understanding of the psychotic experiences they have had and what can make them less vulnerable.

The *therapeutic relationship* with psychotic patients follows a sequence or stages (McGlashan and Keats, 1989), which parallels the evolution of their identity, as we have described.

1   At the beginning, in the relationship of *contact*, the therapist does not exist as such and is included in the patient's psychotic world. It is the time of personal contact, to give the patient a containing relationship, one of safety and trust, of our presence, patience and persistence always preserving the respect and dignity of the patient.
2   Later, we establish *a link*, a very primitive, insecure, ambivalent and unstable relationship. For the patient, this is a relationship that only exists in the present. There is no collaboration or project for the future for the patient but there is a strong presence of unconscious aspects and psychotic transferences.
3   Only later does the patient establish a *personal relationship* of evalu-ation and respect, with some confidentiality and possibilities of having influence, but without a clear therapeutic meaning.

4   Later on, we can establish a *therapeutic relationship* that is stable and consistent, that has motivation, commitment, empathy, trust and therapeutic work; this may only be a therapeutic relationship of support or it may be one of both support and insight.

Our objective in the group dynamics is to favor the best *coping strategies* of the patient which are simultaneously intrapsychic, interpersonal and group ones and that could be falsifying, avoidant, re-evaluating or integrating. We aim to help group members to begin to discard, suppress or modify the most pathological strategies in order to favor the most integrating ones because with the *falsifying strategies*, the patient distorts reality to maintain their image and identity when in crisis. These strategies are fantasies or constructions of a false self that may lead to the creation of a psychotic identity. They are splitting, projection and externalization mechanisms. The delusion is the subjective falsification of the reality experienced.

With the *avoidant strategies*, the subject avoids confronting a painful reality that questions and threatens him or her. The strategies are denial, rejection, forgetfulness, withdrawal, negativistic mechanisms or distraction and occupation in other activities. Alcohol abuse and abuse of other substances are common. The *re-evaluating strategies* attempt to modify the analysis of the threatening reality, focusing on partial aspects of it or making it banal, devaluing others by comparison, re-evaluating oneself, whether with grandiosity and unfounded optimism, or in a catastrophic, fatalistic or resigned way, with disproportioned pessimism.

Favoring *integrating strategies* helps patients to verbalize, communicate, accept and cope, seek information and advice, receive help, mutually review, redefine and restructure their identity again, correcting the most vulnerable aspects and anticipating the most stressing situations possible or other factors. All effective psychotherapies revolve around the best use of coping strategies and group psychotherapy uses the group context and dynamics, mirroring and group therapeutic factors to achieve this.

Group psychotherapy for inpatients

The chronology of psychotherapy interventions from the psychotic episode to recovery starts with group therapy whilst an inpatient and through joint work of all the team in order to obtain better understanding and help from different professional perspectives and therapeutic interventions, not only group but also individual, family and institutional. During the acute psychotic crises or episodes, not all patients fulfil the criteria for inclusion in a psychotherapy group. There is a pre-group stage due to the intensity of the psychotic experiences and non-reflective mirroring (Pines, 1982). In the more intense moments, some patients may have a marked psychotic distortion in their perception of their contextual environment. It is necessary to wait for them to overcome, with the help of neuroleptic treatment, the disorganization, excitation, hostility, anguish or perplexity in order to establish a minimum relationship and communication in the group context. The patient's condition should allow for a certain degree of control and minimum capacity of 'reflective mirroring'. In the first group stage, their mirroring reactions are egocentric and they sometimes try to convert the group into being a psychotic participant in defense of their delusional convictions. The group dynamics act by correcting the perceptive egocentrism and allow for cognitive decentering. Often, the group members reflect better by projecting than by disclosure. They reflect that which they are unaware of, that which they deny, their unconscious conflicts. The groups in the inpatient units are open with frequent sessions held daily or every other day. The therapists are always more active and directive, helping in the cognitive organization of speech, correcting the perceptive egocentrism, paranoid ideation and reducing psychotic reinforcement.

In the first therapeutic interventions, which include groups as well as individual and family interventions, our objective will be to listen, examine and favor self-disclosure of the patient. We should reconstruct together with the patient and the patient's family his or her biographic history and psychotic history, premorbid personality and all the context, relationships and precipitating factors that have led to the identity crisis that is revealed with his or her psychotic manifestations. This is the time to offer help, without humiliation, frustration or rejection of the patient, knowing the mechanisms of this transaction which is to help and to be helped.

The group context should be respectful and safe, in order to help the patients to leave aside the defensive withdrawal, distrust and insecurity and favor self-disclosure and desingularization of the psychosis. In this stage, the purpose is for the patients to know that they are not the only ones who have unique realities and identities. It is to clarify, specify and help express feelings and experiences, to sequence them and place them in the context of the person's biography. It is to separate facts from interpretations, consensually validate reality and introduce other possible hypotheses and perspectives, such as those of close and other significant persons and pathways that have led the patient to the hospital, with all the dynamics experienced in the 'untreated period' of psychosis. We attempt to know the internal world and external reality of the patient, his or her relationships and also the attitudes and reactions of the others regarding the patient's behavior, for example, discrediting and rejecting him or her or trying to understand and help him or her, and to know how the patient hides, expresses or verifies his or her psychotic experiences, what supports the patient has and in what obstacles and distortions we need to intervene therapeutically.

Outpatient group psychotherapy

Our purpose will now be to motivate both the patient and his or her family to follow a therapeutic program with outpatient group psychotherapy that will facilitate the therapist relationship and compliance both with the psychotherapy and medication. This is the time to inform and 'psycho-educate' the patient and his or her family about the psychotic disorder, with realistic hopes and expectations. It is also the time to explain the components of the program, its purposes and approximate duration. The mean duration of our program is approximately four to five years, with a weekly session of 90 to 120 minutes of group psychotherapy and with individual and family sessions that are established according to needs (González de Chávez et al., 1999). All the psychotherapy programs have stages that should not be short-circuited or skipped, in order to achieve the evolution of the identity of the schizophrenic patients. This must first go from the psychotic identity to the acceptance of the patient's identity, then to knowledge of the patient's vulnerability and finally to the integration of his or her identity.

The purpose of all the initial interventions in the psychotherapeutic process is that the patient, after his or her own contradictory internal debate, begins to accept the subjective and psychopathological character of their psychotic experiences. The group functions by contrasting and questioning the psychotic identities and blocking the development of delusional convictions or beliefs in the past truthfulness of the psychotic experiences.

We use both examination as well as confrontation, establishing an interlacing of crossed interventions where the similarities and differences help to advance the disclosure of the objective and subjective worlds, stimulate cohesion and facilitate the observations, analyses and reflections. We support independence and not regression, clear focal communication rather than the verbalization of free associations or vague, abstract, elusive or inferred speech. We avoid long silences and situations of marked anxiety that generate group defenses and cognitive disorganization. We analyze the resistances and transferences when they obstruct the therapeutic process. We make few interpretations and prefer to note questions, contradictions or alternatives, associate sequences and connections and we take an interest in the horizontal observations, opinions or interpretations of the other group members, being always oriented towards improving the degree of the patients' insight.

As the groups are open, with gradual incorporation of new patients, the stages are not the same in all members of the group, but rather different for each patient. The most veteran patients serve to guide and support in their knowledge that those entering a group have suffered a crisis. Mutual identifications permit prospective hope for some and retrospective insight for others. All acquire a sense of continuity of the therapeutic process, the pathway to be covered and that already covered. The group provides a socializing, motivating and altruistic support that makes it possible to analyze and to fight against depression, demoralization and stigma. The patient also has a reference group in the other group members, to have a more objective view of himself or herself and of their progress in a recovery that goes from readaptation to reality, to social life, work, family and intimate relationships. We aim to help our patients gain motivation towards others and for life, for interest in new activities, for positive inter-action patterns in developing relationships, to trust and to be able to become intimate. Living, in both activity and practice, is where the patients reconstruct their identity and become less vulnerable.

Group dynamics and reconstruction of identity in schizophrenia

Group dynamics and the acquisition of knowledge, validation, reconstruc-tion and redefinition through others (Cox, 1973) is no more than a thera-peutically led reactivation and reinitiation of the personal and biographic mirroring process of the subject that has an ongoing creation in his or her external group matrix as lived, leading to the development of the patient's own image, personality and identity.

Since childhood, the family mirroring reactions and then those of other reference groups shape self-observation and self-knowledge together with interpersonal observation and knowledge of many realities. It is a process that is parallel to both the subject's cognitive development and to his or her differentiation and individuation from others, as well as to the capacity to observe, to distinguish and reflect on the external and internal duality of the subject's world and to get to know the characteristics and limits of one's awareness and reality.

A child goes through the process of overcoming the perceptive egocen-trism and achieves cognitive decentering with the capacity of having empathy with the perspective and place of others. The child's cognitive development advances through different stages of logical thinking and overcomes the objective and subjective primitive fusion of magic thinking. Cognitive development and the development of the subject's identity are parallel and are integrated in the same continuous interpersonal mirroring process that the subject has lived since childhood which allows him or her to know reality and know himself or herself through others (Selman, 1980; Pines, 1987; Damon and Hart, 1988).

Altered and conflictive familial dynamics are involved in schizophrenia (Lidz. et al., 1965; Lidz, 1973, 1975; Howells and Guirguis, 1985; Alanen, 1997). Symbiotic, egocentric, hostile, biased, irrational or contradictory dynamics may unfavorably affect cognitive development in one's own image and self-esteem and the attitudes, relationships and understanding of the world surrounding us. The use of strategies or primitive defense mechanisms such as negation, splitting and projection indicates difficulties in differentiation and individualization, fragility and early distortions of identity and significant relationships (Räkkoläinen and Alanen, 1982; Volkan, 1995; Alanen, 1997). This instability, inconsistency and incoherence is reflected in the vulnerable identity and the underlying resort to perceptive egocentrism and cognitive regression against stress factors, circumstances or demands that may break the precarious balance of the poorly integrated subidentities.

Group psychotherapy creates a new mirroring process, allowing one to know and recognize oneself in the others with the help of others who themselves suffer or have suffered the breakdown of an identity that gives rise to fragmentation and alienation of subidentities in psychotic experiences. It is a unique therapeutic context that uses the capacity of insight over others who have also lived or live the subjective transformation of oneself and their own reality. It facilitates a new process of interpersonal and intrapersonal relearning that makes it possible first to accept and recognize the crisis and then that of one's own vulnerability in order to be able to make a more realistic, more stable and more integrated redefinition of one's own identity.

References

Alanen, Y. (1997). *Schizophrenia. Its Origins and Need-Adapted Treatment*. London: Karnac.

Alanen, Y., Räkkoläinen, V., Laakso, J. Rasimus, R. and Kaljonen, A. (1986). *Towards Need-specific Treatment of Schizophrenic Psychoses*. Berlin: Springer.

Anthony, E.J. (1971). Comparison between individual and group psychotherapy. In H. Kaplan and B. Sadock (ed.) *Comprehensive Group Psychotherapy*. Baltimore: Williams & Wilkins, pp. 104–117.

Bloch, S. and Crouch, E. (1985). *Therapeutic Factors in Group Psychotherapy*. Oxford: Oxford University Press.

Bloch, S., Reibstein, J., Crouch, E., Holroyd, P. and Themen, J. (1979). A method for the study of therapeutic factors in group psychotherapy. *British Journal of Psychiatry* 134: 257–263.

Bloch, S., Crouch, E. and Reibstein, J. (1981). Therapeutic factors in group psychotherapy. *Archives of General Psychiatry* 38: 519–526.

Breakwell, G. (1986). *Coping with Threatened Identities*. London: Methuen.

Ciompi, L. (1988). *The Psyche and Schizophrenia*. Cambridge, MA: Harvard University Press.

Corsini, R. and Rosenberg, B. (1955). Mechanism of group psychotherapy: processes and dynamics. *Journal of Abnormal and Social Psychology* 51: 406–411.

Cox, M. (1973). Group psychotherapy as redefining process. *International Journal of Group Psychotherapy* 23: 465–473.

Cullberg, J. (2006). *Psychoses: An Integrative Perspective*. London: Routledge.

Damon, W. and Hart, D. (1988). *Self Understanding in Childhood and Adolescence*. Cambridge: Cambridge University Press.

Dies, R. and Mackenzie, R. (eds) (1983). *Advances in Group Psychotherapy: Integrating Research and Practice*. New York: International Universities Press.

Donlon, P., Rada, R. and Knight, S. (1973). A therapeutic aftercare setting for refractory chronic schizophrenic patients. *American Journal of Psychiatry* 130: 682–684.

Fleck, S. (1982). Group and family therapies: distinctions. In M. Pines and L. Rafaelsen (eds) *The Individual and the Group: Boundaries and Interrelations. Vol I*. London: Plenum Press, pp. 127–137.

Foulkes, S.H. (1964). *Therapeutic Group Analysis*. London: Allen & Unwin.

Free, M.L. (2007). *Cognitive Therapy in Groups*, 2nd edn. Chichester: Wiley.

Gifford, S. and Mackenzie, J. (1948). Review of literature on group treatment of psychoses. *Diseases of the Nervous System* 9: 19–24.

González de Chávez, M. and Capilla, T. (1993). Insight and mirroring in group psychotherapy with schizophrenic patients. Xth International Symposium for the Psychotherapy of Schizophrenia, Stockholm. *Revista de la Asociación Española de Neuropsiquiatría* 13: 29–34, 103–112.

González de Chávez, M. and Garcia-Ordás, A. (1992). Group therapy as a facilitating factor in the combined treatment approach to schizophrenia. In A. Werbart and J. Cullberg (eds) *Psychotherapy of Schizophrenia: Facilitating and Obstructive Factors*. Oslo: Scandinavian University Press, pp. 120–130.

González de Chávez, M., Garcia Cabeza, I. and Fraile, J.C. (1999). Dos grupos psicoterapéuticos de pacientes esquizofrénicos: hospitalizados y ambulatorios. *Revista de la Asociación Española de Neuropsiquiatría* 72: 573–586.

González de Chávez, M., Gutierrez, M., Ducajú, M. and Fraile, J.C. (2000). Comparative study of therapeutic factors of group therapy in schizophrenic inpatients and outpatients. *Group Analysis* 33: 251–264.

Herz, M., Spitzer, R., Gibbon, M., Greenspaan, K. and Reibel, S. (1974). Individual versus group aftercare treatment. *American Journal of Psychiatry* 131: 808–812.

Honest, T. and Yardley, K. (1987). *Self and Identity*. London and New York: Routledge.

Howells, J. and Guirguis, W. (1985). *The Family and Schizophrenia*. New York: International Universities Press.

Hummelen, J. (1994). Group analysis and psychoses. *Group Analysis* 27: 389–391.

Kanas, N. (1986). Group therapy with schizophrenics: a review of controlled studies. *International Journal of Group Psychotherapy* 36: 339–351.

Kanas, N. (1996). *Group Therapy for the Schizophrenic Patients*. Washington, DC: American Psychiatric Press.

Kapur, R., Miller, K. and Mitchel, G. (1988). Therapeutic factors within in-patient and out-patient psychotherapy groups. *British Journal of Psychiatry* 152: 229–233.

Kelman, H.C. (1963). The role of the group in the induction of therapeutic change. *International Journal of Group Psychotherapy* 13: 399–432.

Lapsley, D.K. and Power, F.C. (eds) (1988). *Self, Ego and Identity*. New York: Springer.

Lawrence, R., Bradshaw, T. and Mairs, H. (2006). Group cognitive behavioural therapy for schizophrenia: a systematic review of the literature. *Journal of Psychiatric and Mental Health Nursing* 13: 673–681.

Lazelle, E. (1921). The group treatment of dementia praecox. *Psychoanalytic Review* 8: 168–179.

Levene, H., Patterson, V., Murphey, B., Overbeck, A. and Veach, T. (1970). The aftercare of schizophrenics: An evaluation of group and individual approaches. *Psychiatric Quarterly* 44: 296–302.

Lidz, T. (1973). Egocentric cognitive regression and a theory of schizophrenia. In R. De La Fuente and M. Weisman (eds) *Proceedings of the Fifth World Congress of Psychiatry. Vol. 2*, pp. 1176–1152. Mexico: Excerpta.

Lidz, T. (1975). *The Origin and Treatment of Schizophrenic Disorders*. London: Hutchinson.

Lidz, T, Fleck, S. and Cornelison, A. (1965). *Schizophrenia and the Family*. New York: International Universities Press.

McGlashan, T. and Keats, C.H. (1989). *Schizophrenia. Treatment Process and Outcome*. Washington, DC: American Psiatric Press.

Mackenzie, K.R. (1987). Therapeutic factors in group psychotherapy: a contemporary view. *Group* 11: 26–34.

Mintz, J., O'Brien, C.H. and Luborsky, L. (1976). Predicting outcome of psychotherapy for schizophrenics. *Archives of General Psychiatry* 33: 1183–1186.

Mosher, L. and Keith, S. (1980). Psychosocial treatment: individual, group, family and community support approaches. *Schizophrenia Bulletin* 6: 10–41.

Mullay, P. (1970). *Psychoanalysis and Interpersonal Psychiatry: The Contributions of Harry Stack Sullivan*. New York: Science House.

O'Brien, C.H., Hamm, K., Ray, B., Pierce, J., Luborsky, L. and Mintz, J. (1972). Group vs. individual psychotherapy with schizophrenics: a controlled outcome study. *Archives of General Psychiatry* 27: 474–478.

Parloff, M. and Dies, R. (1977). Group psychotherapy outcome research: 1966–1975. *International Journal of Group Psychotherapy* 27: 281–319.

Pilkonis, P., Imber, S., Lewis, P.H. and Rubinsky, P. (1984). A comparative outcome study of individual, group, and conjoint psychotherapy. *Archives of General Psychiatry* 41: 431–437.

Pines, M. (1982). Reflections on mirroring. *Group Analysis* 15: 1–26.

Pines, M. (1987). Mirroring and child development: psychodynamic and psychological interpretations. In T. Honest and K. Yardley (eds) *Self and Identity*. London and New York: Routledge, pp. 19–37.

Purvis, S. and Mismikis, R. (1970). Effects of community follow up on posthospital adjustment of psychiatric patients. *Community Mental Health Journal* 6: 374–382.

Räkkoläinen, V. and Alanen, Y. (1982). On the transactionality of defensive processes. *International Review of Psychoanalysis* 9: 263–272.

Sadock, B. and Kaplan, H. (1993). Clinical diagnosis in group psychotherapy. In H. Kaplan and B. Sadock (eds) *Comprehensive Group Psychotherapy*, 3rd edn. Baltimore: Williams & Wilkins, pp. 57–72.

Scheidlinger, S., Dies, R., Fuhriman, A. and Mackenzie, K.R. (1997). Group dynamics and group psychotherapy revisited. *International Journal of Group Psychotherapy* 43: 139–182.

Schermer, V. and Pines, M. (1999). *Group Psychotherapy of Psychoses*. London: Jessica Kingsley Publishers.

Scott, D. and Giffith, M. (1982). The evaluation of group therapy in the treatment of schizophrenia. *Small Group Behaviour* 13: 415–422.

Selman, R.L. (1980). *The Growth of Interpersonal Understanding*. New York: Academic Press.

Stotsky, B. and Zolik, E. (1965). Group psychotherapy with psychotics 1921–1963. A review. *International Journal of Group Psychotherapy* 16: 321–344.

Sullivan, H.S. (1962). *Schizophrenia as a Human Process. Collected Works, Vol. II.* New York: Norton.

Toseland, R. and Siporin, M. (1986). When to recommend group treatment: a review of the clinical and research literature. *International Journal of Group Psychotherapy* 36: 171–201.

Volkan, V. (1995). *The Infantile Psychotic Self and its Fates*. Northvale, NJ: Jason Aronson.

Yalom, I.D. (1985). *The Theory and Practice of Group Psychotherapy*, 3rd edn. New York: Basic Books.

Chapter 19

Cognitive behavioural therapy for psychosis

Robert Dudley, Alison Brabban and Douglas Turkington

Introduction

Cognitive behavioural therapy (CBT) is valuable in treating a range of emotional disorders (Beck, 2005). For each of these difficulties there is a unique and specific theory directing understanding and treatment. Nevertheless CBT has much in common across disorders and in this chapter we outline the key characteristics that define CBT. We then review the past development of CBT for psychotic illnesses like schizophrenia, which we refer to as CBT for psychosis (CBTp).[1] Next we review the present status of CBTp in terms of the extent and limits of the current evidence base, as well as outlining the unique and specific characteristics of CBTp. We then offer our view of the future development of CBTp.

Key characteristics of CBT

CBT has a number of characteristic components (Beck, 1995) including the use of a collaborative therapeutic relationship, structured sessions and cognitive and behavioural change techniques. CBT is symptom and problem focused and time limited with between 6 and 20 sessions being common, depending on the nature of the difficulties the person brings.

The defining characteristic of CBT is the cognitive model, which emphasizes the deceptively simple notion that the way a person makes sense of an event determines how he or she feels and behaves. More broadly, the cognitive model accounts for the onset of the emotional disorder by proposing that stressful life events activate core cognitions (termed schemas or core beliefs) that predispose a person to the development of disorder. Whilst CBT focuses on the present, it builds a formulation of the development of the person's problems drawing on this model and incorporating the person's unique and meaningful early experiences that led to the development of these schematic structures of the self, other people, and the world. Within this formulation will be an understanding that the person may have managed these schemas by employing strategies, framed as rules or assumptions that the stressful triggering life events breached or exceeded. This breach of rules in turn accesses the emotion-laden core beliefs leading to the emergence of the emotional disorder. Once developed the problems are maintained by the classic vicious cycle of an unhelpful or biased appraisal of the current situation leading to unhelpful attempts to manage the distress evoked by avoidance, or more subtle but nevertheless unhelpful behaviours. By building a formulation based on the cognitive model, the therapist and client work together to help provide an alternative explanation for the experiences, and introduce the key learning that thoughts are thoughts and not facts, even though they seem true, and that other interpretations may be possible. This learning hopefully leads to a reduction in distress and increased functional behaviour.

Whilst CBT shares some similarities with other approaches which also emphasize the centrality of thoughts (i.e. rational emotive behavioural therapy; Ellis, 1958), it also has key differences, one of which is the emphasis on empiricism.

Empiricism is evident within CBT in two main ways. First, CBT is based on the notion of collaborative empiricism, whereby the client and therapist work together as a team to develop a shared understanding of the problems and test out alternative explanations. Insight is not considered sufficient for change in and of itself. Rather treatment consists of active tests of the appraisal of current experience to help the person evaluate whether there are other possible explanations for their experience.

Second, CBT follows a characteristic research cycle. For any specific disorder the process begins with careful observation and description of the phenomenology to help identify and define key characteristics. Subsequent experimental research studies determine if these characteristics have a role in the development or maintenance of the disorder. Based on this understanding treatments are developed that address these key features. Case studies and case series establish potential value of the treatment, and lead to the refinement of treatment guidelines protocols that inform the full randomized controlled trial (RCT). These rigorous evaluations establish whether CBT is better than no treatment, or better than existing treatments. Reflection on the outcome leads to observation of the problems, client groups, etc. that were not helped sufficiently and the cycle begins again.

We consider the cognitive model as the basis of a formulation, and the emphasis on empiricism as defining features of CBT, and we thus review CBTp[2] in relation to these features.

Past

CBTp begins, as so much of CBT, with Beck. In 1952 he published a case report describing the successful treatment of a man with paranoid beliefs (Beck, 1952). The treatment bears little resemblance to CBT as we know it today as it does not draw on the cognitive model, nor does it measure outcome. However, Beck (2002) considered that the interpretation of delusions within the person's life context led to the development of a plausible alternative explanation for the man's experience, thereby reducing his distress and improving his functioning. Despite this initial success, Beck concentrated on developing his ideas in relation to depression. However, there were continued attempts to offer psychological therapies to people with psychosis that drew on behavioural and cognitive methods. Slade and Haddock (1996) review these approaches and describe their evolution from attempts to manipulate the environment of the person with psychotic experiences through to approaches that aim to empower them to make changes for himself or herself. For example, in the 1960s and 1970s operant conditioning principles used social rewards in order to reduce verbalization of delusions. This was effective in reducing the expression of delusional beliefs with the therapist, but typically did not generalize to other interactions. Other behavioural approaches employed token economies or aversion therapy to help reduce the experience or expression of psychotic symptoms. These approaches declined in use as they did not accommodate the views of the service users, or work to the extent hoped for. Consequently, approaches were developed to help people manage their own experiences and symptoms such as hallucinations, by using distraction and problem solving. Whilst of some value, these approaches do not draw on the cognitive model but did demonstrate that individual psychological approaches could be of value, and encouraged the later use of CBTp. Here we consider the development of CBTp in relation to the research cycle described earlier.[3]

Cognitive phenomenology of psychotic experiences

Dissatisfaction with scientific utility of the concept of 'schizophrenia' (Bentall *et al.*, 1988) led to revision of the view that schizophrenia was qualitatively different from other emotional disorders. This revision encouraged the description and scientific investigations of psychotic symptoms from a cognitive perspective. For example, Bentall *et al.* (1994) found a tendency for people with persecutory delusions to blame others for negative events. This is an attributional style opposite to people with depression. Garety and Hemsley (1994) report a series of investigations that revealed the multidimensionality of delusional beliefs, as well as a characteristic reasoning style in which some people with delusions make hasty or rapid judgements.

With regard to hallucinations, Slade and Bentall (1988) studied psychological processes of voice hearing and found that people who hear voices had a tendency to attribute internal experiences such as their own thoughts to an external source. In addition, Romme and Escher (1996) described how beliefs about voices are crucial to understanding the distress and impact of these experiences. Such descriptive phenomenological and experimental studies began to unpack key cognitive processes that then informed intervention strategies.

Case studies and case series

Watts *et al.* (1973) found that direct confrontation of delusional beliefs only increased conviction, and hence they suggested a strategy of addressing less strongly held beliefs initially, and considering the evidence for and against the belief all the while considering other possible alternative explanations. Chadwick and Lowe (1990) drew on this method when working with 12 people with psychotic symptoms whom they treated using a combination of verbal challenge and active behavioural experimentation (or reality testing). The results were promising with five rejecting their beliefs and five reporting some reduction in conviction and distress. Fowler and Morley (1989) indicated the potential value of work with distraction and other strategies in helping challenge beliefs about voices, and hence directly addressing the mechanism identified by Romme and Escher (1996).

Kingdon and Turkington (1991) reported a case series of 64 people with schizophrenia. Whilst an uncontrolled study, the results indicated benefits for many of the participants, and perhaps more importantly no adverse outcomes from the approach with no severe deteriorations leading to aggressive behaviour or suicide during the treatment. Around this time a series of pilot studies and uncontrolled trials indicated that CBTp was of value for voices (Haddock *et al.*, 1996) and other psychotic symptoms (Garety *et al.*, 1994). These studies enabled the development of treatment manuals (e.g. Fowler *et al.*, 1995) that served as the basis for the intervention in a number of key RCTs.

Randomized controlled trials

To date over 20 RCTs have been undertaken evaluating the efficacy of CBTp. For a full description of this work there are a number of valuable reviews available (e.g. Tarrier and Wykes, 2004). We will not duplicate these reviews; rather we draw attention to some key UK-based studies which are briefly described in Table 19.1 and made reference to in the subsequent sections.

Phases of psychosis

CBTp has different emphases according to the needs of the individuals in the different stages of psychosis. For instance, when working with people who are not actively psychotic but considered to be at ultra high risk of

Table 19.1 Summary of UK-based randomized controlled trials of CBT for psychosis

Author	Year of study	N	Subjects	Control group	Treatment	Therapists	Rating scales used	Outcomes found	Follow-up results (if any)
Phase of psychosis *Pre-psychotic*									
Morrison et al.	2002	58	Considered at ultra high risk of developing a first episode of psychosis. Aged 16–36.	Monitoring.	Up to 26 session of CBT over 6 months.	CBT nurse therapist or clinical psychologist. (1 person seen by a trainee clinical psychologist.)	Rate of transition to psychosis (PANSS). Prescription of antipsychotic medication, probable DSM-IV diagnosis.	Significant reduction in likelihood of developing a psychotic episode, being prescribed antipsychotic medication and meeting criteria for a diagnosis of a psychotic disorder.	
Acute phase									
Drury et al.	1996	40	Inpatients with acute psychosis.	Structured activities and support.	20 weekly sessions (rec'd indiv and group CBT + family engagement).	3 clinical psychologists.	KGV, recovery time.	Overall symptoms and positive symptoms improved. Reduced recovery time. Those with recent onset benefited.	5-year follow-up. Benefits lost.
Haddock et al. (SoCRATES pilot)	1999	36	Acute.	Supportive counselling + psycho-education.	Intervention over 5 weeks during inpatient stay (mean: 10 sessions CBT) + 4 booster sessions (up to 4 months post discharge).	2 clinical psychologists.	Relapse, BPRS, PSYRATS, drop out.	Sig. reduction in symptoms in both groups but no diff. between groups. No sig. diff. found in time till discharge.	At 2-year follow-up: no significant diffs between groups found though relapse rate and time to relapse was better in CBT group.

continues overleaf

Table 19.1 (continued)

Author	Year of study	N	Subjects	Control group	Treatment	Therapists	Rating scales used	Outcomes found	Follow-up results (if any)
Lewis et al. (SoCRATES)	2002	315 (225 f/u)	Diagnosis of schizophrenia or associated disorder. 1st or 2nd acute episode of psychosis: positive symptoms for >4 weeks.	Supportive counselling or TAU alone.	15–20 hours within 5 weeks + booster sessions for 3 months.	CBT therapists.	PANSS, PSYRATS.	Vs. TAU: Sig. improvements at 4 but not 6 weeks on PANSS total, positive symptom subscale Vs. Supportive Counselling: on auditory hallucinations.	Tarrier et al. (2004) report 18-month follow-up. Improvement in symptoms. No benefit for relapse or time till relapse.
Startup et al.	2004	90	Patients suffering acute psychotic episodes admitted to inpatient care.	TAU.	Up to 25 sessions of CBT.	Clinical psychologists.	SFS, BPRS, SANS, SAPS.	Sig. improvement in symptoms and social functioning in CBT group. None of CBT group (vs. 17 per cent of TAU gp) showed reliable deterioration.	Sig. difference found at 12-month follow-up. At 2 years, CBT gp sig. better in neg. symptoms and social functioning, but no s.d. in pos. symptoms.
Relapse phase									
Gumley et al.	2003	144	Diagnosis of schizophrenia: prodrome and early sign of relapse.	TAU.	12 months of CBT.	Clinical psychologist.	Relapse. PANSS, SFS, drop out.	Reduced relapse, reduced admission to hospital. Greater improvements in positive and negative symptoms, global psychopathology, performance of independent functions and pro-social activities.	

Study	Year	N	Sample	Control	Intervention	Delivered by	Measures	Results
Garety et al.	2008	301	Non-affective psychoses who have recently had a relapse of their condition.	TAU, family intervention.	Up to 20 sessions over 12 months.	Clinical psychologists and specialist trained nurses.	PANSS, PSYRATS, BAI, BDI.	CBT and family intervention had no effect on relapse rates, days of hospitalization. At 24 months CBT had some impact on depression. CBT significantly improved delusional distress and social functioning in those people with carers.

Treatment resistant

Study	Year	N	Sample	Control	Intervention	Delivered by	Measures	Results
Tarrier et al.	1993	27	Diagnosis of schizophrenia. Subjects with drug resistant symptoms for at least 6 months. Aged 16–65.	Waiting list.	6 weeks of coping strategy enhancement (CSE) or problem solving (PS).	Psychologists.	BPRS, PSE, KGV, SFS.	Significant reduction in symptoms esp. anxiety and delusions. CSE possibly more beneficial than PS (no impact on negative symptoms or social functioning). 23 followed up at 6 months showed that improvements had been maintained.
Kuipers et al.	1997	60	Patients with stable (drug resistant) psychotic symptoms.	Treatment as usual.	20 sessions: weekly or fortnightly (in up to 9 months).	Clinical psychologists.	PSE, BPRS, MADS, BDI, BAI, BHS, Self-concept Qr, Dysfunction Attitude Scale, SFS.	Sig. improvement in BPRS score (symptoms) in CBT group. At 18 months: no change. Improvement in symptoms is maintained (poss improving).

continues overleaf

Table 19.1 (continued)

Author	Year of study	N	Subjects	Control group	Treatment	Therapists	Rating scales used	Outcomes found	Follow-up results (if any)
Tarrier et al.	1998	87	Diagnosis of schizophrenia, schizoaffective psychosis or delusional disorder. Drug resistant symptoms for >6 months.	Supportive counselling and routine care alone.	20 sessions: 2 per week over 10 weeks (CSE, coping skills and relapse prevention).	Clinical psychologists.	BPRS, relapse rate, time spent in hospital.	CBT group had better outcome in terms of number and severity of positive symptoms and overall symptom reduction (>50 per cent), relapse rates and time spent in hospital.	Benefits remained at 12-months follow-up. At 2-year follow-up no sig. difference between CBT and supportive counselling, though both were sig. better than TAU.
Kemp et al.	1996	47	Diagnosis of schizophrenia or schizoaffective disorder.	Supportive counselling.	4–6 sessions of CBT lasting 20–60 mins, twice a week.	Research psychiatrist or clinical psychologist.	BPRS, GAF, SAI, Drug Attitude Inventory, Attitudes to Medication Questionnaire.	No sig. difference in symptoms but improved insight, compliance and attitude to medication.	Results maintained at 6 months.
Sensky et al.	2000	90	Diagnosis of schizophrenia. Treatment resistant symptoms >9 months, no co-morbid substance misuse, positive symptoms evident.	Befriending.	Weekly: mean of 19 sessions over 9 months.	CBT therapists.	CPRS, MADRS, SANS.	Both expntl and control groups showed sig. improvement in positive and negative symptoms and depression at the end of the study.	9-month follow-up showed CBT group had maintained benefits compared to control group.

Study	Year	N	Inclusion criteria	Control	Intervention	Therapist	Measures	Results	Follow-up
Turkington et al.	2002	422	Diagnosis of schizophrenia receiving secondary care.	TAU.	6 sessions within 2–3 months (+3 family sessions).	CPNs (insight nurses).	CPRS, Insight Rating Scale, Schiz Change Scale, MADRS (PSYRATS).	Improvements in overall symptoms, insight and depression.	Not yet reported.
Durham et al.	2003	66	Diagnosis of schizophrenia or related disorder, persistent positive symptoms, known to services for >6 months.	Supportive psychotherapy or TAU alone.	9 months of CBT (max 20 half-hour sessions).	Clinical nurse specialists.	PANSS, PYRATS, Global Assessment Scale, Clinical Global Improvement, Penn Helping Alliance Qr.	Greater improvement in overall symptom severity in CBT group. Both CBT and SPT groups showed greater improvement in severity of delusions than TAU.	
Haddock et al.	2003	36	Diagnosis of schizophrenia, schizoaffective disorder or delusional disorder + substance misuse (18–65).	TAU.	9 months of motivational intervention, CBT and family intervention.	Specially trained CBT therapists.	GAF, PANSS, SFS, Substance use, relapse.	Sig. improvements in patient functioning (GAF) at 18 months in CBT gp. No sig. diffs found in PANSS or level of abstinence.	
Trower et al.	2004	38	Diagnosis of schizophrenia or related disorder. Command hallucinations >6 months. Recent history of compliance with voice.	TAU.	6 months of CBT.	Clinical psychologist.	Cognitive Assessment Schedule; Beliefs about Voices Questionnaire; Voice Compliance Scale, Voice Power Differential Scale; Omniscience Scale; PANSS, PYRATS; Calgary Depression Scale for Schizophrenia.	Significant improvement in compliance with voices. Sig. reduction in belief of power and omniscience of voice and increase in perceived control over voice. Sig. redn in distress.	Differences in percd power, omniscience and control maintained at 12-month follow-up plus CBT gp sig. less depressed.

developing psychosis, the goal of the work is on helping people better to manage depressive or anxious symptoms and distress, or understand and manage any emerging unusual experiences. Using these approaches, Morrison *et al.* (2002) reported a reduced rate of developing psychosis in such a high risk group.

The evidence is less strong for people who have recently made the transition into psychosis. Lewis *et al.* (2002) found little difference between CBTp and supportive counselling (SC) at the end of treatment in people in their first or second episode of psychosis. This lack of difference was in part owing to the general level of recovery in people in their first episode, meaning that any additional benefit offered by CBTp was hard to demonstrate. However, people receiving CBTp did respond more rapidly and benefit more if they experienced hallucinations than similar people in the control condition. People with delusions appeared to benefit from both CBTp and SC (Tarrier *et al.*, 2004). For people who are acutely unwell and requiring inpatient care, there is evidence of the potential value of CBTp. However, there are not enduring benefits (Drury *et al.*, 1996; Startup *et al.*, 2004; Valmaggia *et al.*, 2005).

Once over the acute phase, specific interventions have been developed to help people as they start to relapse. For instance, Gumley *et al.* (2003) reported reduced admissions for people in comparison to treatment as usual. However, a recently reported study, the Psychological Prevention of Relapse in Psychosis (PRP) Trial, which was a multicentre, randomized, controlled trial of CBTp and family intervention for psychosis, indicated that neither CBTp nor family intervention reduced symptoms or relapse in comparison to treatment as usual. This is a very important study involving over 300 people, and one that indicates that CBTp is not indicated for routine relapse prevention for people recovering from a recent relapse of psychosis (Garety *et al.*, 2008).

At present, the most well supported evidence is for people with long-standing symptoms and who are considered treatment resistant or unresponsive to medications.

CBT for treatment-resistant psychosis typically addresses psychotic symptoms such as hallucinations or delusions that are associated with distress or disruption to the person's life, as well as depressive, anxious or negative symptoms (Fowler *et al.*, 1995). Initial work with treatment-resistant people was undertaken by Tarrier and colleagues (1993) who developed coping strategy enhancement (CSE) which built on the behavioural approaches and aimed to increase functional coping and reduce dysfunctional coping as well as improving problem solving for people with psychotic experiences. This CSE approach was compared to supportive counselling and indicated that CSE was more effective than SC, which in turn was better than treatment as usual (Tarrier *et al.*, 1993). A subsequent analysis of the findings (Tarrier *et al.*, 2001) indicated that people with delusions generally responded better to treatment, whereas people with hallucinations without delusions did not respond.

Sensky *et al.* (2000) offered either CBTp or a control befriending condition (BF) to 90 people with treatment-resistant schizophrenia. In each condition the person was seen by a therapist for sessions on a weekly basis for around nine months, or 20 sessions of treatment. In the BF condition, the therapist engaged in social conversation. Whilst both groups benefited from the intervention, only the CBTp group maintained the benefits at nine-month follow-up. Kuipers *et al.* (1997) reported a trial in which the control was a waiting list and found significant benefits for the CBTp group in terms of reductions in symptomatology. In both of these trials the CBTp was delivered by experienced, highly trained and closely supervised cognitive therapists.

Turkington *et al.* (2002) reduced the amount of training required by the therapists and delivered a more focused treatment package of six individual sessions with the person with treatment-resistant schizophrenia, with three family sessions offered as well. The results indicated that CBTp could be implemented in a real world clinical setting with beneficial results for psychotic and non-psychotic symptoms.

What is startlingly evident is that a supportive and consistent relationship seems to be of great value to many people with psychosis and can help reduce positive symptomatology (Sensky *et al.*, 2000; Lewis *et al.*, 2002). A supportive relationship may have a different mechanism of action than CBT (Milne *et al.*, 2006). Delusions, especially persecutory beliefs, may benefit from the development of trust and intimacy to indirectly challenge beliefs about self-acceptability and the threat of other people, whereas for hallucinations people may need more active and theory-based help (Tarrier *et al.*, 2001).

In summary, there is a strong evidence base for the value of CBTp and the National Institute for Health and Clinical Excellence (NICE, 2002) has recommended that CBTp be available to service users in England. It seems that CBTp is particularly valuable for people with treatment-resistant psychotic symptoms (see also Tarrier *et al.*, 1998).

Present

Tarrier and Wykes (2004) evaluated 20 of the RCTs for CBTp against a number of criteria and concluded that the evidence for CBTp was promising. However, the results should not be accepted uncritically. CBTp has not been properly compared to another empirically supported treatment approach so we do not know if it is better than another psychological approach such as family interventions (see Kennard in Chapter 8) or another individual approach. However, the goal of these initial trials was to demonstrate worth rather than differential benefit. It is important to note though that Tarrier and Wykes (2004) found that the stronger the methodology of the study, the smaller the effect size.

Whilst we have evidence of efficacy, we do not know which, if any, are the important components of treatment; nor do we understand the mechanisms that lead to change. However, despite the lack of clear evidence for the specific features of CBTp, there are generally recognized elements that constitute good CBTp.

Characteristics of CBTp

CBTp shares much in common with CBT for other disorders, but there are some elements given even greater emphasis in CBTp, which include:

- engaging the person in a collaborative and trusting relationship
- developing an understanding of the onset of the psychotic experiences, usually using a stress vulnerability framework
- using theory-guided techniques and methods such as normalization to help address psychotic symptoms like delusions or voice experiences.

These key characteristics are given particular attention in this review. However, for full descriptions of these approaches readers are directed to the many excellent treatment texts (Fowler *et al.*, 1995; Morrison *et al.*, 2004).

Engagement and rapport building

Typically, there is a greater emphasis on engagement and rapport building when developing the therapeutic relationship with a person with psychosis. The reason for this is that a trusting therapeutic relationship is necessary as a vehicle in which to examine the experience of psychosis. The person may have suspicions about the therapist and the broader psychiatric system. Hence, it will take time to regard the therapist as a potential ally in examining these concerns. Unless this trust is established, the use of therapeutic techniques is likely to be of limited utility.

Understanding the onset of the illness

Once a therapeutic relationship is established, time is often spent discussing the first experience of psychosis as the patient went through a change from normality to the psychotic prodrome. The aim is to provide an understanding of the onset of the psychotic illness. Typically this is undertaken by drawing on a stress vulnerability model (Zubin and Spring, 1977). Central to the stress vulnerability understanding is the concept that an individual may have a vulnerability to psychosis owing to genetic and neurological factors, as well as early life experiences. These early vulnerabilities predispose a person to psychosis, which is expressed following exposure to a range of stressors such as life events, substance misuse and trauma. In CBTp the patient is helped to understand how his own unique stressors and vulnerabilities are drawn together in a coherent understanding of what may have led to the development of psychosis. This work also allows the identification of risk factors that may best be avoided in the future to reduce the chance of symptom exacerbation or relapse.

This process of understanding the onset of the illness is then expanded into an individualized formulation of the onset and maintenance of the person's problems and is the basis for work with psychotic symptoms.

CBT with psychotic symptoms

Ideally, formulation of psychotic symptoms uses empirically supported disorder specific models as the basis for a person specific formulation (Beck, 1995) and guides treatment to target key psychological processes using specifically adapted techniques. For example, Morrison (1998) has proposed a model for voice experiences similar to the panic model in which voices are considered to be normal experiences which are catastrophically misinterpreted, and hence the appraisal is the crucial target for intervention. Normalization of these experiences is a crucial treatment approach in this model. The prevalence of voice experiences in stressful or unusual circumstances, and the evidence that people can experience these without undue distress, is used to help the person consider that it is not the experience itself but the appraisal of it that is crucial.

Birchwood et al. (2000) also describe a model in which beliefs about voices are crucial in understanding the distress and impact of these experiences. The beliefs are particularly concerned with the perceived power and omnipotence of the voice, and reflect the social rank of the voice hearer in comparison to the perceived social rank of the voice. We cannot do justice to the range of theories being proposed, and readers are encouraged to access original sources for fuller descriptions of these models. However, what is important is that such models serve as the basis for a formulation that helps explain the onset and maintenance of the psychotic experience and serves as an alternative explanation that can be actively tested in therapy. This is important as the goal is not to prove that the person is wrong (i.e. 'you do not hear voices'); rather the goal is to explain why the person has the distress that he or she does and to provide an alternative explanation for the experience that is then actively tested using collaborative empiricism ('If I too heard the voice of the devil I would feel frightened. However, there seem to be some occasions when you seem to manage to resist the voice and I wonder if this fits with the idea that the voice is so powerful? I wonder if it fits with the view that it could be something you could think yourself? How could we find that out?').

Following work on the antecedents to the development of the illness, development of an individualized formulation and symptom work, attention may turn to more longstanding dysfunctional attitudes, and assumptions that may have led to psychological vulnerability. The aims of CBTp are:

- to reduce the distress and impact of a person's presenting problems
- to provide an understanding of their psychotic experiences
- to change appraisals of these experiences by using normalizing information in conjunction with a formulation to provide a less threatening alternative explanation.

Typically treatment will last for up to 20 sessions, reflecting the longer engagement and rapport building period as well as the severity of the problems a person faces.

Summary of the present

The existing evidence base indicates that CBTp can work. Recent long-term follow-up studies have revealed a mixed picture about the durability of CBTp (Durham *et al.*, 2005). It is clear that there are still many people for whom CBTp is either ineffective or at best a partial solution. CBTp helps some people to some extent some of the time, and not necessarily forever, so modesty is important – as is the need to try to improve what is on offer.

We are now awaiting the results of the second wave of treatments where there is greater focus on the effective components and techniques that create change. A driving force in this process is the development and refinement of models that guide treatment and hopefully increase its efficiency. To date, treatment was largely guided by good clinical judgement, and adaptation of specific interventions to working with psychosis (i.e. normalization). However, increasingly attempts have been made to target the specific processes that should enable more effective and hopefully efficient change (Trower *et al.*, 2004). This state of affairs brings us to consider the future developments in CBTp.

Future

We consider that the further development of CBTp will follow one of four routes:

1   Increasing the specificity of theories and efficiency of treatment of symptoms.
2   Increasing the effectiveness of CBTp by changing the format of delivery.

3   Helping people who have psychotic symptoms in the context of other difficulties.
4   Development of what we term novel approaches.

We consider these in turn.

Increased specification of theories and efficiency of treatments

As described previously, there is an ongoing process of model development and refinement that should produce new theory-guided treatments. This work leads us to models of different symptoms such as command hallucinations (Birchwood *et al.*, 2000), negatively appraised voices (Morrison, 1998), and persecutory beliefs (Freeman *et al.*, 2002). This specification of process continues to challenge the notion that schizophrenia is one single entity and hence we will likely see the development of understanding and treatment of subtypes of psychosis which share similarities with anxiety disorders, and more biological features (such as substance misuse or genetic risk) as well as with trauma-based problems. Increasingly, the role of trauma in the origins and maintenance of psychosis is being understood (Morrison *et al.*, 2003). However, specific treatments for trauma in the context of psychosis are only just emerging (Callcott *et al.*, 2004).

In a similar way, at present we lack knowledge of the psychology of negative symptoms (Rector *et al.*, 2005) or visual hallucinations (Collerton and Dudley, 2004) and it may be that they may need their own treatment approaches.

Changes to the format of treatments

To date there has been limited development of CBTp in group format, despite demonstrating some benefit (Warman *et al.*, 2005). There are many potential benefits of group work besides efficiency of time. Psychotic illness may lead to impacts on social functioning, and group work can help to establish social connections. Moreover, the opportunity to stand back and reflect on other people's experiences and hear corrective feedback and alternative explanations from peers and colleagues of one's own explanations is a potentially powerful experience.

Within the field of CBT there have been substantial efforts made to increase access to a limited resource. One route has been the development of self-help materials and there are now self-help books for people with psychotic experiences (e.g. Freeman *et al.*, 2006). How effective or acceptable these approaches will be, given the emphasis on the development of a therapeutic relationship in CBTp, remains to be seen.

Expanding to whom CBTp is offered

CBTp has been shown to be most efficacious for people with treatment-resistant psychotic symptoms. At present the evidence for working with other phases of psychosis is less well supported. Some encouraging but preliminary evidence supports the use of CBT to help prevent the transition to psychosis (Morrison *et al.*, 2002), and a larger multicentre trial is currently underway to examine whether CBTp can help prevent the transition to psychosis. However, this will not be completed until the end of the decade (Morrison, personal communication).

In addition to offering treatments at different phases of illness, attention is also being paid to the context in which psychosis can present. Recent work combining CBT with motivational interviewing approaches and family intervention may offer the prospect of an intervention for this very difficult to help client group with psychotic illness and substance misuse. Previous pilot work indicates the potential benefit of such an approach (Haddock *et al.*, 2003) and such a trial is underway (MIDAS trial).

Whilst recent evidence has demonstrated the value of CBTp in helping command hallucinations (Trower *et al.*, 2004), psychotic symptoms in the context of forensic settings have not been fully addressed. Once again there is a trial being undertaken to assess the value of CBTp in this setting (PICASSO trial). Similarly, children and adolescents with psychosis may have specific needs that are not currently met within the existing treatment approaches.

Novel treatment approaches

Traditionally in CBT the emphasis has been on addressing the content of thoughts. However, recent developments emphasize that the processes which people engage in to manage their upsetting thoughts, such as ruminating, may actually be unhelpful and can be directly targeted as processes rather than addressing the content of the thoughts. For instance, one area of development with potential promise is the use of mindfulness (Chadwick *et al.*, 2005) and acceptance and commitment therapy (ACT) for people with psychotic illness. These approaches do not engage in critically examining the basis of thoughts or behaviours. Rather the focus is on the decentring from and acceptance of thoughts or images and preventing attempts to suppress, avoid or distract oneself from thinking about such things. A report by Bach and Hayes (2002) indicated that the rate of rehospitalization for people with psychotic illness was significantly reduced following only four sessions of ACT.

Another key development is exciting work undertaken on self-esteem in psychosis by Hall and Tarrier (2003) who found that by using CBT methods to help improve self-esteem they also reduced positive symptoms.

It demonstrates that there are many potential routes to change and direct addressing of psychotic symptoms is not the only way to create a positive outcome.

The above work represents some of the exciting developments being made in the field of CBTp. However, there are still challenges. For instance, despite the success of family interventions there has been little integration of CBTp with family approaches. Also, a particularly important development in the future will be to broaden the range of outcomes measured and not to continue to measure change in terms of symptoms alone. Even where symptoms are addressed it is important that they are measured in the most appropriate manner. For instance, Trower *et al.* (2004) addressed beliefs about voices and found a change in this rather than frequency of the experiences. Of course, even with symptom reduction people may continue to lead limited and isolated lives. In CBTp personally defined goals of treatment often include changing social, occupational and interpersonal functioning as people want to find work, develop friendships and relationships and want more than reduced symptom distress. As CBTp therapists we need to evaluate the impact of our work on these personally defined goals. This can present a challenge to the traditional model of evaluation of symptom change.

Besides the development of these exciting novel treatment approaches, a key challenge remains dissemination of good practice, as it is still the case that psychological interventions are not commonly accessed by people with psychosis. There is a risk that CBTp is offered by poorly trained and inexperienced practitioners. This may lead to poor experiences of therapy and to the perception that the approach cannot help people. It would be a loss for all psychological therapies if CBTp was seen not to work, as it would surely reduce the impetus to develop and offer psychological therapies for people with psychosis.

Finally, the role of CBTp in relation to medication needs further consideration. CBTp is usually considered as an adjunct to medication or a way of increasing adherence (Kemp *et al.*, 1996). However, as CBTp expands to very early (even non-psychotic) stages there are ethical implications in using medications alongside CBTp. Also, where someone remains distressed and disabled by psychotic experiences despite adequate trials of medications, it is important to consider whether CBTp can be offered to people who cannot tolerate antipsychotic medication, or who wish to reduce and stop their medication.

Conclusion

CBTp is of demonstrated value but it is not a panacea. There are substantial gaps in our understanding but there is a tried and tested method to address these and there is reason to be optimistic that CBT-based therapies will continue to grow in their use with people with psychosis. At present CBTp seems most helpful to people with longstanding distressing psychotic symptoms who receive help over 20 sessions or more.

Notes

1 Psychotic disorders is used here to refer to non-affective psychoses, mainly schizophrenia, and does not include CBT for the symptoms of bipolar disorder or prevention of relapse in bipolar disorder. For reviews of CBT for bipolar disorder see Newman *et al.* (2002).
2 Whilst talked about as CBT for psychosis, much of the following review will concentrate on treatment of delusional beliefs and auditory hallucinations which are the most investigated of the features of psychosis.
3 Our focus is on developments in the UK as this is the purpose of the chapter. However, we are aware of the range and quality of research undertaken throughout the rest of the world both in understanding and treating psychosis.

References

Bach, P. and Hayes, S.H. (2002). The use of acceptance and commitment therapy to prevent the rehospitalisation of psychotic patients: a randomised controlled trial. *Journal of Consulting and Clinical Psychology* 70, 5: 1129–1139.

Beck, A.T. (1952). Successful outpatient psychotherapy of a chronic schizophrenic with a delusion based on borrowed guilt. *Psychiatry: Journal for the Study of Interpersonal Processes* 15: 305–312.

Beck, A.T. (2002). Successful outpatient psychotherapy of a chronic schizophrenic with a delusion based on borrowed guilt: a 50 year retrospective. In A. Morrison (ed.) *A Casebook of Cognitive Therapy for Psychosis*. London: Brunner-Routledge, pp. 15–19.

Beck, A.T. (2005). The current state of cognitive therapy: a 40-year retrospective. *Archives of General Psychiatry* 62: 953–959.

Beck, J.S. (1995). *Cognitive Therapy: Basics and Beyond*. New York: Guilford Press.

Bentall, R.P., Kinderman, P. and Kaney, S. (1994). The self, attributional processes and abnormal beliefs: towards a model of persecutory delusions. *Behaviour Research and Therapy* 32: 331–341.

Bentall, R.P., Jackson, H.F. and Pilgrim, D. (1988). Abandoning the concept of 'schizophrenia': Some implications of validity arguments for psychological research into psychotic phenomena. *British Journal of Clinical Psychology* 27: 303–324.

Birchwood, M., Meaden, A., Trower, P., Gilbert, P. and Plaistow, J. (2000). The power and omnipotence of voices: subordination and entrapment by voices and significant others. *Psychological Medicine* 30: 337–344.

Callcott, P., Standart, S. and Turkington, D. (2004). Trauma within psychosis: using a CBT model for PTSD in psychosis. *Behavioural and Cognitive Psychotherapy* 32, 2: 239–245.

Chadwick, P. and Lowe, C.F. (1990). Measurement and modification of delusional beliefs. *Journal of Consulting and Clinical Psychology* 58: 225–232.

Chadwick, P., Newman Taylor, K. and Abba, N. (2005). Mindfulness groups for people with psychosis. *Behavioural and Cognitive Psychotherapy* 33, 3: 351–361.

Collerton, D. and Dudley, R. (2004). A cognitive behavioural framework for the treatment of distressing visual hallucinations. *Behavioural and Cognitive Psychotherapy* 32: 443–455.

Drury, V., Birchwood, M., Cochrane, R. *et al.* (1996). Cognitive therapy and recovery from acute psychosis: a controlled trial: 1. Impact on psychotic symptoms. *British Journal of Psychiatry* 169: 593–601.

Durham, R.C., Guthrie, M., Morton, R.V. *et al.* (2003). Tayside-Fife clinical trial of cognitive-behavioural therapy for medication-resistant psychotic symptoms. *British Journal of Psychiatry* 182: 303–311.

Durham, R.C., Chambers, J.A., Power, K.G., Sharp, D.M. *et al.* (2005). Long term outcome of cognitive behaviour therapy clinical trials in central Scotland. *Health Technology Assessment* 9, 42 (Executive Summary).

Ellis, A. (1958). Rational psychotherapy. *Journal of General Psychology* 59: 35–49.

Fowler, D. and Morley, S. (1989). The cognitive-behavioural treatment of hallucinations and delusions: a preliminary study. *Behavioural Psychotherapy* 17, 3: 267–282.

Fowler, D., Garety, P. and Kuipers, E. (1995). *Cognitive Behaviour Therapy for People with Psychosis: A Clinical Handbook*. Chichester: Wiley.

Freeman, D., Freeman, J. and Garety, P. (2006). Overcoming paranoid and suspicious thoughts. London: Robinson.

Freeman, D., Garety, P.A., Kuipers, E., Fowler, D. and Bebbington, P.E. (2002). A cognitive model of persecutory delusions. *British Journal of Clinical Psychology* 41: 331–347.

Garety, P.A. and Hemsley, D.R. (1994). *Delusions: Investigations into the Psychology of Delusional Reasoning*. Oxford: Oxford University Press.

Garety, P., Kuipers, E., Fowler, D., Chamberlain, F. and Dunn, G. (1994). Cognitive behaviour therapy for drug resistant psychosis. *British Journal of Medical Psychology* 67: 259–271.

Garety, P.A., Fowler, D., Freeman, D., Bebbington, P.E., Dunn, G. and Kuipers, E. (2008). Cognitive behavioural therapy and family intervention for prevention and symptom reduction in psychosis: randomized controlled trial. *British Journal of Psychiatry* 192: 412–413.

Gumley, A.I., O'Grady, M., McNay, L. *et al.* (2003). Early intervention for relapse in schizophrenia: results of a 12-month randomized controlled trial of cognitive behaviour therapy. *Psychological Medicine* 33: 419–431.

Haddock, G., Bentall, R. and Slade, P.D. (1996). Psychological treatment of auditory hallucinations: focusing or distraction. In G. Haddock and P.D. Slade (eds) *Cognitive Behavioural Interventions with Psychotic Disorders*. London and New York: Routledge, pp. 45–70.

Haddock, G., Tarrier, N., Morrison, A.P., Hopkins, R., Drake, R. and Lewis, S. (1999). A pilot study evaluating the effectiveness of individual inpatient cognitive behavioural therapy in early psychosis. *Social Psychiatric Epidemiology* 34: 254–258.

Haddock, G., Barrowclough, C., Tarrier, N., Moring, J., O'Brien, R., Schofield, N. *et al.* (2003). Cognitive-behavioural therapy and motivational intervention for schizophrenia and substance misuse. 18-month outcomes of a randomised controlled trial. *British Journal of Psychiatry* 183: 418–426.

Hall, P.L. and Tarrier, N. (2003). The cognitive-behavioural treatment of low self-esteem in psychotic patients: a pilot study. *Behaviour Research and Therapy* 41, 3: 317–320.

Kemp, R., Hayward, P., Applethwaite, G. *et al.* (1996). Compliance therapy in psychotic patients: randomized controlled trial. *British Medical Journal* 312: 345–349.

Kingdon, D. and Turkington, D. (1991). The use of cognitive behaviour therapy with a normalizing rationale in schizophrenia. *Journal of Nervous and Mental Disease* 179: 207–211.

Kuipers, E., Garety, P.A. and Fowler, D. (1997). The London East Anglia randomized controlled trial of cognitive behaviour therapy for psychosis I: Effects of the treatment phase. *British Journal of Psychiatry* 171: 319–327.

Lewis, S., Tarrier, N., Haddock, G., Bentall, R., Kinderman, P., Kingdon, D. *et al.* (2002). Randomised controlled trial of cognitive-behavioural therapy in early schizophrenia: acute-phase outcomes. *British Journal of Psychiatry* 181: 91–97.

MIDAS trial. http://www.psych-sci.manchester.ac.uk/research/projects/midas.

Milne, D., Wharton, S., James, I. and Turkington, D. (2006). Befriending versus CBT for schizophrenia: a convergent and divergent fidelity check. *Behavioural and Cognitive Psychotherapy* 34, 1: 25–31.

Morrison, A.P. (1998). A cognitive analysis of the maintenance of auditory hallucinations: are voices to schizophrenia what bodily sensations are to panic? *Behavioural and Cognitive Psychotherapy* 26: 289–302.

Morrison, A.P., Bentall, R.P., French, P. *et al.* (2002). Randomised controlled trial of early detection and cognitive therapy for preventing transition to psychosis in high risk individuals. *British Journal of Psychiatry* 181 (Suppl. 43): 78–84.

Morrison, A.P., Frame, L. and Larkin, W. (2003). Relationship between trauma and psychosis: a review and integration. *British Journal of Clinical Psychology* 42, 4: 331–353.

Morrison, A.P., Renton, J.C., Dunn, H. *et al.* (2004). *Cognitive Therapy for Psychosis: A Formulation-Based Approach.* Hove, UK: Brunner-Routledge.

National Institute for Clinical Excellence (NICE, 2002). *Clinical Guideline 1: Schizophrenia. Core Interventions in the Treatment and Management of Schizophrenia in Primary and Secondary Care.* London: NICE.

Newman, C.F., Leahy, R.L., Beck, A.T., Reilly-Harrington, N.A. and Gyulai, L. (2002). *Bipolar Disorder: A Cognitive Therapy Approach.* Washington, DC: American Psychological Association.

PICASSO trial. http://www.psych-sci.manchester.ac.uk/research/projects/picasso.

Rector, N.A., Beck, A.T. and Stolar, N. (2005). The negative symptoms of schizophrenia: a cognitive perspective. *Canadian Journal of Psychiatry* 50: 247–257.

Romme, M. and Escher, S. (1996). Empowering people who hear voices. In G. Haddock and P.D. Slade (eds) *Cognitive Behavioural Interventions with Psychotic Disorders.* London and New York: Routledge.

Sensky, T., Turkington, D., Kingdon, D. *et al.* (2000). A randomised controlled trial of cognitive-behavioural therapy for persistent symptoms in schizophrenia resistant to medication. *Archives of General Psychiatry* 57: 165–172.

Slade, P.D. and Bentall, R.P. (1988). Sensory deception: a scientific analysis of hallucinations. *Behaviour, Research and Therapy* 10: 85–91.

Slade, P.D. and Haddock, G. (1996). A historical overview of psychological treatment for psychotic symptoms. In G. Haddock and P.D. Slade (eds) *Cognitive Behavioural Interventions with Psychotic Disorders*. London and New York: Routledge.

Startup, M., Jackson, M. and Bendix, S. (2004). North Wales randomized controlled trial of cognitive behaviour therapy for acute spectrum disorders: outcome at six and twelve months. *Psychological Medicine* 34: 214–422.

Tarrier, N. and Wykes, T. (2004). Is there evidence that cognitive behaviour therapy is an effective treatment for schizophrenia? A cautious or cautionary tale? *Behaviour Research and Therapy* 42: 1377–1401.

Tarrier, N., Beckett, R., Harwood, S. *et al.* (1993). A trial of two cognitive-behavioural methods of treating drug resistant residual psychotic symptoms in schizophrenic patients. I. Outcome. *British Journal of Psychiatry* 162: 524–532.

Tarrier, N., Yusupoff, L., Kinney, C. *et al.* (1998). Randomized controlled trial of intensive cognitive behaviour therapy for patients with chronic schizophrenia. *British Medical Journal* 317: 303–307.

Tarrier, N., Kinney, C., McCarthy, E., Wittkowski, A. *et al.* (2001). Are some types of psychotic symptoms more responsive to cognitive behavioural therapy? *Behavioural and Cognitive Psychotherapy* 29: 44–55.

Tarrier, N., Lewis, S.W., Haddock, G., Bentall, R., Drake, R., Dunn, G. *et al.* (2004). 18 month follow up of a randomized controlled clinical trial of cognitive behaviour therapy in first episode and early schizophrenia (the SoCRATES trial). *British Journal of Psychiatry* 184: 231–239.

Trower, P., Birchwood, M., Meaden, A. *et al.* (2004). Cognitive therapy for command hallucinations: randomized controlled trial. *British Journal of Psychiatry* 184: 312–320.

Turkington, D., Kingdon, D., Turner, T. *et al.* (2002). Effectiveness of a brief cognitive-behavioural therapy intervention in the treatment of schizophrenia. *British Journal of Psychiatry* 180: 523–527.

Valmaggia, L.R., van der Gaag, M., Tarrier, N., Pijnenborg, M. and Sloof, C.J. (2005). Cognitive-behavioural therapy for refractory psychotic symptoms of schizophrenia resistant to atypical antipsychotic medication. Randomised controlled trial. *British Journal of Psychiatry* 186: 324–330.

Warman, D.M., Grant, P., Sullivan, K., Caroff, S. and Beck, A.T. (2005). Individual and group cognitive behavioural therapy for psychotic disorders: a pilot investigation. *Journal of Psychiatric Practice* 11: 27–34.

Watts, F.N., Powell, G.E. and Austin, S.V. (1973). The modification of abnormal beliefs. *British Journal of Medical Psychology* 46: 359–363.

Zubin, J. and Spring, B. (1977). Vulnerability – a new view on schizophrenia. *Journal of Abnormal Psychology* 86: 103–126.

Chapter 20

Psychopharmacological treatment and psychotherapy in schizophrenic psychoses

Part 1: Challenges of antipsychotic drug treatment in schizophrenia

Jarmo Hietala

Introduction

The first clinical effects of antipsychotic drugs were reported in 1951 by a French surgeon, Henri Laborit, who tried chlorpromazine (4560 RP) in patients in order to find specific forms of anesthesia that he called 'hibernation' (Laborit and Huguenard, 1951). These findings were followed up by the seminal report by Delay *et al.* (1952) showing that chlorpromazine reduced psychotic symptoms, in particular excitation and agitation symptoms, in a heterogeneous sample of patients with mixed psychotic and manic symptoms. These early observations were verified by subsequent controlled studies that convincingly demonstrated the efficacy of this class of drugs, especially in reducing productive psychotic symptoms and the risk of new psychotic episodes in schizophrenia (Casey *et al.*, 1960; Davis *et al.*, 1980).

It was already evident in 1952 that classical antipsychotic drugs did not have specific effects in schizophrenia. Hence these drugs were called 'major tranquillizers' at that time and were already being used for many forms of psychosis. It was equally evident from the very beginning that the clinical effects of conventional antipsychotic drugs or 'neuroleptic' drugs (chlorpromazine, other phenthiazines and butyrophenones) were mostly alleviating the positive symptom dimension of schizophrenia, were frequently associated with partial clinical responses and often induced severe motor side effects limiting the therapeutic usefulness of these drugs. We now know that the central mechanism of action of these drugs is the blockade of specific dopamine receptors (D2) in the brain. We also know that in the first decades these drugs were used in unnecessary high doses that induced excessive dopamine D2 receptor blockade (over 80 per cent blockade) and a full variety of extrapyramidal side effects (EPS) from dystonia to tardive dyskinesia (Farde *et al.*, 1988). The newer generation of antipsychotic drugs such as risperidone, olanzapine and quetiapine have basically the same key mechanism of action, that is dopamine D2 receptor blockade, but are designed to have other pharmacodynamic properties associated with a lower risk for the motor side effects when used in standard doses. Yet, the same problem of limited clinical effectiveness is shared by the new antipsychotic drugs (e.g. Lieberman *et al.*, 2005; Jones *et al.*, 2006). Despite the developments in the antipsychotic drug treatment we still are facing at least three major clinical problems:

1   A small proportion of patients with schizophrenia benefit only marginally from antipsychotic drugs.
2   Even for those patients that do respond, the response is usually partial and all psychopathological domains do not improve in the same manner.
3   The effectiveness of all antipsychotic drugs is limited by side effects and patient compliance.

These issues are discussed below.

Antipsychotic drug treatment: limited clinical effectiveness

The clinical response to antipsychotic drugs is known to be individual. It has been estimated that about 10 to 20 per cent patients respond only marginally or not at all to conventional antipsychotic drugs. These therapy-resistant patients have been convincingly shown to benefit from clozapine in controlled clinical trials. About 30 to 60 per cent of patients refractory to conventional antipsychotic drugs respond to clozapine (Kane *et al.*, 1988). This has been well verified in clinical practice but the use of clozapine is limited due to side effects such as risk for agranulocytosis and also to marked weight gain and metabolic changes in many patients. Clozapine also seems to remain superior to other new antipsychotic drugs in terms of clinical efficacy.

Although some patients with schizophrenia do not significantly benefit from antipsychotic drugs, there is also a proportion of patients that respond exceptionally well to dopamine blocking antipsychotic drugs. Twenty years of brain imaging research has shown convincingly that schizophrenia is associated with a dysregulated dopamine system in the basal ganglia (Hietala *et al.*, 1995; Laruelle *et al.*, 1996). It would be tempting to speculate that the patients with a more pronounced dysregulation of the dopamine system would benefit most from current antipsychotic drug treatment. However, despite extensive research (clinical, brain imaging, genetic) aimed at predicting who is going to respond to antipsychotic drugs, we still have very limited clinical tools for targeting the current antipsychotic drug treatment in schizophrenia. The extensive research on the duration of untreated psychosis and clinical outcome suggests that on average a shorter duration of psychosis is associated with a more favourable response to antipsychotic drugs and a better clinical outcome (see Perkins *et al.*, 2005). Several mechanisms have been suggested for this association including disease progression and the psychosis 'toxicity' hypothesis, but the direct evidence for the latter is scarce. In addition, it is not clear how the dopamine blocking antipsychotic drugs would affect these processes (see Wyatt, 1991; Lieberman *et al.*, 1997; van Haren *et al.*, 2007). It is, however, evident that the association between duration of untreated psychosis and outcome emphasizes the importance of early detection and intervention paradigms.

Yet another problem is that it has been estimated that up to two-thirds of the patients respond to antipsychotic medication only partially, leaving them to cope with residual symptoms, impairment of social and vocational functioning as well as with an increased risk of relapses. A 30 per cent reduction of symptoms (e.g. in PANSS scale) is often used as a response criterion, but this often leaves the patient with significant residual symptoms. We know that antipsychotic drugs affect mostly positive psychotic symptoms, whereas the more relevant negative and cognitive symptom domains and overall prognosis are less affected. Long ago Eugen Bleuler considered auditory hallucinations and delusions as secondary symptoms in schizophrenia that were preceded by a primary disease process affecting associative functions. There is preliminary evidence from short-term controlled trials that some of the newer antipsychotic drugs (e.g. risperidone, olanzapine) may alleviate the negative, cognitive and affective symptoms in schizophrenia, but it is still questionable whether these effects are robust enough to be clinically significant in real-life treatment settings. An unresolved question is even whether any antipsychotic drug, including clozapine, affects the primary negative symptoms of schizophrenia.

Why do patients discontinue antipsychotic drug treatment so often?

It is a well known clinical fact that many patients do not want to continue taking antipsychotic medication. This is also illustrated by the recent naturalistic CATIE study where on average 74 per cent of the patients with schizophrenia had discontinued antipsychotic medication after 18 months (whether the newer drugs or older ones such as perphenazine) due to a variety of reasons including lack of efficacy, intolerable side effects and the patient's own desire to discontinue the medication (Lieberman *et al.*, 2005). Such a high discontinuation rate clearly limits the overall effectiveness of current antipsychotic drugs and deserves further consideration.

After over 50 years of intensive research, the only pharmacodynamic mechanism that is shared by all clinically effective antipsychotic drugs is still the blockade of brain dopamine neurotransmission (Carlsson and Lindqvist, 1963) and in particular the blockade of the dopamine D2 receptor subtype (Seeman and Lee, 1975; Creese *et al.*, 1976; Farde *et al.*, 1988). The most efficacious antipsychotic drug, clozapine, is the most important exception to this rule and indicates that antipsychotic effects can be induced by mechanism(s) beyond dopamine receptors. These mechanisms are likely to involve simultaneous action on multiple neurotransmitter systems such as glutamate and GABA, but unfortunately these mechanisms remain unknown for the time being (see Freedman, 2003).

We know that dopamine blocking antipsychotic drugs are most effective in alleviating productive psychotic symptoms such as auditory hallucinations or delusions. Shitij Kapur (2003) has formulated a clinically meaningful hypothesis on how central D2 receptor blockade results in resolution of psychotic symptoms and in particular delusions. The mesolimbocortical dopamine system and the D2-like receptors are considered to be important for assigning motivational salience to external stimuli or internal representations. Kapur hypothesizes that antipsychotic drugs by blocking D2 receptors reduce the salience of preoccupying psychotic thoughts which results in symptomatic relief. This is well in line with the original observations by Delay *et al.* (1952) describing that neuroleptics induced 'a state of indifference' in patients. In fact, many patients experience the antipsychotic effect so that the delusions or hallucinations do not fully disappear but they do not bother them subjectively so much anymore and have a less marked effect on thinking and behaviour (Mizrahi *et al.*, 2005). If the patient stops antipsychotic medication, the delusions are likely to return almost exactly as they were before taking medication.

The well known drawback of this mechanism of action is that excessive dopamine D2 blockade increases the risk for EPS. It is sometimes hard to distinguish the side effects of antipsychotic drugs from inherent primary negative, cognitive or affective symptoms related to schizophrenia itself. Yet, too high dopamine receptor blockade also increases the risk for overlapping side effect domains such as reduced motivational salience of normal affects (drive), secondary negative symptoms, dysphoric feelings, sexual side effects and possibly cognitive problems such as learning difficulties (see Naber *et al.*, 2005). There are also other probably non-dopaminergic side effects of antipsychotic drugs that also limit patient compliance and contribute to lower well-being and higher discontinuation rates. Weight gain, induced in particular with clozapine and olanzapine, is a good example of this.

Concluding remarks

Research into biological factors and the interaction between biology and environment in schizophrenia is more active than ever (Rapoport *et al.*, 2005; Read *et al.*, 2005) but so far few of the mechanisms that contribute to the core features of schizophrenia are known. Clearly, the biology of schizophrenia involves networks of multiple neurotransmitters. Out of the neurobiological mechanisms glutamate and GABA systems are being extensively investigated, but so far the dysregulated brain dopamine system is the only directly documented neurotransmitter alteration in most (but not all) patients who have schizophrenia (Hietala *et al.*, 1995; Laruelle *et al.*, 1996). Even this dopamine finding is unlikely to be specific for schizophrenia (Hirvonen *et al.*, 2005) leaving room for more specific or 'targeted' psychopharmacological treatments in this disease.

The discovery of antipsychotic drugs remains one of the most important achievements of psychopharmacology. Yet both classical and newer antipsychotic drugs with different side effect profiles share limited clinical effectiveness in the treatment of schizophrenia and current drug treatment options are far from optimal. Despite the improved social prognosis in schizophrenia, many patients suffer from marked functional impairment that leads to decreased quality of life and long-term sickness disability. It has been estimated that about a third of the patients still become chronic and that despite advancements in the pharmacotherapy the overall prognosis of schizophrenia has not improved during the last 20 years. In my opinion, the possibilities of discovering completely new principles for the pharmacological treatment of schizophrenia will be inherently linked to specific advancements of studies into the biology of schizophrenia. These studies focus currently on the details of brain development and environment–biology interactions throughout childhood and adolescence. The major challenge of these studies is to provide a means for early detection and early intervention strategies in prodromal or premorbid phases of the illness. At the same time, there is a need for more advanced psychosocial treatment methods that attend to the individual needs of patients, for example, improving cognitive functioning or abilities for social interaction.

References

Carlsson, A. and Lindqvist, M. (1963). Effect of chlorpromazine and haloperidol on formation of methoxytyramine and normetanephrine in mouse brain. *Acta Pharmacology and Toxicology* 20: 140–144.

Casey, J.F., Bennet, I.F., Lindley, C.J., Hollister, L.E., Gordon, M.H. and Springer, N.N. (1960). Drug therapy in schizophrenia. A controlled study of the relative effectiveness of chlorpromazine, promazine, phenobarbital, and placebo. *Archives of General Psychiatry* 2: 210–220.

Creese, I., Burt, D.R. and Snyder, S.H. (1976). Dopamine receptor binding predicts clinical and pharmacological potencies of antischizophrenic drugs. *Science* 192: 481–483.

Davis, J., Schaffer, B., Killina, G.A., Kinard, C. and Chan, C. (1980). Important issues in the drug treatment of schizophrenia. *Schizophrenia Bulletin* 6: 70–87.

Delay, J., Deniker, P. and Harl, J.-M. (1952). Traitement des états d'exciation et d'agitation par une methode medicamenteuse derive de l'hibernotherapie. *Annals of Medical Psychology (Paris)* 110: 267–273.

Farde, L., Nordström, A.-L., Wiesel, F.-A., Pauli, S., Halldin, C. and Sedvall, G. (1988). Positron emission tomographic analysis of central D1 and D2 dopamine receptor occupancy in patients treated with classical neuroleptics and clozapine. Relation to extrapyramidal side effects. *Archives of Geneneral Psychiatry* 49: 538–544.

Freedman, R. (2003). Schizophrenia. *New England Journal of Medicine* 349: 1738–1749.

van Haren, N.E., Hulshoff Pol, H.E., Schnack, H.G., Cahn, W., Mandl, R.C., Collins, D.L. *et al.* (2007). Focal gray matter changes in schizophrenia across the course of the illness: a 5-year follow-up study. *Neuropsychopharmacology* 32: 2057–2066.

Hietala, J., Syvälahti, E., Vuorio, K., Räkköläinen, V., Bergman, J., Haaparanta, M. *et al.* (1995). Presynaptic dopamine function in striatum of neuroleptic-naive schizophrenic patients. *Lancet* 346: 1130–1131.

Hirvonen, J., van Erp, T.G., Huttunen, J., Aalto, S., Någren, K., Huttunen, M. *et al.* (2005). Increased caudate dopamine D2 receptor availability as a genetic marker for schizophrenia. *Archives of General Psychiatry* 62: 371–378.

Jones, P.B., Barnes, T.R., Davies, L., Dunn, G., Lloyd, H., Hayhurst, K.P. *et al.* (2006). Randomized controlled trial of the effect on quality of life of second- vs first-generation antipsychotic drugs in schizophrenia: cost utility of the latest antipsychotic drugs in schizophrenia study (CUtLASS 1). *Archives of General Psychiatry* 63: 1079–1087.

Kane, J., Honigfeld, G., Singer, J. and Meltzer, H. (1988). Clozapine for the treatment-resistant schizophrenic. a double-blind comparison with chlorpromazine. *Archives of General Psychiatry* 45: 789–796.

Kapur, S. (2003). Psychosis as a state of aberrant salience: a framework linking biology, phenomenology, and pharmacology in schizophrenia. *American Journal of Psychiatry* 160: 13–23.

Laborit, H. and Huguenard, P. (1951). L'hibernation artificielle par moyens pharmacodynamiques et physiques. *Presse Med* 59: 1329.

Laruelle, M., Abi-Dargham, A., van Dyck, C.H., Gil, R., D'Souza, C.D., Erdos, J. *et al.* (1996). Single photon emission computerized tomography imaging of amphetamine-induced dopamine release in drug-free schizophrenic subjects. *Proceedings of the National Academy of Sciences of the USA* 93: 9235–9240.

Lieberman, J.A., Sheitman, B.B. and Kinon, B.J. (1997). Neurochemical sensitization in the pathophysiology of schizophrenia: deficits and dysfunction in neuronal regulation and plasticity. *Neuropsychopharmacology* 17: 205–229.

Lieberman, J.A., Stroup, T.S., McEvoy, J.P., Swartz, M.S., Rosenheck, R.A., Perkins, D.O. *et al.* (2005). Clinical antipsychotic trials of intervention effectiveness (CATIE) investigators. Effectiveness of antipsychotic drugs in patients with schizophrenia. *New England Journal of Medicine* 353: 1209–1223.

Mizrahi, R., Bagby, R.M., Zipursky, R.B. and Kapur, S. (2005). How antipsychotics work: the patients' perspective. *Progress in Neuropsychopharmacology and Biological Psychiatry* 29: 859–864.

Naber, D., Karow, A. and Lambert, M. (2005). Subjective well-being under the neuroleptic treatment and its relevance for compliance. *Acta Psychiatrica Scandinavica* 427: 29–34.

Perkins, D.O., Gu, H., Boteva, K. and Lieberman, J.A. (2005). Relationship between duration of untreated psychosis and outcome in first-episode schizophrenia: a critical review and meta-analysis. *American Journal of Psychiatry* 162: 1785–1804.

Rapoport, J.L., Addingtomn, A.M., Frangou, S. and Psych, M.R. (2005). The neurodevelopmental model of schizophrenia: update. *Molecular Psychiatry* 10: 434–449.

Read, J., van Os, J., Morrison, A.P. and Ross, C.A. (2005). Childhood trauma, psychosis and schizophrenia: a literature review with theoretical and clinical implications. *Acta Psychiatrica Scandinavica* 112: 330–350.

Seeman, P. and Lee, T. (1975). Antipsychotic drugs – direct correlation between clinical potency and presynaptic action on dopamine neurons. *Science* 188: 1217–1219.

Wyatt, R.J. (1991). Neuroleptics and the natural course of schizophrenia. *Schizophrenia Bulletin* 17: 325–351.

Part 2: The principles of using and not using neuroleptics in the Finnish need-adapted approach to the treatment of schizophrenic psychoses

Viljo Räkköläinen and Jukka Aaltonen

General social and biological background to the neuroleptic-free treatment of psychosis

Schizophrenia is almost certainly not one but several related disorders, a manifestation with complex phenomena for which there is no universally accepted definition. This elusiveness of any precise definition seems to be a particular phenomenon of 'schizophrenia' (Aaltonen and Räkköläinen, 1988). Cullberg (2000) states that it is easy to forget that psychosis and schizophrenia are phenomenological concepts that can be defined only by using terms that describe behavioural and subjective changes of the world as experienced.

In biological psychiatry the role of genetics and biology is usually over-emphasized: schizophrenia is considered as a disease of the brain to be treated chemically and electrically. This way of thinking considers life events only as triggers of the manifestation of illness.

Our thesis is that it is not possible to separate schizophrenic behaviour and thinking totally from the contexts of a patient's life and its developmental achievements – past and present. The neglect or disparagement of this fact will lead to many kinds of misunderstandings of human factors and destructive pessimism regarding the possibilities of treatment and recovery, as for example John Read *et al.* (2004) have argued. In the event the contemporary culture defines what schizophrenia is and how it should be treated.

Need-adapted and integrated treatment (Alanen, 1997; Alanen *et al.*, 1986, 1991, 2000; see Chapter 12) has developed in Finland gradually from the 1960s and is based on case-specific needs. The fundamental approach to treatment is the professional use of human interaction. In this context, the purpose of biological intervention, using so-called antipsychotic medication, is to calm the patient down to maximize the possibility for human interaction and psychotherapeutically orientated working. The aim is to help patients better reintegrate the many dimensions of their lives.

Several studies have showed that a great number of first episode cases can recover without neuroleptics. Cullberg (2000) thinks that this could be true of perhaps 50 per cent. It is also known that a great number of patients with psychosis achieve no benefits from antipsychotic medication (e.g. Mosher *et al.*, 2004; Lieberman *et al.*, 2005). According to Cullberg (2000), approximately a third of patients with schizophrenia do not lose their psychotic symptoms from the use of neuroleptics. It has also become more and more clear that both the old and new neuroleptics have serious and often even permanent side effects (e.g. Lieberman *et al.*, 2005) depending on the particular medication, the individual, the dosage and length of time the medication is used. We summarize later in this chapter our promising Finnish results about the treatment of first episode psychotics without using neuroleptics.

Therefore it seems logical, and from the humane point of view ethical, that at least for a group of selected first episode patients, they should be offered the possibility of recovering without the risks of neuroleptics.

The Finnish projects and the neuroleptic-free treatment of psychosis

Pilot study and multicentre API project

In developing further our model of integrated treatment we focused on the possibility of a neuroleptic-free treatment of first episode schizophrenic patients by using an intensive psychosocial need-adapted approach in all cases. An example of this is the Kupittaa pilot project, including a municipal psychiatric hospital with a catchment area of about 80,000 inhabitants in Turku in Western Finland (Räkköläinen *et al.*, 1994; see Alanen *et al.*, 2000).

The findings were that less than half of the unselected group of first episode cases needed neuroleptic medication. That is why we started systematically searching for specific psychological, interactional and social criteria for the use or non-use of neuroleptics in individual cases, and how they responded to different combinations of treatments and we also looked at the prognosis using these different combinations.

That pilot project led to a nationwide clinical research project called the Acute Psychosis Integrated (API) treatment project covering six psychiatric catchment areas (total 600,000 inhabitants) with the cooperation of the National Research and Development Centre for Welfare and Health (STAKES), the University of Jyväskylä (Department of Psychology) and the University of Turku (Departments of Psychiatry and Pharmacology) (Lehtinen *et al.*, 1996, 2000). In all six centres the need-adapted approach to treatment was utilized for all first episode non-affective psychotic patients. Three of the centres (experimental group) with a long treatment culture of the need-adapted approach were also committed to abstain completely from or to use minimal amounts of neuroleptics while the other three centres (control group) used neuroleptics as usual.

There were 135 patients of whom 106 (67 in the experimental group and 39 in the control group) participated in the two-year follow-up study. In the experimental group 43 per cent of the patients had not received any neuroleptics during the entire two-year follow-up period, while the corresponding figure in the control group was 6 per cent. Overall, the patients' condition at the two-year follow-up was relatively good with two-thirds of the patients having 'retained their grip on life'. In the experimental centres the doses and duration of neuroleptics (when needed) were much lower than in the control group. Moreover, at follow-up the experimental group had less psychotic symptoms as well as having needed less days in hospital (Lehtinen *et al.*, 1996, 2000; Bola *et al.*, 2006).

Classification: using or not using neuroleptics as determined by patients' premorbid psychosocial achievements and reaction to the clinical interview

Based on Pao's original classification (1979), built on his long experiences at Chestnut Lodge, we further developed a clinically relevant diagnostic classification, which turned out to be significant also for the indications for neuroleptic medication (Aaltonen *et al.*, 2000; Alanen *et al.*, 2000). In his study Pao (1979) classified the developmental and interactional background and prognosis of people with schizophrenia into three (or four) categories. Our projects leant on Pao's classification, but we gave more importance to the ongoing clinical interactional process in predicting the prognosis of schizophrenia.

The interactional culture was not to regard either the family of origin or the present family network as being the cause of the psychosis but to assess in what way the family could create for the patient scaffolding around which the problems could be approached, and how much they could work with the therapeutic systems and treatment components (Aaltonen and Räkköläinen, 1988). The nature of the ongoing interaction with staff also gave a firm psychological basis for the use or non-use of neuroleptic medication. The classification presented here was first worked out as a result of the Kupittaa project and confirmed in the qualitative analysis of the API project (Aaltonen *et al.*, 2000).

Schizophrenia I: near adequate or adequate premorbid psychosocial achievements

According to Pao (1979), this group of patients with schizophrenia has a good prognosis. While there may have been cumulative traumata in the patient's psychological and social development and achievements, the history of the patient's personality reveals nearly phase adequate development, functioning and identity. The interactional atmosphere of the family is open; the parents do not include the future patient in their struggles. These developmental circumstances form the basis of a good prognosis.

In our project, also, the patients in this group had, in principle, a good prognosis or basis to build a good prognosis because their premorbid identity was rather solid and age appropriate. The patients had achieved developmental capacities for separation and individuation (e.g. in their schooling, vocational training and extrafamilial relationships) that even the psychosis did not root out. These factors remained as their 'psychosocial capital'. Even during their psychosis they had in addition to regressive elements, a history of good psychosocial achievements and individuation. That is why they could make good use of individual psychotherapy, supported by their family members and also family therapy, where the treatment was built on the patient's insight and former capacity for self–object differentiation.

In this group of patients spontaneous remission is also the most probable. A safe, extensive first aid and psychological holding during the psychosis gives space for spontaneous remission and a further maturation of the process of identity. In this group the use of anxiolytics (e.g. lorazepam) was often indicated to alleviate anxiety. Another common feature of this group is that they maintain efforts to be orientated to the future and have the will to achieve goals and satisfactions of adult life in close relationships and in social life. We started to call this feature the maintenance of a grip on life, and this proved to be generally an indicator of a good prognosis in the evaluation of first episode data (Räkköläinen et al., 1979; Alanen et al., 1986; Salokangas et al., 1989).

According to our results it is rather easy, even during the first family meeting, to make a prognostic prediction. In spite of the florid psychotic symptoms, in the first clinical interview these patients often immediately become more coherent when the interviewer (or team members) focused their attention on the patient's former or present constant object relationships.

Conclusion

When there are good premorbid psychosocial achievements and with a broad and intensive psychotherapeutically orientated treatment there was no indication for neuroleptic medication. With many patients in this group, the medication can even be regarded as harmful.

Schizophrenia II: relative lag in premorbid psychosocial achievements, especially in separation development

In this group there has been a prolonged and tortuous separation process during the patients' earlier developmental years; the process has been stormy with often unrealistic attempts at individuation. There has also been a developmental lag (presumably with biological components) or delay in several phases of psychological and social development and achievements. The interactional atmosphere of the family of origin is found not to be an open one. In addition, the parents tended to include the future patient in their own struggles.

According to our results these patients have a rather good overall prognosis, but it is made less favourable by the issues just described with stormy but hopeless trials of separation even in many adult relationships. This means that, compared with the first group of patients, their social network and other psychosocial achievements have remained poorer, and at the onset of psychosis the patients in this group have access to more limited internal and external resources as a consequence of their premorbid adjustment. That is why they end in deadlock in the face of separation situations, sometimes even those separation themes that are aroused in everyday connections.

Intensive family therapy is indicated, especially at the beginning of the treatment process with a specific focus on the creation of the capability to separate for all family members. Later this process can continue within the patient's individual therapy. These patients were found to be susceptible to deep depressive episodes during the treatment process as a part of the separation handicap.

It is typical and diagnostic that in a clinical interview themes that focus on a patient's individuation and separation or themes that are associated in the patient's mind with separation immediately result in an accelerating psychotic disintegration. The patients fall into an experience of bottomless separation, contrasting with the immediate cohering reaction of the first group of patients.

Conclusion

As a part of the need-adapted approach – which for this group was a combination of a longer term intensive family and individual therapy – two-thirds of the group needed neuroleptic medication. In many cases, however, this was only temporary and using low dosages to assist the relinquishing of psychotic solutions to separation issues.

Schizophrenia III: distinctly defective ego functioning from early psychosocial developmental phases

In this group of patients a prolonged symbiosis in the family of origin was manifest as flattened affect, autistic thinking, psychosocial regression and isolation without any clear-cut time to date the onset of psychosis. Even from their early years the patients had lived in an interactional atmosphere in which sparse and constricted communications and emotions in addition to a double-bind intrafamilial culture (Bateson *et al.*, 1956) had been dominant. This led to problematic psychological binding for the future patient and a distortion and handicapping of the patient's psychosocial development and achievements in most areas of their lives. The patients remained in their family of origin without the capacity to make efforts at separation. This background history made for the constituents of a long duration of untreated psychosis, a chronic condition with poor prognosis.

In this group a typical clinical interview finds the patients to be extremely passive and also often – as with their parents – against any psychiatric treatment or any interest in changing their binding mode of interaction. The patients are in need of extensive rehabilitative interventions from the very beginning of the treatment because there is a danger of a continuation, in the treatment context, of the fruitless binding, now towards staff. Structurally oriented family therapy is indicated.

Conclusion

Some patients seemed to derive benefit from neuroleptic medication, especially when it reduced their hypersensitivity enacted by extreme withdrawal from their environment. Special attention is needed as medication can itself foster passivity, negative symptoms and deterioration.

New neurobiological research and clinical classification

With the progress of neurobiological research methods, the functional disorders of neural circuits in psychosis have become more clear and understandable. When a part of the tightly integrated adaptive process collapses, the consequence is useless attempts at reorganizing – manifest at the clinical level by psychotic symptoms. The amygdala, the hippocampus and the frontal cortex form a structural triangle whose adaptive cooperation through neural circuits seems to collapse in psychotic states in different ways.

According to the latest knowledge hypotheses such as that of dopamine excess have to be revised. The simple model of subcortical hyperdopaminergia is not sufficient to explain negative symptoms and cognitive impairment in schizophrenia (Hirvonen, 2005). Hypoactivity in the frontal cortex is associated with negative symptoms. Overactivity of D2 receptors in subcortical nuclei explains positive symptoms and blocking these with neuroleptic molecules is the usual way of dampening positive symptoms.

However, the situation has turned out to be more complicated. Dopamine regulates synaptic interaction in all neural circuits that participate in adaptive reactions. To give a simplified summary: it has become evident that sufficient dopamine flow is needed by receptors in the frontal cortex in order to control dopamine flow between D2 receptors in the subcortex.

From the point of view of the antipsychotic medication, the situation has turned out to be paradoxical. If the inhibiting regulating adaptive function of the frontal cortex is disturbed and decreased through blocking receptors (e.g. by medication), the result could be that negative symptoms, often already existing before treatment, would become exacerbated. It has become gradually apparent that the synaptic effect of dopamine molecules within the systemic triangle of these neural circuits can be both inhibiting and excitatory depending on the ongoing adaptive challenge. If we supply the biological findings to our interactional classification presented in this chapter, our biology-related hypothesis includes the following:

1   *In Schizophrenia I*, the use of neuroleptics should initially be avoided because of the potentially paradoxical effects just mentioned. By doing this the premorbid capacities for recovery are maximized.
2   *In Schizophrenia II*, it is therapeutically indicated to use neuroleptics to control subcortical excessive dopamine flow in order to make more room for adaptive cortical (rational) functioning.
3   *In Schizophrenia III*, it is sometimes possible through biological intervention to loosen excessive cortical inhibitory processes (clinically decreasing negative symptoms).

Concluding remarks

Whether the chaos of psychosis manifests itself in the agony of delusions or isolation, the most adequate response is that of human interaction and a chance for relearning through that interaction. In many cases, achieving this is a tricky journey and neuroleptic medication can be useful to support and calm the patient's situation in order for him to dare to engage again in human interactions.

The *routine* use of both old and new neuroleptics for first episode psychosis cases should now be questioned but for the moment this is a hot issue, causing passionate views in many directions in spite of convincing results. These indicate that in selected cases neuroleptic treatment is not so essential as has usually been considered, if intensive psychosocial treatment measures are provided. It has to be emphasized that a precondition for a successful adaptation of the principles recommended by us is a need-adapted intensive psychotherapeutic context of treatment, based on training and supervision programmes directed to all staff members.

Thorough, need-adapted, case-specific evaluation should be an essential procedure so that neuroleptic medication is neither used for too long nor in too high dosages and does not paralyze the patient's ability to use his or her previous achievements, to learn new ones and to find possibilities for psychological reorganizing and development. As Johan Cullberg (2006) stated: Ask yourself, how you would have your own close relative treated, if met with a first episode of psychosis.

References

Aaltonen, J. and Räkköläinen, V. (1988). On the foundations of family therapy of schizophrenia. [In Finnish.] In J. Aaltonen, V. Räkköläinen and A. Kokkola (eds) *Kokemuksia uusien skitsofreniapotilaiden perhekeskeisestä hoidosta Suomessa* [Experiences about family-centered treatment of first-episode schizophrenia patients in Finland]. Helsinki: Sairaalaliitto.

Aaltonen, J., Koffert, T., Ahonen, J. and Lehtinen, V. (2000). The need-adapted treatment of schizophrenia is team work. [In Finnish with English summary.] *Stakes Raportteja* 257.

Alanen, Y.O. (1997). *Schizophrenia – Its Origins and Need-Adapted Treatment.* London: Karnac.

Alanen, Y.O., Räkköläinen, V., Laakso, J., Rasimus, R. and Kaljonen, A. (1986). *Towards Need-Specific Treatment of Schizophrenic Psychoses.* Heidelberg: Springer-Verlag.

Alanen, Y.O., Lehtinen, V., Räkköläinen, V. and Aaltonen, J. (1991). Need-adapted treatment of new schizophrenic patients: experiences from the Turku project. *Acta Psychiatrica Scandinavica* 83: 363–372.

Alanen, Y.O., Lehtinen, V., Aaltonen, J., Lehtinen, K. and Räkköläinen, V. (2000). The Finnish integrated model for early treatment of schizophrenia and related psychoses. In B. Martindale, A. Bateman, M. Crowe and F. Margison (eds) *Psychosis. Psychological Approaches and Their Effectiveness.* London: Gaskell, pp. 235–265.

Bateson, G., Jackson, D.D., Haley, J. and Weakland, J. (1956). Toward a theory of schizophrenia. *Behavioral Science* 1: 251–264.

Bola, J., Lehtinen, K., Aaltonen, J., Räkköläinen, V., Syvälahti, E. and Lehtinen, V. (2006). Predicting medication-free treatment response in acute psychosis: cross-validation from the Finnish Need-Adapted project. *Journal of Nervous and Mental Disease* 191: 219–229.

Cullberg, J. (2000). *Psykoser, ett biologiskt och humanistiskt perspektiv.* Stockholm: Natur och Kultur. [English edn *Psychosis: An Integrated View.* London and New York: Routledge, 2006.]

Cullberg, J. (2006). Integrated treatment and implications for off-medication periods. *Schizophrenia Bulletin* 32: 299.

Hirvonen, J. (2005). *Brain Dopamine Receptors and Genetic Risk for Schizophrenia. A Twin Study Using Positron Emission Tomography.* Turku: Annales Universitatis Turkuensis.

Lehtinen, V., Aaltonen, J., Koffert, T., Räkköläinen, V. and Syvälahti, E. (1996). Integrated treatment model for first-contact patients with a schizophrenia-type psychosis. The Finnish API-project. *Nordic Journal of Psychiatry* 50: 281–287.

Lehtinen, V., Aaltonen, J., Koffert, T., Räkköläinen, V. and Syvälahti, E. (2000). Two-year outcome in first-episode psychosis treated according to an integrated model. Is immediate neuroleptisation always needed? *European Journal of Psychiatry* 15: 312–320.

Lieberman, J.A., Stroup, T.S., McEvoy, J.P., Swartz, M.S., Rosenheck, R.A., Perkins, D.O. *et al.* (2005). Effectiveness of antipsychotic drugs in patients with chronic schizophrenia. *New England Journal of Medicine* 353: 1209–1223.

Mosher, L., Gosden, R. and Beder, S. (2004). Drug companies and schizophrenia. Unbridled capitalism meets madness. In J. Read, L. Mosher and R. Bentall (eds) *Models of Madness*. New York: Routledge.

Pao, P.N. (1979). *Schizophrenic Disorders. Theory and Treatment from a Psychodynamic Point of View*. New York: International Universities Press.

Räkköläinen, V., Salokangas, R. and Lehtinen, P. (1979). Protective constructions in the course of psychosis: a follow-up study. In C. Müller (ed.) *Psychotherapy of Schizophrenia*. Amsterdam: Excerpta Medica, pp. 233–243.

Räkköläinen, V., Vuorio, K.A., Syvälahti, E. *et al.* (1994). Observations of comprehensive psychotherapeutic treatment of new schizophrenic patients without neuroleptic drugs in Kupittaa Hospital in 1989–92. Paper presented to the XIth International Symposium for Psychotherapy of Schizophrenia, Washington, DC.

Read, J., Mosher, L.R. and Bentall, R.P. (eds) (2004). *Models of Madness*. Routledge: New York:

Salokangas, R., Räkköläinen, V. and Alanen, Y.O. (1989). Maintenance of grip on life and goals on life: a valuable criterion for evaluating outcome in schizophrenia. *Acta Psychiatrica Scandinavica* 80: 187–193.

Chapter 21

Prevention and early intervention in psychosis

Tor K. Larsen

Early detection (ED) is a guiding principle in somatic medicine that has prognostic value for improving outcome for a number of severe illnesses, yet is also problematic due to several methodological and practical considerations. In this chapter, we discuss whether the criticism that has been directed towards screening procedures for diseases such as breast cancer, for example, are applicable and valid for psychosis or pre-psychosis. To this aim, we consider and compare epistemological differences for somatic versus mental disorders. Finally, we describe and summarize our experiences from an intensive early detection programme for psychosis during the past decade in Norway.

In disorders such as breast cancer and abdominal aortic aneurysm, the improved ability to detect anatomical abnormalities has led to increased estimates of the prevalence of the disorder, which may in turn lead to an overestimation of the effects of early intervention (Black, 1998). Three types of biases have been described which relate to the early diagnosis of somatic illness: lead time bias, length bias, and overdiagnosis bias. A *lead time bias* pertains to comparisons that are not adjusted for the timing of diagnosis. For example, if survival time is the primary outcome variable, artificially inflated estimates of better outcome might result. Figure 21.1 provides a graphic example to illustrate this effect.

Since time to survival is the key variable of interest, early detection might appear to lengthen survival time, whereas the majority of early detected cases would never actually lead to illness. When analysing the true effects of early detection, it is important to control for this type of bias, ideally by including comparison groups identified by the same detection method.

The second type of bias, *length bias*, arises when comparisons lack adjustment for the rate of disease progression. As written by Black (1998): 'the probability that a disease will be detected is directly proportional to the length of its preclinical phase, which is inversely related to its rate of progression'.

An *overdiagnosis bias* refers to the failure to control for pseudo-disease, i.e. positively screening cases that are in reality disease free. One example is

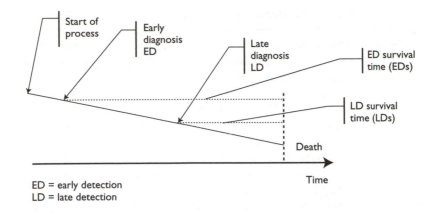

ED = early detection
LD = late detection

Figure 21.1 Early vs. late detection of somatic illness (e.g. breast cancer)

breast cancer, which has a prevalence rate of approximately 1 per cent of females aged 40 to 50 years. Based on this prevalence rate, only 1 per cent of women will become ill due to breast cancer during their lifetime. In one study, however, modern screening procedures such as mammography increased the prevalence rate to 36 per cent simply by detecting smaller tumours (Black and Welch, 1993). As a result, the increase in prevalence in that study equalled 3600 per cent.

The methodological biases outlined above are serious shortcomings which complicate early detection for somatic illnesses. As a consequence, a very intense international debate has arisen regarding how to best avoid, identify and control for these biases. What relevance does this larger discussion and debate have for the early detection of psychosis?

Disease and syndrome: epistemological considerations

In somatic illnesses such as pneumonia, diabetes and breast cancer, a distinction is drawn between symptoms and signs, based on the different levels of description. *Symptoms* are indications of disease based on the subjective experiences of the patient, such as coughing, thirst, or local pain. *Signs* are also indications of disease, but observed from testing or physical examinations, such as chest x-rays, blood sugar levels, or mammography results. Symptoms and signs differ in their levels of description. Signs are considered to be more objective, and can provide confirming or discon- firming evidence to support the validity of the diagnosis suspected based on the patient's symptoms. If a condition has both symptoms and signs at different levels of description it is regarded as an *illness* (Sackett, 2002). In contrast, *syndromes* have signs and symptoms at the same level of description. The majority of conditions in the field of psychiatry are syndromes, reflecting the absence of physical tests available to confirm the diagnosis suspected based upon the subjective and self-reported experience of the patient. This limitation has particular relevance to the application of early detection techniques in mental health. While improved imaging techniques have allowed for the detection of illnesses at the *presymptomatic* level in somatic medicine, this is not yet possible for syndromes such as psychosis or schizophrenia (Larsen and Opjordsmoen, 1996). Early detection for cancer medicine, for example, represents the diagnosis of presymptomatic illness. Early detection for psychiatric diagnoses, however, signifies the detection of symptomatic conditions. This distinction is significant to note when discussing the conceptual, epidemiological and ethical problems related to early diagnosis in psychosis.

Furthermore, the above definitional distinctions have special relevance when viewed in the context of the three biases described by Black (1998). First, the graphic illustration of lead time bias looks considerably different when applied to psychosis. In contrast to cancer, for example, survival time is not commonly used as an outcome measure in mental health. Instead, time to remission is often used to define outcome.

In Figure 21.2, we have graphically depicted the anticipated effects of early detection of psychosis. For the sake of simplicity, we have assumed that the intervention yields no influence on the course or outcome of the disorder. As shown, early detection might artificially appear to worsen outcome, owing to the longer time to remission. Interestingly, this problem stands in stark contrast to the breast cancer example, which is liable to bias in the opposite direction due to the different definitions of outcome (survival time versus duration of illness). If we fail to acknowledge this potential bias, we risk underestimating the positive effects of early treatment. If early detection of psychosis is indeed effective, we should expect the total duration of psychosis to be significantly shorter compared to usual detection methods.

The popular understanding of early intervention

The above considerations correspond to our popular understanding of early intervention. To illustrate, if a patient contracts a virus infection for which no treatment will help, the total duration of illness will be the same regardless of type of treatment received. In accordance with the lead time bias, an ineffective treatment provided earlier might falsely be judged as harmful since the duration of illness post-treatment would be longer. However, if a patient suffers from a treatable condition such as pneumonia, with a natural or untreated course of three weeks, receiving early treatment would significantly shorten the total illness duration, even if the time to remission is not influenced. If the antibiotics relieve symptoms after two days of treatment, a substantial difference exists whether the antibiotics are

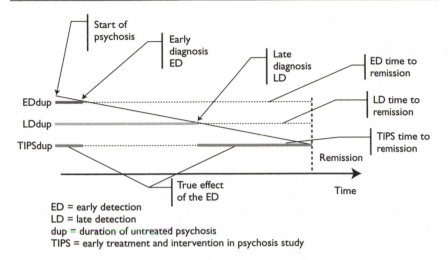

ED = early detection
LD = late detection
dup = duration of untreated psychosis
TIPS = early treatment and intervention in psychosis study

Figure 21.2 Early vs. late detection of psychiatric illness (e.g. psychosis)

taken at day three versus day 13. The resulting effect equals the difference in days between the start of treatment, or ten days.

Similar to somatic illness, one consequence of the length bias when applied to psychosis may be an increased likelihood for both detection and a good prognosis given the often protracted duration of illness. Research on the effects of early detection needs to control for this caveat in multivariate tests. The problem of overdiagnosis, however, is unlikely to pose a threat because diagnosis of presymptomatic illness is not an issue. In a successful early detection programme for psychosis like the TIPS study (see below), no significant increase in the incidence of psychosis has been found, in contrast to those reported for somatic disorders such as breast cancer. It is argued that this result lends support to the theoretical considerations expressed above.

Early detection of psychosis versus early detection of prepsychosis

Until recently, studies have generally focused on efforts for the early diagnosis of psychosis, with little discussion regarding the diagnosis of presymptomatic illness. However, difficult questions have been raised concerning the diagnosis of so-called prodromal or prepsychotic states. Are these studies aiming to diagnose presymptomatic illness, or should we rather assume that we have identified a new syndrome of mental disorder? The international literature appears to be divided over this issue, with mixed arguments to support whether or not we have identified presymptomatic illness (Olsen and Rosenbaum, 2006). Within the German tradition of basic symptoms, which has identified an early and a late prodromal phase, it is argued that early prodromal states can be understood as pre-symptomatic stages (Huber and Gross, 1989). A Scandinavian counterpart to the German basic symptom model has recently been published as an interview guide (EASE). This model focuses on subjective experiences and provides descriptions that might be deemed as an attempt to diagnose presymptomatic illness (Parnas *et al.*, 2005). The authors write: 'What is being talked about is how the patient experiences himself and his world, and not an objectively or medically prescribed "reality" or "morbidity" of these experiences' (p. 238). The subjective aspect is emphasized in a manner that it loses the quality of being described or counted.

However, interview manuals such as the Australian Comprehensive Assessment of At-Risk Mental States (CAARMS; Yung *et al.*, 2005) and the American Structured Interview for Prodromal Symptoms (SIPS; Rosen *et al.*, 2006) regard attenuated positive symptoms as possible prodromal states. Attenuated positive symptom states are clearly symptomatic conditions and the severity of the symptoms is rated on a specific scale to operationally define scores. From our viewpoint, these syndromes could best be labelled as hypopsychosis (Larsen, 2005) and comprise clear psychiatric symptoms which are very close to being psychotic. We argue that in order to avoid the problems of lead time bias and overdiagnosis, it is important to identify and define hypopsychosis as a new symptomatic state. The symptomatic state, or hypopsychosis, would consequently require treatment simply because patients are ill and treatment seeking.

The TIPS study

Background

Over the past decade, we have designed and implemented an ongoing programme for the early detection of psychosis in Rogaland County on the west coast of Norway. The system for early detection consists of the following three elements: information campaigns, early detection teams, and the systematic assessment of all possible first episode psychosis and prodromal (hypopsychotic) cases.

The information campaigns have been developed and designed for the general population, primary health services and schools. On a regular basis, large advertisements have been printed in local newspapers and annually information brochures have been sent to every household in the county. Further, educational seminars and lectures have been provided for GPs, teachers and school psychologists (Johannessen *et al.*, 2005). These information campaigns were intensive between the years 1997 and 2000. During this period, we conducted a research study to compare our early detection programme to other sites in Scandinavia that had no system for early detection (detection 'as usual'). At the present time, we have begun to use information campaigns on a regular and ongoing basis.

The early detection teams are low threshold assessment teams that respond to any referral for a potential case of first episode psychosis. Referrals can be made by anyone by simply calling the team, and we guarantee an assessment within 24 hours. The detection teams consist of three psychiatric nurses/social workers that are on call daily from 08.00 to 15.30. They are trained in use of the Positive and Negative Syndrome Scale (PANSS) interview (Kay *et al.*, 1987), upon which we base decisions regarding the potential for psychosis. At the present time, the early detection teams are an integrated part of the acute ward system at Stavanger University Hospital. If the first screening concludes that a first episode psychosis might be developing, we respond rapidly by conducting a systematic assessment. A thorough baseline assessment is done to measure premorbid functioning, quality of life, social functioning, use/abuse of drugs and alcohol and traumatic experiences, neuropsychological functioning. A diagnosis is made according to *DSM-IV* criteria.

Results from the TIPS studies

The TIPS studies can be divided into four periods: pre-TIPS (1993–1994), TIPS (1997–2005), TIPS II (2001–), and TIPS III starting in 2007. We will briefly describe the results from each period.

Pre-TIPS (1993–1994)

During the pre-TIPS years we conducted an initial study on first episode non-affective psychosis. We included patients ranging in age from 15 to 65 years who resided in our catchment area and suffered from first episode psychosis. The key finding from this study was that duration of untreated psychosis (DUP) was long, with a median of 26 weeks and mean of 104 weeks (Larsen *et al.*, 1996). Greater than 50 per cent of the patients with schizophrenia had been ill for more than 54 weeks with continuous psychosis before they received a diagnosis and treatment.

TIPS (1997–2005)

The TIPS study had an early detection programme located in a single region, Rogaland County, Norway with a population of 370,000. Patients identified via the early detection programme were compared with detection-as-usual methods in two other regions in Scandinavia, the Ullevaal health care sector in Oslo County and the midsector region in Roskilde County, Denmark, with a combined total of 295,000 inhabitants. Patient recruitment was conducted between 1997 and 2000 and follow-ups were carried out at one, two and five years. Inclusion criteria consisted of living in the catchment area of one of the four health care areas, age 15 to 65 years, and meeting the *DSM-IV* criteria for one of the following diagnoses: schizophrenia, schizophreniform disorder, schizoaffective disorder (narrow schizophrenia spectrum disorders), brief psychotic episode, delusional disorder, affective psychosis with mood incongruent delusions, or psychotic disorder not otherwise specified.

Our main results indicate that we succeeded in achieving early detection compared to both the historical control sample from 1993 (Larsen *et al.*, 2001) and the parallel control groups in Oslo (Norway) and Roskilde (Denmark) (Melle *et al.*, 2004). Findings from the parallel control comparison demonstrated a DUP of 16 weeks for patients recruited from the usual detection sites versus 4.5 weeks for the early detection sites. Identification from the early detection sites was significantly correlated with better clinical status at pre-treatment as measured by the Positive and Negative Syndrome Scale and the Global Assessment of Functioning (GAF) Scale. At three months, better clinical status was also found for the PANSS and GAF scores, with the exception of the PANSS positive subscale. Multiple linear regression analyses gave no indication of the potential influence of confounders. The early detected patients were younger, single, more often of Scandinavian origin, and had significantly greater drug abuse. The rate of severe suicidality (plans or attempts) was significantly higher for patients from the usual detection sites, even after adjusting for known predictors of suicidality (Melle *et al.*, 2006).

When we investigated the effects of early detection on outcome, findings demonstrated that patients from the early detection sector had fewer negative symptoms at one-year follow-up, but no effects were found for time to remission or degree of remission related to positive symptoms (Larsen *et al.*, 2006). In accordance with the above discussion of methodological considerations, we maintain that the sum of duration of untreated psychosis and time to remission probably best express the true effect of the early detection efforts (i.e. median of 22 weeks for ED versus 44 weeks usual detection sites). Therefore the results indicate that, on average, the early detected patients with a first episode psychosis suffered half the duration of active psychosis compared to patients from the control sites. From our perspective, we feel this heralds a major clinical achievement.

TIPS II (2001–)

The TIPS II study commenced one year following the termination of funding for the TIPS programme. Luckily, we had the opportunity to continue the early detection teams as an integrated part of the acute ward at our hospital. However, we lacked funding for the continuation of the information campaigns. As a result, we had the opportunity to study the impact of discontinuing the information campaigns while all other components of the ED programme were held constant. Results indicated that the DUP increased (15 weeks compared to five weeks, median) and that fewer patients were detected via the detection teams. The clinical status of the patients was significantly worse, with more positive symptoms and lower GAF scores. In conclusion, findings from the TIPS II study suggest that the information campaigns appear a critical element for the reduction of DUP in first episode psychosis.

TIPS III (2007–)

Recently, we have received financial support to create a research unit specializing in psychosis. Within this framework, we aim to continue our early detection work and apply our knowledge to achieve at least the following three goals:

1   To keep DUP short in our region and to study the long-term effects of early detection (i.e. a ten-year follow-up study of TIPS is currently being planned).
2   To improve early treatment in order to see if more intensive treatment could improve treatment outcome.
3   To study related aspects of early psychosis such as drug-induced psychosis, psychosis in the elderly, etc.

We anticipate that the next phase, TIPS III, will improve our knowledge of early detection of psychosis in the years to come.

Conclusions and final comments

Early detection of psychosis can be successfully achieved through the use of information campaigns directed towards the general population, schools, and primary health services in combination with low threshold detection teams. It is important that the detection teams are mobile and respond rapidly to any call received from potential patients, families or loved ones, GPs, teachers, or others in the community. In Norway, results from our intensive early detection programme have shown that a combination of information campaigns and detection teams can reduce the duration of untreated psychosis to 4.5 weeks (median). We now know that with ongoing and intensive efforts the DUP can be kept short. We must remember that the majority of patients who suffer from first episode psychosis lack insight and disagree with the perception that they are 'ill'. Therefore, it is extremely important that the detection teams respond immediately to referrals, with almost no delay. Individuals suffering from psychosis do not demand immediate treatment, and they typically do not complain about treatment delay. In somatic medicine, the pressure from dissatisfied patients is often a strong factor in facilitating early detection. In psychiatry, on the other hand, it is important that psychiatrists and psychologists assume this responsibility on behalf of the patients and their families.

Based on results from the TIPS study compiled over the past decade, we strongly believe it is imperative that early detection for psychosis be defined as a patient's right. Further, we argue that the responsibility for establishing such an early treatment programme falls upon mental health professionals. So, look around you. Do people in your area have the right and opportunity to receive early treatment for psychosis? If the answer is no, then you have work to do.

References

Black, W.C. (1998). Biases in the assessment of diagnostic innovations. *Acad Radiol* 5 (Suppl. 2): 280–282.

Black, W.C. and Welch, H.G. (1993). Advances in diagnostic imaging and over-estimations of disease prevalence and the benefits of therapy. *New England Journal of Medicine* 328: 1237–1243.

Huber, G. and Gross, G. (1989). The concept of basic symptoms in schizophrenic and schizoaffective psychoses. *Recenti Progressi on Medicina* 80: 646–652.

Johannessen, J.O., Larsen, T.K., Joa, I. *et al.* (2005). Pathways to care for first-episode psychosis in an early detection healthcare sector: part of the Scandinavian TIPS study. *British Journal of Psychiatry* 185 (Suppl. 489): 24–28.

Kay, S.R., Fiszbein, A. and Opler, L.A. (1987). The positive and negative syndrome scale (PANSS) for schizophrenia. *Schizophrenia Bulletin* 13: 261–276.

Larsen, T.K. (2005). A critical discussion of the use of concepts in relation to early intervention in psychosis: do we really know what we are talking about? In M. Colm (ed.) *Schizophrenia: Challenging the Orthodox.* London: Taylor and Francis.

Larsen, T.K. and Opjordsmoen, S. (1996). Early identification and treatment of schizophrenia: conceptual and ethical considerations. *Psychiatry* 59: 371–380.

Larsen, T.K., McGlashan, T.H. and Moe, L.C. (1996). First-episode schizophrenia: I. Early course parameters. *Schizophrenia Bulletin* 22: 241–256.

Larsen, T.K., McGlashan, T.H., Johannessen, J.O. *et al.* (2001). Shortened duration of untreated first episode of psychosis: changes in patient characteristics at treatment. *American Journal of Psychiatry* 158: 1917–1919.

Larsen, T.K., Melle, I., Auestad, B. *et al.* (2006). Early detection of first-episode psychosis: the effect on 1-year outcome. *Schizophrenia Bulletin* 32: 758–764.

Melle, I., Larsen, T.K., Haahr, U. *et al.* (2004). Reducing the duration of untreated first-episode psychosis: effects on clinical presentation. *Archives of General Psychiatry* 61: 143–150.

Melle, I., Johannesen, J.O., Friis, S. *et al.* (2006). Early detection of the first episode of schizophrenia and suicidal behavior. *American Journal of Psychiatry* 163: 800–804.

Olsen, K.A. and Rosenbaum, B. (2006). Prospective investigations of the prodromal state of schizophrenia: review of studies. *Acta Psychiatrica Scandinavica* 113: 247–272.

Parnas, J., Møller, P., Kircher, T., Thalbitzer, J., Jansson, L., Handest, P. *et al.* (2005). EASE: Examination of Anomalous Self-Experience. *Psychopathology* 38: 236–258.

Rosen, J.L., Miller, T.J., D'Andrea, J.T., McGlashan, T.H. and Woods, S.W. (2006). Comorbid diagnoses in patients meeting criteria for the schizophrenia prodrome. *Schizophrenia Research* 85: 124–131.

Sackett, D.L. (2002). Clinical epidemiology: what, who, and whither. *Journal of Clinical Epidemiology* 55: 1161–1166.

Yung, A.R., Yuen, H.P., McGorry, P.-D. *et al.* (2005). Mapping the onset of psychosis: the comprehensive assessment of at-risk mental states. *Australia and New Zealand Journal of Psychiatry* 39: 964–971.

Chapter 22

Psychotherapy and rehabilitation

A comparison between psychotherapeutic approaches and psychiatric rehabilitation for persons with serious and persistent mental illness

Courtenay M. Harding and Dennis J. McCrory

Introduction

Many perspectives have appeared and reappeared across time from biological, psychoanalytic, psychodynamic, learning, cognitive, humanistic-existential, and social and rehabilitative approaches for persons with serious and persistent mental illness. This chapter explores many of the essential similarities and differences between psychotherapeutic and psychiatric rehabilitation approaches in working with persons coping with serious and persistent illness. The authors include a Harvard-trained psychiatrist/psychotherapist (DJMC) and a Vermont- and Yale-trained psychologist (CMH) who have spent their careers working with psychiatric patients with serious and persistent illnesses in need of rehabilitation, conducting research, and helping systems of care.

Over the last 50 years, efforts by many groups have focused on helping the professions widen their interest by adding rehabilitation and/or talking with patients to the provision of medications. We conclude that the fields of psychotherapy and rehabilitation have many more similarities than differences in overall goals, but until recently each field has been conducted in distinctly different ways. It appears that further blending of these approaches would help many more people disabled by their psychiatric disorder, pursue their healing process and improve the quality of their lives.

An assumption that these approaches are contradictory

At first glance, this combination of approaches appears to be quite contradictory. Further, these strategies seem to be provided by different types of people with very different backgrounds and training, using philosophies of care that sound 180 degrees apart. Although many of these differences do indeed exist, their goals have surprising similarities.

Similarities in goals for people seeking care

Everyone, whether psychotherapist or rehabilitation worker, cares that the patient/consumer/user/client/participant has a chance to try and reclaim their lives. We have identified the following as elements which both groups would see as critical factors in achieving that recovery:

- have more understanding of self and life
- experience reduced symptoms
- achieve better relationships
- acquire more skills
- have the unpredictable power of the illness shifted more to the person's control
- resolve the grief over lost opportunities
- promote further adult development
- become less fearful and stronger
- integrate self after trauma
- increase self-esteem and self-confidence
- have hope for a better life.

The classical approaches used to achieve these goals have different languages and emphases

Professionals across both areas tend to have very different emphases, reflected in the language they use to achieve the goals listed above. These factors highlight and reflect the diversity of training, conceptual models, values and traditions. Table 22.1 provides a proposed set of differences between the approaches of the more classical psychoanalytically oriented (especially individual) psychotherapies and rehabilitation. It should be noted that considerable recent movement has been made in the combined integrated treatment of psychotic patients (e.g. surveys by Falloon *et al.*, 1998; Fenton, 2000). This degree of contemporary movement toward integration should be kept in mind when reading Table 22.1.

Psychotherapeutic approaches

Psychotherapeutic approaches have developed across the past three centuries and continue to influence contemporary work. However, one can see origins as far back as Plato (429–347 BCE), who felt that disturbed behaviors grew out of conflicts between the emotions and reason. During the era of eighteenth-century 'rational thinking', Heinroth (1773–1843) proposed that mental illnesses were caused by internal conflicts between

Table 22.1 Early differences between classical psychotherapists and rehabilitation professionals

Psychotherapy professional	Rehabilitation professional
Aiming for insight	Aiming for function
Bases plan on problems, shortcomings, diagnosis of person	Bases plan on strengths, needs and interests of person and environment
Psychotherapist-driven goals	Client-driven goals
Goal – to decrease symptoms and behaviors that get in the way of a life	Goal – to increase behaviors that will net the person a home, a job, friends and social justice
Focuses upon the person's internal reaction to his or her environment	Focuses also upon environmental engineering to make a more nurturing environment
Self-knowledge using a new vocabulary from the therapist's model	Self-determination through psycho-education and regaining control
Learning from the past to improve the present	Learning from today to improve the future
Clinician holding the pain	Rehabilitation worker holding the hope
Knitting a personality back together	Knitting a life back together
Done in individual or group sessions	Done in teams in the community and with peer groups
Training – lengthy, intellectual, and specific models, usually in academic settings or private offices	Training – shorter, practical, problem solving, usually provided in the community or agency
Targets resistance	Targets persistence
Prefers persons who are intelligent and interesting	Prefers a wider range of human functioning
Strict boundary keeping	Few but important boundaries
One-up and one-down relationship	Equal partnership
Office based	Community based
Often uses medications as treatment of choice or as part of the package	Medications seen as adjunctive to rehabilitative strategies
Teaches new ways to see old problems	Teaches self-monitoring and self-management of stress, side effects and symptom exacerbation
Skills to manage ways in which the personality gets in the way in the future	Skills to manage the activities of daily living
Uses professional peer groups to receive more supervision and new ideas	Uses consumer advocacy and public policy
Worries about maintaining separation of boundaries, conducting treatment in a skilled and reliable way	Worries about the effects of poverty, limited literacy, cost containment strategies and stigma/discrimination
Selects strategies for a person	Does activities with a person

unacceptable impulses and the resulting guilt often unknown by the person. Building on past thinking, Sigmund Freud (1856–1939) developed his 'talking cure' and focused on searching for the unconscious meaning of symptoms. As described in various chapters of this book, he has been followed by many other thoughtful clinicians who have further developed classical psychoanalysis and its modifications (e.g. ego psychology, object relations theories, self psychology). Other approaches are based on different theoretical frameworks (e.g. humanistic, phenomenological-existential concepts, systems, behavioral and learning theories).

Each of these schools of thought, concepts and ideas made major contributions to our understanding of humans and their behaviors. Cases of serious and persistent illnesses were often selected by supervisors to provide interesting and illustrative psychotherapeutic training opportunities for psychiatric residents. A necessary component for actual practice has been to establish a relationship between the practitioner and the patient with kindness, hopefulness, careful listening, and empathy. Much of this work has informed rehabilitation workers as a background understanding of the complexities of human beings. Ideas (such as transference, countertransference, denial, projection, repression, regression, turning against self, reaction formation, transitional objects, and the notions of conflictual relationships) have filtered into their practices. However, all of these contributions have often been unacknowledged in the field of rehabilitation as it attempted to differentiate itself from psychotherapy.

Many of the newer treatment/rehabilitative team models are more comprehensive with most of them including strong family and environment centered emphases along with phase-specific work with individuals (e.g. Fenton, 2000).

Biological approaches

Weaving in and out of the use of rehabilitation and psychotherapy across time has been the field of biological psychiatry. Griesinger (1817–1869) fought for the idea that 'mental diseases are brain diseases'. He was followed by Kraepelin (1856–1926) who endeavored to categorize mental disorders as organic processes. The advent of chlorpromazine ushered in a formidable period of psychopharmacology. Currently, most patients with psychoses are residing in the community and the funding is primarily focused on a model of medication, stabilization, maintenance, and entitlements. DeSisto *et al.* (1995) have shown that this model is less helpful in the improvement and recovery process than rehabilitation, self-sufficiency and community integration. Slowly, but surely, we have begun to weave the whole person and the pieces of the work together across fields.

Rehabilitative approaches

The provision of rehabilitation services and psychotherapy appears to alternate with or be adjunctive to biological treatments across the history of mankind. In the earliest history, indigenous peoples had a habit of finding a place in their societies for people struggling with disabilities. Although the Greeks, such as Hippocrates (460–377 BCE), Plato and Aristotle (384–322 BCE), later thought the problems were caused by bodily humors, they also thought that exercise, tranquility, diet and socio-cultural factors would help in their mental health temples. The Romans, with Galen, the Greek physician (129–199 CE), added diagnosis to humane treatment while believing that problems were exaggerated normal processes.

Much later, Pinel (1745–1826) fought for scientific and humane treatment against the terrible incarceration of mentally ill patients in his day by releasing his patients from the dank dark dungeons of the Parisian hospital. At the same time, William Tuke (1732–1822), the English Quaker, began the moral treatment movement by founding the York Retreat on the principles of 'benevolence, comfort and sympathy'. Moral Treatment was based on the 'elevation and reorganization of patients' mental processes' by classroom courses in philosophy, music, art, and literature. Moral Treatment also included a regular and organized schedule of physical and mental activities for the day, kind treatment with minimal uses of restraints, and a stress-free environment. Europe continued to develop the field with the US, Asia, and Africa following its lead.

Psychiatric rehabilitation, as currently practiced, was also influenced during World War II by the tenets of physical rehabilitation and developed through multiple iterations, much in the same way that psychological treatments mentioned earlier have evolved over time. In addition, Anthony *et al.* (2002) point out that the need for return to work by psychiatrically disabled veterans moved the US Congress to pass the 1943 Vocational Rehabilitation Act, which provided the basis for getting people with psychiatric disabilities back to work. Prior to the Act, most patients with serious and persistent mental illnesses were kept in hospital and worked without pay on farms as 'work therapy' or sat listlessly on barren benches in low stimuli institutionalizing environments. Instead of focusing on psychological concepts and symptoms, rehabilitation has focused upon strengths with peer involvement, partnership, and support. It encourages the ability to be productive, with an emphasis upon getting struggling people decent housing, food, clothing, social and occupational skills, friends, exercise, good nutritional and other health practices, reconnection to natural community supports (e.g. church choirs, film clubs, athletic leagues) depending on the interests of the consumer/user/participant.

For years, thoughtful US rehabilitation efforts and community care have been influenced by the Community Support Program Guiding Principles

Table 22.2 Community support principles (National Institute of Mental Health)

Involves consumer, family, community	Normalizing
Enhancement of personal dignity and self-determination	Comprehensive
Available as needed	Targets self-help
Coordinated	Provides continuity
Accessible	Non-discriminating
Confidential	Engages natural supports

for Community Services at the National Institute of Mental Health (see Table 22.2 from the work of B. Stroul, 1984).

More recently, the World Health Organization (2006) has estimated the financial impact of such disablement in terms of 'disability-adjusted life year' (DALY). Such impact grows bigger year by year to the point that by 2020 major depression, for example, will be considered to be the second leading cause of financial loss in the billions of dollars. The impact for schizophrenia is similar. It is this situation with loss of earning power and huge health care costs that provides yet another reason for the importance of providing rehabilitation.

In a move akin to that in other parts of medicine, rehabilitation has begun to provide 'evidence-based practices' such as: Illness Management and Recovery (Mueser *et al.*, 2004a), recently translated into wellness management and recovery (SAMHSA, 2003); Assertive Community Treatment (Stein and Test, 1980); family psychoeducation (McFarlane *et al.*, 1995; Miklowitz *et al.*, 2000); supported employment (Drake *et al.*, 1998); Integrated Dual Disorders Treatment (Drake *et al.*, 1995; Mueser *et al.*, 1998); social skills training (Liberman and Eckman, 1989); as well as social learning inpatient strategies (Paul *et al.*, 1997). Other promising practices include: supported housing (Ridgway and Zipple, 1990); supported education (Bybee *et al.*, 1999); wellness recovery action plan (WRAP; Copeland, 2005); trauma treatment (Mueser *et al.*, 2004b); strength-based case management (Rapp, 1998); shared decision making (Deegan and Drake, 2006); and brief screening neuropsychological protocols such as the NIMH-MATRIC currently being tested across multiple sites (Kirkpatrick *et al.*, 2006). Each of these strategies needs to be considered as part of a clinical team's toolbox to help these complex patients in very specific ways.

Programs should be evaluated on the values shaping the care by promoting hopefulness, empowerment, function, and client-driven decision making, availability of rehabilitation, self-sufficiency, and community integration in addition to fidelity to programmatic structures informed by values (see Anthony, 2003).

Many ideas and values are embedded in programmatic efforts to help patients/clients/users/consumers such as:' reclaiming a life, an active self, taking stock, relying on self, finding supports, learning to love, increase self-esteem, tolerance/acceptance, building on reality, better coping, self-monitoring, spirituality, seeing a process, and reclaiming hope (Spaniol *et al.*, 1999).

Although rehabilitation sciences wish to differentiate themselves from psychotherapy in an effort to establish themselves, many of the latter's contributions have infiltrated and informed the actual practice such as transference, countertransference and the notions of conflictual relationships. Further, people with serious illness say that they need to grieve over lost time and opportunities and get on with adult development, which has already been delayed. The biggest problem is that many patients/ consumers/clients/users/participants often receive only one or two rehabilitative approaches in the same way that they often receive only psychotherapy or only medication. Their individual needs and ongoing life challenges require changing, flexible, and multidimensional systems.

Examples of some integrative approaches

Excluding the pockets of excellence scattered across the world, public systems of care have risked becoming just as custodial as the old state hospitals. What is needed now to reclaim lives from psychosis across the world are simultaneously integrated approaches. Many new strategies have been designed by the caring professions and the consumers of services themselves to blend two seemingly disparate strategies together in order to serve adults with severe and persistent psychiatric disorders such as schizophrenia, major depressions, bipolar disorders, post-traumatic stress disorders, severe anxiety disorders, and disabling or disruptive personality disorders. Recent efforts have also targeted children, adolescents, and youth.

Many innovative rehabilitation programs include the following examples, which have been copied across the world and developed by energetic and visionary psychiatrists, psychologists, and social workers. For example, many readers would be familiar with: Fairweather Lodges (Fairweather, 1980); the Vermont State Hospital Rehabilitation Program (Brooks, see Chittick *et al.*, 1961); Fountain House (Aquila *et al.*, 1999; Beard *et al.*, 1982) in New York; The Trieste Work Cooperatives (Basaglia, 1982) in Italy; the Sopimusvuori Deinstitutionalization Project (Anttinen *et al.*, 1983) in Tampere, Finland; the Parachute Project (Cullberg *et al.*, 2002) in Sweden; Soteria House East and West (Mosher and Menn, 1974; Mosher and Hendrix, 2004) in California and Luc Ciompi (1997) in Switzerland; the PACT Model (Stein and Test, 1980) in Wisconsin; integrated approaches to young adults caught in between the child and adults systems of care (e.g. Clark and Davis, 2000) in the US; recovery-oriented systems (Anthony

2003) in Boston, MA; and The Village (Ragins, 2006) in Long Beach, CA, among many others.

The work from Anthony *et al.* (2002) at Boston University's Center for Psychiatric Rehabilitation highlights seven crucial and common rehabilitation values in such work, which include:

1   Person orientation.
2   Focus on functioning.
3   Support as needed.
4   The specifics of the person's environment.
5   Involvement as full partners.
6   Measuring client outcome.
7   Successes and satisfaction.

All such programs have focused upon helping the struggling person to reclaim his or her life.

Recently, 62 nations have approved a new classification system focusing upon functioning. This classification, known as the International Classification of Function, Disability and Health (ICF), targets: 'human functioning – not merely disability; a universal model not a minority model; an integrative model not merely medical or social; an interactive model not linear progressive; parity not etiological causality; context-inclusive not person in isolation; cultural applicability not just western concepts; operational not theory driven alone; and life span coverage not adult driven' (WHO, 2001).

Illustrations of how a psychiatrist worked with rehabilitation and clinical settings to accommodate both approaches

Below, we present case illustrations of how a clinical setting can become more rehabilitative and a rehabilitative setting can become more clinical.

#1 – How a rehabilitative setting became more clinical

In the mid-1950s there were several important developments in the Massachusetts Rehabilitation Commission (MRC). Two new positions were created; a state-wide mental health coordinator and a psychiatric consultant. Together, they planned and implemented system change. The psychiatrists were hired to act as tutors for the vocational rehabilitation counselors and then served as psychiatric consultants in MRC field offices. The function of these consultants was to perform an 'appraisal' of the background information gathered by counselors of potential clients who claimed a psychiatric disability to assure that the person did indeed have a psychiatric disability and that the information was sufficient to determine whether or not the person had a 'reasonable expectation' of returning to work. The consultants helped the counselors in making vocational plans. Consultation was also to be available at any point in the process when the counselor felt that he or she needed it. The role of 'mental disability supervisor' was also created in each office to support counselors on a day-by-day basis as they worked with this new population.

At the same time, sheltered workshops were opened at many of the state hospital facilities to help prepare inpatients for discharge. The MRC opened 'subdistrict offices' there to 'open cases' and participate in discharge planning. By the mid-1960s, these system changes contributed to a dramatic rise in the number of clients receiving vocational rehabilitation services. The findings showed the rate went from less than one person a year to 15 per cent of open cases.

By the mid-1970s these workshops moved into the community and the MRC programs had done the same. Over time, these workshops were being replaced by a heavy emphasis on supported employment and returning the person to the real workforce. Worthy of note was the fact that these developments were simultaneous with other developments in the mental health system, the impact of the introduction of chlorpromazine in the first case, and the early beginnings of 'deinstitutionalization' in the second.

#2 – How a clinical setting became rehabilitative

A 35-year-old woman with a psychotic disorder was improving and she expressed an interest to return to work. A vocational rehabilitation counselor confirmed that her functioning was stable and that she wished to return to secretarial work which she had enjoyed some years before. Her skills were rusty and she was frightened of public transportation, her only means of travel. The counselor suggested a stepwise rehabilitation plan including learning to take a bus without panicking, a brush-up course at a local secretarial school, and job placement.

The client liked this plan and discussed it with her therapist, who angrily called the counselor, insisting that she had referred the client for a job. The counselor explained that she believed the client could return to work, but that she needed 'a process', a series of steps, to reach the goal. The clinician reluctantly agreed to support the plan. Six months later, the client was adjusting to her new job as a secretary.

Clearly the psychotherapist had helped her client in her recovery to the point that she could think seriously of returning to work and made a timely referral for vocational rehabilitation services. The counselor conducted an assessment and proposed a plan of action to actualize this interest. The therapist was initially not prepared to hear 'a process' as the outcome of the referral. A conversation between the two service providers made clear the value of the approach: the client was not 'ready' to pursue her goal immediately without preparatory steps and the plan was successful in the long run. The therapist learned an important lesson from this experience about interest/strengths/needs-based assessment and stepwise planning that she was able to apply to her work with other patients. This experience also led to in-service training between the two programs on the rehabilitation alliance (McCrory, 1991).

The stories demonstrate the clinical development of vocational rehabilitation counselors and the rehabilitation practices of clinicians. Further, in one of the MRC offices, the counselors became interested in how their consultant, when appraising the background information, had predicted the risk of several of their clients needing rehospitalization. A review of the material revealed that there had been a repetitive pattern of regressions and remissions in the histories. A person with schizophrenia had a recurrence of his psychosis. Another client who was a person with a borderline personality disorder had again become suicidal. Prior to these rehospitalizations, both of them had been doing very well as far as their counselor could tell when, without warning, they became overwhelmed and needed inpatient care.

This intrigued the counseling staff and they wanted to learn to be prepared for this risk and to prevent it, if possible. So, for a number of months each 'case review' was focused on this possibility. By the end of a year, the office had discovered what they called 'the rehabilitation crisis' (McCrory et al., 1980). More importantly, they had learned to pay attention to this risk, especially with clients who were making significant changes in their lives. Such a shift from disabled to 'able' people and the experience of the conflict and stress which accompanied these changes were important indicators to take into consideration.

The following story further is illustrative. The agency's rehabilitation counseling staff held a workshop on the rehabilitation crisis. A man in his forties with a diagnosis of schizophrenia was discussed, who was about to start a transitional employment position. Two previous attempts had been unsuccessful with the client becoming psychotic, assaultive and required rehospitalization.

At their next appointment, the therapist raised the matter and learned that this 'progress step' made her patient so uncomfortable that on the previous two occasions he had stopped his medication in an effort to sabotage his success. Having had a chance to discuss the matter, the patient chose to go ahead with the change in program, and actually asked to increase the dose of the medication and successfully started his new competitive job. Eventually, use of sheltered workshops was discontinued for persons with persistent and serious illness.

The rehabilitation counseling staff learned to pay more attention to the risks of transition for their vulnerable clients. They became attuned not just to their clients' symptomotology but to situations that heightened stress.

They learned to recognize these situations as triggers and to offer support before the stress became overwhelming. The psychotherapist also discovered that patients with serious psychiatric disorders could indeed return to work, and in the process of transition they might indeed become more symptomatic as natural and predictable responses to the heightened stress. And, moreover, with the support of the rehabilitation alliance, they can master the challenge and enhance their self-esteem and confidence as a result.

These examples illustrate successful collaborations between rehabilitation counselors and clinicians. Newer approaches are now provided by integrated clinical and rehabilitative teams working together as partners with persons who are experiencing serious and persistent illness, using a wide range of evidence-based and promising practices as needed and desired.

Conclusion

This chapter began with an exploration of the many essential similarities and differences between psychotherapeutic and psychiatric rehabilitation approaches in working with persons coping with serious and persistent mental illness, drawing attention to the basic compatibility of these two approaches. It went on to briefly survey the many developments in each field over time with some reference to the development of biological approaches. Finally, it spoke of the value of integrating these approaches and gave examples of how this was achieved with psychotherapists and rehabilitation counselors working together.

The authors are convinced of the value of integrating approaches, working and learning from each other in clinical practice, training and research, as both fields participate with psychopharmacologists in understanding and serving the needs of people with these disabling conditions. This message is very timely as much attention has become focused in recent years on the 'fragmentation' of the mental health systems of care. Many systems have grown very much like the nursery rhyme 'house that Jack built' over the past five decades. These systems have built separate, often competing, service programs/service models and funding streams developing out of very different traditions, focusing on different needs, with differing language, goals, and methods. Yet the persons with serious and persistent illness need access to a wide variety of options at different points in their recovery process. Thus, systems and practice need to catch up to the offerings of science and the available knowledge base.

This chapter is yet another 'call' for the spread of core integrative strategies across the world. Whether or not a clinician or rehabilitation worker is conducting evidence-based, values-based, integrative, phase-specific, titrated, flexible strategies, the bottom line continues to be the importance of a working collaborative relationship with the person seeking restoration to a life.

Acknowledgment

The authors would like to thank attendees at our presentation of the first draft of this chapter at the fifteenth ISPS meeting in Madrid for their helpful feedback which helped to reshape the work.

References

Anthony, W.A. (2000). A recovery oriented service system: setting some system level standards. *Psychiatric Rehabilitation Journal* 24: 159–168.

Anthony, W.A. (2003). Editorial: bridging the gap between values and practice. *Psychiatric Rehabilitation Journal* 28: 105.

Anthony, W.A. Cohen, M., Farkas, M. and Gagne, C. (2002). *Psychiatric Rehabilitation*, 2nd edn. Boston, MA: Center for Psychiatric Rehabilitation, Sargent College, Boston University.

Anttinen, E.E. (1983). Can the vicious circle of chronicity and institutionalization be broken? *Psychiatria Fennica Yearbook*. Helsinki: Foundation for Psychiatric Research in Finland, pp. 21–31.

Aquila, R., Santos, G., Malamud, I. and McCrory, D.J. (1999). The rehabilitation alliance in practice: the clubhouse connection. *Psychiatric Rehabilitation Journal* 23: 19–23.

Basaglia, F. (1982). Riabilitazione e controllo sociale. In F. Basaglia and F. Basaglia Ongaro (eds) *La maggioranza deviante*. Torino: Einaudi.

Beard, J.H., Propst, R.N. and Malamud, T.J. (1982). The Fountain House model of psychiatric rehabilitation. *Psychosocial Rehabilitation Journal* 5: 47–53.

Bybee, D., Collins, M. and Mowbray, C.T. (1999). Supported education for individuals with psychiatric disabilities: long-term outcome from an experimental study. *Social Work Research* 23: 89–100.

Chittick, R.A., Brooks, G.W., Irons, F.S. *et al.* (1961). *The Vermont Story: Rehabilitation of Chronic Schizophrenic Patients*. Burlington, VT: Vermont State Hospital.

Ciompi, L. (1997). The Soteria concept: theoretical bases and practices: 13 year experience with a multitherapeutic approach to acute schizophrenia. *Psychiatria et Neurologica Japonaca* 9: 6334–6350.

Clark, H.B. and Davis, M. (2000). *Transition to Adulthood: A Resource for Assisting Young People with Emotional or Behavioral Difficulties*. Baltimore, MD: Paul H. Brookes.

Copeland, M.E. (2005). *WRAP: Step by Step*. http://www.copelandcenter.com.

Cullberg, J., Levander, S., Holmqvist, R. *et al.* (2002). One-year outcome in first episode psychosis patients in the Swedish Parachute project. *Acta Psychiatrica Scandinavica* 106, 4: 276–285.

Deegan, P.E. and Drake, R.E. (2006). Shared decision making and medication management in the recovery process. *Psychiatric Services* 57: 1636–1639.

DeSisto, M., Harding, C.M., McCormick, R.V. *et al.* (1995). The Maine-Vermont three decade studies of serious mental illness: matched comparison of cross-sectional outcome. *British Journal of Psychiatry* 167: 331–338.

Drake, R.E., Noordsy, D.L. and Ackerson, T. (1995). Integrating mental health and substance abuse treatments for persons with severe mental illness. In A.E. Lehman and L.B. Dixon (eds) *Double Jeopardy: Chronic Mental Illness and Substance Abuse*. New York: Harwood, pp. 251–264.

Drake, R.E., McHugo, G.J., Clark, R.E. *et al.* (1998). Assertive community treatment for patients with co-occurring severe mental illness and substance abuse disorder: A clinical trial. *American Journal of Orthopsychiatry* 68: 201–215.

Fairweather, G.W. (ed.) (1980). The Fairweather Lodge: a twenty-five year retrospective. *New Directions for Mental Health Services* 7.

Falloon, I.R.H., Held, T., Roncone, R. *et al.* (1998). Optimal treatment strategies to enhance recovery from schizophrenia. *Australian and New Zealand Journal of Psychiatry* 32: 32–49.

Fenton, W. (2000). Evolving perspectives on individual psychotherapy. *Schizophrenia Bulletin* 26, 1: 47–72.

Kirkpatrick, B., Fenton, W.S., Carpenter, W.T. *et al.* (2006). The NIMH-MATRICS consensus statement on negative symptoms. *Schizophrenia Bulletin* 32: 214–219.

Liberman, R.P. and Eckman, T.A. (1989). Dissemination of skills training modules to psychiatric facilities: overcoming obstacles to the utilization of a rehabilitation innovation. *British Journal of Psychiatry* 155 (Suppl. 5): 117–122.

McCrory, D.J. (1991). The rehabilitation alliance. *Journal of Vocational Rehabilitation* 1: 58–66.

McCrory, D.J., Connolly, P.S., Hanson-Mayer, T.P. *et al.* (1980). The rehabilitation crisis: the impact of growth. *Journal of Applied Rehabilitation Counseling* 11: 136–139.

McFarlane, W.R., Lukens, E., Link, B. *et al.* (1995). Multiple-family groups and psychoeducation in the treatment of schizophrenia. *Archives of General Psychiatry* 52: 679–687.

MedMAP and other Evidence-Based Practices (2003). www.samhsa.gov.

Miklowitz, D.J., Simoneau, T.L., George, E.L. *et al.* (2000). Family-focused treatment of bipolar disorder: 1 year effects of a psychoeducation; program in conjunction with pharmacology. *Biological Psychiatry* 48: 582–592.

Mosher, L. and Hendrix, V. (2004). *Soteria: Through Madness to Deliverance*. San Diego, CA: XLIBRIS.

Mosher, L.R. and Menn, A.Z. (1974). Soteria: An alternative to hospitalization for schizophrenia. In J.H. Masserman (ed.) *Current Psychiatric Therapies*. New York: Grune and Stratton, pp. 287–296.

Mueser, K.T., Drake, R.E. and Noordsy, D.L. (1998). Integrated mental health and substance abuse treatment for severe psychiatric disorders. *Practical Psychiatry and Behavioral Health* 4: 129–139.

Mueser, K.T., Corrigan, P.W., Hilton, D.W. *et al.* (2004a). Illness management and recovery: a review of the research. *APA Focus* 2: 34–47.

Mueser, K.T., Rosenberg, S.D., Jankowski, M.K. *et al.* (2004b). A cognitive-behavioral treatment program for posttraumatic stress disorder in severe mental illness. *American Journal of Psychiatric Rehabilitation* 7: 107–146.

Paul, G.L., Stuve, P. and Menditto, A.A. (1997). Social-learning program (with token economy) for adult psychiatric inpatients. *Clinical Psychologist* 50: 14–17.

Ragins, M. (2006). http:/www.thevillage-isa.org.

Rapp, C.A. (1998). *The Strengths Model: Case Management with People Suffering from Severe and Persistent Mental Illness.* New York: Oxford University Press.

Ridgway, P. and Zipple, A.M. (1990). The paradigm shift in residential services: from linear continuum to supported housing approaches. *Psychosocial Rehabilitation Journal* 13: 11–32.

Spaniol, L., Gagne, C. and Koehler, M. (1999). Recovery from serious mental illness: What is it and how to support people in their recovery. In R.P. Marinelli and A.e. Deu Orto (eds) *The Psychological and Social Impact of Disability* (fourth edition). New York: Springer.

Stein, L.I. and Test, M.A. (1980). Alternative to mental hospital treatment. *Archives of General Psychiatry* 37: 392–397.

Stroul, B. (1984). *Principles of Community Support Systems.* Rockville, MD: National Institute of Mental Health.

Substance Abuse and Mental Health Services Administration (SAMHSA, 2003). *Wellness Management and Recovery.* Rockville, MD: SAMHSA (http://mentalhealth.samhsa.gov/).

World Health Organization (WHO, 2001). *International Classification of Functioning, Disability, and Health.* Geneva: WHO.

World Health Organization (WHO, 2006). *(DALY) Disability Adjusted Life Years.* http://www.who.int/healthinfo/boddaly/en/index.html.

Chapter 23

Soteria

A treatment model and a reform movement in psychiatry

Volkmar Aderhold (Translated by Peter Stastny)

In honour of Loren Mosher

Everyone is much more simply human than otherwise.
(H.S. Sullivan, *The Interpersonal Theory of Psychiatry*, 1953)

Introduction

The Soteria treatment model was initiated by the American psychiatrist Loren Mosher during the early 1970s. Between 1968 and 1980, as director of the Schizophrenia Branch of the National Institute of Mental Health (NIMH) he developed two federally funded research demonstration projects: 'Soteria' (1971–1983) and 'Emanon' (1974–1980). The aim was to investigate the effects of a supportive milieu therapy ('being with') for individuals diagnosed with 'schizophrenia', who were experiencing acute psychotic episodes for the first or second time in their lives. In these programmes neuroleptics were either completely avoided, or given in low dosages only.

Since the founding of Soteria Berne by Luc Ciompi in 1984, similar programmes have been developed in Europe, mostly in the form of residential facilities situated in proximity to psychiatric hospitals. To this day, the Soteria model remains particularly encouraging for the consumer/ survivor movement. It represents a concrete alternative to traditional treatment which is dominated by neuroleptic use, demonstrates the self-healing potential of individuals experiencing acute psychoses, and constitutes a major attempt to humanize psychiatry.

Personal roots – Loren Mosher (1934–2004)

As a student, Mosher discovered existentialism and phenomenology in approaching unavoidable human suffering and developed a great appreciation of subjectivity, openness and divergent theories. His psychiatric training at Harvard was strongly influenced by Elvin Semrad, who was less determined to cure patients than to jointly explore their lives guided by pride, respect and empathy. Semrad promoted the experiential confrontation of the insecurity, unpredictably, and unintelligibility that are fundamental to psychiatric problems, and which trigger anxiety among 'treaters' and patients alike. Another important source of influence on Mosher was Sullivan's (1962) way of presenting therapeutic human relationships in his interpersonal theory and applied in his specially designed milieu for persons with schizophrenia at Sheppard-Pratt Hospital in the late 1920s.

Following his residency, Mosher spent the years 1966–1967 as a fellow at the Tavistock Clinic in London, where he met John Bowlby and Anna Freud. At the same time, he kept in contact with Kingsley Hall (1965–1970), a therapeutic community for individuals diagnosed with 'schizophrenia' led by R.D. Laing. This environment was designed to permit going through the experience of psychosis without unduly pathologizing influences. Mosher ultimately felt like an outsider at Kingsley Hall, and the institution seemed rather helpless in confronting the difficulties of its residents. Kingsley Hall nevertheless became a guiding post for the development of the Soteria model in both positive and negative ways.

Mosher adopted an applied phenomenology from the clinical studies of R.D. Laing (1960, 1967) and the Existential (Daseins) Analysis of Medard Boss (1963). During these years, he was also interested in the labelling theory proposed by Scheff (1966), suggesting that the condition of those suffering from mental disorders usually worsens after they have been given the label of 'crazy'. Mosher was also well acquainted with Irving Goffman's (1961) analysis of the rigid structure in psychiatric hospitals, clarifying the overarching institutionalizing processes and the deleterious consequences for the patients. He was also familiar with community psychiatric approaches such as that of Fairweather Lodge (Fairweather *et al.*, 1969).

An understanding of psychosis

Mosher had a life-long scepticism vis-à-vis models of 'schizophrenia', amongst other reasons because these obscured an open phenomenological view, particularly since use of this term has not diminished the enigma of the phenomena to this day. Mosher saw psychosis as a coping mechanism and a response to years of various events that were subjectively experienced as traumatic and led the person to retreat from reality. The experiential and behavioural attributes of 'psychosis' – including irrationality, terror, and mystical experiences – are seen as the extremes of basic human qualities.

The Soteria setting

A 'homelike' environment in a 12-room house with garden within a fairly poor neighbourhood in San José, California, offered intensive milieu therapy for six or seven individuals, called residents or clients. For research reasons they were unmarried persons newly diagnosed with 'schizophrenia', with one or two new residents admitted each month.

About seven full-time staff members plus volunteers were selected for their individual rather than formal qualifications, and characterized as psychologically strong, independent, mature, warm, and empathic. Soteria staff were significantly more intuitive, introverted, flexible, and tolerant of altered states of consciousness than the staff on the general psychiatric inpatient unit (Mosher *et al.*, 1973; Hirschfeld *et al.*, 1977). These personality traits seem to be highly relevant for success in this kind of work.

Former residents could become regular staff members and did so on several occasions. Soteria employed a quarter-time psychiatrist, who visited the house once a week, and was available on call. Twenty-four or forty-eight hour shifts gave the opportunity of being with residents for long periods of time and thereby experiencing complete biological/psychological psychotic cycles of clients while avoiding disruptive separations due to staff turnover – an experience only family members or significant others have under ordinary circumstances. At times of high activity – mostly afternoon until midnight – Soteria tried to have a 50/50 mix of relatively 'organized' and disorganized persons in the house including recovering clients and volunteers (Mosher *et al.*, 2004).

Procedures

The staff's primary duty is to 'be with' disorganized clients without the expectation that they need to be doing something specific. If frightened, they should call for help. Partial recovery of clients can generally be achieved within six to eight weeks, and the average length of stay was four or five months. Soteria was an open social system which allowed easy access, departure and return, if needed. Everyone shared the day-to-day running of the house as far as they were able. Roles were only minimally differentiated to encourage flexibility with little emphasis on hierarchy, which meant relatively informal day-to-day functioning. Integration into the local community was paramount (Mosher, 1972, 1992).

Instead of traditionally defined, formal in-house 'therapy', yoga, massage, art, music, dance, sports, outings, gardening, shopping, cooking, etc. were offered and much appreciated. Special meetings were scheduled to deal with interpersonal problems as they emerged, and family mediation was provided as needed. Continuity of relationships after moving out of the house was greatly encouraged.

General guidelines for behaviour, interaction and expectation:

The general guidelines for behaviour were as follows:

- Do no harm.
- Treat everyone, and expect to be treated, with dignity and respect.
- Guarantee asylum, quiet, safety, support, protection, containment, interpersonal validation, food and shelter.
- Expect recovery from psychosis, which might include learning and growth through and from the psychotic experience.
- Provide positive explanations and optimism.
- Identify plausible explanations: emphasize biography, life events, trigger factors instead of vulnerability; promoting experiences of success.
- Encourage the patient to develop his or her own treatment plan; he or she is considered the expert.
- Identify meaningful aspects of life beyond being a patient.
- Do not assume responsibility for anything the clients might be capable of achieving – trust in self-help.
- No use of the labels 'schizophrenia' or 'schizophrenic'.

Rules

Rules were established as follows:

- Violence to self or others is forbidden.
- Visitors are not allowed without prearrangement and agreement of the current residents of the house. Family members and friends are welcome, but it is preferred that they plan their visits in advance.
- No illegal drugs are allowed in the house (in practice residents rarely used illegal drugs, certainly not in the house).
- No sex between staff members and residents is permitted (a form of incest taboo).
- As long as residents were not a threat to themselves or others, extremes of human behaviour were tolerated.

Three phases

1. Acute crises

During this phase 'being with' is used as a practice of interpersonal phenomenology. The use of a special room (like the 'soft room' in Berne) was soon abandoned in favour of a fluid interpersonal way of 'being with' in a variety of physical and social settings.

> The most basic tenet is 'being with' – an attentive but non-intrusive, gradual way of getting oneself 'into the other person's shoes' so that a shared meaningfulness of the subjective aspects of the psychotic

experience can be established within a confiding relationship. This requires unconditional acceptance of the experience of others as valid and understandable within the historical context of each person's life – even when it cannot be consensually validated. Soteria also paid thoughtful attention to the caregiver's experience of the situation (not unlike the psychoanalytic concept of 'transference' [and counter-transference]). The method aimed to keep in focus the whole 'being' ('Dasein') in relation to others.

(Bola *et al.*, 2005: 370)

Detailed case reports are given in Mosher *et al.* (1994, 2004).

2. Restitution of the fragmented personality in a protected context

During this phase, the resident is expected to get involved in daily routines. For the staff it signals a role change from being a 'parent' to a more symmetrical peer relationship. In order to normalize the experience of psychosis, it is related to the person's biographical context, framed in positive terms, and described in everyday language.

Developing relationships is of great importance to facilitate a process of imitation and identification among clients, and for the staff to be able to acknowledge any precipitating events and the painful emotions that stem from them. Usually, these emotions are disavowed, but at Soteria they were discussed until they could be tolerated.

3. Orientation to the outside world

This included role diversification and growing competence and the development of new relationships inside and outside the house: cooperation, planning, arrangement. It was common to reach a consensus among the entire group before a resident was discharged.

The naturally developing social network of peers continued after discharge to support recovery and to facilitate community integration, which included direct help with housing, education, work and social life. Once someone was a member of the Soteria community, she or he was always welcome back in case they were having difficulties, as long as space at the house was available. Everyone was equally welcome even if he or she was not having any problems and only wanted to socialize or help with activities. Over time both residents and staff were socializing outside the facility itself.

Mosher believed that this network was of crucial importance for the long-term outcome of the Soteria work. The 'Soteria community' was still active at least ten years after the programme was closed. It was never formally researched since it was an unplanned development.

Voyce Hendrix estimates that approximately 5 per cent of the residents were hospitalized during their stay at Soteria because staff felt that they were not able to refrain from harming themselves or others, but such decisions were often made by the entire group.

Medication

Whenever possible, no neuroleptics were used during the first six weeks of treatment. However, benzodiazepines were permitted. If there was insufficient improvement after six weeks, chlorpromazine (thorazine) was initiated in dosages of 300 mg or more (Mosher and Menn, 1978). Basically, the medication was supposed to remain under the control of each resident. Dosages were adjusted based on self-observation and reports to staff. After two weeks, the patient could decide whether they wanted to continue the medication or not (Mosher et al., 1994).

> Today my position is that, since no real alternatives to antipsychotic drugs are currently available, to be totally against them is untenable. Thus, for seriously disturbed people, I occasionally recommend them – as part of collaborative planning with my client – but in the lowest dosage and for the shortest length of time possible. Instead of anti-psychotics, however, I prefer to calm acute psychosis and restore sleep/wake cycles with an initial course of minor tranquilizers accompanied by in-home crisis intervention.
>
> (Mosher et al., 2004: 303)

Supervision

The psychiatrists and the principal investigator were charged with supervising the staff. Feelings that seem to cause the staff to shift from the 'being with' to the 'doing to' mode are explored in detail (Mosher et al., 1973: 393).

Direction and funding

Alma Menn became the programme director of Soteria. During the following years until Soteria and Emanon were closed, Voyce Hendrix worked as the programme coordinator. Initially, Soteria was funded for 18 months only. Over the next ten years, eight progress reports were requested and submitted, and five site visits by federal reviewers took place. 'Our grant was reviewed more times by more committees than any grant in the history of the NIMH' (Mosher et al., 2004: 304).

In 1976, Mosher was terminated as the principal investigator of Soteria, and the research design was changed from that of the first cohort in which treatment was assigned (1971–1976 with 79 subjects) into an experimental design with random assignment in the second cohort (1976–1979 with 100 subjects).

In 1980 Mosher was removed as the Chief of the Schizophrenia Center at the NIMH while he was on sabbatical in Italy writing a book on community psychiatry: 'All of this occurred because of my strong stand against the overuse of medication and their disregard for drug-free, psychological interventions to treat psychological disorders' (Mosher *et al.*, 2004: 305). Once NIMH funding had ceased, despite careful data collection methods and positive results, Emanon and Soteria only remained open until 1980 and 1983, respectively.

Research design

The Soteria project used a quasi-experimental treatment comparison with consecutive admissions and space available treatment assignment in the first cohort (1971–1976; n = 79) and an experimental design with random assignment in the second cohort (1976–1979; n = 100). Data were collected for two years post-admission. Subjects for the study or control groups were recruited from two county hospital psychiatric emergency screening facilities in the San Francisco Bay area. All persons meeting the criteria were asked to sign informed consent (Mosher and Menn, 1978; Bola and Mosher, 2003).

Inclusion criteria (to the second cohort)

- Ages 15–32, and not currently married (relatively poor prognosis group).
- Initial diagnosis of schizophrenia by three independent clinicians (*DSM-II*).
- Judged to be in need of hospitalization.
- One or no previous hospitalization with a diagnosis of schizophrenia for less than four weeks.
- Post-discharge treatment was uncontrolled.

Control group

- Treated in well-staffed general hospital psychiatric wards supporting a medical model.
- Ninety-four per cent were treated continuously with antipsychotic medication (average 700 mg chlorpromazine-equivalents per day).
- Post-discharge medications prescribed for nearly all.

- Post-discharge placement in other parts of the psychiatric network if needed.
- Post-discharge treatment was uncontrolled.

Results

Six-week outcomes

Results for both groups – measured with the Global Psychopathology Scale – were similar and showed significant improvement. Since only 33 per cent of the Soteria subjects received neuroleptics during the initial six weeks (12 per cent continuously), Soteria proved to be equally effective for the majority of clients as neuroleptics for acute symptom reduction (Mosher *et al.*, 1995).

Two-year outcomes

The separate analyses of the two experimental cohorts yielded equally favourable overall results in comparison with the control group, and significantly better results with regard to their independent living status. While the first experimental cohort showed a significantly lower relapse and medication rate over two years (Mosher and Menn, 1978), the second cohort showed only a non-significant trend in this direction. Mosher suggested that this might have been due to the demoralizing effect on the staff of the programme's financial instability, and in particular the dissolution of the social networks that had developed around both houses (Soteria and Emanon).

The positive impact of the Soteria intervention on relapse prevention, or rather the prevention of rehospitalizations, was demonstrated for the first cohort over a period of two years (Matthews *et al.*, 1979), utilizing survival analysis. Soteria residents (n = 32) showed significantly better survival rates after two years, especially those who were treated without neuroleptics (92 per cent in the first cohort), in comparison with those 50 per cent of control subjects (total n = 36) who received neuroleptics continually over the two years.

In their comprehensive re-analysis of both cohorts (see Bola and Mosher, 2003 for methodological details), all study completers were included and divided into several subgroups, taking into consideration the higher attrition rates among control subjects. Of the control subjects 28 per cent (50 of 179) were lost to follow-up after two years.

Drug-free responders

At the two-year follow-up, the drug-free group (43 per cent of all Soteria subjects) was performing well above the overall group mean (at +0.82 of a standard deviation) on a composite outcome scale, representing the dimensions of rehospitalization, psychopathology, independent living, social and occupational functioning. As summarized, the key results for Soteria subjects who completed the study were (Bola *et al.*, 2005):

- For *all subjects*, Soteria had a moderate effect size advantage (+0.47 SD; t = 2.20; p = 0.03).
- For *schizophrenia subjects*, Soteria had a large effect size advantage (+0.81 SD; t = 2.42; p = 0.02).
- The subjects diagnosed with *schizophreniform disorder* also had better outcome when treated at Soteria; however, the difference was not statistically significant (+ 0.34 SD; t = 1.22; n.s.).

Of subjects who went through the Soteria programme 43 per cent did not receive antipsychotic drugs during follow-up and had strikingly good outcomes (+0.82 SD of a standard deviation on a composite outcome scale representing the dimensions of rehospitalization, psychopathology, independent living as well as social and occupational functioning).

Luc Ciompi and Soteria Berne

Theory of schizophrenia

For Ciompi, as well as Mosher, all theories of schizophrenia should be grounded in the basic and fundamentally human element of 'schizophrenic being'. All aspects of schizophrenic experience make sense from the perspective of biography. In his book *Affektlogik* (1982) Luc Ciompi developed a sophisticated view of the Soteria approach in an intelligent and comprehensive blend of empirical findings and theoretical perspectives, all with the aim of making psychosis more understandable. He integrated the phenomenological and psychopathological, subjective and objective, affective and cognitive, the biological and the social aspects. Central elements in Ciompi's presentation are: the longitudinal studies of patients with schizophrenia (Ciompi and Müller, 1976); referring to the key influence of psychosocial factors on the course of illness (Ciompi, 1980, 1988); Piaget's developmental psychology; system theory; psychoanalytic individual and systemic family therapies; and neurobiology. Subsequently, Ciompi gave further attention to the important role of affects in the organization of (intra)psychic processes (Ciompi *et al.*, 1991; Ciompi, 1997), and complemented his model of psychosis with considerations based on chaos theory as a theory of non-linear and chaotic system dynamics (Ciompi, 1989; Ciompi *et al.*, 1992a).

According to 'affect logic' (with its double meaning of 'the logic of affects' and of the 'affectivity of logic'), Ciompi understands an acute psychosis as an anxiety-ridden type of disintegration of diffuse 'affective and cognitive relational systems' or 'programs concerning feelings, thoughts, and behaviours' with the possible outcome of forming relatively isolated 'affective and cognitive realms', i.e. delusional ideas. The transition into frank psychosis can be understood from a chaos theoretical perspective as a non-linear phase jump (bifurcation) given an excess of affect, and accordingly remission can be seen as a reversal of this jump under conditions of relaxation.

The guiding image for the treatment of acute psychosis according to Ciompi is a 'good mother, who intuitively knows how to calm her child who is caught up in frightful fits of delirious fever' (Ciompi *et al.*, 2001: 60). He assigns great importance to the protection from stimuli, emphasizing enduring emotional relaxation, the calming of anxiety, and continuous relationships, which led him to reintroduce the 'soft room' in the treatment of acute states. Unequivocal and non-contradictory communication is another important treatment element (Ciompi *et al.*, 1991, 1992b; Ciompi and Hoffmann, 2004).

Development of Soteria Berne

In 1984 Ciompi founded Soteria Berne, having been 'infected' during a stay at Soteria California seven years earlier. He was in charge of the project until 1998 and was then followed by Holger Hoffmann. In distinction to Mosher, Ciompi considered himself a 'psychiatric reformer' (Ciompi *et al.*, 2001: 46) and wanted to integrate Soteria Berne from the beginning into the community-based mental health services network, establishing it as a theoretical framework within a bio-psycho-social model of psychosis. In Berne, more than half of the staff consisted of mental health professionals.

Principally, the phase-specific process is laid out similarly in Berne as in California. Relaxation and protection from stimuli are emphasized in the acute phase. Soteria Berne added the stimulus reducing 'soft room' for the initial treatment phase, where residents and supporters spend most of their time during the first days and weeks of their stay. The diagnosis of schizophrenia is used and openly discussed with patients and relatives.

Compared to Soteria California, Berne uses more prophylactic medication maintenance during the reintegration phase, and a more systematic approach in individual and family treatments. Soteria Berne reports that only 10 to 15 per cent of individuals who experience a first psychotic episode cannot be treated in their programme, which indicates a fairly low level of selectivity (Ciompi and Hoffmann, 2004).

Research evaluation

Research evaluation has led to a replication of the Soteria studies in a new programme structure that was completely independent of its American predecessors. To this end, Ciompi chose a prospective two-year study design that included 22 first episode psychosis subjects who met *DSM-III* criteria for schizophrenia and compared them with a pair-wise matched control group consisting of 22 individuals with statistically similar age, sex, premorbid social adjustment and predominant positive or negative symptoms, recruited from four different clinical services.

The results of this effort were not as impressive as in the original Soteria study, given that the outcomes in the areas of psychopathology, social and vocational reintegration, and relapse rates were no better than in several other well-functioning control sites. One remarkable difference was the fact that after two years – not unlike California – only 9 per cent of Soteria subjects lived in their parental home, compared to 34 per cent in the control group, a finding pointing towards increased capabilities for independent modes of living.

The proportion of first episode subjects who were not treated with neuroleptics was 30 per cent. However, among control subjects the dosages were three to five times higher (Ciompi *et al.*, 1993).

The treatment costs per patient in the pilot study were initially higher, but were ultimately lowered to 90 per cent of the cost of acute inpatient treatment by reducing the average length of stay in Soteria Berne to three months (Ciompi *et al.*, 2001).

Particularly positive treatment effects will most likely be found in the domain of subjective experiences: satisfaction, self-worth, positive self-concept, long-term personality development, less stigmatization and discrimination among residents and their relatives ('soft data' from qualitative research yet to be formally completed).

Soteria Berne succeeded to become firmly established within the psycho-social service system of Berne, serving as a model programme. Since its foundation, Soteria Berne has provided encouragement for service users and providers as a model programme and training site. Another unique feature of Soteria Berne is the regular referral of former residents to outpatient psychotherapy, especially utilizing the services of Elizabeth Aebi, a former Soteria staff member who is a highly experienced psychoanalyst.

Further developments

In recent years the length of stay has been shortened to three months in response to pressures from third-party payers. This led to use of the 'soft room' being more time limited. The therapeutic focus lies more on relaxation and providing protection from overstimulation than an interactive 'being with' the psychotic experience. Concerning pharmacotherapy, Ciompi prefers low doses to a drug-free treatment. In recent years, neuroleptics were being given within two or three weeks, if symptoms persisted. Furthermore, low dose maintenance neuroleptics are prescribed as a rule to prevent relapse, given that relapse rates were only moderately reduced at Soteria California (first cohort), and not at all in Berne.

The rather low readmission rate of 12 per cent and the essentially routine administration of neuroleptics indicates a rather close connection to the traditional service system (maybe suggesting that Soteria is still a singular experience with rather limited impact).

Ciompi's concepts of psychosis and of acute treatment as providing an enduring emotional relaxation are striving for a high degree of scientific objectivity, by virtue of its tendency to lay out practice guidelines – in a considerably more structured fashion than Mosher's open phenomenological approach. However, even Ciompi himself shares some scepticism about scientific explanations in a subsequent personal reflection about Soteria, expressing a 'deep respect before the unsolved riddle of schizophrenia':

> Over the years, mysteries have been purportedly uncovered too many times, or rather violated by some partial truth, be it from a genetic, eugenic, psychopharmacologic, social or family dynamic perspective. Not unlike Loren Mosher I have come to the conclusion, after frequent and hardly innocuous dogmatic excesses, that the theoretical uncertainty and emotional immediacy of an engaged and empathic lay person – certainly within a steady dialogue with equally empathic experts – can come closer to a deeper truth of this enigmatic 'disturbance' (or at least cause less harm) than any highfalutin theory.
>
> (Ciompi *et al.*, 2001: 179)

Attempts at explaining the effectiveness of Soteria

Mosher

Promoting new relationships

> Relationships were the decisive elements: if they did not develop at Soteria, nothing changed. But it was near impossible to avoid forming some kind of relationship at Soteria. The only question was, what kind of relationships needed fostering.
>
> (Mosher *et al.*, 1994: 15)

Developing a more independent identity

> Without the supportive network of basic interpersonal relationships, clients were not capable of developing an identity independent from their families of origin. If this did not succeed, these young people who had just emerged from their parental homes in the midst of a psychotic episode, were bound to head for another crisis.
>
> (Mosher *et al.*, 1994: 67)

Beyond this there is a fair amount of overlap between the Soteria approach and salient therapeutic elements as generally defined:

• An environment experienced as healing.
• A trusting relationship with a therapist.
• Developing plausible explanations for the problems that had occurred.
• Promoting positive expectations for the future, largely through the personal qualities of the therapist.
• Promoting the possibility for positive experiences as part of the therapeutic process.

Ciompi

In explaining the effects of Soteria, Ciompi builds on his concept of affect logic. The main element is the persistent reduction of tension which contains several other not clearly identifiable 'more subtle components' (Ciompi et al., 2001). This main factor corresponds theoretically with the concept of 'affective logic' in Ciompi's understanding of psychosis, since it influences the capacity of 'affects to have impact on thinking and behavior' (Ciompi et al., 2001: 50) and it also imitates the effects of neuroleptics in such a milieu (p. 65).

Dissemination and replicability of the Soteria approach

Since the founding of Soteria in 1971, there have been approximately 12 similar projects around the world, most of them in Europe. Currently, there are projects in Berne (Switzerland), Zwiefalten and Munich Haar (Germany), Stockholm North (Sweden), and several in Denmark, with one starting in Alaska in 2009. An additional 11 initiatives to replicate Soteria have faltered due to the lack of cooperation of area hospitals. Clearly, a successful implementation of Soteria hinges on close collaboration with a regional hospital (Ciompi et al., 2001).

The greater popularity and replication of Soteria in European countries is probably a result of Luc Ciompi's more integrative approach. Ciompi speculates that Loren Mosher's antipsychiatric attitude and the critical stance towards neuroleptics have been an important hindrance to its replication in the USA.

Additionally, the Soteria model has contributed to the establishment of acute inpatient units within the established mental health system, which employ so-called 'Soteria elements' (Kroll, 1998). Early examples were two wards at the psychiatric hospital in Gütersloh (closed in 2001 due to a change in administration) and Gießen. At least a further eight similar inpatient units and crisis residences followed, each explicitly promulgating a Soteria concept.

Both Mosher and Ciompi have welcomed this development in principle. In the meantime, a certain level of polarization between the original Soteria concept and these acute inpatient units that employ Soteria elements has become notable. There is a conflict regarding the spread of Soteria principles by integrating them within the standard treatment system, which might mean risking a dilution of the treatment effect and false labelling. On the other hand, there is also concern that holding on to the original idea with its considerable therapeutic potential and its aversion to neuroleptics bears the risk of further marginalization and ultimately its extinction.

Under ideal circumstances I assume that both of these approaches might be valid, especially if the intentions are clearly shown. However, at this point I would primarily champion the establishment of bona-fide Soteria programmes to support research and further programme development. Obviously, such a position does not take into account the level of wide-spread opposition to such efforts.

Soteria as an 'ideological movement' and a guiding idea

Beyond all this, the Soteria idea has contributed to the fact that milieu and interpersonal aspects of treatment, especially in German-speaking countries, are taken a bit more seriously:

> In the past 15–20 years we have been continually accompanied, overtly or not, by the Soteria model. It has become a measure of humane treatment methods, a humane approach towards patients, even a measure of the appropriate conduct of doctors.
>
> (Ciompi et al., 2001: 219)

The influence of the Soteria idea and its applications is also prevalent in the Northern European countries (see Chapter 12). As part of the Swedish multicentre Parachute Project, small crisis apartments outside of the hospital were successfully introduced in several regions to provide short-term crisis intervention. Patients who made use of these apartments did significantly better than control subjects in their psychosocial functioning, and along with their families were especially satisfied with their treatment (Cullberg et al., 2002, 2006). The special contextual conditions of Soteria-type programmes can be created in a family home, a non-family residence, or a network meeting held nearly anywhere. Such care has been pioneered in Finland (Alanen et al., 2000; Lehtinen et al., 2000; Seikkula et al., 2003) and is now also being studied in Sweden (Cullberg et al., 2002; see Bola et al., 2005).

Especially following the broad success of dehospitalizing long-term patients from large institutions, the need for a fundamental retooling of acute treatment has emerged. The Soteria concept remains of predominant importance for this work in progress.

Personal assessment and outlook

The Soteria model has provided a notable impulse for improving the therapeutic milieu within the acute care system, especially in German-speaking countries, and thereby has made an essential contribution towards enhancing the quality of the services and the lives of individuals suffering from psychoses. In addition, several model programmes have emerged and have successfully implemented some of the Soteria elements within routine services. However, a continual 'being with' that goes beyond a few hours can almost never be provided. Classical Soteria programmes have not been established during recent years.

Presently, there is a risk that Soteria development comes to a halt at this point, or even takes a gradual turn backwards Under increasing financial constraints we are witnessing a reduction of psychosocial treatments within services offered to individuals with psychoses. On the other hand, the recent disappointment about the long-term effects and side effects of the 'atypical' neuroleptics might give way to stronger efforts for better psychosocial treatment programmes including Soteria, helping to lower dosages of neuroleptics or to avoid them at all.

In my view, the historical and therapeutic potential of the Soteria concept is far from exhausted. Quite possibly, the combination of Soteria facilities with community-based psychosis treatment teams that work according to the need-adapted model might offer the best chance to facilitate its survival. (Alanen, 1997; Alanen et al., 2000; Aderhold et al., 2003). Such an approach would significantly lower the average length of stay at Soteria, and thereby its costs. Lehtinen et al. (2000) and Seikkula et al. (2003, 2006) have demonstrated that such a primarily ambulatory service system can offer treatment without neuroleptics for 40 to 70 per cent of individuals experiencing a first psychotic episode (see also Bola et al., 2006). In three regions and two historical cohorts, these subgroups achieved best results compared to their controls. This model was also successfully evaluated in Sweden (Cullberg et al., 2002, 2006).

It is my assumption that the further refinement of neurobiological methods will provide more clarity about the 'antipsychotic' effects of therapeutic relationships and relaxing environments on neuronal systems that are altered by psychosis, and will thereby provide further rationale for including the Soteria model among the key treatments of psychosis.

It is also quite likely that an increasing awareness of the toxicity of the atypical neuroleptics – along with the drug-induced deficit syndrome, obesity, raised cholesterol levels, diabetes and neurodegeneration with increased cell death (apoptosis; e.g. Bonelli et al., 2005; Liebermann et al., 2005) and mortality (Correll et al., 2006), especially when prescribed in combination with other drugs (Henderson et al., 2005; Joukamaa et al., 2006) – will promote the reconsideration of psychosocial treatments to their full potential. The aim would be to avoid drugs completely for at least 40 per cent of the patients, or alternatively to use the lowest possible dosage and thus contain the possible risks.

Neuroleptics should be seen as elements of a historical compromise and not as a curative solution. An open ethical debate concerning their use must be held with service users and their organizations. Further Soteria services combined with community-based teams that use the need-adapted treatment model would enable multicentre studies with large sample sizes.

Such a treatment model as that of Soteria can become a rallying point for service users and relatives, especially in Europe. Professionals still seem thwarted by economic dependency on the pharmaceutical industry that has invaded the entire medical system in an insidious fashion (Angell, 2004), together with one-sided beliefs determined by biological reductionism. Currently there is a notable effort, especially in England (House of Commons Health Committee, 2005), to contain the influence of the pharmaceutical industry on the medical system. There is a growing international movement to promote and disseminate Soteria and similar alternative treatment programmes (i.e. http://www.soterianetwork.org/; www.intar.org). I am optimistic and trust in the frequently dialectical movements in history.

References

Aderhold, V., Alanen, Y., Hess, G. and Hohn, P. (eds) (2003). *Psychotherapie der Psychosen Integrative Behandlungsansätze aus Skandinavien*. Gießen: Psychosozial.

Alanen, Y.O. (1997). *Schizophrenia – Its Origins and Need-Adapted Treatment*. London: Karnac.

Alanen, Y.O., Lehtinen, V., Lehtinen, K. *et al.* (2000). The Finnish model for early treatment of schizophrenia and related psychoses. In B. Martindale, A. Bateman, M. Crowe and F. Margison (eds) *Psychosis: Psychological Approaches and their Effectiveness*. London: Gaskell, pp. 235–265.

Angell, M. (2004). *The Truth about the Drug Companies – How They Deceive Us and What To Do About It*. New York: Random House.

Bola, J.R. and Mosher, L.R. (2003). Treatment of acute psychosis without neuroleptics: two-year outcomes from Soteria project. *Journal of Nervous Mental Disease* 191: 219–229.

Bola, J.R., Mosher, L.R. and Cohen, D. (2005). Treatment of newly diagnosed psychosis without antipsychotic drugs: The Soteria project. In S. Kirk (ed.) *Mental Disorders in the Social Environment: Critical Perspectives from Social Work*. New York: Columbia University Press, pp. 368–384.

Bola, J.R., Lehtinen, K., Aaltonen, J. *et al.* (2006). Predicting medication-free treatment response in acute psychosis: cross-validation from the Finnish need-adapted project. *Journal of Nervous Mental Disease* 194: 732–739.

Bonelli, R.M., Hofmann, P., Aschoff, A., Niederwieser, G., Heuberger, C., Jirikowski, G. *et al.* (2005). The influence of psychotropic drugs on cerebral cell death: female neurovulnerability to antipsychotics. *International Clinical Psychopharmacology* 20: 145–149.

Boss, M. (1963). *Psychoanalysis and Daseinsanalysis*. New York: Basic Books.

Ciompi, L. (1980). Ist die chronische Schizophrenie ein Artefakt? Argumente und Gegenargumente. *Fortschritte der Neurologie und Psychiatrie* 48: 237–248.

Ciompi, L. (1982). *Affektlogik*. Stuttgart: Klett-Cotta. [English edn *The Psyche and Schizophrenia. The Bond between Affect and Logic*. Cambridge, MA: Harvard University Press, 1988.]

Ciompi, L. (1988). Learning from outcome studies. Towards a comprehensive biological-psychological understanding of schizophrenia. *Schizophrenia Research* 1: 373–384.

Ciompi, L. (1989). The dynamics of complex biological-psychosocial systems. Four fundamental psycho-biological mediators in the long-term evolution of schizophrenia. *British Journal of Psychiatry* 155: 15–21.

Ciompi, L. (1997). *Die emotionalen Grundlagen des Denkens. Entwurf einer fraktalen Affektlogik*. Göttingen: Vandenhoek & Ruprecht.

Ciompi, L. and Müller, C. (1976). *Lebensweg und Alter der Schizophrenen. Eine katamnestische Langzeitstudie bis ins Senium*. Heidelberg: Springer.

Ciompi, L., Dauwalder, H.-P., Maier, C. and Aebi, E. (1991). Das Pilotprojekt 'Soteria Bern' zur Behandlung akut Schizophrener. I. Konzeptuelle Grundlagen, praktische Realisierung, klinische Erfahrungen. *Nervenarzt* 62: 428–435.

Ciompi, L., Ambühl, H. and Dünki, R. (1992a). Schizophrenie und Chaostheorie. *System Familie* 5: 133–147.

Ciompi, L., Dauwalder, H.-P., Maier, C. *et al.* (1992b). The pilot project 'Soteria Berne': clinical experiences and results. *British Journal of Psychiatry* 161 (Suppl. 18): 145–153.

Ciompi, L., Kupper, Z., Aebi, E. *et al.* (1993). Das Pilot-Projekt 'Soteria Bern' zur Behandlung akut Schizophrener. II. Ergebnisse einer vergleichenden prospektiven Verlaufsstudie über 2 Jahre. *Nervenarzt* 64: 440–450.

Ciompi, L., Hoffmann, H. and Broccard, M. (eds) (2001). *Wie Wirkt Soteria?* Bern: Huber.

Ciompi, L. and Hoffmann, H. (2004). Soteria Berne. An innovative milieu therapeutic approach to acute schizophrenia based on the concept of affect-logic. *World Psychiatry* 3: 140–146.

Correll, C.U., Frederickson, A.M., Kane, J.M. and Mann, P. (2006). Metabolic syndrome and the risk of coronary heart disease in 367 patients treated with second-generation antipsychotic drugs. *Journal of Clinical Psychiatry* 67: 575–583.

Cullberg, J., Levander, S., Holmquist, R. *et al.* (2002). One-year outcome in first episode psychosis patients in the Swedish Parachute project. *Acta Psychiatrica Scandinavica* 106, 4: 276–285.

Cullberg, J., Mattsson, M., Levander, S. *et al.* (2006). Treatment costs and clinical outcome for first episode schizophrenia patients: a 3-year follow-up of the Swedish 'Parachute Project' and two comparison groups. *Acta Psychiatrica Scandinavica* 114: 274–281.

Fairweather, G.W., Sanders, D., Cressler, D. and Maynard, H. (1969). *Community Life for the Mentally Ill: An Alternative to Institutional Care*. Chicago: Aldine.

Goffman, E. (1961). *Asylums*. Garden City, NY: Anchor.

Henderson, D.C., Nguyen, D.D., Copeland, P.M. *et al.* (2005). Clozapine: diabetes mellitus, hyperlipidemia and cardiovascular risks and mortality: results of a 10-year naturalistic study. *Journal of Clinical Psychiatry* 66: 1116–1121.

Hirschfeld, R.M., Matthews, S.M., Mosher, L.R. and Menn, A.Z. (1977). Being with madness: personality characteristics of three treatment staffs. *Hospital and Community Psychiatry* 28: 267–273.

House of Commons Health Commitee (2005). *The Influence of the Pharmaceutical Industry*. http://www.parliament.the-stationary-office.co.uk/pa/cm200405/cm select/cmhealth/42/42.pdf.

Joukamaa, M., Heliovaara, M., Knekt, P. *et al.* (2006). Schizophrenia, neuroleptic medication and mortality. *British Journal of Psychiatry* 188: 122–127.

Kroll, B. (1998). *Mit Soteria auf Reformkurs*. Gütersloh: Jokob van Hoddis.

Laing, R.D. (1960). *The Divided Self*. Chicago: Quadrangle.

Laing, R.D. (1967). *The Politics of Experience*. New York: Ballantine.

Lehtinen, V., Aaltonen, J., Koffert, T. *et al.* (2000). Two-year outcome in first episode psychosis treated according to an integrated model. Is immediate neuroleptisation always needed? *European Psychiatry* 15: 312–320.

Lieberman, J.A., Tollefson, G.D., Charles, C. *et al.* (2005). Antipsychotic drug effects on brain morphology in first-episode psychosis. *Archives of General Psychiatry* 62: 361–370.

Matthews, S.M., Roper, M.T., Mosher, L.R. and Menn, A.Z. (1979). A non-neuroleptic treatment for schizophrenia: analysis of the two-year postdischarge risk of relapse. *Schizophrenia Bulletin* 5: 322–333.

Mosher, L.R. (1972). A research design for evaluating psychosocial treatment for schizophrenia. *Hospital and Community Psychiatry* 23: 17–22.

Mosher, L.R. (1992). The social environmental treatment of psychosis: critical ingredients. In A. Webart and J. Culberg (eds) *Psychotherapy of Schizophrenia: Facilitating and Obstructive Factors*. Oslo: Scandinavian University Press, pp. 254–260.

Mosher, L.R. and Menn, A.Z. (1978). Community residential treatment for schizophrenia: two-year follow-up. *Hospital and Community Psychiatry* 29: 715–723.

Mosher, L.R., Hendrix, V. *et al.* (1994). *Dabeisein: Das Manual zur Praxis in der Soteria*. Bonn: Psychiatrie-Verlag.

Mosher, L.R., Reifman, A. and Menn, A.Z. (1973). Characteristics of non-professionals serving as primary therapists for acute schizophrenics. *Hospital and Community Psychiatry* 24: 391–396.

Mosher, L.R., Vallone, R. and Menn, A. (1995). The treatment of acute psychosis without neuroleptics: six-week psychopathology outcome data from the Soteria project. *International Journal of Social Psychiatry* 41: 157–173.

Mosher, L.R., Hendrix, V. with Fort, D.C. (2004). *Soteria – Through Madness to Deliverance*. Philadelphia, PA: Xlibris.

Scheff, T. (1966). *Being Mentally Ill*. Chicago: Aldine.

Seikkula, J., Alakare, B., Aaltonen, J. *et al.* (2003). Open dialogue approach: treatment principles and preliminary results of a two-year follow-up on first episode schizophrenia. *Ethical and Human Sciences and Services* 5: 163–182.

Seikkula, J., Aaltonen, J., Alakare, B. and Haarakangas, K. (2006). Five-year experience of first episode non-affective psychosis in open-dialogue approach: treatment principles, follow-up outcomes and two case studies. *Psychotherapy Research* 16: 214–228.

Sullivan, H.S. (1953). *The Interpersonal Theory of Psychiatry*. New York: Norton.

Sullivan, H.S. (1962). *Schizophrenia as a Human Process*. New York: Norton.

Chapter 24

Deinstitutionalization and neuroleptics

The myth and reality

Robert Whitaker

Most histories of psychiatry attribute the emptying of mental hospitals in the United States and other western countries to the development of chlorpromazine and other antipsychotic drugs in the 1950s, and view this as a watershed moment in society's care of the mentally ill. In his (1997) book *A History of Psychiatry*, Edward Shorter neatly summarized this belief: 'Chlorpromazine initiated a revolution in psychiatry, comparable to the introduction of penicillin in general medicine.' With this drug, he said, schizophrenia patients 'could lead relatively normal lives and not be confined to institutions' (Shorter, 1997). This is a comforting story of progress, and it enables the United States and other western countries to believe that, however flawed modern care may be, it is light years better than what came before.

Yet there are many reasons to question this story of progress, at least in the United States. Since the arrival of chlorpromazine, the percentage of Americans disabled by mental illness has jumped fivefold (Whitaker, 2005). There are hundreds of thousands of mentally ill people who are homeless or locked away in prisons in the US. And even those who remain fairly stable on antipsychotic drugs are regularly beset by a host of physical problems, which may include tardive dyskinesia, obesity, diabetes, blood disorders, impotence, and cardiovascular problems. There is also evidence that the drugs may lead to early death.

So have we made progress in treating the seriously mentally ill or not? It is, in fact, fairly easy to put together an alternative history of psychiatry, one that doesn't tell a story of progress at all. One can make the case that the most progressive form of care we've ever had, at least in the United States, both in terms of its humanity and its capacity for helping people recover, occurred in the early 1800s, when Quakers championed the idea of moral treatment, where the mad could be cared for in small retreats.

Moral treatment

Although we may think of Philippe Pinel as the father of modern psychiatry, it was the Quakers in York, England who provided the model of care that was adopted in the United States in the early 1800s. The York Retreat (see Chapter 2) was a simple place, with gardens and walks where the ill could get their fill of fresh air. The Quakers fed their patients four times daily, and held tea parties, at which the patients were encouraged to dress up. During the day, patients were kept busy with a variety of tasks – sewing, gardening, and other domestic activities – and given opportunities to read, write and play games like chess. This method of care, the York Quakers reported in 1813, produced good results. During the Retreat's first 15 years, 70 per cent of the patients who had been ill for less than 12 months recovered, meaning that they had been discharged and never returned to the Retreat. Even 25 per cent of the patients who had been chronically ill before coming to the Retreat, viewed as incurable, recovered (Tuke 1813/1996).

Philadelphia Quakers opened the first moral treatment asylum in the United States in 1817, and soon such facilities were established in Boston, Hartford, New York and other cities. The first public asylum opened in Worcester, MA in 1833, and by 1841, there were 16 private and public asylums in the United States that promised to provide moral treatment to the insane.

The blueprint for a moral treatment asylum was fairly sharply defined. The facility was to be kept small, providing care to no more than 250 patients. It was to be located in the country, the grounds graced by flowerbeds and gardens, where the mentally ill could take their fill of fresh air and find solace in tending to plants. The building itself was supposed to be architecturally pleasing, as the insane were said to be particularly sensitive to aesthetic influences. The asylum was to be governed by a superintendent who was 'reasonable, humane . . . possessing stability and dignity of character, mild and gentle . . . compassionate' (Scull, 1989). And finally, the patients were to be kept busy with a variety of tasks – gardening, reading, playing games, and educational pursuits – that could divert their minds from their obsessive and mad thoughts.

Historians who have gone back and examined the archival records of the early moral treatment asylums have concluded that this form of care did help many to heal. In the first decades of moral treatment, 35 to 80 per cent of all admitted patients were discharged within a year, and the majority of those discharged were viewed as having been cured (Dain, 1964; Grob 1973, 1983; Scull, 1989). At Pennsylvania Hospital, presided over by Thomas Kirkbride for over 40 years, 45 per cent of 8546 'insane' patients during his tenure were discharged as cured, and another 25 per cent discharged as improved (Morton, 1895). Meanwhile, a long-term follow-up study of 984 patients discharged from Worcester State Lunatic Asylum from 1833 to 1846, which was conducted in the 1880s, found that 58 per cent had remained well throughout their lives. Seven per cent had relapsed at least once but had subsequently returned to the community. Only 35 per cent had become chronically ill or had died while still mentally ill (Bockoven, 1972).

We have no way of knowing, of course, what diagnoses these patients would be given today. Yet certainly they were quite sick upon admittance. Worcester asylum preferentially admitted 'lunatics furiously mad, and dangerous to the peace and safety of the community' (Torrey, 2001). Moreover, in 1850, only one in every 5000 people in the United States was in an asylum, and so clearly the patients were, in terms of their disturbed behavior, at the far end of the spectrum (Torrey, 2001).

The downfall of asylum care: 1850–1950

The downfall of moral treatment was set in motion in the 1840s, when the reformer Dorothea Dix, a Massachusetts woman who had suffered her own breakdown years earlier and recovered after a year of rest, lobbied state governments to build moral treatment asylums so that this humane form of care could be made available to all. In 1840, there were only 2561 patients in the United States being cared for in hospitals and asylums, and thus many 'mad' people were being kept in miserable jails and poorhouses (Deutsch, 1948). In response to Dix's emotional appeals, states generously responded with a wave of asylum building, and by 1880 there were 139 private and public mental hospitals in the United States. However, as this wave of asylum building occurred, states began dumping people with all kinds of illnesses into the institutions. The small 'retreats' turned into crowded and poorly funded hospitals that housed 500 or more patients, and those with organic illnesses – old age senility, cerebral arteriosclerosis, brain tumors, and dementia associated with end-stage syphilis – naturally had no hope of recovery. The institutions filled up with chronic patients. Moral therapy came to be seen as a failed form of care.

The 'science' that most directly shaped society's care of the mentally ill over the next half century was eugenics (a term coined in 1862 by an Englishman, Sir Francis Galton). Eugenicists argued that those with 'good genes' should be encouraged to breed, while those with bad genes should be prevented from having children, and the mentally ill, of course, were at the head of this 'unfit' category.

In 1896, Connecticut approved a law prohibiting the 'insane' from marrying, and other states quickly followed suit. In 1907, Indiana became the first state to pass a compulsory sterilization law. By 1945, 21,311 people in American state mental hospitals had been operated on in this way (Robitscher, 1973). At the same time, states began segregating the insane for ever longer periods of time. For example, only 42 per cent of first episode patients admitted to New York state hospitals between 1909 and 1911 were discharged over the next 17 years (Grob, 1983). With so few patients being discharged, the number of hospitalized mentally sharply ill rose from 151,507 in 1903 to 272,527 in 1929 (Myerson, 1936), leading the

Journal of Heredity to happily editorialize that 'segregation of the insane is fairly complete' (Popenoe, 1923).

Neuroleptics and deinstitutionalization

With the end of World War II and the full revelation of the horrors of Nazi Germany, eugenics became a shamed science. No longer was it acceptable to argue that the insane needed to be segregated because of their bad 'germ plasm' and at that moment states began talking about pursuing alternatives to mental hospitals. The number of hospitalized mentally ill was creeping past 500,000, and their collective expenditures for these patients had reached $500 million, an expense they were eager to reduce. In the early 1950s, the Council of State Governments articulated a vision of reform. 'There are many persons in state hospitals who are not now in need of continuing psychiatric hospital care', the council announced. 'Out-patient clinics should be extended and other community resources developed to care for persons in need of help, but not of hospitalization' (Council of State Governments, 1950; Rusk, 1954).

Over the next few years, the states began developing community care initiatives, funnelling at least a few mentally ill into nursing homes and halfway houses. In 1955, the patient census at state mental hospitals hit an all-time high of 558,600, and then, over the next six years, it declined slightly to 528,000. Since the decline had coincided with the introduction of neuroleptics – the use of thorazine (chlorpromazine) began in the USA in 1954 – two researchers at the New York State Department of Mental Hygiene, Henry Brill and Robert Patton, concluded that this modest decline was due to the new neuroleptics. They did not refer to the change in policy announced by the states prior to this (Brill and Patton, 1962).

However, California did compare discharge rates for schizophrenia patients treated with and without neuroleptics, and their results belied the conclusion drawn by Brill and Patton. In a study of 1413 first episode male schizophrenics admitted to California hospitals in 1956 and 1957, researchers found that 'drug-treated patients tend to have longer periods of hospitalization; furthermore, the hospitals wherein a higher percentage of first admission schizophrenia patients are treated with these drugs tend to have somewhat higher retention rates for this group as a whole' (Epstein *et al.*, 1962).

The true period of deinstitutionalization in the United States was from 1963 to the late 1970s, the exodus driven by a change in social and fiscal policies. In 1963, the federal government began picking up some of the costs of care for the mentally ill not in state institutions, and two years later Medicare and Medicaid legislation increased federal funding for care of mental patients in non-hospital settings. Naturally, states responded by discharging their hospitalized patients to nursing homes and shelters. In

1972, an amendment to the Social Security Act authorized federal disability payments to the mentally ill, which accelerated the transfer of hospitalized patients into private facilities. As a result of these changes in fiscal policies, the number of patients in state mental hospitals dropped from 504,600 in 1963 to 153,544 in 1978 (Scull, 1984).

Neuroleptics and chronic illness

The first well-designed study of the efficacy of neuroleptics was conducted by the National Institute of Mental Health (NIMH) in 1961. It was a nine-hospital trial of 344 schizophrenia patients, and at the end of six weeks, 75 per cent of the drug-treated patients were 'much improved' or 'very much improved' compared to 23 per cent of the placebo patients. The NIMH research concluded that neuroleptics should no longer be considered mere 'tranquilizers' but 'antischizophrenic' agents, suggesting that science had developed something akin to a magic bullet for the disease (Cole *et al.*, 1964). This finding nicely complemented the story of medical progress advanced by Brill and Patton (1962), and it also helped prompt John F. Kennedy to announce a national plan for replacing state mental hospitals with a matrix of community care. The new drugs, he said, made 'it possible for most of the mentally ill to be successfully and quickly treated in their own communities and returned to a useful place in society' (*New York Times*, 6 February 1963).

That six-week study is still cited today as proving the efficacy of neuroleptics for curbing acute episodes of schizophrenia. However, the follow-up study done by the NIMH investigators told a very different story. They found, much to their surprise, that at the end of one year 'patients who received placebo treatment were less likely to be rehospitalized than those who received any of the three active phenothiazines' (Schooler *et al.*, 1967). This result raised an unsettling possibility: While the drugs were effective over the short term, perhaps they made people more biologically vulnerable to psychosis over the long run, and thus the higher rehospitalization rates at the end of one year?

Other reports soon deepened this suspicion. Drug-treated patients were cycling in and out of hospitals, and researchers reported that it appeared that 'relapse during drug administration is greater in severity than when no drugs are given' (Gardos and Cole, 1977). Bockoven and Solomon (1975) reported that 45 per cent of patients treated at Boston Psychopathic Hospital in 1947 with a progressive model of care did not relapse in the five years following discharge, and that 76 per cent were successfully living in the community at the end of that follow-up period. In contrast, only 31 per cent of patients treated in 1967 with neuroleptics at a community health center remained relapse-free over the next five years, and as a group they were much more 'socially dependent' on welfare and needing other forms of support than those in the 1947 cohort.

With debate over neuroleptics rising, the NIMH funded three studies in the 1970s that looked at whether early episode schizophrenia patients could be successfully treated without drugs. In each instance, the non-medicated patients fared better. In 1977, Carpenter *et al.* reported that only 35 per cent of the non-medicated patients (treated following an intensive psychotherapeutic approach) relapsed within a year after discharge, compared to 45 per cent of those treated with neuroleptics. The non-medicated patients also suffered less from depression, blunted emotions, and retarded movements (Carpenter *et al.*, 1977). Rappaport *et al.* (1978) reported that in a trial of 80 young male schizophrenic patients admitted to a state hospital only 27 per cent of those treated without neuroleptics relapsed in the three years following discharge, compared to 62 per cent of the medicated group. The final study came from Loren Mosher, then head of schizophrenia research at NIMH (see Chapter 23; Bola and Mosher, 2003). Together, the results of the studies by Mosher, Rappaport and Carpenter pointed to an unnerving conclusion: exposure to neuroleptics increased the long-term incidence of relapse. Carpenter's group defined the conundrum:

> There is no question that, once patients are placed on medication, they are less vulnerable to relapse if maintained on neuroleptics. But what if these patients had never been treated with drugs to begin with? . . . We raise the possibility that antipsychotic medication may make some schizophrenic patients more vulnerable to future relapse than would be the case in the natural course of the illness.
>
> (Carpenter *et al.*, 1977: 14)

In the late 1970s, two physicians at McGill University in Montreal, Guy Chouinard and Barry Jones, offered a biological explanation for why this was so. The brain responds to neuroleptics – which block 70 per cent to 90 per cent of all D2 dopamine receptors in the brain – as though they are a pathological insult. To compensate, dopaminergic brain cells increase the density of their D2 receptors by 30 per cent or more. The brain is now 'supersensitive' to dopamine, and this neurotransmitter is thought to be a mediator of psychosis. The person has become more biologically vulnerable to psychosis, and is at particularly high risk of severe relapse should he or she abruptly quit taking the drugs (Chouinard *et al.*, 1978; Chouinard and Jones, 1980).

Thus, by 1979, the research picture was pretty complete. Neuroleptics were known to cause a dizzying array of physical and emotional side effects, and even on the target symptom of psychosis, drug-treated patients fared worse than placebo patients over the long term. Two years earlier, Jonathan Cole, one of the pioneering figures in psychopharmacology, who

had led the initial NIMH trial, published, with G. Gardos, a paper pro-
vocatively titled 'Maintenance Antipsychotic Therapy: Is the Cure Worse
than the Disease?'. They concluded that 'an attempt should be made to
determine the feasibility of drug discontinuance in every patient' (Gardos
and Cole, 1977).

Other confirming evidence

All of that evidence was in place 25 years ago, and there have been a
number of studies since that confirm that the standard of care in the United
States – which involves telling all schizophrenia patients that they have an
incurable brain disease and must be on antipsychotic drugs for the rest of
their lives – has been an abysmal failure, and does not arise from 'evidence-
based medicine'.

Perhaps the most damning findings came from the World Health
Organization (WHO), which in the 1970s and 1980s conducted two studies
comparing schizophrenia outcomes in 'developed' and 'undeveloped' countries. In the first study, initiated in 1969, the WHO investigators found that
patients in three poor countries – India, Nigeria, and Colombia – were
doing dramatically better at two-year and five-year follow-ups than patients
in the US and four other developed countries. At five years, about 64 per
cent of the patients in the poor countries were asymptomatic and functioning well. In contrast only 18 per cent of patients in the rich countries were
in this best outcomes category. The difference in outcomes was such that
the WHO researchers concluded that living in a developed nation was a
'strong predictor' that a schizophrenic patient would never fully recover
(Leff et al., 1992).

These findings stunned western psychiatrists, and so the World Health
Organization conducted a second study to see if the findings would hold up.
This time it compared two-year outcomes in ten countries, and it focused
on first episode schizophrenics, all diagnosed by western criteria. The
results were the same. In the poor countries, 63 per cent of schizophrenics
had good outcomes. Only slightly more than one-third became chronically
ill. In the rich countries, the ratio of good-to-bad outcomes was almost
precisely the reverse. Only 37 per cent had good outcomes and the
remaining patients did not fare so well (Jablensky et al., 1992).

The WHO investigators did not identify a cause for the stark disparity in
outcomes. However, they did note that there was a difference in the medical
care that was provided. Doctors in the poor countries generally did not
keep their patients on neuroleptics, while doctors in the rich countries did.
In the poor countries, only 16 per cent of the patients were maintained on
the drugs, compared to 61 per cent of the patients in the rich countries.
Once again, the evidence pointed to the same conclusion: there is a

correlation between the use of neuroleptics on a continual basis and poor long-term outcomes.

Other studies of this sort abound. In 1994, Courtenay Harding reported that one-third of all schizophrenics who had been on a back ward in a Vermont hospital in the 1950s had eventually recovered as a result of a rehabilitation program, and that this recovered group all shared one characteristic: they had all stopped taking neuroleptics (McGuire, 2000). She concluded that it was a myth that patients must be on medication all their lives, and that 'in reality it may be a small percentage who need medication indefinitely' (Harding and Zahniser, 1994). That same year, Harvard Medical School investigators reported that long-term outcomes for schizophrenia patients had declined over the past 20 years, and were now no better than they had been in 1900, when water therapies were the treatment of the day (Hegarty et al., 1994). The Harvard researchers also reported that in studies where neuroleptics were gradually withdrawn from patients, only a little more than one-third relapsed within six months, and that those who reached this six-month point without becoming sick again had a good chance of remaining well indefinitely. 'The later risk of relapsing was remarkably limited,' they wrote (Viguera et al., 1997). Finally, in a study of schizophrenia patients in the Chicago area, researchers at the University of Illinois Medical School reported in 2007 that 40 per cent of those who refused to take antipsychotic medications were recovered at five-year and 15-year follow-up exams, versus 5 per cent of the medicated patients (Harrow and Jobe, 2007).

The failure of the psychopharmacology revolution, with its emphasis on 'drugs for life', can also be seen more broadly in the ever-growing number of disabled mentally ill in the United States. Up until the 1950s, the number of hospitalized mentally ill provided a rough estimate of this group, and that year there were 559,000 people in state hospitals, or 3.38 people per 1000 population. Today, the disabled mentally ill typically receive either a disability payment from the Social Security Disability Insurance (SSDI) program or the Supplemental Security Income (SSI) program, and many live in residential shelters or other subsidized living arrangements. Thus the hospitalized patient of 50 years ago receives either an SSDI or SSI payment, and in 2003 there were 5.726 million people in the United States who received one of these payments (or both). That is a disability rate of 19.69 people per 1000 population, which is more than five times what it was in 1955.

A model for reform

There are, of course, people with schizophrenia who benefit from neuroleptics, and thus the challenge is to extract from the outcomes research a different paradigm for their use. And what the research literature suggests is this. First, early episode patients should initially be treated without drugs, as this would allow many – 50 per cent or more based on the studies done by Carpenter, Rappaport, and Mosher in the 1970s – to recover from psychosis without undergoing the drug-induced changes that make a person more vulnerable to psychosis over the long term. Second, every person stabilized on the drugs should be given a chance to gradually withdraw from them, as many – nearly two-thirds according to the Harvard researchers – would not relapse and have a good chance of remaining well indefinitely. In other words, the evidence calls for selective, cautious use of the drugs, and not surprisingly, Finnish and Swedish investigators who have followed this approach in a psychotherapeutically oriented treatment context have reported good results (Cullberg, 1999; Cullberg *et al.*, 2002; Lehtinen *et al.*, 2000; Lehtinen, 2001).

Society must also provide a safe haven for psychotic people, and this is where moral treatment could serve as a guide. Small retreats modeled after the moral treatment asylums of the early nineteenth century could be built, with neuroleptics used in the selective, cautious manner described above. Loren Mosher's Soteria experiment showed that this approach could work today. The patients, even though most were unmedicated, slept in unlocked bedrooms, and they were expected to help cook and do other chores around the house. The staff were expected to treat them with dignity and respect, and to 'be with them' as they struggled with their minds. Mosher's good results led Luc Ciompi in Switzerland to set up a Soteria home (see Chapter 23), and in 1992 Ciompi concluded that first episode patients treated with no or very low doses of medication 'demonstrated significantly better results' than patients treated conventionally (Ciompi *et al.*, 1992). This of course was the signature of good science. Mosher's results were replicated by a second investigator.

However, none of this is going to happen in the United States. The accepted wisdom is that drugs enabled deinstitutionalization, and that this kicked off a modern era of 'scientific' care that has greatly improved the lives of the severely mentally ill. While this story is not supported by psychiatry's own research, it is a comforting myth for modern society, and one that brings great profits to drug companies and to a psychiatric establishment that sells it to the public. Myths do exact a toll, however, and the research literature shows quite clearly who is paying the price.

References

Bockoven, J. (1972). *Moral Treatment in Community Mental Health*. Woodstock, CT: Spring, pp. 14–15, 55–67.

Bockoven, J. and Solomon, H. (1975). Comparison of two five-year follow-up studies: 1947–1952 and 1967–1972. *American Journal of Psychiatry* 132: 796–801.

Bola, J. and Mosher, L. (2003). Treatment of acute psychosis without neuroleptics:

two-year outcomes from the Soteria project. *Journal of Nervous Mental Disorders* 191: 219–229.

Brill, H. and Patton, R. (1962). Clinical-statistical analysis of population changes in New York State mental hospitals since introduction of psychotropic drugs. *American Journal of Psychiatry* 119: 20–35.

Carpenter, W., McGlashan, T. and Strauss, J. (1977). The treatment of acute schizophrenia without drugs: an investigation of some current assumptions. *American Journal of Psychiatry* 134: 14–20.

Chouinard, G. and Jones, B. (1980). Neuroleptic-induced supersensitivity psychosis: clinical and pharmacological characteristics. *American Journal of Psychiatry* 137: 16–20.

Chouinard, G., Jones, B. and Annable, L. (1978). Neuroleptic-induced super-sensitivity psychosis. *American Journal of Psychiatry* 135: 1409–1410.

Ciompi, L., Dauwalder, H., Maier, C., Aebi, E., Trutsch, K., Kupper, Z. *et al.* (1992). The pilot project Soteria Berne. *British Journal of Psychiatry* 161 (Suppl. 18): 145–153.

Cole, J., Klerman, G. and Goldberg, S. (1964). The National Institute of Mental Health Psychopharmacology Service Center Collaborative Study Group. Phenothiazine treatment in acute schizophrenia. *Archives of General Psychiatry* 10: 246–261.

Council of State Governments (1950). The mental health programs of the forty-eight states. *The Council*, p. 5.

Cullberg, J. (1999). Integrating psychosocial therapy and low dose medical treatment in a total material of first-episode psychotic patients compared to treatment as usual: a three-year followup. *Medical Archives* 53: 167–170.

Cullberg, J., Levander, S., Holmqvist, R., Mattsson, M. and Wieselgren, I.-M. (2002). One-year outcome in first-episode psychosis patients in the Swedish Parachute project. *Acta Psychiatrica Scandinavica* 106: 276–285.

Dain, N. (1964). *Concepts of Insanity in the United States, 1789–1865*. Piscataway, NJ: Rutgers University Press, pp. 120, 132.

Deutsch, A. (1948). *The Shame of the States*. New York: Harcourt Brace.

Epstein, L., Morgan, R. and Reynolds, L. (1962). An approach to the effect of ataraxic drugs on hospital release rates. *American Journal of Psychiatry* 119: 36–47.

Gardos, G. and Cole, J. (1977). Maintenance antipsychotic therapy: is the cure worse than the disease? *American Journal of Psychiatry* 133: 32–36.

Grob, G. (1973). *Mental Institutions in America*. New York: Free Press, p. 68.

Grob, G. (1983). *Mental Illness and American Society*. Princeton, NJ: Princeton University Press, pp. 193–196.

Harding, C. and Zahniser, J. (1994). Empirical correction of seven myths about schizophrenia with implications for treatment. *Acta Psychiatrica Scandinavica* 90 (Suppl. 384): 140–146.

Harrow, M. and Jobe, T. (2007). Factors involved in outcome and recovery in schizophrenia patients not on antipsychotic medications. *Journal of Nervous and Mental Disease* 195: 406–414.

Hegarty, J., Baldessarini, R., Tohen, M., Waternaux, C. and Oepen, G. (1994). One hundred years of schizophrenia: a meta-analysis of the outcome literature. *American Journal of Psychiatry* 151: 1409–1416.

Jablensky, A., Sartorius, N., Ernberg, G., Ansker, M., Korten, A., Cooper, J. *et al.* (1992). Schizophrenia: manifestations, incidence and course in different cultures. A World Health Organization ten-country study. *Psychological Medicine* 20: 1–95.

Leff, J., Sartorius, N., Korten, A. and Ernberg, G. (1992). The international pilot study of schizophrenia: five-year follow-up findings. *Psychological Medicine* 22: 131–145.

Lehtinen, K. (2001). Finnish need-adapted project: 5-year outcomes. Madrid: World Psychiatric Association International Congress.

Lehtinen, V., Aaltonen, J., Koffert, T., Räkköläinen, V. and Syvälahti, E. (2000). Two-year outcome in first-episode psychosis treated according to an integrated model. Is immediate neuroleptisation always needed? *European Journal of Psychiatry* 15: 312–320.

McGuire, P. (2000). New hope for people with schizophrenia. *APA Monitor* 31, 2.

Morton, T. (1895). *The History of the Pennsylvania Hospital.* Philadelphia, PA: Times Printing House, p. 243.

Myerson, A. (1936). *Eugenical Sterilization.* Basingstoke: Macmillan, p. 24.

New York Times (1963). President seeks funds to reduce mental illness. 6 February.

Popenoe, P. (1923). In the melting pot. *Journal of Heredity* 14: 223.

Rappaport, M., Hopkins, H., Hall, K., Belleza, T. and Silverman, J. (1978). Are there schizophrenics for whom drugs may be unnecessary or contraindicated? *International Pharmacopsychiatry* 13: 100–111.

Robitscher, J. (ed.) (1973). *Eugenic Sterilization: A Biomedical Intervention.* Springfield, IL: Charles C. Thomas, p. 123.

Rusk, H. (1954). States map a new attack to combat mental illness. *New York Times*, 21 February: 46.

Schooler, N., Goldberg, S., Boothe, H. and Cole, J. (1967). One year after discharge: community adjustment of schizophrenic patients. *American Journal of Psychiatry* 123: 986–995.

Scull, A. (1984). Decarceration: community treatment and the deviant, a radical view. Piscataway, NJ: Rutgers University Press.

Scull, A. (1989). *Social Order/Mental Disorder.* Berkeley: University of California Press, pp. 90, 102, 110.

Shorter, E. (1997). *A History of Psychiatry.* Chichester: Wiley, p. 255.

Torrey, E. (2001). *The Invisible Plague.* Piscataway, NJ: Rutgers University Press, pp. 208, 350.

Tuke, S. (1813/1916). Description of the Retreat. Process Press, 1996, reprint of 1813 edition, pp. 201–203.

Viguera, A., Baldessarini, R., Hegarty, J., Van Kammen, D. and Tohen, M. (1997). Clinical risk following abrupt and gradual withdrawal of maintenance neuroleptic treatment. *Archives of General Psychiatry* 54: 49–55.

Whitaker, R. (2005). Anatomy of an epidemic. *Ethical Human Psychology and Psychiatry* 7: 23–35.

Chapter 25

Further development of treatment approaches to schizophrenic psychoses

An integrated view

Yrjö O. Alanen, Manuel González de Chávez,
Ann-Louise S. Silver and Brian Martindale

We will sum up the message of this book with four points:

1   The dominant biological models of schizophrenic psychoses and the treatment approaches based on them have upheld one-sided and fatalistic views of this disorder that frequently provoke low levels of help, health care and professional dedication for psychotic patients and their families. Nevertheless there is an increasing development towards a more integrated understanding of the character and treatment of these disorders based on both neurobiological and psychodynamically oriented research.
2   Improved quality of treatment and social care for these persons has been proven to be possible and is now a necessary aim.
3   This book contains extensive reviews of psychological treatments that are effective with patients with schizophrenic psychoses illustrating their multidisciplinary character and utilizing a variety of approaches and perspectives.
4   This book intends to be a useful tool to increase the spread of integrated programmes and to inform the teaching and training of mental health professionals in psychotherapeutic interventions and treatment modalities for psychotic patients.

Preconditions for integrative development have increased

The contradictory and antagonistic views with regard to schizophrenic psychoses have been very detrimental to efforts in developing treatment. There is an obvious need for more integrated approaches, emphasizing the demand for comprehensive premises necessary for successful treatment settings.

The preconditions for a more integrated development of the treatment of schizophrenic psychoses have grown in comparison with earlier decades. The reasons for this are twofold. The therapeutic approaches that have gradually developed are both more diverse but at the same time more complementary to one another. Furthermore, during the last ten years, the progress of neurobiological research has approached the views previously developed by psychoanalytic and other psychotherapeutic investigators so as to make an integrative development more possible at the theoretical level. We will first refer to the latter.

Integrative development in the field of neurobiology

The biomedical study of schizophrenic disorders has not been able to find an unambiguous organic or genetic cause of schizophrenia. The focus has transferred to multifactorial hypotheses. The division of mental disorders into explanatory and understanding psychology presented by Jaspers almost one hundred years ago (see Chapter 1, pp. 3–4) has, with the development of brain studies, become a less categorical doctrine. Most neuroscientists are now emphasizing the holistic nature of all brain functions:

- superior significance of neural webs or circuits compared with individual centres
- the plasticity and modifiability of these functions
- perhaps most significantly, the brain's development and functioning is dependent on the individual's interaction with the human environment.

These views became familiar especially as a result of the five principles of the neurobiologist and psychiatrist Eric Kandel, a Nobel Laureate, presented in 'A New Intellectual Framework for Psychiatry' (Kandel, 1998), and its extension dealing with the relationship between brain studies and psychoanalysis (Kandel, 1999). Genes are important determinants of neuronal interconnections in the brain, Kandel states, but gene expression is crucially affected by developmental and social factors, especially human interaction. Learning modifies gene expression and neuronal networks. Due to the plasticity of central nervous system functions, psychotherapy and psychosocial support as well as medication may effect changes in the neuronal networks, and the interconnections between neurons. Biological and psychological phenomena reciprocally affect each other.

The interaction between genetic and psychological environmental factors in the development of schizophrenic disorders was clearly shown by the results of the large Finnish adoptive family study (Tienari *et al.*, 2003, 2004; Wahlberg *et al.*, 2004; Wynne *et al.*, 2006), briefly referred to in Chapter 1. Kandel's view concerning the dependence of gene expression on interaction with the human environment was thus now verified with regard to the aetiology of schizophrenic psychoses.

A more detailed review of the development of the integrated neurobiological and psychosocial research, also relevant to the study of schizophrenic psychoses is included in Chapter 16, by Koehler and Silver.

Looking toward the future, another set of exceptionally interesting observations will most probably be developed by the research on the brain's mirror neurons and their functioning, found by Rizzolatti and Gallese (Gallese *et al.*, 1996; Rizzolatti *et al.*, 1996). They are supposed to be significant for the early development of the human personality, especially the development of mutual empathy and identifications during interactions between the baby and his mother (or other caretaking persons). Further studies on mirror neuron functions may shed more light on our knowledge of the early interaction between individual genetic characteristics and the effects of early emotional interplay. Their potential relevance to the study of schizophrenia vulnerability is obvious (c.f. Gallese, 2006; Olds, 2006).

Many psychoanalysts and/or psychodynamically oriented researchers and clinicians have addressed the integration of biological and psychological approaches to schizophrenic disorders. Michael Robbins' (1993) and Johan Cullberg's (2006) books are excellent examples of this.

Integrative development of treatment approaches

The treatment of schizophrenic patients is a complex issue, which in the majority of cases can be best accomplished within the public health care system. This is due to the heterogeneous nature of schizophrenic psychoses, implying the availability of a comprehensive treatment context, as well as the need for cooperation with other psychosocial activities, such as early detection of disorders and rehabilitation.

Psychodynamic and cognitive approaches and their relation to each other

Two major orientations with starting points differing from each other can be discerned, the psychodynamic (psychoanalytically oriented) and the cognitive behavioural. They are both applied to individual, group and family-centred therapeutic work (in the latter often combined with systemic theoretical standpoints).

As pointed out in several chapters of our book, since Freud's pioneering work several generations of psychoanalysts have developed the psycho-analytic – or, with its more extended meaning, psychodynamic – under-standing and treatment methods so as to make them be suitable for psychotherapy with psychotic patients. The starting point is to study together with the patient the problems that contributed to his becoming ill and their connections to the deeper ground of his personality development. In the individual therapeutic process, the transference–countertransference relationship, established with an empathic listening on the part of the therapist, has crucial significance. In that way the therapist may help the patient to become able to renew a developmental process of his personality and human relationships. Concurrent with this development, the insight into the meaning of psychotic symptoms would increase. They would lose their importance and the danger of their recurrence be diminished.

Intensive psychoanalytically oriented individual therapeutic relationships require from the patient both a capacity for internal exploration and motivation for this (which may often only be clarified when an empathic therapeutic relationship has been established). The therapeutic process is usually lengthy and not suitable for all schizophrenic patients. This sets limits to its use in community psychiatric centres. However, this matter has also been exaggerated. Psychodynamically based knowledge is also successfully used in connection with less intensive psychotherapeutic relationships. And, as pointed out by Murray Jackson (Chapter 8), such knowledge is also of the utmost importance for the general atmosphere in a hospital community – as well as open care unit – treating schizophrenic patients.

The cognitive behavioural therapeutic methods (CBT; see Dudley et al., Chapter 19 and Kennard, Chapter 8) are based on learning theories. CBT is symptom and problem focused from the beginning, more directed to factors that maintain the patient's symptoms than those related to their psychological origins. The number of sessions is limited, between six and 20 sessions being common. The goal is to develop a better control of psychotic symptoms, especially encouraging the patient to look for alternative explanations for his hallucinations and delusions. With first episode patients, special attention is paid to the precipitating experiences preceding the onset of the psychosis, in order to teach the patient (and/or his family members) to manage the risk of relapse. Behavioural methods are also used to aid the rehabilitation of the longer term patients to cope better with their life environment.

Compared with psychodynamic therapy, the use of cognitive behavioural methods is easier to apply to a greater number of patients. The weakness of CBT therapies is their more superficial character, usually sliding over the deeper nature of the patients' problems. The restricted length may prevent long-term effects of the therapy (a danger sometimes alleviated by so-called booster sessions). Many behavioural therapists connect their work with a denial of the part that psychological factors play in the developmental history of the psychosis. Continued use of neuroleptic drug treatment is usually regarded as a necessary adjunct to behavioural therapies with psychotic patients.

However, there are also common features between psychodynamic and cognitive (if not those strictly behavioural) therapists, including the shared aim of helping the patients. Cognitive therapists also aim to understand the problems of their patients, and psychodynamic therapists give 'alternative explanations' to their patients with regard to their psychotic delusions in the form of interpretations and translations of the psychotic language to a more common level. In some European centres the term 'cognitive-analytic psychotherapy' has been established as this involves the use of cognitively based techniques in connection with a psychodynamically oriented psycho-therapy, or involvement of deeper psychological understanding in a cognitively oriented psychotherapy.

The evolution of cognitive therapies over the last ten years is interesting. This is well represented by the personal evolution of Paul Chadwick, one of its principal developers (Chadwick *et al.*, 1996; Chadwick, 2006). There appeared – with the help of important iconoclasts of schizophrenia such as Bentall (1990) or Boyle (1990) – a reorientation to the person who suffers from psychotic symptoms. The ABC analysis of delusion, voices and paranoia (Chadwick *et al.*, 1996) was developed through the *Person-Based Cognitive Therapy for Distressing Psychosis* (Chadwick, 2006) with greater emphasis on the therapeutic relationship (of the Rogerian type). This includes a mindful meditation to alleviate distress that arises from experi-ences and their meanings, a metacognitive perspective and insight into internal experiences, and working with a unifying self-concept and schemata as a process, as well as with the central goal of self-acceptance (Chadwick, 2006).

This may be a significant step towards easier dialogue and a possible future convergence with psychodynamic therapies that also consider the unconscious and the person as a whole, in their specific biographical dynamics and situation. Perhaps we can now take a more open attitude and exchange and reflect on our mutual conceptions of the psychotic disorders and therapeutic processes. Besides Chadwick's approach, such reflection may even help to get a perspective on the 'neo-phenomenology of the self' in schizophrenia (Zahavi, 2000; Cheung Chung *et al.*, 2006). We are in adjoining rooms. We only need to open the door.

Evidence-based evaluations and the field of psychotherapy

There are some factors in current psychiatric research whose influence has been detrimental especially to the development of psychodynamic psychotherapy. The DSM classification, as important as it is for research purposes, is apt to transfer the focus of the psychiatric teaching too much on to symptom-based phenomenology that often seems to undermine the interest in psychodynamic understanding of the patients. We may hope that the efforts to renew the international psychiatric classification on the grounds of 'Psychiatry for the person' (Mezzich, 2007; Mezzich and Salloum, 2007) will have a positive impact on this situation.

Another factor is evidence-based evaluation (EB) of therapeutic results, the importance of which is at present much emphasized even in psychiatry, with mixed opinions amongst psychotherapists. EB evaluations strictly mean those based on randomized controlled trials (RCTs), usually having quite rigid premises with regard to the definition of the therapeutic methods. The criteria for follow-up results are based on easily defined and measurable external facts or observations. It is easy to recognize that the use of external agents such as medications are better suited to these kind of evaluations than the appraisal of psychotherapeutic approaches. This is especially true of psychoanalytically oriented therapies. In them, the crucial goal is a gradual inner development of the patient's personality in which the individual character of the particular therapeutic relationship is always very significant (see e.g. Hinshelwood, 2002). It is easier to make an EB evaluation of the results of simple CBT approaches that are following clearly predefined techniques and criteria. To make an evaluation of a psycho-dynamically oriented therapist's work, a qualitative case-specific study focused on the patient's and therapist's experiences of the treatment relationship is necessary.

Concerning schizophrenic psychoses, this kind of evaluation is further complicated by several factors. The comprehensive and heterogeneous nature of this patient group is not well served by a restricted therapeutic intervention defined in advance. For the success of therapy, a more comprehensive treatment approach including – in one way or another – the patient's nearest human environment is often necessary, as well as modification of treatment plans at each stage. Such an approach cannot be studied by a rigid EB method – and is usually therefore left outside of the recommendations based on EB methods. In their book dealing with network-centred approaches, Seikkula and Arnkil (2005) succinctly state that recommendations based on EB evaluations which do not take notice of the complex and need-adapted nature of the psychotherapeutic work with psychotic patients 'are not recommendations for the practical therapeutic work but recommendations for an artificial reality brought about by the research setting'.

The difficulties due to the heterogeneous nature of the schizophrenia group of psychoses may also be exemplified by follow-up studies on psychodynamic individual therapy with randomized populations of schizophrenic patients. It is well known that most of such studies have yielded rather pessimistic results. However, if this kind of therapy suits some patients well, with good results, but is unsuitable for others – a great deal of them even lacking any motivation for this kind of therapeutic relationship – the good and bad results cancel each other out in a statistical analysis. Still, a mode of treatment cannot be considered ineffective if it only benefits some of the patients. Rather, we should investigate for which patients this treatment is indicated.

It should be added that it is still possible to evaluate results of comprehensive psychotherapeutic approaches as an entity – e.g. the need-adapted treatment whose content varies from case to case – in an evidence-based way, even if not in a rigid RCT setting. This can be made by comparing the outcome of patients in catchment areas in which this treatment model has been carried out with areas where other kind of models have been applied, or by following prognostic developments in chronologically successive cohorts in catchment areas in which the new model has been established (see the Finnish and Swedish projects described in Chapter 12).

Developing a comprehensive and integrated treatment of schizophrenic patients

During the last century, the psychiatric sector of public health care was widely regarded to be of secondary importance. Its needs for development have easily been ignored and economic savings made by restricting its activities. In the light of the great importance of mental health disorders, both with regard to the perspectives of well-being and economic factors, including the loss of working days, this has been a most disastrous policy. During the new century this situation should be rapidly changed – a matter further justified by the development of psychotherapeutic knowledge and activities.

In the chapters of this book, various examples of psychotherapeutic approaches to schizophrenic psychoses, established in countries with different social and cultural climates, have been described. In what follows, we will bring forward some matters that we find especially crucial for further development.

The psychotherapeutic attitude

It is very important to encounter our schizophrenic patients as our fellow human beings, listening to them and appreciating their personality and difficult position. The self-esteem of most of these patients is weak, and admission to treatment – especially hospital treatment – is a further blow, often leading, besides the psychotic break, to post-traumatic stress symptoms (Shaw *et al.*, 1997). As pointed out very emphatically by many psychosis psychotherapists – e.g. by Frieda Fromm-Reichmann in her classic book *Principles of Intensive Psychotherapy* (1950) – a respectful and sincere attitude towards the patient is the necessary foundation for the therapist's successful work as the builder of the bridge between the patient and reality. Openness is very important. It should be put into practice also by the patient's participation in all meetings dealing with the planning of his treatment. Involuntary admission should be avoided as far as possible and where this is regarded as necessary, it should be as short as possible and the reason for it should be clarified with the patient and access to the documents connected with this be secured for him.

A psychotherapeutic attitude, shared among the staff members and based on efforts to understand what has happened to the patient and how we could use this understanding as a basis for approaching and helping him, should be the starting point and continued characteristic of the treatment. In our opinion, a psychodynamically oriented study should be a necessary part of the first phase of treatment – even in cases in which another kind of treatment orientation may be the decision. In this way the emphasis for a deeper understanding of the patients' problems can be spread among the members of treating community and become a characteristic of its general climate.

The extension of the psychodynamic study to the patient's closest interpersonal environment – usually the family – is an important part of the early phase of the treatment, as we will see later while describing the so-called therapy meetings. Corresponding to this environment-centred approach, the more specific cultural background of the patient should also be taken into consideration while planning and carrying out the treatment. The significance of understanding the cultural background of the patient and his interpersonal environment has been described in a very illustrative way by Lyn Chua, Chan Hee Huh and Jim Geekie and his colleagues in Chapters 14 and 15 of our book, describing the development of treatment activities in cultural conditions somewhat different from the western countries. This is a matter not limited to specific areas but gaining more and more importance both in European countries and in the US, because of the growing cultural dispersion of the global population.

Prevention and early intervention

Many schizophrenic patients come late to treatment. In the Norwegian study preceding the TIPS project described by Larsen (Chapter 21), the mean duration of untreated psychosis (DUP) was 114 weeks and the median 26 weeks (Johannessen et al., 2000). The delay is often due to the patient's denial of his illness and/or the prejudice and feelings of shame present in the family. The time lag, however, is apt to impair the prognosis because psychotic symptoms as part of the patient's inner dynamics tend to become more fixed, and the attitudes of the family and other environment worse, thus consolidating the patient's role as a mentally ill person.

Preventive activities and efforts towards earlier interventions are therefore of major significance. Rightfully, their development has been increasingly in the limelight over the past few years (see e.g. Gleeson and McGorry, 2004). The excellent results of Falloon's (1992) pioneering project in Buckinghamshire, England attracted much attention, and similar results were achieved in the Finnish Western Lapland study (Chapter 12 and Chapter 17). Both of these projects were carried out in rather small rural catchment areas. However, the clinical results of Larsen's TIPS project in the catchment area around the town of Stavanger were impressive compared with its control sites. McGorry et al. (2002) have shown that impressive preventive work can also be done in a metropolis like Melbourne in Australia.

Projects dealing with early detection of psychoses have been described by Larsen (Chapter 21) and Kennard (Chapter 8). The preventive work should be detached from the stigma of 'looking out for schizophrenia', to lessen the danger of possible harmful consequences. According to an early work by McGorry *et al.* (1995), such prodromal features are 'extremely prevalent' among older adolescents and unlikely to be specific for subsequent schizophrenia. A highly careful and empathic attitude is necessary in the preventive psychiatric work. It would be a fateful error, for example, to order neuroleptic treatment for many a 'hypopsychotic' youngster instead of a psychologically oriented interview and support. Heinimaa and Larsen (2002) have published an overview of the conceptual and ethical aspects of early diagnosis and intervention.

In our book, early intervention centres with a many-sided human approach have been described especially in Chapters 14 (Lyn Chua) and 15 (Geekie *et al.*). We also refer to the family-centred approach developed in connection with the Finnish need-adapted treatment model (Alanen *et al.*, 2000; see Chapter 12). The initial conjoint meetings ('therapy meetings') of the patient, members of his family and the treating team had a surprisingly advantageous effect on the patient's outcome, even in the long term (Lehtinen, 1993). Listening to the patient at the same level as other participants is apt to diminish the tendency to label him as hopelessly ill and the consequent psychological isolation, the 'closure' as aptly described by Scott and Ashworth (1967). At the same time, it is possible to support the family members in their often very stressful situation. Psychotic persons are far more dependent on their families and their outcome is much more influenced by family attitudes than that of less severely disturbed personalities (as even indicated by the EE studies; Leff *et al.*, 1985). In the initial phase, most of the families are very motivated to attend these meetings, which are usually continued during the next days and weeks, sometimes in connection with home visits.

Treatment facilities

Towards the end of the twentieth century, a typical feature of the psychiatric care in western countries was a very marked reduction in the number of hospital beds. This was partly based on the decrease of patients with serious psychotic symptoms, brought about by the development of the combination of psychosocial and drug treatment, partly on economic premises and sometimes indifference to the fate of chronically psychotic patients. In some countries (see Chapter 11, on Italy) this gave a welcome stimulus for the development of outpatient treatment, including the establishment of diverse facilities further supporting the patients' well-being and living circumstances. However, especially in large cities it sometimes led to the abandonment of many psychotic patients to their own devices.

Development of comprehensive outpatient care is of prime importance for future treatment of schizophrenic patients. The outpatient centres, preferably decentralized according to a sectorized model, should be equipped with appropriate staff from different disciplines with the quantitative and qualitative resources able to provide expansive and diversified therapeutic work. Close cooperation with hospitals is essential and most likely if the outpatient centres and the hospitals are parts of the same decentralized organization. This may increase the coherence of activities and give better possibilities to avoid unnecessary breaks and changes of psychotherapeutic relationships. Besides individual therapy, group therapy and various kinds of group activities should be developed. Equally important is the need for family- and environment-centred therapeutic activities, with an increase of home visits, most likely to occur in a decentralized open care network.

However, for many first admitted young schizophrenic patients a sufficiently long inpatient period is a necessary precondition for the establishment of a lasting therapeutic relationship. This can best be established in a ward characterized by an unhurried atmosphere, open mutual communication, various group activities, family-centred therapy meetings and development of supportive therapeutic relationships with personal nurses (an example of such a psychotherapeutic community was described by Alanen, 1997: 144–145, 191–195). The present hurried atmosphere of many acute wards is not very suitable for such purposes, a fact that should be considered very seriously in future developments. The best solution may be the foundation of separate treating homes for first admitted and also for recurrent psychotic patients, in the frame of community psychiatry, following the Soteria model and its applications (see Aderhold, Chapter 23). The experiences from Soteria Berne as well as those from the Swedish Parachute Project (see Chapter 12) may here serve as examples to be followed.

Family approaches

Family-centred approaches should usually be continued after the initial interventions. They can be based on either a psychodynamic or a cognitive orientation, often depending on available resources (however, the opinions and needs of the patients and their families should also be regarded as an indicator). A longer lasting family-centred intervention is most needed in the treatment of young patients with an acute onset of psychosis associated with conflicts with parents, as well as – if possible to establish – among patients who have become psychotic while married or living in a long-term couple relationship. However, continued family meetings or other kind of family-centred treatment are also indicated in cases where the only interpersonal relations of a severely ill, withdrawn patient occur in the home. With patients in danger of chronicity, CBT methods can help both the patient and family members to more easily notice the signs of a threatening recurrence or worsening of symptoms and be better able to avoid this danger (e.g. Gumley *et al.*, 2003; see also Chapter 19). Particularly positive experiences have been reported of psycho-educational work with multi-family groups (McFarlane, 2000).

While examining the development of family-centred approaches to schizophrenic psychoses, Helm Stierlin (Chapter 17) regrets the extremist viewpoints presented by some family researchers and therapists that, for their part, stimulated ill-founded ideas that family students and therapists blame parents for their children's illness. In some countries like the USA this led to an understandable opposition led by the parents' associations. Unfortunately, also the attitudes of several psychiatric researches tended to consider family dynamic investigation and therapy in this field as taboo – an attitude based on moralizing, not science. There are biologically oriented researchers for whom the term 'environment' is restricted to the external effects which the baby has experienced during the intrauterine life and delivery. It may be appropriate for clinicians to avoid the term 'family therapy' and rather speak of family meetings or consultations, but the continuation of understanding, non-blaming meetings with families of psychotic patients is most important.

During the last years, relationships between trauma and psychosis have aroused much interest (see review by Morrison *et al.*, 2003), culminating in the studies revealing the great frequency of physical and sexual abuse experienced by future schizophrenic patients in their childhood (Read *et al.*, 2005). However, such findings are not specific to schizophrenia but are also found in other psychiatric disorders. There is reason to hope that the results of these studies should not be exaggerated and reactivate blaming. The starting point of family therapists is to help families. We know that the origins of schizophrenic psychoses, as well as most other mental disorders, are multifactorial, multifaceted and multilayered, involving both genetic and other biological factors (including the precipitating effect of drugs like cannabis), as well as early interactional relationships and experiences during later phases of life. We also know that many schizophrenic patients are particularly important children for their parents. A successful psycho-dynamic family therapy may help parents who have unconsciously cherished overly symbiotic relations with their children – often stimulated also by the children's innate inclinations – to support their child's developmental process towards a more integrated personality and independent life. For such a result, it is necessary for the therapists to see the events through empathic understanding of each family member, to 'take everybody's part' ('Allparteilichkeit', Stierlin *et al.*, 1977). A positive contact between the therapist and the parents, established during preceding family meetings, is often important, sometimes even crucial, for the success of subsequent individual therapy.

Individual psychotherapy

A long-term psychodynamic individual therapy may still be the mode of treatment that best helps a schizophrenic patient to re-establish his personality. However, it is not indicated for all cases of schizophrenia. The chances of success are most optimal for patients who are included in the better half of schizophrenics – those who have made better progress in life than schizophrenic patients in the average. The outbreak of their psychosis is usually acute, at least relatively, and an initial motivation to study one's own problems easily arises. Many of these patients are rather quickly able to establish a symbiotic-type transference relationship with their therapist, which then serves as foundation for a successful therapeutic process. We have to regret the still widespread consequence of Freud's erroneous views that the narcissistic retreat in psychosis does not allow for a fruitful therapeutic relationship.

On the other hand, for many schizophrenic patients it is difficult to develop the motivation for introspection needed in a psychodynamic psychotherapy. This is true especially of the most seriously ill patients and those with tenacious paranoid delusions. In these cases, a CBT-oriented therapy is usually a better alternative (see Iso-Koivisto's (2004) study described in Chapter 12). However, the guidelines should not be rigid. The treatment plan of every patient should be studied and followed up individually, in a 'case-specific' way. We have above pointed out the signs of an increasing congruence between psychodynamic and cognitive approaches. And there is always the question of the resources available.

The possibilities of increasing the amount of psychoanalytically oriented individual therapies in the context of public health care have usually been considered poor. In the Northern European countries some individual therapies of schizophrenic patients, when indicated, are purchased from therapists practising outside the public health care service. But we should realize that psychodynamic individual therapy of a psychotic patient does not require the same frequency of sessions as classical psychoanalysis. Two hours a week is recommended, and many staff therapists find this quite feasible. In his instructive book *Weathering the Storms – Psychotherapy for Psychosis*, Murray Jackson (2001) gives many examples of good results of long-term therapies with relatively low frequency, achieved even by nursing staff members with the help of competent supervision. Therapy takes place face to face, which provokes a better scope for mutual empathy and introjection, 'mirroring', to use the term favoured by Benedetti (1976).

Group therapy and group activities

The importance and benefits of group psychotherapy in schizophrenia are stressed in Chapter 18. Group psychotherapy characteristics differ from those of other psychotherapies. These differences may provide some therapeutic factors that favourably affect the experiences and behaviours of schizophrenic patients. This type of therapy should form an essential ingredient in all psychotherapy programmes, providing all the patients with the opportunity of a group dynamic context with persons who are having or have had these unique experiences. They can express themselves, make comparisons, validate their experiences and know themselves better. It is also a place where they can acquire insight about their distinctive characteristics and difficulties, thanks to group mirroring, and where they can reconstruct their identity and their world in a stable and realistic way. Other group activities or peer group meetings may also have the same kind of functions in a less specific form.

Rehabilitation and psychotherapy

In Chapter 22, Harding and McCrory make a call for more integrative strategies between psychotherapeutic and rehabilitating interventions. They illustrate this with interesting examples of the ways in which these approaches can – and should – support each other. It should be past history to sequence these two types of interventions with parsimonious strategies that consider rehabilitation only after an evolved period of the disorder and when the patients clearly showed their 'defective mark'. One of the most beneficial teachings obtained from early interventions in psychoses is a clearer awareness of the difficulties many patients already have during their premorbid period – of their problems in social relationships and intimacy, and in the adaptation and adjustment to the educational, vocational and working world. These premorbid difficulties that undoubtedly influenced the patient's becoming ill also demand an early rehabilitating intervention. We now know better the need for complementarity and simultaneousness of psychotherapy and rehabilitation and we should facilitate the adjustment and personal development of our patients in both directions, supporting their own actions and vocational settings. In the Finnish National Project, the newly admitted patient's 'grip on life' – by which we mean whether the patient has maintained or lost his effort to achieve the goals and modes of satisfaction associated with the interpersonal relationships and social life of an adult person – appeared to be one of the most important factors predicting the outcome (Salokangas et al., 1989).

On neuroleptic treatment

From a global perspective, during the latter half of the last century the use of neuroleptic medication has been regarded as the most crucial element in the treatment of the patients of the schizophrenia group. However, the question of the beneficial and deleterious effects of neuroleptics has become more and more a matter of debate. Even if the neuroleptic medication alleviates so-called positive symptoms in about two-thirds of the patients and helps them to cope better in the community, the meta-analysis by Hegarty *et al.* (1994) and many other studies have shown that the number of fully recovered people with schizophrenia has not increased since the advent of neuroleptics. We know that the side effects of these drugs are harmful to patients if they are used with an unnecessary high dosage, still a regrettably general practice in many countries. The harmful side effects have not disappeared with the development of the 'new generation' of neuroleptics, even if somewhat changed in their nature (e.g. Lieberman *et al.*, 2005; see also Aderhold in Chapter 23 pp. 342–343). There are many patients that are non-compliant with long-term use of neuroleptics, just because of the side effects. There is an increasing opposition to compulsion to take these drugs, firmly supported, for example, by the Mind Freedom movement in the USA (mindfreedom-news@intenex.net).

The use of neuroleptics, especially in high doses, may also be motivated more by defensive needs of the psychiatrists and other staff members than by the patient's best interests. This may include the unconscious wish to avoid encountering the deep-rooted, anxiety-provoking problems of psychotic patients (see Chapter 1), or – more consciously – the staff's desire for calming down the atmosphere of a psychiatric ward for their own comfort.

The effect of neuroleptic drugs is crucially based on the blockade of brain dopamine (especially D2 dopamine) transmission. Positron emission tomography (PET) studies have shown that blocking of dopamine transmission at the level of 60 to 80 per cent should be considered sufficient and that this will be achieved with a rather low dosage of neuroleptics (see Hietala, Chapter 20). A higher dosage is a misguided choice, because it no longer improves the outcome of the treatment but notably increases the number of adverse side effects. As pointed out by Whitaker (Chapter 24), long-term intake of neuroleptics also produces a compensatory increase of the density of the D2 receptors in the brain. The result is that the danger of a relapse of psychotic symptoms is increased after the discontinuation of drugs, especially if done abruptly.

The claims that the neuroleptic medication should protect the brain from the ostensibly harmful effects of schizophrenia have not been confirmed. On the other hand, we know that neuroleptics themselves have harmful effects on brain. It is also important to remember that dopaminergic transmission is very important for the brain function in learning and thus also for psychotherapeutic interaction (a fact emphasized, e.g. by Braus, 2005). Even because of this, neuroleptic treatment with higher dosage is incompatible with psychotherapeutic activities. The calming effect of a lower dosage of neuroleptics may be used as a support for psychotherapeutic relationship, but it is important that the dosage will be gradually reduced in the course of therapy and even finished if no longer needed. As shown by Räkköläinen and Aaltonen (Chapter 20), many acute psychotic states can be satisfactorily calmed with a psychotherapeutic approach combined with benzodiazepines for a shorter time. In their chapter Räkköläinen and Aaltonen present pilot experiences on the indications of the use or non-use of neuroleptics in the treatment of first admitted schizophrenic patients in an intensive, psychotherapeutically oriented treatment context, classified in three groups on clinical and psychodynamic premises. For the integrated treatment of schizophrenic group patients we will emphasize here the following viewpoints with regard to the use of neuroleptic drugs:

1   The treatment of first episode psychosis patients should begin with an (approximately) three-week-long period during which an intensive psychotherapeutic contact with the patient and the people making up his personal interactional network should be given the prime importance. If possible, the use of neuroleptics should be postponed and the anxiety and agitation of the patient controlled with benzodiazepine medication. If an inpatient treatment is needed, this should preferably be carried out in a hospital ward or treatment home in which sufficient time and resources could be secured. If at home or in other outpatient environment, the intensity of the treatment and the safety of the patient and his family members should be guaranteed.

2   After this period, neuroleptic treatment with small or moderate doses is indicated to support the continuing psychotherapeutic intervention for patients whose psychotic state has been found to persist and be deep-rooted. With many patients recovering from an acute psychosis, neuroleptic treatment can be avoided. This will help to prevent unnecessary and even stigmatizing use of neuroleptic drugs, which once begun is often prescribed indefinitely. For this reason alone these patients should be carefully followed and the indication for the need for neuroleptics be reviewed at regular intervals.

3   With all patients with schizophrenia group psychoses, the use of high dosage of neuroleptic drugs is contra-indicated. Medication and its various effects should be regularly discussed with the patient, the doses gradually diminished and the medication even finished when considered possible.

Training and supervision

Because of the longstanding undervalued position of the mental health sector, both the quantity and quality of resources remain insufficient in most countries. We would like to emphasize especially the importance of increasing the quality of resources. During the National Schizophrenia Project in Finland, e.g. (see Chapter 12), a real development of activities became possible only after increasing the quality of resources through supervision and training activities connected with the project work and this was also so in catchment areas in which the quantity of staff members was better than average.

The first step to develop the psychotherapeutic abilities of staff is on-the-job training and the establishment of supervision given by experienced therapists. Concurrently, public health organizations should support possibilities for staff members to participate in psychotherapy training programmes, with psychotherapy of psychoses included. We firmly advocate training programmes built on a multiprofessional basis, including members of nursing staff alongside physicians and psychologists. Nurses specialized in psychiatry and working in community psychiatric centres form an important psychotherapeutic resource whose contribution to the psychotherapeutic work has usually not been adequately noticed – despite early pioneers such as Gertrude Schwing, the pupil and coworker of Paul Federn (see Chapter 5). The same applies to social workers, especially as members of family therapeutic teams.

Because of the great diversity of psychotherapeutic activities with schizophrenic psychoses it is not advisable to develop rigidly standardized programmes and/or recommendations; some negative experiences have occurred. Rather, different kinds of psychotherapy training programmes should be developed, with an awareness of the need of their mutually complementary character. Nevertheless, general standards defining the qualifications for psychotherapeutic work (special level) and for the status of trainer and supervisor (advanced special level) are recommended.

Training of individual psychodynamic therapy with psychotic and other severely regressed patients has usually not been included in psychoanalytic training programmes. An example that could be followed might be the advanced special level training in psychodynamic psychotherapy with severely disordered patients described by Aaltonen et al. (2002). In cognitive psychotherapy, training programmes for psychotic patients should also be developed further. In team-based group and family therapy training programmes work with patients with psychosis is often included.

In his views on the future development of the International Society for the Psychological Treatments of the Schizophrenias and other Psychoses (ISPS), Gaetano Benedetti (2006) dealt with the reasons why many of his seminars – even despite an enthusiastic response from their participants – did not lead to organizational efforts and long-lasting therapeutic activities. He then writes of the importance of creating, within psychiatric and psychotherapeutic institutions, therapist groups that could share their experiences, including preverbal communications and therapists' resistances caused by daily symbiotic-type relationships with psychotic patients. This could be seen as a call for cooperation and mutual sharing of experiences also at the wider level, to be better able to further develop psychotherapeutic approaches to schizophrenic patients and their problems.

Concluding words

It is very difficult to foretell the future of any developments in a world facing great problems demanding common global resources during the next decades: the continuing population expansion, increasing inequality between rich and poor people and countries, pollution problems and lack of fresh water, and the threatening climate change with its various consequences. To be able to manage such challenges, we should sincerely hope that a common solidarity between different countries should gain more foothold than it has now.

The development of psychotherapeutic approaches to schizophrenic psychoses described in the various chapters of this book also has many special challenges to manage. Biological psychiatry in its reductionistic forms still has dominance in psychiatric research and teaching, supported by the general interest in biological and technical sciences as well as by the economic world, represented by the pharmaceutical industry. In the medical field, the research and treatment approaches connected with expensive technical equipment are often experienced as more impressive targets of economic support than psychotherapeutic projects and training activities.

Our knowledge of the essence of schizophrenic psychoses is still split and incomplete. Welcome and tangible signs of a more integrated development in the future are still visible, both in theory and practice. The diversification of psychotherapeutic treatment modes has increased our possibilities of helping a greater number of our patients and led the development of treatment activities to a more integrative course. We hope that such development will continue and, for its part, increase the position of psychotherapeutic approaches to schizophrenic patients. We do not think that the patient's 'stabile remission with minor symptoms' (as defined by some influential researchers), maintained with the help of a continuing neuroleptic medication, would be a satisfactory goal for our treatment activities (even if necessary with a hopefully diminishing number of our patients). We believe that early and intensive treatment based on psychological understanding would in future support increasing numbers of patients to be able better to overcome their deep-rooted problems and help their growth as human beings and their interpersonal and social capabilities.

There are signs that may forecast a better future. Among them is the continuing and diversified development of the ISPS. Over 50 years the ISPS has enlarged from small (if important) symposia to a lively international organization with large congresses (the last one, in Madrid 2006, had 1200 participants) and with active local associations in different parts of the world (see Alanen *et al.*, 2006). We hope that a new generation of psychotherapists from different professional disciplines would witness a rise of a more integrated – and more humanistic – age in schizophrenia research and therapy. We would be happy if our book played its part in stimulating such development.

References

Aaltonen, J., Alanen, Y.O., Keinänen, M. and Räkköläinen, V. (2002). An advanced special-level training programme in psychodynamic individual psychotherapy of psychotic and borderline patients: the Finnish approach. *European Journal of Psychotherapy & Counseling & Health*, 5: 13–30.

Alanen, Y.O. (1997). *Schizophrenia – Its Origins and Need-Adapted Treatment*. London: Karnac.

Alanen, Y.O., Lehtinen, V., Lehtinen, K., Aaltonen, J. and Räkköläinen, V. (2000). The Finnish integrated model for early treatment of schizophrenia and related psychoses. In B. Martindale, A. Bateman, M. Crowe and F. Margison (eds) *Psychosis: Psychological Approaches and their Effectiveness*. Glasgow: Gaskell (ISPS), pp. 235–265.

Alanen, Y.O., Silver, A.-L.S. and González de Chávez, M. (2006). *Fifty Years of Humanistic Treatment of Psychoses*. Madrid: Fundácion para la Investigación y Tratamiento de la Esquizofrenia y otras Psycosis.

Benedetti, G. (1976). Curative factors in psychotherapy with schizophrenic patients. In J. Jorstad and E. Ugelstad (eds) *Schizophrenia 75. Psychotherapy, Family Therapy, Research*: 15–27.

Benedetti, G. (2006). My views for the future development of the ISPS. In Y.O. Alanen, A.-L.S. Silver and M. González de Chávez (eds) *Fifty Years of Humanistic Treatment of Psychoses*. Madrid: Fundácion para la Investigación y Tratamiento de la Esquizofrenia y otras Psycosis, pp. 327–330.

Bentall, R. (1990). *Reconstructing Schizophrenia*. London and New York: Routledge.

Boyle M. (1990). *Schizophrenia. A Scientific Delusion*. London and New York: Routledge.

Braus, D.F. (2005). Aktuelle neurobiologische Forschungsergebnisse, die von der Bedeutung für die Psychotherapie sind. Paper presented at the Kongress Brennpunkte der Psychiatrie, Hamburg, 28–30 April.

Chadwick, P. (2006). *Person-Based Cognitive Therapy for Distressing Psychosis*. Chichester: Wiley.

Chadwick, P., Birchwood, M. and Trower, P. (1996). *Cognitive Therapy for Delusions, Voices and Paranoia*. Chichester: Wiley.

Cheung Chung, M., Fulford, K. and Graham, G. (2006). *Reconceiving Schizophrenia*. Oxford: Oxford University Press.

Cullberg, J. (2006). *Psychoses. An Integrated Perspective*. London and New York: Routledge.

Falloon, J.R.H. (1992). Early intervention for first episodes of schizophrenia: a preliminary exploration. *Psychiatry* 55: 4–15.

Fromm-Reichmann, F. (1950). *Principles of Intensive Psychotherapy*. Chicago, IL: Chicago University Press.

Gallese, V. (2006). Mirror neurons and intentional attunement. Commentary on Olds. *Journal of American Psychoanalytical Association* 54: 47–57.

Gallese, V., Fadiga, L., Fogassi, L. and Rizzolatti, G. (1996). Action recognition in the premotor cortex. *Brain* 119: 593–609.

Gleeson, J.F.M. and McGorry, P.D. (eds) (2004). *Psychological Interventions in Early Psychosis. A Treatment Handbook*. Chichester: Wiley.

Gumley, A.I., O'Grady, M., McNay, L. *et al.* (2003). Early intervention for relapse in schizophrenia: results of a 12-month randomized controlled trial of cognitive-behaviour therapy. *Psychological Medicine* 33: 419–431.

Hegarty, J.D., Baldessarini, R.J., Tohen, M. *et al.* (1994). One hundred years of schizophrenia: a meta-analysis of the outcome literature. *American Journal of Psychiatry* 151: 1409–1411.

Heinimaa, M. and Larsen, T.K. (2002). Psychosis: conceptual and ethical aspects of early diagnosis and intervention. *Current Opinion Psychiatry* 15: 633–641.

Hinshelwood, R.D. (2002). Symptoms or relationships. *British Medical Journal* 324: 292–293.

Iso-Koivisto, E. (2004). *'Pois sieltä, ylös.takaisin'* – *ensimmäinen psykoosi kokemuksena*. ['Away from there, upwards, back again' – meaning given to the experience of first psychotic episode. Finnish with English summary.] Turku: Annales Universitatis Turkuensis.

Jackson, M. (2001). *Weathering the Storms. Psychotherapy for Psychosis*. London: Karnac.

Johannessen, J.O., Larsen, T.K., McGlashan, T. and Vaglum, P. (2000). Early intervention in psychosis: the TIPS project, a multicentre study in Scandinavia. In B. Martindale, A. Bateman, M. Crowe and F. Matgison (eds) *Psychosis: Psychological Approaches and their Effectiveness*. Glasgow: Gaskell (ISPS), pp. 210–234.

Kandel, E. (1998). A new intellectual framework for psychiatry. *American Journal of Psychiatry* 155: 457–469.

Kandel, E. (1999). Biology and the future of psychoanalysis: a new intellectual framework for psychiatry revisited. *American Journal of Psychiatry* 156: 505–524.

Leff, J., Kuipers, L., Berkowitz, R. and Sturgeon, D. (1985). A controlled trial of social intervention in the families of schizophrenic patients: two-year follow-up. *British Journal of Psychiatry* 146: 594–600.

Lehtinen, K. (1993). Need-adapted treatment of schizophrenia. A five-year follow-up study from the Turku project. *Acta Psychiatrica Scandinavica* 87: 96–101.

Lieberman, J.A., Stroup, T.S., McEvoy, J.P. *et al.* (2005). Clinical antipsychotic trials of intervention effectiveness (CATIE). Effectiveness of antipsychotic drugs in schizophrenia. *New England Journal of Medicine* 353: 1209–1223.

McFarlane, W.R. (2000). Psychoeducational multi-family groups: adaptations and outcomes. In B. Martindale, A. Bateman, M. Crowe and F. Margison (eds) *Psychosis – Psychological Approaches and their Effectiveness*. Glasgow: Gaskell (ISPS), pp. 68–95.

McGorry, P.D., McFarlane, C., Patton, G.C. *et al.* (1995). The prevalence of prodromal features in adolescence: a preliminary survey. *Acta Psychiatrica Scandinavica* 92: 241–249.

McGorry, P.D., Yung, A.R., Phillips, R.J. *et al.* (2002). A randomized controlled trial of interventions designed to reduce the risk of progression to first episode psychosis in a clinical sample with subthreshold symptoms. *Archives of General Psychiatry* 59: 921–928.

Mezzich, J.E. (2007). Psychiatry for the person: articulating medicine's science and humanism. *World Psychiatry* 2007: 1–3.

Mezzich, J.E. and Salloum, I.M. (2007). Towards innovative international classification and diagnostic systems: ICD-11 and person-centered integrative diagnosis. *Acta Psychiatrica Scandinavica* 116: 1–5.

Morrison, A.P., Frame, L. and Larkin, W. (2003). Relationships between trauma and psychosis. *British Journal of Clinical Psychology* 42: 331–353.

Olds, D.D. (2006). Identification: psychoanalytical and biological perspectives. *Journal of American Psychoanalytical Association* 54: 17–46.

Read, J., van Os, J., Morrison, A.P. and Ross, C.A. (2005). Childhood trauma, psychosis and schizophrenia: a literature review and clinical implications. *Acta Psychiatrica Scandinavica* 112: 330–350.

Rizzolatti, G., Fadiga, L., Gallese, V. and Fogassi, L. (1996). Premotor cortex and the recognition of motor actions. *Cognitive Brain Research* 3: 131–141.

Robbins, M. (1993). *Experiences of Schizophrenia. An Integration of the Personal, Scientific, and Therapeutic.* New York: The Guilford Press.

Salokangas, R.K.R., Räkköläinen, V. and Alanen, Y.O. (1989). Maintenance of grip on life and goals of life: a valuable criterion for evaluating outcome of schizophrenia. *Acta Psychiatrica Scandinavica* 80: 187–193.

Scott, R.D. and Ashworth, P.L. (1967). 'Closure' at the first schizophrenic breakdown: a family study. *British Journal of Medical Psychology* 40: 109–145.

Seikkula, J. and Arnkil, R.E. (2005). *Dialogical Meetings in Social Networks.* London: Karnac.

Shaw, K., McFarlane, A. and Bookless, C. (1997). The phenomenology to traumatic reactions to psychiatric illness. *Journal of Nervous and Mental Diseases* 187, 6: 250–253.

Stierlin, H., Rücker-Embden, I., Wetzel, N. and Wirsching, M. (1977). *Der erste Familiengespräch.* Stuttgart: Ernst Klett.

Tienari, P., Wynne, L.C., Läksy, K. *et al.* (2003). Genetic boundaries of the schizophrenia spectrum: evidence of the Finnish adoptive family study of schizophrenia. *American Journal of Psychiatry* 160: 1–8.

Tienari, P., Wynne, L.C., Sorri, A. *et al.* (2004). Genotype-environment interaction in schizophrenia-spectrum disorder: long-term follow-up study of Finnish adoptees. *British Journal of Psychiatry* 184: 216–222.

Wahlberg, K.-E., Wynne, L.C., Hakko, H. *et al.* (2004). Interaction of genetic risk and adoptive parent communication deviance: longitudinal prediction of adoptee psychiatric disorders. *Psychological Medicine* 34: 1531–1541.

Wynne, L.C., Tienari, P., Sorri, A. *et al.* (2006). I. Genotype-environment interaction in schizophrenia spectrum: genetic liability and global family ratings in the Finnish adoption study; II. Genotype-environment interaction in the schizophrenia spectrum: qualitative observations. *Family Process* 45: 419–447.

Zahavi, D. (2000). *Exploring the Self.* Amsterdam: John Benjamin.

Name index

Aaku, T. 169, 170
Aalto, S. 292
Aaltonen, J. 153, 158, 164, 166–78, 169, 170, 171, 174, 175, 177—8, 295, 295–303, 296, 297, 341, 342, 354, 371, 372
AAVV 16
Abba, N. 282
Abi-Dargham, A. 289, 292
Abraham, K. 26, 31, 38, 46–7, 67, 78
Achte, K.A. 167
Ackerson, T. 319
Aderhold, V. 127, 130, 211, 328–45, 342, 366
Adler, A. 125
Aebi, E. 337, 338, 354
Agar-Jacomb, K. 211
Ahonen, J. 173, 174, 297
Akabane, Y. 222
Akhtar, S. 74, 84, 224
Alakare, B. 174, 341
Alanen, Y.O. 3–9, 7, 23–37, 29, 51–5, 114, 130, 153, 158, 159, 160, 164, 166–77, 167, 169, 170, 171, 172–3, 177–8, 217, 224, 225, 240, 252, 256, 258, 262, 263, 295, 296, 298, 341, 342, 357–76, 365, 366, 369, 372, 374
Aleman, A. 225

Alessandrini, M. 145–52
Alexander, F. 39, 40
Alport, G.F. 84
Aluffi, G. 147
Ammar, S. 15
Andersen, T. 161, 239–40
Anderson, C. 159
Ang, M. 204–13, 364, 365
Angell, M. 343
Anhert, L. 225
Anker, M. 191
Annable, L. 351
Ansker, M. 352
Anthi, P. 160
Anthony, E.J. 253, 256
Anthony, W.A. 318, 319, 320, 321
Anttinen, E.E. 167, 172, 320
Appel, J.W. 224
Applethwaite, G. 274, 283
Aquila, R. 320
Argyle, N. 211
Arieti, S. 74
Aristotle 13, 318
Arlow, J. 67
Armelius, B.Å. 160
Arnkil, R.E. 362
Arundale, J. 85
Aschoff, A. 342
Ashworth, P.L. 365
Auestad, B. 161, 310
Aulagnier, P. 142
Austin, S.V. 270
Avikainen, S. 359

Bach, P. 282
Bachrach, B. 15
Badaracco, J. 84
Badura, W. 187
Bagby, R.M. 291
Bak, I.R. 161
Bakalar, N. 90n10
Baldessarini, R. 353, 370
Bally, G. 110–11, 120
de Barbaro, B. 187, 188
Barnes, T.R. 289
Barret, R.J. 10
Barrois, C. 143
Barrowclough, C. 275, 282
Basaglia, F. 109, 145, 148, 320
Bateman, A. 100
Bateson, G. 95, 234, 300
Battegay, R. 113
Beard, J.H. 320
Beavan, V. 211
Bebbington, P.E. 273, 276, 281
Bechgaard, B. 74, 164, 166, 178n1
Beck, A. 68, 267, 268–9, 279, 281, 284n1
Beckett, R. 273, 276
Beder, S. 296
Beebe, B. 225
Beers, C. 56, 57
Begley, S. 225
Bell, D. 82, 85
Belleza, T. 351
Bendix, S. 272, 276
Bendix, T. 163

Subject index

Aarhus 162, 163
ABC analysis 361
abuse 85, 207, 209, 222, 367
acceptance and commitment therapy
  (ACT) 282
access to health services 101
ACT *see* acceptance and commitment
  therapy
Acute Psychosis Integrated (API)
  treatment 173–4, 296–7
adolescence 241, 365
'affect logic' 336–7, 340
alcohol abuse 259
American Psychiatric Association
  (APA) 5, 56, 69, 75, 217, 224
American Psychoanalytic Association
  57, 58–9
American Psychopathological
  Association 60
American Relational school 224
anthropology 222
anti-psychiatry movement 98
anxiety 73, 80, 220, 225, 298
APA *see* American Psychiatric
  Association
API *see* Acute Psychosis Integrated
  treatment
Arbours Crisis Centre 98, 103
archetypes 78
arts therapies 100, 133, 149
Asia 191–8
asylums 17, 18, 19, 347–9; *see also*
  hospitals
attachment 82, 220, 225
Austen Riggs Center 73, 137
Austria 124, 132–4
autism 4, 299
autoeroticism 30, 34

autopoesis 220
avoidant strategies 259

Bechkterev Institute 186
befriending 277
'being with' 328, 331–2, 333, 342
beliefs: confrontation of delusional 270;
  cultural 195, 197; voice hearing
  269–70, 279, 283
Bellevue Sanatorium 44, 45, 46, 110, 115
benzodiazepines 333, 371
Berlin 46–7, 129–30, 132
Berne Soteria 119, 337–9, 354, 366
bio-psychosocial approach 191, 194,
  196–7, 223, 337
biological factors 3, 7, 222–3, 357,
  358–9; Germany and Austria 134;
  medication 291–2; rehabilitation
  317; social support influence on 220;
  Sweden 157; *see also* brain;
  neurobiology
biological reductionism 217–19, 224,
  225–6, 343, 373
biomedical treatment: Eastern Asia 191,
  196; New Zealand 204; Singapore
  193; *see also* medical model
bipolarity 132
borderline personality disorder 4–5, 83
Boyer House 73
brain 20, 222, 233, 358–9; biological
  reductionism 217; dopamine
  blocking drugs 288, 289, 290–1, 292,
  300–1, 351, 370; family therapy 238;
  Griesinger 124; neurobiological
  research 300–1; psycho-education
  239; psychotherapy impact on
  225–6; social factors impact on 223
British Psychoanalytic Society 83